State, Nation and Ethnicity in Contemporary South Asia

State, Nation and Ethnicity in Contemporary South Asia

Ishtiaq Ahmed

PINTER
London and New York

PINTER
A Cassell Imprint
Wellington House, 125 Strand, London WC2R 0BB
215 Park Avenue South, New York, NY 10003, USA

First published in Great Britain 1996

British Library Cataloguing-in-Publication Data
A catalogue record for this book is available from The British Library.

ISBN 0–86187–747–0

Library of Congress Cataloging-in-Publication Data
Ahmed, Ishtiaq, 1947–
    State, nation, and ethnicity in contemporary South Asia / Ishtiaq Ahmed.
        p.   cm.
    Includes bibliographical references and index.
    ISBN 0–86187–747–0
    1. South Asia – Politics and government. 2. Ethnicity – South Asia.
3. South Asia – Ethnic relations. I. Title.
DS341.A38   1996
305.8'00954–dc20   95–36993
                                                                                             CIP

Typeset by Mayhew Typesetting, Rhayader, Powys
Printed and bound in Great Britain by Biddles Limited, Guildford and King's Lynn

Contents

For Meliha and our boys,
Sahir and Selim

Preface

In 1986 I applied for a grant from the Swedish Agency for Research Co-operation with Developing Countries (SAREC) to do research on Sikh separatism in India. SAREC lays stress on co-operation between researchers based in Sweden and those of the developing countries on which the research is to be done. The procedure at SAREC is that applications are sent for remarks to the Swedish missions on which the research is proposed. The mission has to assess, among other things, whether the concerned developing country will allow such research to be done on its territory.

My guess is that it was felt that India would not look with favour upon somebody probing into its Punjab problem, and therefore not allow a foreigner to visit Punjab. Nevertheless I was granted a small amount by SAREC to investigate possibilities of doing work on the Sikh problem. Naturally I called the Indian Embassy and requested documents which it might think important to represent the Indian position. This request was granted and I received some material, but simultaneously the Indian ambassador lodged an oral complaint at the Swedish Foreign Office, alleging that my research was detrimental to Indian interests and SAREC's decision to support it conflicted with its aim of promoting co-operation between Sweden and a developing country.

I must say that such a reaction by the Indian diplomat deeply shocked me. My interest in the Indian Punjab had actually been kindled by my concern for Punjab, which once again was being bled in the name of religious nationalism. However, the Indian officers seemed to have taken notice only of my Pakistani-Punjabi origin and my Muslim name and concluded that I was bound to be biased against India. In any case, I managed to interview some of the leaders of the Khalistan Council in the United Kingdom, and along with a short historical background submitted the report to SAREC.

In the meantime the situation in South Asia began to turn from bad to worse. By 1987 the Sinhalese—Tamil confrontation in Sri Lanka had escalated drastically. In India the Sikhs persisted with their struggle. In Bangladesh the tribal people of the Chittagong Hill Tracts continued their low-intensity armed struggle against the state. In 1988 Muslim Kashmiris also began to agitate against India. The same year the Sindhi–Mohajir ethnic conflict took an extremely violent turn in Pakistan. It was quite clear that the relationship between state, nation and ethnicity in South Asia was causing serious disturbance. Existing explanations on the subject were usually case studies confined to particular states. It seemed necessary for someone to look at the problem in its interconnectedness: without a regional, comparative-historical approach sense could not be made of this new tragedy unfolding in South Asia.

Now it so happens that researchers, like detectives, do not usually give up their investigations half way. I had just begun to understand what ethnicity means when the SAREC grant ran out. With the experience of hindsight I can now say that it proved to be a blessing in disguise. I learnt one crucial fact at the very beginning: states are haunted by anxieties and fears about threats to their existence, and, therefore, South Asian states have all reason to be suspicious about anybody prying into matters concerning their unity and security. Doing research on ethnic conflicts and separatism surely means stepping on many toes. Having realized this fact, I accepted that I would have to conduct my investigation under rather atypical circumstances.

Thus in 1989 when my application for a three-year grant to investigate ethnic conflict and separatism in South Asia was approved by the Swedish Council for Research in the Humanities and Social Sciences (HSFR) I embarked upon the investigation very much the wiser. The completion of the book, however, took much longer — five instead of three years — because the research problem proved to be much more complicated than anything I could imagine and required collection of data on an extensive scale.

Two aspects of the book need to be mentioned specifically. Firstly, since a few times in the original source the amount of money is given in rupee or taka values I have chosen not to attempt to convert these South Asian currencies into the US dollar or English pound, because the values of the South Asian currencies have varied enormously over time and it is, therefore, rather frustrating to attempt such conversions. Roughly between 1970 and 1990 the rupee and taka exchange rates against the US dollar have varied from 7–15 rupees or takas to a dollar in the 1970s to 25–40 rupees or takas to a dollar in the early 1990s; hence, for example, the problem for a non-economist of converting to the US dollar values an amount of 1000 million rupees or takas spent during the period 1975–90. Secondly, in covering the events in South Asia I have chosen not to go beyond 1993. The analysis proferred upon the basis of the data collected until the end of 1993 holds also for 1994 and the first half of 1995. No dramatic change took place in the South Asian situation as a whole or in the specific cases which are examined in this investigation. The exception is, perhaps, the withdrawal of the army from

Karachi in 1994, and the subsequent sharp escalation of violence in that bleeding city. One can, of course, keep on collecting more horrendous details of ethnic violence from Karachi and other parts of South Asia, but such a task by itself is not interesting for analysis. Fluctuations in the intensity of violence occur many times in the course of protracted ethnic conflicts. More crucial is the identification and understanding of the underlying causes and roots of these on-going struggles.

Many people have contributed to the completion of this book. My dear friend and colleague Associate Professor Björn Beckman was extremely helpful with comments on the various drafts of the theoretical chapters 1–4. Professor Peter Schalk at the Department for the History of Religions, University of Uppsala was a great help with material and comments on my chapter on Sri Lanka. Don Odom, a former student of mine and now editor at the Stockholm International Peace Research Institute (SIPRI), was very kind with editorial advice and very useful comments on the manuscript. These three have been extremely generous and kind to me. I benefited greatly from talking about Sri Lanka to Dagmar Hellmann-Rajanayagam at the German Institute in London and on the Sikh problem to Roger Ballard at the University of Leeds. Gabriele Winai-Ström spared time to look at the pre-independence section on Sri Lanka. Lars Lindström provided useful comments on my theoretical formulations. Ms Nicola Viinikka and Dr Iain Stevenson at Pinter Publishers warmly encouraged me to continue with my work.

The Nordic Institute for Asian Studies (NIAS) and the Working Group for the Study of Developing Strategies (AKUT) provided small grants for travelling. The AKUT group has also been a forum where I could share some ideas on ethnic conflict and separatism with my peers Lars Rudebeck, Gunilla Andræ, Olle Törnquist, Inga Brandell, Kenneth Hermele, Bosco Parra and Gunnel Cederlöf. Olle in particular is to be thanked for helping me with contacts in India. In the autumn of 1992 AKUT organized an International Workshop on Social Movements, State and Democracy in Delhi in co-operation with Delhi University and the Indian Statistical Institute. I was able to participate in that workshop thanks to AKUT. At the Indian end, I owe many thanks to Professor Partha Mukherji and his assistant Mr Sahoo.

Here in Stockholm, I owe thanks to my elder brother Mushtaq Ahmad for his very useful comments on Chapter 5 dealing with the cultural and political heritage of the Indian subcontinent. Syed Sirajus Salakin had very useful information to share with me about the socio-political situation in Karachi soon after independence. Rafiq Khan helped with his vast knowledge about the PPP and Punjab and Sindh situations. Ahmed Faqih helped with material and information on PPP and general intellectual stimulation. Manzoor Manghi provided material and information on the Sindhi position. Riaz Cheema and I discussed many aspects of contemporary South Asian politics, agreeing most of the time on our assessment of past and present events. Ilyas Khan and I discussed problems of the oppressed classes in South Asia. Feroz Dar, Khawaja Khalid, Tamiz Rahman, Dr Parwazi, Imran, Sajjad, Humanyun, Naim, Bashir, Mansoor, Khalida Malik, Ninder Gill, Ram Kishen and Charanjiv Mehta have been participating in our monthly social gatherings. I have surely benefited from their company. Shaikh Jawaid dropped out of our group but remained in touch. To all of them many thanks.

In South Asia I was helped by scholars, journalists, politicians, old friends and many other people I met in connection with my investigation. The list is too long to be given here. Some of the names are given at the end of each country chapter. I owe special thanks to my younger brother Zubair Ghazi, who helped me with material and contacts in Pakistan. Nadeem Khalid at Karachi went out of his way to help me with material and contacts in Sindh. My old friends Fayyaz Bedaar, Alauddin, Zakir Mohammad Salim, Jawaid Sarfraz, Pervaiz Shah, Haji Ghiasuddin, Murad Bodla, Ishaq, Ayub and others extended their warm hospitality when I visited Lahore. In Bangladesh Professor Talukder Maniruzzaman helped me with contacts.

In the Department of Political Science, University of Stockholm, my colleagues have been helpful in so many different ways. I especially thank Donald Lavery.

From my father, Mian Ghulam Muhammad Ghazi, I learnt a lot about pre-Partition Punjab.

Despite incurring so many favours from many sides I alone bear responsibility for the interpretations and analysis presented in this book.

At home, Meliha and our two boys, Sahir and Selim, provided all the love, warmth and, of course, necessary diversions. I am very pleased that the completion of this book coincides with Selim's third birthday.

ISHTIAQ AHMED
Sollentuna, 7 June 1995

1

Introduction

This book explains *why* and *how* nation-building by India, Pakistan, Bangladesh and Sri Lanka is resisted by some cultural groups, which instead claim a separate national identity and demand special rights over a territory they claim to be theirs by historical and cultural right, but which allegedly has been pre-empted by the state. The emergence of nationalist claims against the state, however, is a process, usually gradual and by no means moving in only one direction or always ending up in armed conflict. Separatist nationalism may fail to mobilize substantial support among members of the group on whose behalf it is staked, or it can wither away under the impact of overall socio-economic change, or be accommodated within some autonomy formula, or assume threatening proportions in the form of secessionist bids. The important thing to note is that states almost invariably resist breakaway attempts.

The ethnic revival and separatism

Group tension and conflict in modern multi-ethnic societies underlie political separatism. Ethnic tension has been growing the world over in the post-war period, but towards the closing decades of this turbulent century it has displayed increasing malignancy. Among the protracted historic movements, the Irish and Basque national movements have from time to time taken the form of terrorist outbursts. In Canada, sections of the French-Canadian population have shown a proclivity towards the idea of a separate French-speaking state. Similar echoes can be heard occasionally from Scotland and Wales against union with England. Racist discrimination was widespread in the southern USA until the civil rights movement, exemplified in the 1960s by the leadership of Dr Martin Luther King, compelled the federal government to legislate against institutionalized discrimination. Ethnic riots, however, do occur in the United States, the most recent being those in Los Angeles in 1992. High unemployment and police brutality are usually the underlying causes of such riots. In Latin America, the Indian peoples have risen in revolt a number of times, only to be brutally suppressed by the ruling creole élites.

In West Asia, the Kurdish national question constitutes a major concern for Iran, Iraq, Turkey and to a lesser degree Syria. The Israel—Palestine confrontation became the focal point around which Arab and Muslim nationalism crystallized against Western domination. China, which has been seen as a homogeneous society, is having trouble with the Muslim peoples of Sinkiang, and there is, of course, the Tibetan issue. In North Africa, tension between Arabs and Berbers comes to the surface from time to time. In sub-Saharan Africa loyalty to the state is seriously compromised by the pull of tribe, language and religion. This is exemplified by the rivalry between the Hutu and Tutsi peoples spread over Rwanda and Burundi. Its most recent outburst in April 1994 has claimed the deaths of hundreds of thousands of people. Nigeria, Ethiopia and several other multi-ethnic states have been rocked by separatist struggles. In the Ethiopian case, the separation of Eritrea stands out as the solitary example of successful separatism. The most notorious case of sustained comprehensive racist and ethnic violence, of course, has been the apartheid regime in South Africa.

The most gruesome kinds of ethnic conflicts have flared up in the former multi-ethnic states of the Soviet Union and Yugoslavia. On the other hand, the dissolution of the former Czechoslovakia and the coming into being of two ethnic nation-states instead stands out as a peaceful resolution of the ethnic tangle. The reunion between the two German states is an example of a divided people coming together. The ugly nature of the contemporary ethnic revival should not, therefore, be construed to mean that ethnically diverse societies are destined to end up in violent conflict and disruption. Ethnic diversity is almost universal and has existed throughout history. Most of the time, human societies have managed to maintain the ethnic peace, though usually by imposing severe restrictions and disabilities on defeated and subordinate groups. In recent years a new form of resistance has been growing the world over among marginalized indigenous peoples against ever-increasing encroachment and usurpation of their land and natural resources by settlers, prospectors, private industry, multinational companies and the state.

Ethnic conflict and separatism in South Asia

In pre-colonial South Asia, ethnic and communal peace was largely maintained through, on the one hand, the caste system, which ideologically prohibited social mobility and largely succeeded in restricting it, and, on the other hand, the plurality of religions, sects and syncretic cults which provided scope for peaceful co-existence. The stability of this framework was underwritten by an essentially subsistence agrarian economy which furnished little scope for dynamic change. During the colonial period, ethnic tension began to mount as the various cultural groups competed with one another for the various opportunities which capitalist change and the system of representation instituted by the British offered to them. The most dramatic expression, and thus far the only successful one, of separatist nationalism in post-colonial South Asia was the break-up of Pakistan in 1971 which resulted in the creation of Bangladesh.

In India, the Sikh and Kashmiri separatist movements currently pose the most powerful separatist challenges to the state. Separatist tendencies are to be found in other parts of India too. In Pakistan, the ethnic conflict in the southern province of Sindh between indigenous Sindhis and Urdu-speaking migrants from India, called Mohajirs, is the most recent major separatist confrontation to take place. In Bangladesh, a separatist movement has been active since 1972 among the tribal peoples of the Chittagong Hill Tracts. The bitter Sinhalese–Tamil civil war in Sri Lanka, which inevitably dragged in the Muslim minority, has created deep cleavages among these groups.

The leaders of the hill tribes of Chittagong expressed a desire to join India but were placed in Pakistan and Kashmir, where the opinion of the Muslim majority remained unknown, but the Muslim leadership preferred union with India instead of Pakistan. In all the other cases mentioned above the cultural minorities had accepted or openly supported joining the state against whom they were later to start agitating. Simple explanations such as economic deprivation being the root cause of separatism are clearly inadequate because the Sikhs are one of the most prosperous communities in India. In this instance it seems more a case of rising expectations of Sikh upper classes and intelligentsia rather than economic exploitation. Explanations based on the primacy of primordial factors such as religious identity are also unsatisfactory because the Sindhis overwhelmingly and the Mohajirs almost exclusively belong to the same religion but are severely divided by linguistic differences. More crucially, the state is the central actor — and in the perceptions of the separatists the arch villain — in all the separatist dramas being enacted in South Asia.

Perhaps the most typical feature of recent ethnicized political tension in South Asia is its proclivity towards violence and extremism. All the paraphernalia contributing to extremism are available in abundance: widespread poverty, illiteracy, a rapidly growing population and high unemployment, bad and corrupt government, erosion of the moral framework of society, drugs and narcotic gangs, the easy availability of weapons and ammunition, and most crucially the interference of external actors. Brutal and bloody attacks by one cultural group on another without regard or mercy for anyone — women, children, the old or the disabled — epitomize the most extreme forms of such conflict. The state has not only failed to protect its citizens from such attacks but has itself been the perpetrator of many such crimes, and is invariably the main prize which different competing groups intend to win, either by capturing it or breaking it and making one of their own. *Why* and *how* this has happened is the puzzle this book sets out to solve.

As a preliminary explanation it can be stated that the pressures and forces which thrust India, Pakistan, Bangladesh and Sri Lanka towards ethnic conflict and separatism are internal as well as external, regional as well as global, with linkages extending over both time and space. In other words, the contemporary conflicts are neither sudden nor isolated disruptions of state and society, rather they are the expression of an intricate interplay between structural tensions and political omissions and commissions of influential political actors.

Nationalism and the doctrine of the right to national self-determination

Although the idea of community and a sense of belonging to a human group are ingrained in the human condition it is difficult to say if these are naturally inborn or socially acquired characteristics. In a way the distinction between the natural and the social is largely artificial in that human beings are generally gregarious and this quality compels them to associate with others. The ability to communicate through shared symbols and signs has been a precondition for the various forms of societal organizations which human beings have devised in order to live together. Most centrally through language, but also various other cultural means, communication has advanced among human beings. The propensity to associate with those that one identifies with has simultaneously involved the exclusion of exogenous groups and peoples. Such identification and classification has been practised in all human societies whatever their level of development, structuration and stratification. Such practice could not have been of much consequence were it not to serve also as a way of laying claims to territory, property and other possessions and privileges in opposition to the claims of other groups. Group identity and claim to specific territory can be described as the essence of the nationalist sentiment. Its echo can be heard throughout the ages and in almost all stable societies the world over.

It was, however, towards the end of the feudal epoch that national consciousness based on the incident of language and sectarian divisions of Christianity, often in combination with each other, was given expression in political thought. Marsilius, Machiavelli, Luther, Calvin and a host of other political and moral theorists argued against the domination of the Church of Rome and for greater political autonomy and independence of their immediate societies (Sabine and Thorson, 1973: 271–346). These were followed by other theorists such as Bodin and Hobbes, who stood for a strong central state. Mercantilist ideas provided the motive force of the earliest moves of European states to maximize their advantage in trade *vis-à-vis* others and to adopt protectionist measures (P. Anderson, 1983: 145).

The Glorious Revolution in England in 1688 and the influential defence by Locke of limited government added a democratic dimension to national consolidation. Rousseau's idea of direct democracy and general will of a people presaged the peculiarity of future nationalism: that it refers to the collective self-determination of a group of people and not necessarily to individual autonomy (Rousseau, 1990: 200−28). It was, however, the industrial revolution and the growth of capitalism which provided nationalism and nation-building with the strongest impetus. Out of these cataclysmal changes evolved both the rational spirit of the Enlightenment, premissed on universalism and faith in science, as well as anti-rational and militarist doctrines.

The French Revolution did away with the feudal order in France and delegitimized the system of hereditary privileges. People were no longer to be regarded as subjects. Rather they were to be treated as citizens with equal rights to participate in the political process. As regards the question of nation, the position taken was that all those who lived within French territory were entitled to the same rights. The centralized bureaucratic French state, particularly during the Jacobin period, set upon a concerted course of homogenization through the French language. Non-French-speaking regions under its jurisdiction were made to learn French. It arranged the dissemination of standard cultural and political values through processions, music, theatre and an array of other artistic means. The aim was to consolidate a French identity which was both ethno-cultural and political. Thus the ethnic dimension that was added to French identity modified the original universalism of the French Revolution ideology. Similar standardization policies were adopted by Prussia, England, Spain, Sweden and other west European states (Smith, 1986: 133−4). The system of public education based on a main language helped to solidify national cultural identity. In the case of Sweden, liquidation of parochial powers and the establishment of a strong central state were achieved through the application of considerable force by Gustav Vasa in the sixteenth century. Catholicism was suppressed and people were converted to the Lutheran faith. The reformed State Church and the Swedish language became the cultural symbols of Swedish national identity. By the middle of the nineteenth century the school system disseminated a standardized version of the Swedish language throughout the realm. The tiny Finnish-speaking groups settled in Sweden tried unsuccessfully to resist the imposition of Swedish language (Jonsson, 1991: 5−33). Similarly the Sami minority of northern Sweden was also made to learn Swedish.

In this early round of nationalism, therefore, the state took the initiative in nation-building. The logic underlying such endeavour was that nation and state should be congruent. Nowhere, however, were nation and state completely congruent: minorities both big and small survived as distinct cultural entities among them. Wherever recalcitrant regions and cultural groups resisted conformity to standardization measures of the state, they were subjected to severe violence by the authorities. Ultimately the modern state acquired greater control over society through the expansion and consolidation of a large centralized administrative and military system (Giddens, 1985: 112–16; 172–92).

On the other hand, the German-speaking peoples, divided among several petty states, were attracted to nationalism as the ideology for pan-German unity. In particular it was a reaction to Napoleonic expansion. Herder was to develop the idea of national life as an organic growth that comes into being through centuries of shared culture and experience. He laid great stress on the long historical roots of the German folk and national spirit and made the German language the measure of this distinctive cultural character (Smith, 1983: 181–2). However, for Herder nationalism was a universal sentiment shared by all people and, therefore, not just a German urge. The universality of nationalism could, therefore, serve as the basis for peaceful co-existence among nations. On the other hand, for Hegel the destiny of the German nation was to be united under the leadership of Prussia and to carry forward the spirit of Western civilization (Sabine and Thorson, 1973: 572–9). More aggressive versions of nationalism also appeared in Germany under the influence of the so-called German Romantic Movement. For example, Fichte simply assumed that the German nation existed and that individuals had to subordinate themselves to the nation, while the nation had to strive to achieve a sovereign state (Smith, 1983: 198–9). Generally the Romantics exalted faith and intuition instead of reason and intellect. Ideas about the superiority of the Aryan race were also expressed. German nationalism found its first forceful expression under Bismarck. Later, National Socialism emerged as an awesome form of militarism, expansionism and racism. Thus German nationalism, which originated as a defensive reflex against French hegemony, instead turned later into a veritable militarist doctrine of expansion and conquest.

Benedict Anderson (1983: 52–65) argues that modern nationalism based on the notion of equal rights of all citizens and democracy appeared as a political project first in Latin America and not in Europe as is commonly believed. The creole upper classes began to demand freedom from metropolitan Spain (in the case of Brazil from Portugal) in the early nineteenth century, and Latin America could win freedom already in the last century. The founding of new states also served as the basis for the abolition of slavery. Interesting in this connection is the fact that, except for Brazil, all regions of Latin America were predominantly Spanish-speaking, but this did not help bring about a single united Spanish-speaking super-state. Rather the old administrative boundaries established earlier by Spain became the boundaries of the new states. These had also been treated historically by Spain as discrete economic zones. However, under the imperial system most superior appointments went to European Spaniards and the colonies were forbidden to trade independently. Spain monopolized the trade of its colonies. Consequently the creoles were alienated from political power and denied economic gains. Under the circumstances the creoles began to distinguish themselves from their European kins and instead developed a national identity which included rather than excluded the aboriginal Indians (B. Anderson, 1983: 52).

About Anderson's remark that Latin American nationalist leaders proclaimed equal rights of all citizens it can be said that the practical significance of such declarations was the abolition of slavery; a revolutionary act as such. However, after several hundred years of violence and suppression the surviving native Indians and the Africans had been reduced to an inferior position in the social hierarchy. The creoles occupied the upper layer and the mestizos the middle position above the Indians and Africans. Thus an ethnical social and power hierarchy had been firmly consolidated and the enjoyment of equal citizen rights was not substantial for the subordinate classes and ethnic groups.

In Europe, nationalism expressed as the demand for self-determination belongs to the period from the latter half of the nineteenth century onwards. The Italians Mazzini and Garibaldi presented nationalism in terms of humanitarian liberalism and as revolutionary patriotism respectively, as an integral element of democracy and social justice enshrined in the notion of self-rule. It followed logically from such theorizing that the highest level of self-rule was the possession of sovereign power. In short, the hallmark of nationhood was the achievement of statehood. However, these liberal theorists who supported the idea of national self-determination had in mind a threshold in terms of size when they supported or opposed the right of self-determination. A large nationality which could sustain a big state and ensure development was entitled to separate statehood, but not smaller groups, which were thought to play a divisive and negative role. Thus Mazzini was opposed to Irish, Sicilian, and Welsh petty nationalisms (Hobsbawm, 1992: 31).

As a political doctrine of self-determination, nationalism was put to use extensively in Europe rather late in history: in the late nineteenth century and early twentieth century. At that time, the huge land-based multinational, multi-ethnic Austro-Hungarian, Czarist and Ottoman empires comprised a great variety of confessional and linguistic nationalities which were kept in submission by a tiered land-owning nobility and the imperial bureaucracy. The nationalist movements that cropped up in central and eastern Europe were of several varieties — movements aiming for freedom of particular nationalities within specific and limited territories as well as irredentist and Great Nation pan-Slavic and pan-German movements.

Early in the twentieth century, W. Wilson and V.I. Lenin (1969) came out forcefully in support of the right to national self-determination for linguistic nationalities and colonized peoples. Consequently many independent states came into being in central eastern Europe after the First World War as a result of the dismemberment of the Austro-Hungarian, Czarist, German and Ottoman empires. During this later phase of European nationalism it was some people claiming to be a nation which was allotted a state. In other words, this time nation preceded state. The process of reconstruction of the map of central and eastern Europe, however, entailed forced expulsion and extermination of those unfortunate nationalities and cultural groups which were either wrongly placed or too small to be given consideration. Notwithstanding the bloodshed which ensued the formation of these new so-called nation-states, minority nationalities and cultural groups continued to be found in them. On the other hand, many Asian possessions of the Czarist empire were retained by the Bolsheviks following the 1917 Revolution.

Nationalist ideologies invoking the right of self-determination also began emerging in the twentieth century among the peoples of Asia and Africa. The anticolonial movements which they inspired were fired with democratic passion about self-rule and national sovereignty reminiscent of the positive ideals of the French Revolution. After the Second World War, the process of decolonization began in earnest. Between 1945 and 1960 much of Asia and Africa secured their freedom by various peaceful and violent means.

The dialectical nature of nationalism

Most central to note with regard to nationalism is that both as a political movement and as an ideology it harbours a dialectical relationship between two opposite tendencies. On the one hand, it is the manifestation of a rational and democratic — and by that token universal — principle originating in the libertarian spirit of the Enlightenment: if individuals have a right to autonomy, then by analogy nations and peoples have the right to self-rule. On the other hand, nationalism is a particularist outlook whose chief purpose is to draw sharp lines between people on the basis of some cultural distinction, and upon such a basis claim the right of self-determination, and by that token power, for a particular group over a specific territory (Wittrock, 1988: 299). Which of the two tendencies dominates in a particular nationalist claim can be identified only empirically, in its historical context and in relation to counter-claims.

A perverted logical corollary of the particularist type of nationalist claim can be that non-members have to be expelled from its territories to make the claim more real and the nation-state viable. Classically, in modern times, the creation of Israel was accompanied by such drastic measures against the Arabs. In South Asia, the division of the Indian subcontinent into India and Pakistan was attended by communal pogroms. The most infamous present-day case of ethnic cleansing is the Bosnian situation in which Serbian excesses against Muslims have become proverbial. In contemporary South Asia the claimants to self-determination against the established states have also been carrying out ethnic cleansing against minority groups settled among them; Sikhs against Hindus in Punjab, Muslims against Hindus in Kashmir; Mohajirs and Sindhis against each other and against other settlers; the tribals of the Chittagong Hill Tracts against Bengali settlers from the plains; and Tamils against Sinhalese and Muslims. Such acts are, of course, mostly retaliations to the brutality of the state. The important thing to note is that the application of the right of self-determination in modern multi-ethnic multi-cultural societies can be extremely unsafe for minorities, because it seldom happens that wholly homogeneous societies are co-extensive with specific territories.

Post-colonial claims to national self-determination against established states

The exercising of the right of self-determination by many colonized peoples of Asia and Africa in the postwar period did not result in a neat transfer of power to consolidated nations. This statement is a commonplace, but it captures a significant flaw in the anatomy of the post-colonial state: decolonization split tribes, communities, peoples and nationalities and placed them oddly and arbitrarily into successor states carved out of empires. At the same time, the anti-colonial ideology could mobilize a wide assortment of patriotic opinion consisting of social classes, peoples, communities and nationalities and a wide variety of political organizations who wanted the colonial power to leave. Thus both involuntarily as well as out of free choice diverse cultural units and political organizations were subsumed under the potential nation and allotted to the post-colonial states. An implicit stipulation of decolonization was that these several entities were to work for the realization of their rights and aspirations within the framework of the new states.

The current international system and the principle of self-determination

The subsequent appearance of separatist nationalist movements against established states in the postwar period was poorly anticipated both in international law and in academic development theory. While recognizing the general principle of self-determination, the United Nations Charter of 1945 based itself essentially on the notion of sovereign rights of states over their territories (Article 2.—7). The system of representation in the General Assembly was also constituted primarily in terms of member states while the people permanently residing in them were described as the nation. The United Nations Universal Declaration of Human Rights of 1948 took up an individualistic and not a group standpoint on human rights. The United Nations International Covenant on Economic, Social and Cultural Rights (1966: Article 1.—1,2,3) and the United Nations International

Covenant of Civil and Political Rights (1966: Article 1.—1,2,3), however, explicitly recognize the right of self-determination of a people. This right is envisaged in particular for Non-Self-Governing and Trust territories, in other words for existing colonies and other similar areas. Yet simultaneously the right of the 'nation-state' to ensure its survival, and by that token to prevent secession, is accorded primacy in the United Nations International Covenant on Civil and Political Rights (Article 4.—1). Confusion has existed therefore in UN discussions and documents on the usage of the terms 'peoples' and 'nations'. Sometimes they were used interchangeably, but later 'peoples' came to be accepted as a wider term while 'nation' was used in a more reserved manner for political entities possessing a state of their own. Self-determination for peoples was understood in a positive sense of right to exercise self-rule while for nations it applied negatively, in the sense of non-interference from outside powers. Such distinctions did not help to resolve the question of concrete application of such a right, once decolonization had been achieved and it was raised against an established state (Davidson, 1993: 14–15).

That this has happened is not surprising since in principle the international political order has generally been indifferent if not directly hostile to demands to national self-determination raised by disgruntled cultural groups against sovereign states whose territorial integrity is sanctioned by international law, conventions and treaties. On the other hand, notwithstanding a bias in favour of the status quo, the asymmetry and anarchy in the global power balance provided hostile neighbours, regional powers, big powers and superpowers ample opportunities to exploit the internal ethnic conflicts of newly formed or unstable states; hence the clash between principles and *real-politik* and the inevitable arbitrary and opportunistic handling by external actors of conflicting nationalist claims.

Territorial state: the norm

The interesting point to note is that, notwithstanding the controversial nature of many individual states in Asia and Africa, the territorial state system itself has been accepted as the legitimate and desirable framework for organizing society. Nobody seriously envisages the reversal of the modern state system to some pre-colonial loose political order, without fixed borders and absence of central authority. At any rate, such a possibility is wholly impractical in the contemporary international state system which leaves no scope for territorial ambiguity. On the contrary, possession of state authority has become the norm for effective exercise of political influence and the pursuit of economic interest. Thus whereas reversal of the territorial state to some idyllic non-state or extra-territorial community is out of the question, this does not detract from the fact that the authority of specific individual states has been challenged both from within and from outside. Consequently claims to national self-determination have been staked against some states in the Third World by groups claiming to be nations by themselves.

The modernity of nation and nationalism

Ernest Gellner (1983: 1) asserts: 'Nationalism is primarily a political principle, which holds that the political and the national unit should be congruent.' The term originated during modernization and industrialization and was not to be found in pre-modern societies. Anthony Smith (1986) disagrees about the modernity of nations and points out that nationalism is a sentiment as old as history. The ethnic roots of modern nations are to be traced back into their collective memories and myths. The historically derived ethnic identity serves as the basis of nation-formation in moments of revolutionary change. Therefore nations can more appropriately be considered ethnic groups politicized during modernization. John Breuilly asserts that it is misleading to think of nationalism in cultural terms. Nationalism 'is, above all and beyond all else, about politics, and that politics is about power. Power, in the modern world, is primarily about control of the state' (1982: 1–2).

Karl Deutsch (1966: 86–106) lays emphasis on communications as the chief factor in the modernization process. Smaller units of society which are fed with a standardized code of communication, particularly language, become a people. When a people is organized for political action to acquire a measure of effective control over its members it becomes a nationality. A nationality graduates to a nation when it acquires the power to back up its aspirations. The consummation to full nationhood occurs when it achieves sovereign status in a state of its own. Benedict Anderson (1983) emphasizes the role played by the print revolution and capitalism in forming modern nations. The literate middle classes became the bearers of national consciousness centred upon the vernacular languages rather than Latin which was cultivated by the priestly and aristocratic classes.

Orthodox Marxism also conceptualizes the nation as a configuration resulting from assimilation of diverse smaller cultural groups under the impact of modernization. According to Joseph Stalin: 'A nation is a historically constituted, stable community of people, formed on the basis of a common language, territory, economic life, and psychological make-up manifested in a common culture' (1972: 60). Moreover, the presence of all these conditions is considered necessary. Most centrally, common religion or ethnic origin as the sole basis of nation is rejected while common language is stressed. Furthermore, the development of communities and nationalities into nations is related primarily to the level of economy. When capitalist relations of production and exchange become the dominant mode of production, less advanced nationalities move on to become nations. In principle nations are entitled to sovereign rights over specific territory.

The question of congruence between nation and state

The idea that nation and state should be congruent underlies modern Western political theory and is reflected in the power struggles which raged in Western Europe during the eighteenth and nineteenth centuries and later (Snyder, 1976). The influential theory of nationalism propounded by Ernest Gellner (presented first in 1964 and elaborated subsequently, especially in 1983) states that industrialization has the in-built logic of bringing nation and state into congruence. Such is not the case in agrarian society, which is based on the division of labour between a vast peasantry and a small but variegated upper class. The prevalent ideology legitimizes inequality and stratification within the group and there is no interest in promoting homogeneity. Rather, variegated sub-units based on dialectal and ritual diversity can be found within cultural groups. Furthermore, high culture is the exclusive domain of literary specialists belonging to the power élite within each cultural group. Thus each group is insulated from the other by cultural particularism (1983: 8–13).

In contrast to agrarian society, the new high culture of modern society deriving from the logic of expansive industrialization requires the dissolution of specializations in the division of labour and their replacement by functioning individuals equipped with general skills who can be put to use on a wider basis. Thus the high culture of the industrial age encompasses the mass of the population. It stands for equality and homogenization of society. Mobility is the essence of the industrial division of labour. It does not mean that specialization ceases to exist. Rather, specialization remains considerable but changing from one type of activity to another within comparable branches of production is easier and a matter of retraining (1983: 24–38).

The modern system of education is the chief medium through which the state equips the people with general skills that can be put to use everywhere. Only a nation-size educational system can produce citizens equipped with modern education. A small village or any other minor unit is inadequate for such a purpose. Acquisition of literacy in the official language opens the door to membership in the nation. Those produced by one educational system employing a particular language cannot serve easily in another society employing another language. Hence education and language become the basis of the new nationalism centred on the state. Industrialization and modernization do not proceed evenly, however. Rather, greater differentiation takes place with the increased momentum of modernization. In these circumstances, the intelligentsia of cultural groups which are distinguishable from mainstream society in a marked sense — in terms of language or other primordial factors — can develop a sense of separate identity and nationalism and invent a nation (Gellner, 1964: 147–78).

The incessant pursuit of growth inevitably brings about centralization of state power. The centralized state cannot tolerate other centres of power. Most cultural groups, however, do not develop a strong separatist movement and are in the course of time broken down and dissolved. Thus, although nationalism is a strong force, not all cultural groups cross the threshold and become nations. In any case there are some 8000 language groups in the world and each cannot possibly be provided with a separate state (Gellner, 1983: 43–50). Moreover, the creation of a new state does not fulfil the aspirations of all group members. The two main social bases of nationalism are the intelligentsia and the proletariat. For the former national independence brings enormous advantage in terms of access to important decision-making positions and other jobs in the political system. For the latter independence is usually a disenchantment and may even bring about more harsh treatment at the hands of the national bourgeoisie. As regards the alleged irrational nature of nationalism, Gellner chides liberals and Marxists for seeing only rational, enlightened and universalist features in modern people. People are equally swayed by passions, ethnic loyalties and unreason. This explains how in the real world both reason and passion affect human behaviour (Gellner, 1964: 147–78).

The growth-maximizing processes nevertheless continue unabated, and under mature industrialization become predominant, rendering nation and state congruent. However, complete congruence may never occur, and several groups may retain their separate cultural identity beside the nation, unless the state is willing to exterminate them wholesale. The diversity that may remain can be accommodated in the mainstream since high culture disseminated by the state includes the inculcation of the main rules of the political game which are shared and respected by all.

A critique of Gellner's theory

While Gellner's views on uneven development are most instructive in understanding the appearance of separatism, his theory about nation-state congruence is essentially derived from the historical experience of Western Europe. As a generalization it is somewhat teleological with a metaphysical tinge about it, and some dangerous implications follow from it for the multicultural regions of the developing world. For what is to be done if most parts of the Third World (where agrarian society is currently in the process of dissolution) remain only partially or incompletely industrialized for a long time to come? How should the plurality and diversity of culture which are likely to survive partial industrialization be handled by the state? What if the weak push of industrialization is compounded by extra-industrial compulsions such as the sudden proliferation of ideas dysfunctional to national unity, or the emergence of internal rebellions, or the appearance of external threats? Under such circumstances, the state will have to work out some sort of a congruent nation or else perish. On the other hand, state-led homogenization may not have a basis in a burgeoning industrial expansion. Rather it may stem from security fears or ideological rigidity or even economic stagnation. Moreover those groups which may succeed in breaking away in the process are also likely to suffer the same disabilities of peripheral capitalism: incomplete industrialization.

More fundamentally, there is no guarantee that successful and complete industrialization and the dissemination of high culture preclude all future regressions. The international economy is known better for its periodic ups and downs than for some eternal state of stability and growth. Gellner himself has argued against the prevalent belief in total human rationality and stressed the recognition of the irrational dimension in the human kind (1964: 147–78). Under stress the irrational dimension tends to assert itself in all societies. Even in the most homogeneous of Western societies such as Sweden the recent inflow of large numbers of immigrants and political refugees is likely to complicate the question of congruence. At any rate, nationalism as ethnic congruence is an unrealistic perception of the modern global processes of mobility and migration.

On the other hand, in theory, orthodox Marxism recognizes the possibility of several nations living together in a single state out of free will, but reserving the right to withdraw and establish their own states. The USSR was formally organized as a voluntary federation of various nations, nationalities and national groups. In practice, however, the state remained highly centralized. The various republics enjoyed cultural autonomy in terms of preserving and developing their respective languages, but were under strict political control of the centre dominated by ethnic Russians.

The point is that all states seek to develop effective mechanisms for controlling society, and *some type of congruence* between nation and state is necessary for the orderly and systematic reproduction of the material and emotional needs of people. How this can possibly be managed by Third World states is a question which is addressed in the final section of this book.

An historical-comparative regional analysis

According to Partha Ghosh, 'a region may be broadly termed as a particular geographical area of the world the constituent states of which have shared historical, cultural and economic features and which, in foreign affairs, behave as interrelated units' (1989: 7).

South Asia qualifies very well as a region according to the above definition. In the present study, however, only the four post-colonial states of India, Pakistan, Bangladesh and Sri Lanka in the South Asian region have been included. Nepal and tiny Bhutan on the Indian subcontinent are kingdoms which escaped colonial occupation and could retain many characteristics of traditional societies. Modernization and industrialization have thus far made only a token appearance in them. Although ethnic tension has come to the surface, in Nepal especially, there is no significant separatist movement present in these states. Similarly the minuscule Maldives in the Indian Ocean, with a population of only 200,000 form a homogeneous society where separatism does not appear to be an option of any sort. Afghanistan is sometimes included in South Asia, but culturally and politically remains more a part of south-west Asia.

Not only are India, Pakistan, Bangladesh and Sri Lanka located in the same geographical region but their pre-colonial cultural and political heritage stems from common, though quite variegated, ancient and medieval roots. More crucially, they owe their origins to the processes of change and transformation — uneven but interconnected — wrought by the same colonial power. The British intervention in a marked sense separated state from society. The élites which took over power at the time of British withdrawal were compelled by a host of internal and external pressures to reduce or eliminate the existing incongruence between state and society. Consequently all these four states have been engaged in nation-building. Each has sought socio-economic modernization and development as essential components of nation-building. On the other hand, each of them differs in terms of size, level of socio-economic development, ethno-cultural mix, dominant cultural tradition, élite ideology and emplacement in the regional and global political order.

Notwithstanding these similarities and differences, the nation-building processes in all these four countries have been confronted by serious separatist challenges. Each case of separatism constitutes a unique specimen of state–society contradictions with its own history and dynamics. However, these challenges invariably connect with the politics of the neighbouring states and, therefore, can be understood only in relationship to each other and to the wider global system. These processes, connections and linkages are analysed in an historical-comparative manner. The main focus is on ethnic conflict and separatism after independence, particularly during the 1980s and until the end of 1993. The historical context is, however, traced back to the colonial period and beyond. In the case of the Sikhs, their historical background is given in greater detail as their origins as a religious group are relatively less known. By 1993 the various states had gained the initiative and a low ebb in separatism could be observed except for the Kashmir situation. The struggle over Kashmir was the last to emerge in the form of a violent separatist movement and continues at a high conflict level.

The following are the main questions examined. What are the historical roots of the contemporary ethnic conflict and separatist movements in South Asia? What is the relationship between modernization and nation-building? What is the relationship between state, nation and ethnicity? Under what conditions does ethnic tension assume separatist or secessionist direction? What type of social forces are involved in these struggles? What type of mechanisms do the state and the separatist challenger employ to advance their demand for loyalty, submission and support from the people? What is the role of external actors in such conflict? What role does violence play in such confrontations? Furthermore, what measures can be taken to reduce ethnic tension and to facilitate peaceful settlement of armed conflicts between the state and the separatists?

Reliability of official statistics and documents

The 1981 censuses of India, Pakistan, Bangladesh and Sri Lanka provide the basis for statistics on population and a breakdown in terms of religious and linguistic composition, sectorial distribution of the economy, and so on. A study on nationalism, ethnic conflict and separatism includes centrally the question of numbers. Such numbers and figures must invariably be obtained from government sources. However, information on population, religion, language and ethnic origin given in the census reports are sensitive matters and the states are likely to manipulate such data. Most typically, government figures on minorities are almost always challenged by the minorities. The latter claim to be more than what the government reports. For example the 1981 Indian Census gives the number of Muslims as 75.5 million. Indian Muslims claim to have been more than 80 million at that time. Similarly the Pakistan Census of 1981 gives the Ahmadiyya sect's following in Pakistan as a mere 104,244. A senior member of the Ahmadiyya sect in Sweden, a humanitarian refugee from Pakistan, claimed the incredible figure of six million for his community in Pakistan.

Hazards of data collection

Doing research on armed conflict between the state and separatist movements is both daunting and risky. The researcher must learn to conduct the inquiry amid the suspicion and hostility of both the concerned states and their bureaucracies, including their various secret services, as well as that of the separatist movements and their spokespeople. Much of the ethnic violence carried out by various agents are acts of sheer terror and brutality, for which no state official or spokesperson for a separatist movement is willing to take direct responsibility. It is not uncommon for a visa to travel to a particular country to be refused outright or restricted to some few places removed from the troubled areas. The ethnic origin of the researcher plays an important role in how states and separatist movements deal with pleas for access to research material.

Interviews with spokespeople of separatist movements

Interviews are a vital experience for the researcher in this field. Government officials almost never agree to be interviewed and invariably refer to their official publications and to newspaper reports. Those who venture to speak request not to be identified or quoted. On the other hand, interviews with informed politicians, academics and journalists are very useful for sharpening the focus of the inquiry. They also served as the author's sources for coming into contact with the relevant organizations involved in the separatist struggles. All interviews were tape-recorded. The spokespeople dwelt upon their nationalist cause at their own pace. Questions and clarifications were kept to the minimum and not all were responded to by the interviewees. Only summaries of these interviews are presented in this book. Publications of the separatist organizations are also an important source for understanding their ideology, programme and strategy, and their version of truth.

Face-to-face talks with spokesmen of the secessionist movements, if obtained, are perhaps the most valuable part of research on separatism. Not so much as reliable sources for ascertaining objective truth but for learning about the circumstances in which the separatists operate. The ideologue or militant activist is convinced about the righteousness of his cause, holds his opponents in hatred and contempt and can provide excruciating details concerning the horrific ills meted out to his people. However, despite the possibility of disinformation and deception which these interviews can contain they are also the main channel through which these actors hope to inform and influence others, particularly the larger public.

Two of my interviewees were murdered before this book went into print. Krishnakumar alias Kittu, the International Secretary of the Tamil Tigers of Eelam, died in January 1993 when his boat was blown up in the Palk Strait. The chairman of the Mohajir Quomi Movement (the ethnic party of the Muslim refugees who left India and settled in Pakistan), Azim Ahmed Tariq, was assassinated in May 1993. Here one is confounded by a strange dilemma — the same person, group or organization can be seen as the perpetrator as well as the victim of ethnic-based hatred. Therefore, without theoretical understanding and historical context we cannot make sense of these conflicts. Consequently theoretical works have been consulted extensively to develop the framework and to integrate the empirical data.

Structure of the book

The problem being investigated has been introduced in Chapter 1. This is followed by a conceptual discussion on ethnicity, state, society and nation in Chapter 2. Chapter 3 deals with a theoretical discussion on the contradictions which arise between the state and disgruntled cultural groups in the form of ethnic clashes and separatist movements, as the former proceeds with nation-building in the context of the internal and external balance of power. In Chapter 4 a summary of the theoretical discussion conducted in Chapters 1–3 is presented and a theory of ethnic conflict and separatism in multicultural post-colonial states is proposed. Chapter 5 is an historical sketch of the evolution of state and society in the Indian subcontinent before India, Pakistan and Bangladesh emerged as independent states. Chapters 6 to 9 present state–separatist conflicts in India, Pakistan, Bangladesh and Sri Lanka. Chapter 9 on Sri Lanka also includes a sketch of Sri Lankan cultural and political history. Chapter 10 is devoted to a comparative analysis within a regional perspective of the main features of the state–society incongruence in each of these four states, ending with recommendations on how to manage ethnic conflict and separatism.

References

Anderson, B. (1983) *Imagined Communities*, London: Verso.

Anderson, P. (1983) 'Absolutist states of Western Europe' in D. Held *et al.* (eds), *States and Societies*, Oxford: Martin Robertson and Company.

Breuilly, J. (1982) *Nationalism and the State*, Manchester: Manchester University Press.

Davidson, S. (1993) *Human Rights: Law and Political Change*, Buckingham: Open University Press.

Deutsch, K.W. (1966) *Nationalism and Social Communication*, Cambridge, Mass.: MIT Press.

Gellner, E. (1964) *Thought and Change*, London: Weidenfeld and Nicolson.

Gellner, E. (1983) *Nations and Nationalism*, Oxford: Basil Blackwell Ltd.

Ghosh, P.S. (1989) *Cooperation and Conflict in South Asia*, New Delhi: Manohar Publications.

Giddens, A. (1985) *The Nation-State and Violence*, Cambridge: Polity Press.

Hobsbawm, E.J. (1992) *Nations and Nationalism Since 1780*, Cambridge: Cambridge University Press.

Jonsson, P. (1991) 'Svensk överhet och finska undersåtar' in *Finsk-Ungriska Småskrifter*, Lund: Finsk-ugriska Institutionen.

Lenin, V.I. (1969) *The National Liberation Movement in the East*, Moscow: Progress Publishers.

Rousseau, J.-J. (1990) *The Social Contract and Discourses*, London: Everyman.

Sabine, G.H. and Thorson, T.L. (1973) *A History of Political Theory*, Hinsdale: Dryden Press.

Smith, A.D. (1983) *Theories of Nationalism*, London: Duckworth.

Smith, A.D. (1986) *The Ethnic Origins of Nations*, Oxford: Basil Blackwell Ltd.

Snyder, L.L. (1976) *Varieties of Nationalism: A Comparative Study*, New York: Holt, Rinehart and Winston.

Stalin, J.V. (1972) 'Marxism and the National Question' in B. Franklin (ed.), *The Essential Stalin*, New York: Anchor Books.

The United Nations Charter, 1945.

The United Nations International Covenant on Civil and Political Rights, 1966.

The United Nations International Covenant on Economic, Social, and Cultural Rights, 1966.

The United Nations Universal Declaration of Human Rights, 1948.

Wittrock, B. (1988) 'Kulturell identitet och den moderna staten' in G. Winai-Ström (ed.), *Konfliktlösning i det flerkulturella samhället*, Uppsala: Uppsala Universitet.

2

Ethnicity, State, Society and Nation

This chapter examines the relationships between ethnicity, state, society and nation. The following questions are posed to elicit the relationships: What constitutes the ethnic category? Does ethnicity invariably serve as a rallying point for political action or is it contingent upon a set of situational and historical factors to gain political significance? When do ethnic differences result in violent conflict? What is the relation between ethnicity, state, society and nation?

The concept of ethnicity

Human beings act individually or in groups in the pursuit of their goals and interests. This is a matter of common observance. Individual action, however, rarely suffices to make effective demands on state and society. Political parties, pressure groups, class and professional organizations, ethnic group, caste and kinship lineages are some of the channels, other than the family, which are employed for influencing larger societal entities. Both Marx and Weber were convinced that in modern industrial society social consciousness based on ties of affection will be supplanted by rational affinities. In the case of the former it was class and in the latter nation which was to replace primordial identity. This optimism has subsequently coloured a wide variety of social science theories. Recurrent ethnic behaviour patterns in many parts of the world, not least significantly in advanced industrial societies such as the United States, therefore, has been a perplexing intellectual riddle for social scientists trained to believe in the triumph of reason and universalism. To them, ethnically oriented behaviour has seemed an anachronistic irritant — primordial and atavistic — out of place with the overall development of society.

The post-war ethnic revival therefore has been some sort of an intellectual provocation which theories and concepts prevalent in social science at that time could not explain adequately. It was in 1953 that the term ethnicity was first employed in social science to denote the character or quality of an ethnic group (Banton, 1983:

114). The concept of ethnicity was advanced as a generic term covering tension and conflict arising out of the cultural heterogeneity in a territorial state. In many senses it was put forth as a replacement for class to conceptualize social stratification in society. Theories of ethnicity suggested interaction between cultural groups, vertically structured with their own ranking systems, as a more reliable measure of social behaviour than social class in post-industrial mass consumption societies.

Two main types of theories of ethnicity were put forth: those emphasizing primordiality and those laying stress on situational and contextual factors. The primordialists considered the ethnic identity as a given. Because of primordial affinities deriving from race, skin colour, tribe, caste, language, religion and other such factors each ethnic group has a different historical experience and consequently its position in society is likewise determined. The primordialists argued that human beings have always been grouped together on the basis of given primordial characteristics (Geertz, 1963; Shils, 1957: 113–45). Other writers pointed out the situational nature of the ethnic identity. Identity is multidimensional and consists of several ingredients — skin colour, religion, language and so on. Which of them is relevant depends on the requirements of the situation (Phadnis, 1989: 14–15). Young (1976) goes so far as to describe ethnic identity as a fluid concept. Alavi (1989: 223) contrasts ethnicity with class and asserts that class membership is based on the division of labour and is not, therefore, amenable to subjective manoeuvre. On the other hand the ethnic identity contains no permanent boundaries. It is essentially a reactive awareness formed in a given situation and, therefore, not a given category. In other words ethnicity is elusive, an epiphenomenon, while class deriving from status and location in the system of production is real and rational.

Donald L. Horowitz (1985: 21–54) stresses the salience of ethnic conflict in heterogeneous Third World societies. People identify themselves with their ethnic group rather than the nation or state. Especially important to note is the distinction between ranked and unranked groups. Where ethnic origin and social class coincide it is a case of a ranked system. Unranked groups are cross-class. If ethnic groups are structured in a hierarchy, with one group superordinate and the other subordinate, and constitute a single society the ranked group will seek greater equality so that vertical differences are minimized or eliminated and the group can move up. When armed conflict or war takes place between two ranked groups it takes the form of a social revolution. The Hutu uprising against the Tutsi in 1959 in Rwanda and the African uprising against Arab domination in Zanzibar in 1964 are cases in point.

On the other hand, in an unranked system parallel ethnic groups co-exist, each group stratified internally. Unranked groups constitute whole societies by themselves. Between two unranked groups the problem of superiority can exist, but it is not settled. As they are autonomous societal units they can display quite different types of leadership. This can be problematic if they have to interact on a regular basis. The problem is not so much about subordination, but of inclusion and exclusion. Competition and conflict between unranked groups can be likened to interaction between two sovereign states. Disgruntled unranked ethnic groups talk in terms of being nations, and separatism is likely to be present among them. However, neither ranked nor unranked groups are static. Rather, on the global level, ethnic subordination is on the decline. Even ranked groups can rewrite their histories and aim at higher status as unranked groups.

Horowitz concentrates mainly on the competition between unranked ethnic systems. On the role of the state in ethnic competition, the author distinguishes between a dispersed polity and a centralized polity. It is not, however, clear if it is a question of ethnic dispersion that the author has in mind or whether it is a question of how the state is ideologically and politically constituted to deal with the ethnic factor. At any rate, the argument is that dispersed systems facilitate inter-ethnic co-operation while centralized systems impede it.

Paul Brass (1974: 8) distinguishes ethnic group, community and nationality/ nation on the basis of the level of consciousness. An ethnic group is an objectively distinct group, but its members do not necessarily attach subjective importance or political significance to that fact. A community is an ethnic group whose members have developed an awareness of common identity and have sought to draw boundaries of the group. A community becomes a nationality or nation when it mobilizes for political action and attains political significance. However, not all groups move in such a direction: some disintegrate or merge into the larger society, others retain their separate identity. Brass (1991: 23–36) emphasizes the role of élite competition as the basis for ethnic groups developing subjective consciousness and making political demands. The author presents an instrumentalist view of ethnic identity which is constructed (though not invented) from objective differences and is not, therefore, simply given.

The subjectivity of ethnic rationality

While ethnicity is certainly an important feature of modern politics, it can be asserted that its most conspicuous characteristic is its subjective rationality. This behaviour may be reactive to real discrimination practised by the state, but the important point is that it tends to draw sharp lines between the rights of the group and those of others. Not only groups which in an objective sense have been badly treated by the state but also those which may have benefited in a tangible and manifest sense can develop a very strong sense of dissatisfaction against the state. Consequently in competition between unranked groups, or between the state and unranked groups, ethnicity can play the role of masking objective contradictions deriving from class and social rank within society as a whole and its various constituent units. In periods of socio-economic or political stress and crisis, ethnicity is subject to easy manoeuvre by opinion-builders. This subjective rationality of ethnicity or rather its emotional and irrational nature can hinder communication between the parties to a dispute.

Ethnic identity: a product of 'objective differences' and situational factors

The view taken in the present investigation is that ethnic identity needs to be conceptualized as multidimensional, comprising 'objective characteristics' some or all of which can gain relevance in certain situations and become 'objective differences' and be employed by a set of individuals to mobilize those who share these characteristics for some societal action. In other words, ethnic identity is situational, contextual and in terms of basis for collective action constructed. In an historical conjuncture particular identity markers may acquire political or social relevance and serve as the basis for allocation of differential rights, access to opportunities and affect personal safety.

The author's personal impressions of British South Asian society are quite interesting. Under normal conditions immigrants from South Asia in the UK — Indians, Pakistanis, Bangladeshis, Sri Lankans — tend to feel solidarity with each other in the face of racism in white British society. The assertion of South Asian identity in these circumstances is situational, essentially reactive and in response to the concrete circumstances. It is relevant in the UK, but does not correspond to the actual politics of South Asia where considerable tension and hostility exists between the various states, and no doubt their citizens are influenced by official propaganda and entertain a certain amount of antipathy against each other if not actual hostility.

Paradoxically, while retaining a state-oriented patriotism in the UK, they simultaneously socialize with one another across religious and state-ascribed nationality on the basis of their language and popular culture. Thus Punjabi Muslims, Sikhs and Hindus or Gujrati Hindus and Muslims interact often socially, sometimes regularly, in a deeply affectionate manner. This happens in the other direction too. Indian, Pakistani and Bangladeshi Muslims or Bangladeshi and Indian Hindus develop lasting fraternal ties. These multifarious relationships are, of course, subject to variation and fluctuation. Muslim—Hindu—Sikh clashes in the subcontinent tend to sour and embitter relations in the UK. On the other hand, the new generation of South Asians born and brought up in the UK inevitably internalize many norms and values upheld by British culture. A clash of identity and values, therefore, occurs between the new Britons of South Asian origin and their parents and elders. These apparently conflicting propensities obtain within each Hindu, Muslim or Sikh family settled in Europe, North America and elsewhere outside their own societies. Besides these sectional divisions there exist also movements among leftist non-white intellectuals living in Europe to unite Africans and Asians around a common black identity in relation to white society.

While such behaviour reflects the significance of objective characteristics and their role in identity formation, at the same time it shows that these differences serve as the basis of social consciousness and mobilization only in relation to concrete situations: group identities expand and contract, and at the same time new ones are formed and old ones weaken or dissipate altogether.

The limits of ethnic mutability

While the multi-dimensionality and flexibility of ethnic identity is important to bear in mind, a distinction between its immutable and mutable elements is worth remembering. Biologically fixed characteristics cannot be acquired, transformed or abandoned at will. On the other hand, other so-called objective identity markers are amenable to change. A new language can be learnt or a different religion adopted. A change of language and/or religion is more practicable on the individual level, however. Large groups of people sharing a culture evolved around a language or religion or a combination of both rarely make such adjustments on a voluntary basis. Objective identity markers therefore need to be conceptualized as both fixed and flexible.

Ethnicity and state

In multi-ethnic societies unequal distribution of influence and resources between and among different ethnic groups is more of a rule than an exception. Two influential proponents of an instrumentalist theory of ethnicity, Glazer and Moynihan (1975: 10), write: 'The strategic efficacy of ethnicity as a basis for asserting claims against government has its counterpart in the seeming ease whereby government employs ethnic categories as a basis for distributing its rewards.' Rather than dismissing ethnicity as a primitive hangover, inconsistent with a liberal democratic environment, Glazer and Moynihan emphasize its normal place in modern US politics. In a similar vein Enloe (1980: 12–22) argues that the ethnic factor is of paramount importance in the security planning of states. Recruitment to the armed forces, deployment of troops and filling of sensitive and strategic positions are carefully screened on an ethnic basis.

However, what may be normal practice for states need not be the normal expectation of their people. If employment of ethnic criteria for distributing rewards is perceived as discriminatory by citizens, some type of protest can come along sooner or later. The state can mitigate ethnic tension if people can find employment on the basis of their qualifications and if political parties based on class or ideology or some other rational criterion exist which provide a forum for people to come together and make political demands on a universal basis. On the other hand, the state can severely limit the possibility of adjustment for people by adopting explicit policy to discriminate against some groups. In such circumstances ethnic identity may be objectified, leaving little or no room for manoeuvre and adjustment.

An apt example of this process was the apartheid system which until 28 April 1994 debarred non-whites in South Africa from equal civil and political rights. Limitations on non-Muslims to participate in politics in Pakistan are another example. A state legalizing discrimination on the basis of ethnic differences is involved in some sort of segregational policy. It may be total or limited, based on racist myth or religious injunction. In such circumstances a clear-cut ethnic response is likely but not necessary. Through political efforts opposition to the state can be grounded on ideology rather than primordiality. The ANC represents such an effort to transcend ethnic differences and seek a universal democratic basis for its politics. Equally, a political party or group leaders can seek to objectify an ethnic distinction and claim special treatment or rights on that basis. During the freedom struggle against the British in India the Muslim League represented a purely ethnic response. The Inkatha movement in contemporary South Africa represents such a tendency.

The majoritarian principle and ethnicity

It can be argued that, because states are entities representing organized power, the most powerful group or groups are likely to be those who not only constitute the majority but also dominate the state. In all heterogeneous societies usually the biggest group dominates the state both in terms of political and military power and in terms of cultural identity. Where this is not the case and small but militarily strong minorities are in power, as was the case in Uganda under Idi Amin, South Africa under the apartheid system, or in present-day Iraq (20 per cent Sunni Arabs) and Syria (11 per cent Alawite Arabs), the employment of force by the state to control the majority is very likely. The large-scale ethnic violence in Burundi and Rwanda during 1993–94 is also reflective of the same problem, though in a different form. The Tutsi minority (15 per cent) dominates the army in both the states but the Hutu majority (85 per cent) has been expanding its influence through political and electoral means. Consequently the Hutu were emboldened in Rwanda to challenge the state and in 1994 they attacked the Tutsi and killed them in the thousands. The Tutsi army, however, managed to regain control and the Hutu were made to flee in large numbers to the neighbouring states. The situation continues to be explosive.

Where the ethnic distribution is such that the majority and the minority are not too unevenly balanced in numbers, other factors such as economic power, representation in the army, distribution in society (dispersed or concentrated in regions) assume importance. Malaysia and Nigeria are examples of such a situation. Such states have to work out some system of democratic power sharing or face the possibility of ethnic confrontation and possibly break up of the state. The role of ethnic numbers and control over state power, particularly the army, are important to consider in analyses of modern-day politics. However, any attempt to propound a grand theory of ethnicity and its relationship to national stability is fraught with oversimplification because historical legacy, cultural, socio-economic and external factors also contribute to the actual dynamics of specific societies.

Some general rules can be stated nevertheless for contemporary states: the 'normal' form of the state is that the ethnic majority dominates the state. Such a situation helps stabilization of power. On the other hand, the most explosive situations are those where a large ethnic majority is ruled by a small ethnic minority. Yet the apparent ubiquity of ethnicity in shaping state power in the sense that the biggest group is likely to dominate the state belongs to the modern nation-state. In the past, ethnic minorities could establish their hold over much larger societies and maintain it for long periods of time. The Muslim ruling class of South Asia was very often comprised of people of Turkish, Afghan or Persian origin who were few in numbers but controlled military power. European colonial empires of Asia and Africa were classical cases of minuscule minorities of Europeans ruling over vast numbers of natives. It was not until modernization, uneven development and rapid communications and the parallel development of the ideas of individual rights, nationalism and democracy had gained legitimacy that the very central political relevance of ethnicity was acknowledged. The notion of government by consent which was instituted in terms of free periodic elections ensured that the majority ethnic group was well represented in the government and the state. In theory democracy did not recognize ethnic majority as the basis of political majority. The majority principle was supposed to be based on the support which different political factions, later modern political parties, could receive from the electorate, which initially was restricted and later expanded to become universal finally. However, such developments took place in societies which were already consolidated ethnic entities such as the French, Swedish, Dutch and so forth. Therefore the ethnic factor did not play a significant role in their divisions of majority and minority. On the basis of the election result the French or Swedes could be part sometimes of the majority and at other times of the minority because the ascendance of the majority ethnic group was not threatened by such fluctuations.

At any rate, the majoritarian ethnic dimension has now become the standard and has consequently impacted on the state–society relationship all over the world.

Thus attitudes about legitimate authority are not permanent but subject to change along with other features of society. Any given conception of legitimate state, therefore, reflects historical conjunctures between cultural legacy, political awareness and concrete interests. What might be considered legitimate and proper at one point in time may appear grossly unfair and unacceptable in another. Consequently contemporary societies which are ruled by ethnic minorities unwilling to relinquish their dominant position have had to evolve some ideology which apparently transcends the majoritarian aspect of one type of ethnic identity and endeavours to replace it with another. Thus the Bathists of Iraq and Syria invoke pan-Arabism as a supra-ideology of all Arabs which debunks the ethnic identity based on sect, as for example that of the Shia Arab majority in Iraq, or the Sunni Arab majority in Syria. The degree of success of such ideological invocation is an empirical question.

Ethnicity and interests

At any rate, ethnic identity is an important variable in societal interaction. It serves an important psychological and emotional role in social life and also as a basis for collective action. However, human beings and their collective organizations rarely approach the question of identity in abstract terms. Rather it is their concrete needs and aspirations which determine the choice of identity. The multidimensionality of ethnicity usually enables people to make adjustments in their self-definition as they interact with others in the pursuit of their goals. Similarly states take cognition of the ethnic factor. It is one of the factors that the state and the political system must handle.

A definition of ethnicity

In the light of the above discussion ethnicity may be defined as: the tendency of human beings to associate with one another around shared religion, sect, language, cultural tradition, belief in common ancestry and a host of other particularist ties. The feeling of belonging together, of sharing common symbols and a structure of discourse is usually multidimensional, constituted by more than one so-called objective characteristic. Ethnic identity can, therefore, usually be rather pliable, facilitating adjustment to varying situations and contexts. Ethnicity necessarily involves feelings of solidarity and loyalty towards fellow members and, by that token, of detachment and indifference if not hostility towards 'others'. Very often ethnicity derives from some real or felt sense of deprivation and denial.

The terms ethnic group, cultural group and communal group are used interchangeably in the present study as they all represent the same sort of group feeling deriving from primordial ties.

State and society

Whereas the state is primarily a political entity represented by its officialdom and institutions, society pertains to the regular interactions between people which are sustained by customs, traditions, beliefs and values inherited from a common past, and includes the division of labour, production processes and the wider social order. Culture refers to common, stable, habitual preferences and priorities in thought and action (Deutsch, 1966). Society, however, is difficult to define in terms of exact boundaries. Family, tribe, caste, religious community, linguistic and regional groups and so on are social units within society. These possess a personality of their own while belonging simultaneously to the larger society. This means that amid the main body of customs, traditions, beliefs and values a huge variation can be found at individual level of societal unit.

In contrast to the vague nature of societal boundaries, the modern state is primarily a territorial entity with definite boundaries. Its boundaries become inevitably the framework within which society and its various units are produced and reproduced. However, as the state possesses organized power it has greater advantage in acting in a deliberate and specific way upon society. On the other hand, society consisting of various autonomous units cannot ordinarily act upon the state in a similar fashion. The ability of the state to act upon society in a deliberate manner, however, does not mean that it will always act successfully. To a large extent the state can act successfully if interpenetration between state and society has proceeded in some depth over a fairly long period of time and in the process have both come to acquire common politico-cultural features.

State—society consensus

Writing in the context of modern Western civilization, Weber defines the state as a societal organization which claims authority over a given population in a specific territory. It imposes its will through a system of administration and law modifiable by statute. The executive staff can legitimately use force on behalf of the state, within limits permitted or prescribed by its regulations (Weber, 1978: 41).

The idea of legitimate use of force implies that people habitually accept the authority of the state, and that it does not have to resort to force routinely to compel people to obey (Easton, 1965: 278–90). It also means that arbitrary use of power is not permitted and that the rule of law prevails. Further, it is presumed that legitimate authority derives from popular consent. The forms of organized authority (republic, constitutional monarchy and so on) can, however, differ from society to society, depending on cultural heritage and prevailing norms and values. In other words, the state is conceived ideally as an arbiter which society has created to resolve recurring disputes among members according to accepted universal rules and procedures (Skinner, 1978). Implicit in the consensus standpoint is the presumption that state and society in the West have developed symmetrically, in symbiosis with each other, and that improving the stability of this equilibrium through necessary change and adjustment is self-evident.

State–society tension

In the Marxist tradition, the state is not considered a neutral umpire settling disputes among individual, groups and classes according to law. Rather the main purpose of the state is to preserve the dominant economic mode of production and to promote the interests of the ruling class. It makes possible the exploitation of the labour of the real producers: slaves, serfs, workers and others through the threat or use of force as well as ideology (Engels, 1970: 461–583). Ideology created by the ruling class generates false consciousness among the exploited classes (Marx and Engels, 1976: 59). Antonio Gramsci (1976: 210–12) presents the idea of false consciousness as hegemony of the ruling class.

Intrinsic to the Marxist standpoint — which has been formed mainly in the context of the historical evolution of state and society in the West — is the presupposition that the state reflects the overall evolution of class society. It is part of the society and not outside or above it except in an ideological sense. Thus Marxist analysis of the capitalist state focuses on unmasking its class character with the intention of convincing the oppressed classes to change the situation to their advantage; in the ultimate sense by smashing the bourgeois state.

State pre-eminence

Theda Skocpol emphasizes the autonomy of the state in relation to social classes and the international system. She writes:

> The state properly conceived is no mere arena in which socioeconomic struggles are fought. It is, rather, a set of administrative, policing, and military organizations headed, and more or less well coordinated by, an executive authority. Any state first and fundamentally extracts resources from society and deploys these to create and support coercive and administrative organizations. Of course, these basic state organizations are built up and must operate within the context of class-divided socioeconomic relations, as well as within the context of national and international economic dynamics. (1979: 29)

Skocpol's main contention is that states are organizations which control people and territories. For the survival of the state it is not popular legitimacy which is essential, but legitimacy accorded to it by politically powerful and mobilized groups, including, crucially, its own cadres. Even when a loss of legitimacy occurs as a result of new tasks being thrust upon the state it can remain quite stable if its coercive organizations remain coherent and effective. If the state maintains the status quo, most social groups will accept it. In other words, it is primarily the question of a state's own organizational and coercive capacity, in relation to both the internal class structure and the international system, which determines its capability to stall breakdown. Loss of popular legitimacy is not sufficient for the collapse of the state (Skocpol, 1979: 24–33).

This assertion captures an important aspect of the apparent durability of all states: they can survive even when popular legitimacy does not exist if the crucial state organs remain loyal. However, specific historical conjunctures can lend legitimacy a very central role and may serve as a contagion affecting several states. Thus decolonization in Asia and Africa after the Second World War came about largely as a loss of popular legitimacy by the colonial powers. Similarly the loss of popular legitimacy sealed the fate of the Soviet system and of its Eastern European socialist states. The state as an organization was largely intact but proved ineffective in stopping popular insurrection. Thus, while popular consent is not necessary for the continued survival of a state, its absence can lead to easy collapse of the state system in a period of upheaval and turmoil.

The state as supreme reason and universal altruism

The Greeks reposed supreme reason in the state and both Plato and Aristotle were convinced about its superiority to the men who lived in it. In modern times, Hegel was to reinvest the state with supreme reason (Avineri, 1991: 196–200). Such pre-eminence given to the state undoubtedly facilitated the emergence of totalitarianism in the twentieth century. However, his more important notion of the state as universal altruism needs to be re-evaluated. For Hegel, the state was the basis of universal solidarity based on universal citizenship: 'A man counts as a man in virtue of his humanity alone, not because he is a Jew, Catholic, Protestant, German, Italian, etc.' (quoted by Avineri, 1991: 197). This aspect of Hegelian thinking has been eclipsed by his more perfectionist notions of the state. However, the link between higher reason and universal altruism is logically an interdependent one. Higher reason is intrinsic to the cognition and acceptance of universalism.

While the concept of the state as higher reason may be an abstract philosophical position, it seems correct to assert that all states are the expression of some collective reason or will. Real states may approximate to universalism, in which case they come close to Hegelian standards, or they may not.

The state as legitimate power: consent and tension

Power exists whenever two or more human beings come in contact and establish a relationship which makes them change their positions in action or thought. It may be momentary or long-lasting, trivial or significant. An agent, for example A, possesses power if he can influence the behaviour of another agent, B, in accordance with A's wishes. In a raw sense, A can terrorize B into submission, but according to one point of view this would not mean that A has power over B, because it is indicative of a weak relationship. A powerful relationship is one in which A and B are agreed on the fundamentals defining their asymmetrical equation, though they may differ about its details (Ball, 1980: 81–105). Therefore power as a relationship based on consent should be distinguished from force and terror which are employed by an agent whose power is challenged by an agent who is denied power and has to resort to non-agreed means and methods to acquire it. Power is thus the ability to influence in a legitimate manner so that the complying agent accepts to change position peacefully though not necessarily happily.

Such a view is rather problematic in that if compliance is the essence of power the most dramatic and unequivocal demonstration of the absence of power would be successful defiance or non-compliance by the opposing agent. In other words, power exists only when compliance can be exacted. Under all circumstances, therefore, power, in order to be meaningful as the ability to influence in a desired direction the behaviour of an agent, requires the ability or capacity to be able to do so in practice.

This brings us to the question of tension. All states are expressions of organized power and are invariably headed by power élites and dominant classes. Although in democratic society various devices have been constructed to check abuse of power there is no question of such power being equally distributed. Consequently, the power élite and dominant classes constitute the centre while the rest of society ends up in some distant position removed from the centre, the vast majority of them constituting the periphery. Thus all states have to invest in mechanisms of socio-political control. On the one hand, ideology, political socialization, political participation, the distribution of socioeconomic benefits and, on the other hand, building up the punitive, intelligence-gathering and military capacities have to be attended to by the state in order to ensure its ability to exact compliance.

In the ultimate sense then, the power of the state is manifest in its ability to handle internal and external challenges. In this connection the question of territory and population is significant. Possessing large territory and a big population enhances the sense of power of a state. As regards the population, it is important for it to be obedient and loyal, for no state can hope to survive in the long run through the employment of coercion alone. Obedience is relevant not only in relation to the general requirements of law and order but also in the regulation and orderly sustenance of the production, ownership and distribution of the material needs of society. A structure of loyalty which transcends other emotional bonds to which individuals are tied — family, religious community — and links them to the state has to be attended to in some form. Such a function is commonly described as nation-building.

The state as consent and tension as well as collective will and reason

The position taken in the present enquiry is that the state is based on consent to the extent that people are by habit used to living in a state. The majority of people are used to performing their routine tasks and transactions within the precincts of a state. For most people the state in which they reside is their permanent homeland. If the state, however, continually expresses its 'will' through bad government, an overall deficit in its emotional capital in society is a likely outcome. On the other hand, individuals, groups and classes which are oppressed by the state or rather develop such an awareness and want to change the situation can no longer be considered as rendering habitual consent to the state. Equally, criminals and anti-social elements practically violate the principle of consent. Thus tension is intrinsic to the state system. However, tension may remain undetected during periods of overall stability and prosperity.

At the same time, the state remains an abstraction and concentration of collective reason — perhaps more correctly that of the dominant élites and classes and their components. Such reason may be universalistic or particularistic, democratic or authoritarian, pluralistic or regimental, coherent or chaotic, rigid or flexible and so on. Such reason is not reducible to economic rationality or military doctrine, but is a larger question of ideals and visions. The ideas and convictions of leaders and dominant parties, the interpretation of history, the laws and constitution are some of the sources from which the organizing ideology of a state can be deduced. The 'two faces of the state' (one is an organizing element, the other a coercive element), as Barry Buzan (1991) puts it, are an important variable in the underlying logic of state practice towards its citizens, neighbours and other states.

Population, ethnicity and nation

One can distinguish various types of social groups in the population of a modern state. While some will be foreigners, aliens of one type or the other, the majority will in principle be people with permanent legal rights and claims in the state. This body we can label as the citizenry, but only in a broad sense because most of them may be rural people with little sense of identification with the urban power centres and of participation in its affairs, which is what citizenry actually implies. In principle this vast body of citizens will be entitled to a number of civil rights and political rights. States may not, however, confer equal political rights on all individuals and groups. Some may be excluded on the basis of religion or race. Such a group or groups will be less than citizens. Even in the citizen body there may be some ethnic and religious minorities with no interest in assimilating with the larger society. Others may be so small that their participation in politics may have no significance. Finally there may be a number of naturalized citizens, ethnically and culturally quite removed from the main population body. These may enjoy full political rights and in this sense will be citizens proper, but would still be quite detached from the indigenous cultural ethos. Consequently, quite varied ethnic associations and experiences are to be found among the populace. The question is, can one conceptually include all such categories of people in the all-inclusive nation?

Statist versus ethnicist conceptions of nation

The widespread practice in scholarly literature of including all the legal and permanent members of the population in the nation, irrespective of whether they are given equal rights, can be described as the statist approach. On the other hand, the ethnicists reject citizenship, which is a legal relationship between an individual and the state, as a valid basis for membership in the nation. For them, the nation is an ethno-cultural bond between those sharing some primordial characteristics. Primordial associations and identifications cannot be changed or given up and nations are simply enlarged ethnic groups. When groups bound together by primordial ties confront a political or social threat they organize themselves for political action and become nations. Nationalism as a form of consciousness and the nation as a political category are therefore an enlargement of sentiments and organizational units found earlier in history, according to the ethnicists (Greetz, 1963; Shils, 1957).

Formal statist definitions are unsatisfactory as they do not adequately cover real situations. Substantial sections of the population may be denied equal citizenship rights through both legal restrictions and social practice. On the other hand, ethnicist definitions ignore the possibility that ethnic identity may dissipate, dissolve or assimilate into something else in the historical process. This approach underrates the capacity of states to cull a nation out of their existing ethno-cultural mix. Through the education system particularly, but also the extension of communications and economic development, states do manage to dissolve many parochial ties and integrate and assimilate quite diverse peoples into a nation. Such transformation, however, takes place over a fairly long period of time.

The properties of nation

To begin with, the question of size — conceptualized as population or in terms of economic output or geographical area — deserves careful consideration. Although the exact size of a nation is impossible to determine, a group a few hundred or thousand strong is very unlikely to make its claims to national identity be taken seriously. A reasonably large number of people related to each other through the division of labour in the production process and/or common culture is a likely candidate to the claim of nation. Geographical location and concentration in a specific area are also important to press the claims to separate national identity. Groups dispersed in a larger society make a weaker case for a nation than those located in specific border regions.

More crucially, the claims of a group to being a nation need to be distinguished from what the state defines as the nation. In newly founded multicultural states it is not uncommon for more than one version of nationalism to exist besides the one promoted and projected by the state. The claim to nationness is therefore contestable and controvertible. Benedict Anderson (1983) has aptly defined a nation as 'an imagined political community — and imagined as both inherently limited and sovereign'. Elaborating upon this rather brief definition he points out that the members of a nation in reality have no chance of getting to know each other and yet in their minds they share a sense of belonging together. Further, even if such a group comprises millions of members there is also a sense of limitation of the boundaries of the nation, howsoever elastic these may be, beyond which exist other nations. Notwithstanding actual inequality and exploitative relations that may exist between members and classes within the nation, it is conceived as a horizontal comradeship bound together by deep emotional ties. It is this force of communitarian feelings that explains why people are willing to die in large numbers on behalf of the imagined community (Anderson, 1983: 15–16).

In one sense then the nation is both a universal and a particularist group. It is universal in that it transcends immediate emotional ties and aims for unity on a larger impersonal emotive plane, particularist because it is a declaration of group boundaries which exclude others. In the latter sense the nation resembles an ethnic group in that it refers to a feeling of belonging together. Like the nation the ethnic group is also an imagined community (Phadnis, 1989: 21).

An historical view of nation

An historical vision on citizen and nation is in place. The American Declaration of Independence and the French Revolution converted subjects into citizens. At that time the concept of nation was not in use. It developed out of the concept of citizen: the nation was simply the sum total of citizens. However, the citizen — as one qualified to take part in elections — was initially a man; in the case of the USA a white man. It took another 150 years before women and non-white men were enfranchised. In fact only after the Second World War has the era of universal rights and citizen gained global ramifications. In between the French Revolution and the Second World War intercontinental wars, extermination or genocide of minorities, mass pauperization of the peasantry, ruthless exploitation of the working class, colonial plunder and many more evils were visited upon hapless people.

On the positive side, parochial culture and subsistence economy were swept away and an industrial economy of growth emerged, and more or less stabilized in the West. The hegemony of science in terms of applied knowledge was firmly established (Wittrock, 1993: 132). As a mode of knowledge metaphysics was relegated to the private sphere. It did not mean the end of ideology in the sense of obfuscation, only one won the right to dissent and disagree on received wisdom and to propose alternatives. Primary school education became universal. Education in general became secular. The motive force of such change were the middle classes as well as the proletariat. The end result was mass participatory democracy. Thus in the historical evolution of citizens into nations consisting of men and women with equal rights economic change towards capitalism and industrial society has been crucial. Such change cost a great deal in human life, and many heroic popular struggles had to be waged before those rights were conceded to women, religious minorities and lower-class working people.

To recapitulate the historical evolution of modern Western nations, it is to be remembered that first the notion of citizen supplanted that of subject, but its content changed only gradually and became truly co-extensive with whole populations of the Western democracies only after the Second World War. Thus although communities and cultural groups have existed since the dawn of history and have founded states based on their specific traditions and practices, and possession of political power has been important for practising freely their own social and political codes, what characterizes the modern Western conception of nation deriving from the French Revolution is the emphasis on the equality of all citizens: that is, of the potentially active free agents in society.

Nation and the problem of group rights versus individual rights

Now, the fundamental principle deriving from the French Revolution, that a nation confers equal human rights on its members, is not without complications when applied to groups claiming to be nations by invoking some non-Western criterion. For example, according to the Muslim fundamentalists and traditionalists, Muslim women are an integral part of the Muslim *Umma* (Muslim nation), but are not by virtue of that fact entitled to the same political, civil and economic rights as Muslim men. Muslim female fundamentalists may concur in such a view and submit voluntarily to male domination. According to these Muslim men and women they would be part of a nation, but with differential rather than identical rights. They may even assert that such is proper equality whereas the notion of equal and same human rights is a Western distortion which does not take correct cognizance of the natural differences between men and women. Moreover, in their point of view Western values are not authoritative for Muslims.

This train of reasoning is quite typical among the fundamentalists who never run short of scholastic sophistry to sustain such a thesis. A situation can well be imagined that if a fundamentalist Muslim group is awarded a piece of territory in consonance with the principle of self-determination it may employ its sovereign will to abolish individual autonomy and may relegate women to some second-rate status. Similarly Hindu fundamentalists may want all Indian Muslims to be treated as *mleccha* (impure or unclean) and thus driven out of chaste society, in accordance with the sacred canons enunciated by Manu more than two thousand years ago. In the final analysis, therefore, the concept of self-determination or self-rule of a collectivity or group is not necessarily consonant with democratic values. In some situations the self-determination of a group may actually liquidate individual autonomy and militate against gender equality, racial harmony and religious tolerance. Thus collective self-determination may or may not include individual autonomy. To the extent it does not it is not consistent with the libertarian spirit and ideals of the French Revolution.

A definition of nation

It is manifest from the above discussion that attempting an 'objective definition' of nation is rather problematic. Shared cultural characteristics and a long continuous residence in a specific territory tend to make the claim of nationness of a group a strong one, but it is not so simple. Other groups may also be living in the same area. More crucially, it is very difficult to determine what length of continuous residence is appropriate for judging between conflicting claims. The approach taken in the present study is that the claim to nation is a political claim to rights and power, and like all political claims to rights and power it can be made sense of only in terms of what its exponents say about it and how it relates to the historical and contemporary situation.

A nation can, therefore, be defined as: a relatively large group of people — vertically-linked and stratified by class and social rank — which identifies itself in terms of some cultural particularity and associates itself with a particular geographical area (usually one where it resides) over which it assumes it has original rights. Such a group is either exercising self-rule or aspires to it.

The above definition refers to a feeling — not to why and how such a feeling develops or whether such a claim is legitimate and reasonable or not. At any rate, unless such a feeling obtains the nation does not exist in any practical sense of the word. It is, however, normal that members of the nation identify themselves with an array of subgroups in day-to-day life and the national identity is not a regular reference. Moreover, the feeling of nationness may be deliberately demonstrated in terms of various activities related to self-rule, or it may be subdued and routinized in terms of institutional arrangements about self-rule in an established nation-state. A final word on nation is in order. It is argued that the feeling of nationness is a construction. People sharing long historical associations do not automatically develop a sense of common political destiny. This has to be cultivated by the dominant élite and leadership. At some historical moment such a project has to be undertaken by the political leadership.

The so-called historical nations such as the British, French, Swedish and so on were constructed during the seventeenth, eighteenth and nineteenth centuries through various peaceful as well as violent means. Several different variants and models of nation were put forth during this period, and in the historical process some gained acceptance. Such processes are under way currently in Third World societies and the new states of Eastern Europe. The situation of the Arabic-speaking people is a case in point. Pan-Islam, pan-Arabism and national identity based on state of origin such as Egyptian, Jordanian, Saudi Arabian, Tunisian and so on are various competing frameworks for constructing national identity which have informed Arab nationalist politics in recent times. The processes of transformation of people into a nation in a Third World situation is discussed at length in the next chapter.

Nation and state

A conceptual difference between nation and state is in place. While the nation is a politico-cultural entity identifiable by its 'character' and collective rights, the state is a politico-juridical entity identifiable by its sovereign right over a territory. The two may coincide, and the term nation-state captures this relationship. The relationship between nation and state, however, needs to be put into perspective. States may come into being without anything resembling a nation having emerged among the people. Termination or collapse of existing states and empires provides opportunities for the formation of new states. In some cases this may lead to rather odd constructions resulting in arbitrary divisions of people and territory.

Ethnicity, state, society and nation

As is clear from the above discussion, a state can exist without a coherent nation just as a nation can exist without a separate state of its own. On the other hand, all states strive towards the establishment of a stable socio-political base in society for their survival and have to work it out of the available ethnic pool. Nation-formation in some form is, therefore, inherent in the state—society relationship. The relationship between state and nation, however, has no set or fixed pattern.

Whereas complete and permanent disharmony between the two cannot but end in the destruction of an existing state, complete harmony is rather rare. The problem of ethnicity, that is of groups of people associating around a cultural tie and making demands on the political system, can come into conflict with the state, its idea of nation and also other groups in society. In its extreme form ethnicity can take the shape of separatist nationalism. Lastly, external actors may impinge upon the internal affairs of states and upset their strategies of nation-building and development. These we shall examine in the next chapter.

References

Alavi, H. (1989) 'Politics of ethnicity in India and Pakistan' in H. Alavi and J. Harriss, *Sociology of Developing Societies: South Asia*, London: Macmillan.

Anderson, B. (1983) *Imagined Communities*, London: Verso.

Avineri, S. (1991) 'Hegel, Georg Wilhelm Friedrich' in D. Miller, J. Coleman, W. Connally and A. Ryan (eds), *The Blackwell Encyclopaedia of Political Thought*, Oxford: Blackwell Reference.

Ball, T. (1980) *Transforming Political Discourse*, Oxford: Basil Blackwell.

Banton, M.P. (1983) 'Ethnicity, ethnic group' in Michael Mann (ed.), *Macmillan Student Encyclopedia of Sociology*, London: Macmillan.

Brass, P.R. (1974) *Language, Religion and Politics in North India*, Cambridge: Cambridge University Press.

Brass, P.R. (1991) *Ethnicity and Nationalism: Theory and Practice*, New Delhi: Sage Publications.

Buzan, B. (1991) *People, States and Fear*, London: Harvester Wheatsheaf.

Cashmore, E. (1988) *Dictionary of Race and Ethnic Relations*, London: Routledge.

Deutsch, K.W. (1966) *Nationalism and Social Communication*, Cambridge, Mass.: MIT Press.

Easton, D. (1965) *A System Analysis of Political Life*, New York: John Wiley and Sons.

Engels, F. (1970) 'The origin of the family, private property and the state' in *Marx and Engels: Selected Works*, Moscow: Progress Publishers.

Enloe, C.H. (1980) *Ethnic Soldiers*, London: Penguin.

Geertz, C. (1963) 'The integrative revolution' in Geertz (ed.), *Old Societies and New State*, New York: The Free Press.

Glazer, N. and Moynihan, D.P. (1975) 'Introduction' in Nathan Glazer and Daniel P. Moynihan (eds), *Ethnicity: Theory and Experience*, Cambridge, Mass.: Harvard University Press.

Gramsci, A. (1976) *Selections from the Prison Notebooks*, London: Lawrence and Wishart.

Horowitz, D.L. (1985) *Ethnic Groups in Conflict*, Berkeley and Los Angeles: University of California Press.

Marx, K. and Engels, F. (1976) *Collected Works*, vol. 5, Moscow: Progress Publishers.

Phadnis, U. (1989) *Ethnicity and Nation-Building in South Asia*, New Delhi: Sage Publications.

Shils, E. (1957) 'Primordial, personal, sacred and civil ties', *British Journal of Sociology*, vol. 7.

Skinner, Q. (1978) *The Foundations of Modern Political Thought*, vols 1 and 2, Cambridge: Cambridge University Press.

Skocpol, T. (1979) *States and Social Revolutions,* Cambridge: Cambridge University Press.

Snyder, L.L. (1976) *Varieties of Nationalism: A Comparative Study*, New York: Holt, Rinehart and Winston.

Weber, M. (1978) 'Basic categories of social organisation' in W.G. Runciman (ed.), *Weber Selections in Translation*, Cambridge: Cambridge University Press.

Wittrock, B. (1993) 'Polity, economy and knowledge in the age of modernity in Europe' in *AI & Society,* London: Springer-Verlag London Limited.

Young, C. (1976) *The Politics of Cultural Pluralism*, Madison: University of Wisconsin Press.

3

The Nation-State Project versus the Separatist Project in South Asia

This chapter examines the relationship between nation-building and separatist movements. A fundamental assumption underlying the discussion is that a weak interface between state and society, originating during the colonial period, compounds the post-independence efforts of the South Asian states to stabilize control over society. The gaining of independence was the high point of popular support among the people for their states. Subsequently, such support has fluctuated — diminishing among some sections and increasing among others. Therefore the post-colonial South Asian state is conceptualized both as a fixed entity — in terms of its bureaucratic structures — and as a variable entity engaged in a process of improving its support base in society. In a way all states are engaged in this dual activity and there is no perfect state–society congruence which once achieved can be preserved for ever. In the case of the post-colonial states of South Asia, state-building and nation-building constitute extraordinary compulsions because the historical conjuncture of several internal and external factors since the mid-1960s has been unfavourable to state–society harmony.

The post-colonial state–society incongruence

The modern state was an imposition of colonialism on Asian and African societies. Social scientists and historians of different persuasions have interpreted that relationship in a variety of ways. Hamza Alavi (1973: 145–95) proffers a modified Marxist theory of the relative autonomy of the post-colonial state under peripheral capitalism. The fundamental thesis is that the state in the former Asian and African colonies is an external imposition: its structuration and formation rooted in the interest of imperialist class interests. The end of colonialism does not mean the demise of the colonial state system. Rather it is taken over by the indigenous ruling élite and applied to the peculiar requirements of post-colonial society, which stands in a relationship of dependence and marginalization to the international capitalist system. Owing to its origins in the advanced capitalist system, the state is relatively 'overdeveloped' in relation to society. Not only is society in general less developed than the state but also the indigenous dominant classes consisting of the bourgeoisie and landowners are less advanced than the state. Consequently the state has to mediate the competing and conflicting interests of the metropolitan bourgeoisie, the indigenous bourgeoisie and the landowning class. It is not, therefore, simply a creature or instrument of any one class. Rather it is 'relatively autonomous' in relation to the three dominant classes. Whatever economic development the state is able to achieve perpetuates its dependent relations to imperialism while simultaneously seeking to preserve the system of private property internally. Important in Alavi's theory is the identification of a fundamental incongruence between state and society in post-colonial societies, which he attributes to colonialism.

Joel Midgal (1988: 1—41) looks at the capabilities of states to achieve change which their leaders seek to realize in society through state planning, policies and actions. Strong states are those with high capabilities to penetrate society, regulate social relations, extract resources and appropriate or use them in determined ways. Weak states are those lacking such capabilities. His main thesis is that Third World states represent a duality: whereas they are successful in penetrating society, they are rather ineffective in bringing about goal-oriented change. The reasons for this ineffectiveness are to be found in the fact that the values upon which the developing state bases its social control are inherited from the colonial period. Only the ruling élite internalizes the modernist values and norms of the colonial legacy. However, the experience and orientation of the élite is much less spread out in society than the vastly diverse sets of beliefs and recollections upheld by the multifarious units of the larger society. Midgal writes: 'The strength of shared memories and beliefs within various subunits — the clans, tribes, linguistic groups, ethnic groups, and so on — suggest an image for many societies of the Third World quite different from the centralized, pyramidal structure found, say, in many European countries' (1988: 37). Midgal regards ethnic diversity as a particularly serious problem in developing societies. It tends to promote conflict since the state cannot respond adequately to the multifarious claims and demands which crop up from a fractionalized society. He mentions the shared fear of foreign aggression by people as a factor helping to consolidate a strong socio-political base for the state. In other words, states become strong in terms of social control if their security concerns are widely shared by society.

The idea of the Third World state as a neo-patrimonial entity — based formally on rational—legal universal principles but functioning in practice as a great vehicle of patronage and personal aggrandizement of powerholders — has been put forth to explain an inherent paradox typifying Third World states: they are both strong and fragile at the same time (Clapham, 1985). The strength of the state derives from the vast resources it has at its command to repress a civil society composed of a patchwork of heterogeneous cultural groups; its fragility from the fact that it is not deeply anchored in a cultural sense in the society and is considered an alien being by many of its constitutive units. Consequently, the collapse of a ruling coalition and the end of a regime can severely strain the state system and may even bring about its dissolution. Hence the paradox that the state is both strong and fragile simultaneously.

South Asian post-colonial state–society relationship

Rasheeduddin Khan (1989: 42–5) describes the Indian state as a 'Total State'. As compared with the totalitarian state, the total state is not based sheerly on terror and one-party dictatorship. Rather the term refers to the unlimited range, extent and exercise of legitimate power by the state over the rest of society. In the Indian context it refers to four characteristics: (*a*) unlimited state authority over group and individual life; (*b*) the decisive impact of the state in determining the direction of national life; (*c*) the preponderant coercive–consensus power of the state in relation to the aggregative civil power available to collectivities of people, such as classes and cultural groups; and (*d*) the role of the state as a unified apparatus of politico-legal hegemony of the dominant classes based on a multi-class electoral support obtained periodically by the ruling parties. Khan's emphasis is on the overwhelming nature of state power in India. The dominant Congress Party reflects in the political sphere the paradoxical ethos of Hindu culture: it is tolerant, accommodating and capable of internalizing dissent and yet maintaining social hierarchy and inequality. In short, Khan lays stress on the capability of the state and the political system to control society effectively, with the aid of Hindu cultural trappings, within the bounds of class hierarchy.

Hamza Alavi's (1973) notion of an 'over-developed state' is derived largely from his analysis of the Pakistani state of the 1960s. He argues that a predominantly Punjabi military–bureaucratic oligarchy dominates Pakistan. This oligarchy is linked to the powerful landowning class and the bourgeoisie. Although Alavi analyses the state–society incongruence essentially in class terms, he does draw attention to the ethnic dimension of such incongruence: the strongest resistance to the centre comes from the non–dominant nationalities (Alavi, 1973: 145–95). However, on the whole his theory is about the strong state in relation to the weaker classes.

As against theories emphasizing the domination of the South Asian state over society, there are approaches in the reverse direction too: the state is seen as relatively weak in relation to society. Writing on South Asia in the late 1960s, Gunnar Myrdal (1968: 277) coined the term 'soft state' to describe the inability of the state to make people obey laws and regulations made by it, and to impose discipline over them. Hans Blomquist (1988: 185–220; 299–335) reverses the argument and describes the Indian state as a particularist state — a state not bound by its own formal rules and laws. He traces the roots of such a state system in the wider established historical tradition of political and social patronage. The particularist state is, however, conceived as a soft state in that it lacks capacity to implement effectively the policies it devises. Writing on the Sri Lankan state, Mick Moore (1990: 155–82) argues that although development of state and society in Sri Lanka has been parallel the state has not been able to maintain its autonomy *vis-à-vis* the society. On the contrary, society has been able to penetrate the state apparatuses through electoral politics. The governments that have come to power had to build up a system of patronage and reward in order to sustain their support base in society. Such an approach inevitably undermined the autonomy of the state. In relation to Bangladesh, Ben Crow (1990: 193–222) puts forth the idea of a weak state. He conceptualizes this weakness, firstly, on the level of the state apparatuses, particularly the army, which, in contrast to the Pakistani army from which it descends historically, is not a monolithic, centralized hierarchical structure but is constituted by several groupings and factions. Revolts and rebellions against army rule have, therefore, come from rival groups within the army. Secondly, the weakness of the Bangladeshi state is apparent from its inability to tax the large rich peasantry.

The South Asian state both strong and weak

The idea of a dual character of the Indian state as both strong and weak is suggested in an historical perspective by Subrata Kumar Mitra (1990: 73–93), who distinguishes, on the one hand, a high degree of 'stateness' in the more than 2000 years old Indian political tradition and, on the other hand, the breakdown of state authority as a result of social disorder, political upheavals and foreign rule. Consequently a residual sense of uncertainty exists about the legitimacy of the state notwithstanding its manifest strength. The modern state is, therefore, a 'successor to a mixed legacy of phases of high stateness' (1990: 73). He discusses critically the scope and limits of the policy of accommodation of primordial interests which the Indian state followed after independence, and argues in favour of the state controlling the social agenda and providing resolute leadership rather than submitting to the pressure of contentious sectional interests (1990: 93).

In the present enquiry the idea of a dual character of the state — both strong and weak — is assumed also for Pakistan, Bangladesh and Sri Lanka, because they have been formed by the same historical processes. In a theoretical sense the Islamic political tradition is one of a high degree of stateness and the Buddhist that of a low one, but the British takeover of South Asia effected a drastic rupture with the past and transformed both state and society. The 'strength' and 'weakness' of the contemporary South Asian states, therefore, are more immediately rooted in the state–society incongruence which occurred during the colonial period. This duality became manifest in the ways and means through which these states tried to realize their will in society: this will may be described as modernization and development within a capitalist framework with a view to generating more wealth, consolidating the nation and making the state strong against internal and external threats.

The nation-state project

Björn Hettne asserts that the 'nation-state project' is intrinsic to the modern state system. In the sense of a project, it is a complex of several processes which are set in motion by the central élite. It refers to a set of obstacles to be surmounted, a pool of resources to work with and, most crucially, the possibility that the project may fail to succeed. Ideally the objectives the project is meant to achieve are: consolidation of exclusive political–military control of the state over certain territory, building up a defence structure to thwart external claims to such territory, creation of political legitimacy, material welfare, and a degree of cultural homogeneity. A failure of the project would be the state abandoning universal criteria and instead investing its efforts in creating a purely ethnic nation. The latter type of project is intrinsically unstable and leads ultimately to the disintegration of the state (Hettne, 1993: 78).

Interesting implications follow from Hettne's conception of the nation-state project. As regards the need for consolidation of exclusive political–military control over territory and building up a defence structure is concerned, these refer to state-building. In its bare outline state-building is relatively easier to describe. Recognizing the authority of a government over a specific territory and the people who live there constitutes the formal establishment of a state. Such change is usually accompanied by recognition of the sovereign and independent status of the new state by the world community. This is followed by admission into international organizations and bodies. A territorial framework, a bureaucratic and military infrastructure and a body of political institutions represent the state. Thereafter the state has to adopt a recruitment policy to replenish its cadres and a policy to regulate its various functions. In an apparent sense the state is complete and in gear to proceed with its multifarious activities.

However, as regards the processes whereby the political system acquires legitimacy, and thereby predominance, this needs to be seen as a continuous process. It is contested and challenged by societal units not willing to assimilate into the nation-building project of the state. Hettne rejects selective or ethnic nation-building as commensurate with the nation-state project. Nation-building has to be universal and democratic, otherwise it tends to promote instability. Such a standpoint is somewhat normative and deals with the democratic implications of nation-building. It is possible that selective nation-building may still include within its span an overwhelming majority of the people, and powerless discriminated minorities may not be in any position to challenge the state in a serious manner. The situation of non-Muslim minorities in Pakistan is a case in point. They are officially subjected to political discrimination, but because of their small numbers and paucity of resources lack the strength to challenge the state. It is correct, however, that ethnic nation-building militates against democracy and the rights of minorities and to that extent is repressive.

On the other hand, universal nation-building which requires secularization of culture and identity in the political sphere may be resisted by substantial sections of society who may be unwilling or unprepared to assimilate into the nation. Under the circumstances, the nation-state project can be destabilized because of such cultural obstacles. In the context of South Asia, the universal and democratic nation-state project was put forth by the Indian élite led by Nehru, but sections of Hindu society and minorities such as Sikhs and Muslims have had great difficulty in accepting such a concept of nation. Logically, therefore, nation-building by the state can proceed into two opposite directions: either the whole population is considered as equal members of the nation, or some cultural particularity shared by part of the population is selected as basis of nation. In the former case a policy of equal rights for all people and in the latter differential rights — more for the nation and less for the others — follows.

Project formulation and implementation

Assuming that the nation-state project is imperative for Third World states, it does not follow necessarily that all states have one ready for themselves at the time of their founding. In some cases, the nation-state project may remain unclear or undefined except in some vague sense of a commitment to education, economic development and national integration. It does not mean either that, even if some consensus obtains among the ruling élite on the project, it would be formulated and implemented in a single-minded and effective manner. Much of the lofty proclamations of politicians and political leaders may be just rhetoric. Incompetence, apathy, corruption and other distortions may be widespread among the state officials, making the notion of project somewhat overstated.

At any rate, the nation-building processes proceed in the context of existing cultural heritage, class structure, internal power distribution, and external pressures. This means that allocation of resources, employment opportunities, and influence over the state will hardly be even and equal for all groups, classes and people. In such a situation, whereas the nation-state project in an abstract logical sense remains intrinsic to the state's own survival, the actual content and form of the project are likely to be modified, compromised or even supplanted in the light of the actual dynamics of change and stability attendant upon the state.

Ideological inputs

States have to generate organizing ideologies as part of the processes of consolidating control over society. The national identity sanctioned is woven out of the patronage and selection of popular myths, symbols, emblems and a variety of other rites and rituals which are calculated to forge closer links between the political establishment and society. It is disseminated through the school system and mass media. In so far as South Asia is concerned, an Indian, Pakistani, Bangladeshi or Sri Lankan nation had never existed before either in the statist or in the ethnicist sense. Scholars of South Asian societies usually employ phrases such as multinational states, state-nations, nations-in-the-making and nations-in-the-becoming to conceptualize the processes current in the multi-ethnic and multi-cultural South Asian states towards consolidation and integration (Mukherji, 1992: 23–4). The emphasis is on the state as creator of nation.

The élites that came to power at the time of independence in India, Pakistan and Sri Lanka proclaimed in their euphoric independence addresses a general commitment to democracy, modernization and development. The Indian ruling élite waxed eloquent on the superiority of liberal democracy and secularism, while the Pakistani élite indulged in an extravagant ideological fantasy combining idealized Islam and liberal democracy. Sri Lanka expressed similar high hopes about uninterrupted national integration and economic development. Bangladesh, which came into existence later, also started on a note of general optimism about democratic development. Thus the erstwhile central élites were committed to the idea of democracy. Their success in establishing democratic hegemony over society has, however, met with varied success.

Political inputs

The post-colonial South Asian states in principle recognized the electoral process and universal adult franchise as the legitimate means of forming governments, although in practice elections have been held consistently only by India and Sri Lanka. The legitimacy of civilian rule, however, is established as a norm. Thus, despite constant military takeovers, Pakistan and Bangladesh have returned to civilian rule (one variant of civilian rule being that the military generals acquire civilian positions and recruit ministers from the public rather than the army). A dictatorship with totalitarian characteristics has never been established in any South Asian state, including Pakistan, the most authoritarian of the four states in the region. The free press has existed in all the four states, despite various degrees of restrictions.

Socio-economic inputs

The overall basis for modernization and development is, however, material change. In its essence a modern society is one which is prepared to accommodate social change and achieve material welfare. Most crucially needed are appropriate skills for functioning and communicating with a technologically advanced world (Apter, 1968: 197). Promoting education, industrialization and agricultural modernization were the three-pronged development goals adopted by the South Asian states. An economy of growth was to supplant traditional subsistence agriculture. The UN developmental agencies such as the WHO and UNESCO and financial institutions such as World Bank and the IMF also supported such thinking. The logic was quite simple: education and economic development would create prosperity, which in turn would ensure political stability and promote loyalty to the state. As a result the state would become strong in the face of internal and external threats.

A flaw in conventional development thinking was the concentration on economic growth without adequate measures to encourage population control through proper incentives and family planning. The system of mass vaccinations against cholera, malaria, typhoid and other such diseases and the extension of other basic health-care facilities greatly reduced the overall rate of mortality. In subsequent decades this omission in planning was to enormously strain the developmental potential of the South Asian countries as a population explosion took place. Between 1947–48 and 1981 the population of South Asia doubled.

However, the achievements of the post-colonial state during the period 1947–65 were by no means unimpressive. In education, industrial production and agricultural modernization substantial gains were made. In particular the problem of shortage of food grain, which constituted a major problem at the time of independence, was by the mid-1960s very much under control. India led the region because of size as well as because of political stability achieved through periodic elections, the pre-eminence of the Congress Party and the ideological hegemony of the secularist Nehruvian central élite.

In one sense, however, the South Asian states continued to reproduce an imbalance already present during the colonial period: between economic transformation and cultural change. Disintegration of the old society exceeded integration and consolidation of a modern one. As a process, therefore, modernization — educational, socio-economic and political — generated its own dialectics of integration–disintegration; assimilation–exclusion; upward–downward mobility and accordingly affected the relationship between the state and its variegated populace.

Intervening factors modifying the nation-state project

Whatever strategy a state adopts to create a nation, the survival of the state itself against internal and external dangers is a paramount consideration in such calculations. The survival of the state, of course, means the survival of the social order or social hierarchy it upholds. In this connection, the question of collective identity is significant. It may be easier for the state to convince mainstream society that a common destiny binds them together if the central power élite ethnically and culturally stems from the same stock as mainstream society. In other words, the state can ensure support for the nation-state project rather easily from main-stream society. On the other hand, cultural groups which are different from mainstream society or the dominant cultural group in a marked sense, for example in terms of religion, may be considered with caution in the nation-state project. Not necessarily in an ideological sense, but in a political one. For example, Muslims in India are treated with suspicion because their recognized leaders opposed the unity of India and created Pakistan. In the post-independence period this suspicion has been kept alive because of alleged sympathies of Indian Muslims for Pakistan rather than for India. The credibility of such allegations is a matter of conjecture, but state security planning is sensitive to such factors. On the other hand Indian Christians do not bear such stigma and are culturally more in tune with the secularism of the Indian state. They have, therefore, not faced similar suspicion from the state. There is nothing to suggest, however, that states cannot win over the loyalty of suspect groups.

More importantly, defence and security considerations, which are uppermost in state planning, are essentially organized in terms of external dangers (Buzan, 1991). Nationalism and patriotism in the context of the state are virtues relevant essentially in connection with the external interests of a state and reflect its percep-tion of the danger and threat posed by external factors more than purely domestic concerns for greater integration. The state can also employ fear-of-foreign-aggres-sion and exploit ethnicity as a strategy to attain internal unity. Such considerations tend to have modifying repercussions on the nation-state project.

Ethnic ties and nation-building

The historically evolved social structure in South Asia is mediated by ideas about race, religion, caste, *biradari* (kinship lineage), tribe and clan which have been sig-nificant in past South Asian history as ties around which social identity was formed. However, in present times, except for indigenous peoples who employ tribe for cultural identity, in most other cases caste, *biradari*, tribe and clan are not of much use in large-scale identity formation. The cultural factors that the ruling élites have had to come to terms with in connection with nation-building are race, language and religion — covering large numbers of people with their own ranking and hierarchy.

As regards race, notwithstanding popular mythology about Aryan—non-Aryan types the observable evidence clearly testifies to considerable intermixing. Shades of brown are more typical than clear-cut divisions of black and white. Race has, however, been invoked obliquely in the nation-building discourse in Sri Lanka and figured prominently in the Aryan–Dravidian debate in India. Basing nationality on a particular language is essentially a European political concept. There is no historical record of purely language-based movements in earlier South Asian history. Regional forces challenging the centre have existed, however. Linguistic nationality as opposed to religious nationality has been put forth in the modern period by both liberals and Marxists, and the Indian Congress Party had adopted it already before independence as the future basis of reorganization of provincial boundaries.

On the other hand, the religious basis of popular movements against the state existed before the colonial period. The state also made use of Hindu or Islamic symbols to legitimize itself. The Hindu, Muslim, Buddhist and Sikh communal revivals in the form of organized political communities, however, are modern phenomena. Modern communication networks established by the British made communal organization possible on an all-India scale. Moreover, the colonial state gave recognition to religion as basis of group representation. Religious nationalism finally led to the division of the British Indian empire into India and Pakistan.

For the post-colonial state the employment of either language or religion as identity markers in nation-building is not without complications. As Gellner (1964) has correctly pointed out, language is the centrepiece of national identity in modern states. In a purely technical sense a language is a neutral medium that makes possible developed communication among human beings. It is, however, also a cultural factor. It is the chief outlet for expression of emotions, feelings, views, serious thought and the whole range of social consciousness. Neither the production of the material needs of a society nor its other multifarious functions can be performed without language making possible regular and systematized communication. Most states, however, give preference to one language out of many (Gellner, 1964: 147–78). This fact has direct bearing on the ability of people to seek employment: those whose language is chosen for official use have an obvious advantage over others. Separatist nationalism is often an attractive proposition for groups whose language does not enjoy official status.

The role of religion is different. As a body of beliefs about spiritual and mundane matters religion usually tends to prescribe a whole range of rites, rituals, symbols, doctrines and dogma to its followers. Rules permitting entry into and exclusion from the community are laid down. Standards of good and bad are prescribed. Law covering social behaviour with appropriate punishments for offences may also be present. Such a community is potentially capable of functioning as a political entity. Literate historical religions consisting of elaborate social systems and with millions of followers, such as Hinduism, Islam, Buddhism and Sikhism, can be put to political use rather easily and therefore constitute proto-nations as such. In so far as Islam is concerned there is no doubt about its strongly political propensity. The patronage of a specific religion or sect by the state in a multi-religious or multi-sectarian society can provoke separatism among those ignored.

Modernization and social change

In a now classic work, Barrington Moore Jr (1966) analyses the drive of a number of societies towards modern industrial change. The argument is arranged in terms of strategic classes and class alliances and their overall position in the balance of power in an historical context. India (and by that token the whole of South Asia) is included as an exception to successful modernization achieved by the other cases: as a case of weak and incomplete modernization. In opposition to conventional Western and Marxist theories which concentrate upon the bourgeoisie and the working class to explain modernist change, Moore considers the nature of the landlord—peasant relationship as the key factor in deciding which road to modernization a society will tread. Although the author brings in the question of political values and attitudes as an important variable in influencing the choice between dictatorship or democracy, he does not associate them with a specific class in a general sense. Historically, the bourgeoisie of England, France and the USA were favourably inclined towards democracy, but so were also the commercial landowning classes of England, and the French peasants made common cause with the bourgeoisie to defeat the feudal landowners. The main thrust of the author's thesis is that modernization is the inevitable direction and goal of all societies, but different routes, democratic or dictatorial, are open to them. An important dimension in his argument is the prominent, even decisive, role violence has played in their democratic or dictatorial passage from pre-modern to modern society.

As regards India, the author argues that it did not produce an ascendant bourgeoisie which could in communion with commercially oriented landlords (as happened in England), or by aligning with the peasantry against reactionary landlords (as in France), or independently (as in the USA) bring about capitalistic industrialization within a liberal democratic political framework. The pre-colonial economic and political systems were based on an economy of waste and despotism, which proved dysfunctional to capital formation and thereby thwarted the road to modernization.

The second possibility of a revolution is also from above, but led by an alliance between a weak bourgeoisie and a strong landowning class (as happened in Germany and Japan). Such transformation is achieved within a fascistic framework because the dominant social classes need the power of the state to modernize. This did not happen because British colonialism, on the one hand, patronized the land-owning classes and, on the other hand, opposed the Congress Party which represented the Indian bourgeoisie. As a result the weak but growing Indian bourgeoisie and the vast landowning classes could not work out an alliance in favour of modernization. The third possibility is that of a revolution from below in the form of a peasant-based Communist revolution against centralized bureaucratic states, as happened in Russia and China. This path to modernization did not evolve in the Indian case because the caste system subverted peasant mobilization on a large scale. The post-independence Indian development is a continuation of the weak modernization impulse and, therefore, India has not become a modern capitalist–democratic state despite such a commitment of its political leadership.

A critique of Moore's thesis

In Moore's analysis of the Indian case a systematic explanation of the role which British colonialism played in class and state formation is not properly attempted. Rather the analysis is somewhat eclectic. For example, for the absence of a strong bourgeoisie the author looks back into the pre-colonial socio-economic system; for the absence of an alliance between the weak bourgeoisie and the landed classes the British period and its policy of dividing the bourgeoisie and the landowning class is pointed out; while the absence of a strong peasant movement is explained in terms of the perennial caste system.

The role of the colonial intervention is understood differently in the present study. The British imposed an advanced political order on South Asia, but left much of society dependent upon pre-modern production processes, cultural forms and socio-political values. On the other hand, the development of an indigenous industrial class was restrained (Martinussen, 1980: 1455–61). The industrial sector remained weakly developed as a whole and unevenly spread in the various regions. On the other hand, the main linchpin of the colonial system, the landed classes, came out rather unscathed. Their position was greatly strengthened as proper proprietary rights were conferred on them. Additionally, the British followed a policy of rewarding loyalty from the locals by conferring landed property on them. As regards the peasantry and other rural working people, caste, sect, religion, ethnic ties which in the past had kept them divided were exploited also by the colonial administrators when needed. When the British left, India (with the other South Asian states) was placed in a peripheral, dependent relationship to the international capitalist system. Consequently it is argued that the ability of the post-colonial state to modernize in a democratic manner has been seriously constrained not only by powerful internal landowning interests but also by the disadvantageous terms of trade for developing societies in the international market. As producers mainly of raw materials or semi-manufactured and manufactured goods of simple quality the South Asian states have been in no position to compete with the industrialized countries the prices of whose products have risen much faster than that of developing countries.

Lloyd I. Rudolph and Susanne Hoeber Rudolph (1987: 3–4) assert that India has not been dependent on the international market for its development. Rather it has pursued development on a protectionist basis and has aimed at self-reliance. Of course India sought self-reliance and was less dependent until the end of the 1970s on the international system for its development, but the lack of indigenous investments and capital formation in the 1960s (Bardhan, 1984: 17–31) meant an increasing reliance on foreign aid (Frankel, 1978: 293). Thus lack of capital formation frustrated attempts at self-reliant development. This problem applied to both productive industry and the defence sector which India began expanding after the 1962 border war debacle with China. At the beginning of the 1980s India changed course, and liberalization of the economy was undertaken. The result was a huge foreign debt, which is one of the biggest in the Third World. The notion of a peripheral capitalist economy therefore remains applicable to India notwithstanding its efforts at self-reliant development in the 1960s and 1970s.

At any rate, in order to overcome the worst effects of such structural weakness industrialization was given priority by the four South Asian states. The bourgeoisie was extended ample help with finance and infrastructure. India possessed a relatively strong big bourgeoisie. Pakistan did not have a proper bourgeoisie of its own. It had to be fostered by the state. In Sri Lanka the central political élite was also owner of sizeable commercial plantation farms. But nowhere in South Asia were the state and the bourgeoisie able to push through rapid and cumulative industrialization. The position of the other dominant classes on such transformation had to be taken into account. Soon after independence (except for Pakistan where big landlords formed a powerful class but were by no means independent feudal owners of the Western type with local power bases), in India and Sri Lanka the traditional landlord system was liquidated. On the other hand a broad section of middle-range capitalist farmers and rich and middle-range peasants not only survived but were assisted to consolidate and expand through the so-called Green Revolution strategy. To these landowning classes, castes and *biradaris* (kinship lineages) concessions had to be made since they exercised considerable political clout at the local level and were therefore important for electoral purposes as well as the general maintenance of control (Alavi, 1973: 145–72; Bardhan, 1984: 40–53; Kohli, 1989: 69–72; Moore, 1985: 50–77).

Not seeking alliance with these entities would have required the big central bourgeoisie to mobilize the poorest sections of rural society and the working class for a prolonged social revolution to smash the old order. Such a drastic revolution made no sense to the bourgeoisie and the central élites as its radical implications were beyond calculation. In any case, the institution of private property seemed threatened by such drastic strategy in a world where peasant and working-class revolutions had come to be associated with anti-property Marxist notions. Thus modernization was sought in alliance with rural property-owning classes. In the case of India and Sri Lanka, where the élites adopted social-democratic ideology, land reforms were more radical than in Pakistan where big landowners constituted a powerful political factor. Under the so-called Green Revolution strategy adopted by India, Pakistan and Sri Lanka, agricultural modernization promoted by the state encouraged commercial farming. Capitalist farmers as well as rich and independent peasants were the beneficiary of such change. Thus substantial benefits accrued from industrialization, based on the import substitution strategy, and agricultural modernization to the propertied classes: preferential loans, tax holidays and rebates, import licences, subsidies, price support and a number of general infrastructural facilities.

On the other hand, the impact on the poor of modernization and development was much more complicated. Initially a part of the poor peasantry released from agriculture could be absorbed by industry; some poorer urban and rural households attained even more dramatic upward mobility as their sons acquired modern education. However, as typically happens in most developing countries, modernization and development could not proceed much further after a short period of ascendant growth and expansion, because neither the internal nor the external markets were favourably structured for sustained growth. Consequently the volatile intelligentsia, educated but unemployed and, therefore, frustrated, was available in large numbers for political agitation when the overall modernization crisis hit South Asia in the 1980s. The majority of people remained, however, dependent, but in an increasingly precarious manner, on agriculture.

Proliferation of revivalist tendencies

The changes brought about by the mid-1960s gave more smaller entrepreneurs, capitalist farmers and rich peasants a share in power and the allocation of resources by the state. A significant degree of democratization in ownership structure did occur, not only in India and Sri Lanka but also in a milder form in Pakistan. In terms of cultural change and new sources of political influence the direction taken by society was different, however. The induction of the middle strata brought puritanical religious values and attitudes into the political process. Similarly the intelligentsia, which has been recruited into the state services from these mobile rural and urban classes, carried with it traditional culture and attitudes. Emerging from traditional moorings and seeking respectability and prestige to harmonize its improved status, it turned to familiar but idealized versions of precolonial cultural identity. Thus anti-liberal and undemocratic impulses were inducted into the

political process at the middle and mass level. These tendencies gradually manifested themselves in the political system when the social and political crisis of
uneven and weak development began to mount from the second half of the 1960s
onwards. Under pressure and threat the state tended to succumb to neo-fascistic
overtones even when the top élite remained committed to democracy or some
form of rational government. In an important sense, therefore, the balance of
power was somewhat altered; the traditional middle strata creating a space for
themselves at the level where state and society interacted regularly. Zoya Hasan
observes:

> Belated and retarded capitalism in newly liberated countries of the Third World
> . . . is conditioned by its inability to destroy pre-modern forms. . . . A significant
> aspect of this situation is not just the incompatibility between the old and the new
> but the fact that the social and cultural force of pre-capitalist forms is much
> greater in the political sphere than in the sphere of production. (1989: 25)

Prelude to the separatist challenges of the 1980s

From the mid-1960s the problems of uneven and insufficient development began
to plague South Asia in a chronic manner. Domestic investments were insufficient
while the external debt — incurred to finance development and military expansion
— began to mount. A veritable population explosion greatly strained the development process. Moreover, the impressive achievements in higher education during
the 1960s had produced a large number of college and university degree holders,
mostly in the field of humanities. For them employment opportunities grew only
slightly, so unemployed young men were to be found in large numbers during the
late 1960s and early 1970s. These recently arrived members of the intelligentsia,
often of peasant and lower middle-class origins, were not willing to return to
their humble surroundings. By that time the disruption of the subsistence
economy had proceeded in some depth and the restoration of the old order was
wellnigh impossible. The state was, therefore, compelled to continue expanding
its instrumentalist role as the main solver of societal social crisis, but it failed to
meet the demands of the growing population. Unemployment therefore rose
sharply. For example, in India unemployment went up between 1954 and 1974
from 5.3 million to over 15 million (Hiro, 1976: 85). In Pakistan the economy
first expanded rapidly between 1959–60 and 1964–65, then slowed down and
declined sharply in 1969–70 (Ahmed and Amjad, 1984: 90). Unemployment,
especially among educated young men, was also an acute problem in Sri Lanka in
the late 1960s and early 1970s. In 1969 there were 14,000 university graduates and
112,000 young adults with the general certificate of education, ordinary level
qualification, without employment (Wilson, 1974: 62). As the crisis deepened, ad
hoc and stopgap arrangements became routinized as responses to sprawling social

distress and political unrest. The period 1965–75 saw political and social unrest come to a head all over South Asia.

The first major upheaval, however, was an interstate confrontation. A 17-day stalemate war was fought by India and Pakistan in September 1965. Both sides portrayed it to their people as a victory. The propaganda in Pakistan was particularly effective. However, the euphoria of largely fictitious successes was soon eclipsed by the economic hardships which followed. Pakistan's impressive economic development was suddenly menaced by price hikes, and unemployment multiplied as the costs of war-making were shifted to the public. From 1966 onwards Pakistan was gripped by mass hysteria against the government of Field Marshal Ayub Khan. Complaints about authoritarian rule, lack of provincial autonomy, illegitimate modernization of Islamic law, growing economic hardship and above all failure to defeat India and liberate Kashmir were added to the growing list of grievances. Agitations and protests led by the combined opposition parties representing fundamentalists, regionalists, centrists, Marxists and other elements began to gain pace from 1966 onwards. Finally the government fell in 1969. It was succeeded by a military regime under Yahya Khan.

During the Pakistani election campaign of 1970 the urban and rural lower middle classes of Punjab were attracted to the radical rhetoric of the Pakistan People's Party led by Zulfikar Ali Bhutto. More dramatic during General Yahya's period was the civil war in East Pakistan which culminated in the emergence of Bangladesh as a separate state in December 1971. The break-up of Pakistan had been made possible by Indian military intervention. Victory by India accentuated Hindu big nation nationalism while in Pakistan the old slogan of 'Islam in danger' received renewed vigour both because of defeat at the hands of India and because the Islamic socialist Z.A. Bhutto had come into power. Elsewhere also in South Asia mass democratic urban movements and peasant-based uprisings began to emerge. The urban democratic movements were directed against rising prices, unemployment, corruption, authoritarian rule and arbitrary use of state power. India's euphoria over military success and successful detonation of an atomic device in 1974, however, proved inadequate to stem the growing economic crisis which followed on the heels of the global oil crisis of 1973–74. Consequently it was rocked by growing urban unrest during 1974. In 1975 Prime Minister Mrs Indira Gandhi imposed a state of emergency which suspended many civil and political liberties. It finally led to her being ousted from power as a result of a crushing electoral defeat in 1977. However she was returned to power in 1980 as the joint opposition alliance led by the Janata Party failed to establish a credible alternative ruling coalition. In Sri Lanka the various Sinahalese-dominated governments alienated the Tamil minority through discriminatory laws and violent actions.

Within sections of South Asian society radical ideas had been gaining strength since the mid-1960s when China took a radical line in international politics.

Revolutionary Marxist-Leninists and unemployed youths tried to mobilize popular support for armed revolution and overthrow of the established socio-political orders. Peasant-based guerrilla movements such as the Naxalites in India (Banerjee, 1984) and the insurrection of poor Sinhalese youths in Sri Lanka in 1971 (Gunaratna, 1990) were the most powerful challenges to the state during this period. Reverberations of peasant radicalism were also felt in the North-West Frontier Province of Pakistan where local skirmishes took place between landlords and peasants led by the Mazdoor—Kisan Party. In all these cases the brutal response of the state and dominant classes against the radical challengers was merciless and the resistance collapsed. Following the cultural revolution debacle in China, and particularly after the death of Mao in 1976, general demoralization and pessimism descended upon South Asian revolutionaries. On the other hand, the repressive state organs emerged strongly armed with draconian laws, expanded and modernized paramilitary and anti-insurgency facilities and general optimism about the efficacy of military solutions. Such a change was particularly noticeable in India and Sri Lanka, where the insurrections were the most intense but the state had won. Thus nothing changed fundamentally in South Asia despite a decade of widespread agitations and revolutionary activity against the regimes in power.

In the political climate of the second half of the 1970s, therefore, neither liberal democracy nor Marxist ideology any longer made sense to the frustrated and disgruntled sections of society. Young people raised in a dismal political atmosphere saw very little hope of a secure future for themselves. Under the circumstances, accumulated grievances were left with few channels of the modern rational variety: elections through political parties or class-based revolution. It is not surprising that a region experiencing such gigantic political convulsions, along with natural disasters and a galloping population explosion, should begin to lose direction. The emergence of separatist ideas and movements was indicative of a serious socio-political malaise which threatened to rip society and state apart.

The prestige of the erstwhile Westernized élites gradually began to wane as corruption and favouritism mounted in the corridors of power. The central élite and the vast bureaucracy which controlled scarce capital resources were tempted to exploit such advantage. This contrasted sharply with the strong control exercised during the colonial period by the British ruling élite over the rest of society. Ethnic alienation of the British from South Asian society in a curious way gave them the advantage of acting as neutral arbiters of conflicting claims of the various indigenous groups. Neutrality was backed by rational—legal rules and a general purity of conduct of British officials.

Now the post-colonial state was headed by indigenous élites who could be accused of a religious, sectarian or ethnic bias depending on who was in government and which group dominated the state services. Corruption practised by the élites could now be seen through an ethnic prism. Identification with the state and against it assumed an important political significance in South Asian politics. The weak interface with its diverse cultural units rendered the state particularly vulnerable on the question of identity and identification. Consequently the contradictions which arose in South Asian societies were strongly manifest in the realm of cultural incongruence, even if the contradictions themselves constituted a much more complex reality deriving from socio-economic and political grievances.

Thus the growing contradictions of peripheral capitalism severely jolted the nation-state project. Indian secularism was compromised and its peaceful Gandhian ideological trappings were stigmatized, Sri Lankan social democracy was tainted by state terrorism against Sinhalese youths and ethnic assaults on Tamils, Pakistan's Muslim nationalism was a shambles as East Pakistan seceded. More of Islam rather than less of it was adopted by the Pakistani state to quell popular unrest. Having won independence from Pakistan, the Bengali Muslim leader Sheikh Mujibur Rahman dismissed the demand for special rights of the tribal people of the Chittagong Hill Tracts as seditious. None of these developments augured well for democratic development in South Asia.

During the 1980s the internal crisis along the centre–periphery axis was lent a peculiar primordial character by events taking place along the north-western flank of South Asia. India and Pakistan in particular had to adjust to the impact of the Communist coup in Afghanistan in April 1978 followed by the Iranian Revolution of early 1979 and the Soviet intervention in Afghanistan later the same year. Likewise adjustments followed for Bangladesh and Sri Lanka. In particular the growing rootlessness and insecurity which pervaded South Asia lent a new type of respectability and relevance to revivalist ideologies and millenarian movements.

The separatist project

Separatism may be defined as: a tendency present among members of a cultural group who come to feel that their objective identity markers — race, skin colour, language, religion or some other such ascriptive factor — render them extraneous to mainstream society, which thereby allegedly treats them in a prejudiced and anomalous manner. In essence it is indicative of an apprehension of a real or perceived threat to the well-being of the group posed by other groups, usually those superior in numbers or holding dominant positions in the state.

However, although the feeling of being discriminated against by the state may be present among several cultural groups in a country, it is often those groups, or rather those members of a large unranked cultural group, which are concentrated in substantial numbers in a particular region that can employ separatism in a spatial sense to undo their real or alleged discrimination, exploitation and oppression in a larger socio-political whole. Inevitably such separatism includes a claim to special rights over territory and the recognition of that group as a separate nation. Whether such a claim is about autonomy within the state or independence from it is often unclear. It can be assumed that the state is normally willing to go as far as autonomy while the most ardent separatists aim for independence.

Élite competition

Whatever the class composition of a society or a group within it, a rather small number of people constitutes the élite which exercises power and influence (*Demokrati och Makt i Sverige*, 1990: 301–57). More importantly, because of its prestige, the élite sets standards of public conduct which serve as a model to the wider society. It is useful, however, to break down the élite into various clusters. In terms of location in a multi-ethnic, regionally diverse state one can distinguish between, on the one hand, a central élite which includes decision-makers and other key figures heading the dominant social, economic, political and bureaucratic orders and, on the other hand, regional or group élites which either occupy peripheral power positions or simply command influence because of high status accorded to them in traditional terms. In any case, power in society is concentrated around élite clusters who exercise it over society, either in communion or in conflict with one another. The rationale of political separatism in the form of nationalist struggles against the state are disputes and grievances about power and resource sharing.

The socio-political dynamics of separatism

Cultural groups as such are not actors, rather they provide the material from which a leadership and organization emerge. Ranked groups such as depressed castes, minor tribes, poor religious communities and sects may possess a greater sense of alienation from the state and mainstream society. Their grievances and suffering may be much greater but they would rarely be in a position to challenge the state in a serious manner. Only large unranked groups with some sort of historical continuity and cultural distinctiveness can possibly launch a powerful challenge to the state.

A leadership and an organization would be needed to mobilize support, coordinate activities, and work out an ideology and programme for the alleged nation. The nationalist organization has to convince its members that its ethnic peculiarity marks it off from mainstream society in a dramatic manner and that exploitation, discrimination and oppression of group members by the state is a result of it. Additionally it has to convince members that it could lead them out of such suffering if given support. In case the ethnic difference is not dramatic and the leadership lacks resources, the ability to mobilize support may prove feeble even if the group has a long catalogue of grievances against the state. Such considerations are often matters of calculation, and, just as the nation-state project can end in failure, the claim to a separate nationality is also a project and can founder, even as merely an idea. The state applies all the means available to counter the separatist organization with its own barrage of propaganda and threats. At any rate, the ability of the political leadership to evolve a cogent ideological formula is a significant dimension of separatist struggles.

Intellectuals

The construction of a national identity and ideology is attempted by a rather special group of opinion-builders which includes a leader and a coterie of devoted intellectuals. This group is articulate and innovative and specializes in emotive narration of grievances in a cultural discourse (Smith, 1983: 93–5). Additionally, it is the repository of the collective memory, deriving from both real and fictive sources, of a pristine past. Lawyers, writers, journalists, poets, divines and a host of other miscellaneous cultural and social specialists are engaged in warping such memories into heroic tales about the group's past glory or suffering or both.

Intelligentsia

Since élites and intellectuals are removed from the mass of society, in political systems which are not based simply on autocratic hereditary leadership, a need exists to build networks to disseminate the separatist message in the larger society. The presence of a broad intermediary stratum which is closely linked to society becomes crucial. This stratum is the intelligentsia. It can be described as that section of the society which is employed in professions and positions requiring literary skills to perform routine tasks. Engineers, doctors, teachers, office clerks, minor priests, bureaucrats and other such actors constitute the intelligentsia (Smith, 1983: 81–2). In a way, in a largely illiterate society the lower sections of the intelligentsia comprising clerks, school teachers, minor priests and unemployed youths are like a junior élite — separated from the upper classes but prominent in mainstream society because of the ability to read and write and the intellectual pretensions which such skills obviously bring along. Thus while the top portion of the intelligentsia may be part of the élite, most will be functionaries of rather modest standing; the 'clerkly' class as Gellner (1964: 169–70) has described it. In Gellner's theory of nationalism the intelligentsia and proletariat are considered the two prongs of the nationalist movement. However, it is the intelligentsia which stands to gain the most from the creation of a separate state as it secures positions of influence in the state. On the other hand the proletariat is sidelined from a share in the gains (1964: 147–78).

As regards developing societies, some peculiarities of the intelligentsia need to be noted. With the spread of the modern school system, literary skills become available to a broader segment of society than the rather narrow traditional priestly and aristocratic élites. Consequently the intelligentsia evolves out of a mixed rural and urban cultural and class background. Such an intelligentsia is reflective of a rather bewildering variation in norms, values and general cultural orientation; hence the paradox that despite exposure to modern, universal values its cultural horizon remains narrow and parochial. Ethnic awareness receives its strongest political articulation within the intelligentsia, as its members have to compete with the intelligentsia of other social groups and communities over jobs and other opportunities within the framework of the modern territorial state. Because of its strong cultural particularism the intelligentsia can easily begin to perceive the competition in ethnic terms. It is, therefore, not surprising that this stratum is very often the most noticeable element in ethnical conflicts.

More crucially, societies and groups lacking a sizeable intelligentsia are seriously handicapped in sustaining a prolonged separatist struggle. Building up mass consciousness effectively and efficiently is dependent on skills which can counter the state's propaganda and ideological indoctrination. This skill is generally available with the intelligentsia. In political terms the most dramatic impact of modernization, particularly of the spread of modern education, on peasant societies and neglected areas is the evolution of an intelligentsia which can articulate their grievances effectively. Because of the intelligentsia, popular group concerns such as employment, food prices and so forth figure more prominently in the catalogue of group grievances. On the other hand, because of its education and literary skills, the intelligentsia tends to be less docile and submissive towards the upper classes and élite strata. Whereas the élite needs the assistance of the intelligentsia to undertake important political missions requiring mass support, the latter renders such a task from some sort of a bargaining position; promises of jobs and other economic opportunities being the most significant.

Hamza Alavi (1989: 228–9) has been tempted to describe ethnic conflict in South Asia as a special characteristic of the 'salariat', which the British created with the sole purpose of manning the lower echelons of the colonial administration and army. The argument is that since government jobs were the main source of employment — the private sector being insignificant — most educated people (the potential salariat) had to seek employment with the state. Ethnic groups (e.g. Muslims) removed from influence over the state found their way blocked by other dominant ethnic groups (e.g. Hindus), and so were led to believe that their chances of getting jobs would improve with the creation of a state of their own.

Research on the Pakistan movement shows, however, that the Muslim salariat could penetrate the countryside, particularly the key province of Punjab, only after the traditional Muslim élite consisting of landlords and religious divines had been won over to the idea of Pakistan (Gilmartin, 1989: 200−5; Sayeed, 1980). It is, therefore, wiser to approach the separatist project as a multi-layer undertaking of leading strata striving to animate ordinary group members with faith in cultural exclusiveness and mobilizing them for political action on such a basis.

Intervening external factors facilitating the separatist project

The internal contradictions propelling South Asian societies towards ethnic tension and separatism were facilitated considerably by the type of external political regime consisting of hostile power blocs and regional systems formed in the shadows of the Cold War. However, first the general economic situation obtaining in the world at that time needs to be remembered. The dramatic increase in the price of oil after 1973−74 put into disarray the earlier advantageous position of the Western states. For some of them, exporting weapons to the Third World became a significant means to mitigate their economic difficulties. The Soviet bloc also made full use of this source of income. Notwithstanding widespread poverty and underdevelopment, the tension-ridden South Asian states of India and Pakistan began acquiring quite advanced conventional weapons. The smaller states also directed considerable resources to the modernization of their armed forces.

On the other hand, notwithstanding an inherent bias in favour of the status quo, the international system as formed by the logic of bipolar superpower competition during the Cold War lacked cohesion and a core or centre capable of regulating interaction between different parts. If anything, the international system tended to push or pull the various states towards either of the two poles constituted by the superpowers. Consequently, the United Nations, as the formal centre of the international system, lacked power and authority and the capability to prevent recurrent disturbances in the system. In many senses of the word, the international system was a mere patchwork of territorial states which while commanding vastly different levels of influence in regional and global politics nevertheless interacted with one another either on a regular or occasional basis and formed clusters and subsystems as a result. A certain amount of anarchy was thus inherent to the 'international political system' (Buzan, 1991).

Hence neither internal attempts at exiting from a state nor external connivance and assistance to such movements could be successfully controlled by the international system. As a less developed region of the Third World, South Asia was particularly vulnerable to external influence and pressure. Ethnic diversity, cultural plurality, religious differences, widespread poverty, unequal development and the cumulative effect of bad government meant that big powers, hostile neighbours and many international political movements found easy access into South Asian societies.

South Asia an unstable regional system

After the demise of British colonialism, South Asia came to constitute a regional system of hostile states which was conspicuous for the absence of common strategic thinking and political objectives. Such a situation has unavoidable negative repercussions on socio-economic development notwithstanding mass poverty and a basic cognizance by the states that development has to be given priority. The balance of power in a military sense was heavily tilted in favour of India, but Pakistan, the second major state in the region, sought to offset it by seeking support outside the region. In the 1950s Pakistan sought membership in Western military pacts and received massive economic and military aid. In the early 1960s when Zulfikar Ali Bhutto served as Pakistan's foreign minister it started to cultivate close links with China and the conservative but rich Muslim countries of the Persian Gulf region. Disputes over territory and sharing of the assets of British India, and the religious tension between Hindus and Muslim which accompanied the Partition of the Indian subcontinent into India and Pakistan, kept the relationship between the two states charged with tension. Wars in 1948, 1965 and 1971 and recurring intermittent skirmishes along their borders has meant that both states have directed enormous resources to brace their military machines (Brzoska, 1986: 264—5; Johal, 1989; Wulf, 1986: 125—8). The two states have thus actively followed a policy of hostility and confrontation against each other. As part of security maximizing strategy — which has included looking for ways and means of weakening each other — the two states have tended to take a keen interest in the separatist movements going on across their borders and very often supported them. Tension also exists between India and its other South Asian neighbours. Sri Lanka, Bangladesh and even Nepal have had serious disputes with India. Its neighbours accuse India of hegemonic designs.

Lloyd I. Rudolph and Susanne Hoeber Rudolph (1987: 10—11) have taken up India's large size as compared to the other South Asian states and its relative independence of the world economic system and political order as indicators of its strength. What is missing in such analyses is a realization of India's considerable sense of cultural isolation which contributes to its security fears. Although the largest country in South Asia, it is also the only major Hindu-majority one (the only other Hindu-majority state is Nepal) in the world. Just as on the island of Sri Lanka the Buddhist Sinhalese make up a vast majority but nevertheless suffer from a minority complex in relation to the Hindu Tamils, who are in a minority but would make up a vast majority if the Tamils of India are also counted in and the backing of the Indian state to them is taken for granted, similarly India suffers from a profound minority complex in relation to the Muslim world, whose backing to Pakistan and Bangladesh is also assumed to be forthcoming. The reality in both situations is quite different. Neither has India backed the Tamil separatists to the extent that they may get their separate state on the island nor has the Muslim world as one body supported Pakistan in its various disputes with India. In the present world order, state interests weigh heavier than ideological rhetoric. However, perceptions and fears play an important role in state behaviour just as they do in the behaviour of human individuals and other societal entities. Thus we find India entering into a 25-year peace treaty with the Soviet Union in 1971, which included assurance of military assistance in case of external attack upon it.

Moreover there are cultural and ethnic links which cut across borders in South Asia and thus connect their peoples and cultural groups to ideologies and movements in conflict with the interests of the states. Consequently, economic co-operation, which is the backbone of regional stability, is absent in a substantial sense from the interaction of these states. At any rate, in the absence of an agreed security arrangement among the various states a high level of tension obtains in South Asia (Buzan and Rizvi, 1986). The formation of the South Asian Association of Regional Co-operation (SAARC) in 1985 has meant that a forum exists where the South Asian states can discuss their problems and disputes. But thus far SAARC has failed to function as a proper regional organization because of a lack of agreement on political and fundamental strategic interests of the states in the region (Ghosh, 1989: 8–14). Hence, South Asia is a highly unstable regional system.

The religious dimension

The Islamic connection links substantial sections of the South Asian populace to West Asia and the Persian Gulf region. The Iranian Revolution of 1978–79 appeared in world politics as almost an indictment of global politics dominated by the superpowers. Led by a Shia priest, the Ayatollah Khomeini, whose vision of a puritan Islamic society was inspired by medieval piety and rabid anti-modernism, the new revolution seemed to convey the general message that ideologies based on Western rationalism, both liberal and Marxian, could not move the masses of Asia and Africa in any profound sense. People had to recover from their own cultural past ideas of revolution and moral revitalization. The sense of community based on ties of affection had to be retrieved and reinstalled in the urban centres where cultural rootlessness, vulgar display of wealth and corruptions in terms of prostitution and other morally degrading forms of social life were rampant. The resultant anomie invited the appearance of millenarian ideologies and movements.

The new model of mass politics illustrated by the Iranian Revolution combined genuine grievances against dictatorship and international capitalism with a bewildering admixture of religious fervour, bigotry and outright unreason. Instead of rational political doctrines, the new era heralded in revivalist ideas deriving from reified and romanticized, idealized, selective narrations of cultural history. Religious and mystical beliefs and myths, and a variety of other such cultural factors were resuscitated to create new forms of agitational politics. It is not unreasonable to assume that the Iranian Revolution played a significant role in changing the direction of mass politics in South Asia. Muslim, Sikh, Buddhist and Hindu and various other types of religious nationalisms that had always existed in South Asia, at different stages of ferment, emerged with great force during the 1980s. Both the state and separatist movements were vulnerable to this new type of ethno-cultural nationalism. As the crisis deepened, violence on a large scale burst out in South Asia.

The religious factor impacted on South Asia also in the form of a hectic competition between the rich oil-producing fundamentalist Muslim regimes of Iran and Saudi Arabia to promote their rival brands of Islam in South Asia. An active missionary policy in India provoked a Hindu reaction. In the case of Pakistan, the Iranian–Saudi rivalry deepened the sectarian rift between Shias and Sunnis. On the whole, it has meant a boost to revivalist religio-political movements among several apprehensive religious communities of South Asia. In particular the rise of Hindu nationalism in India can be seen as a reaction to the perceived threat posed by the Islamic revival around her.

The Cold War dimension

During the Cold War, the superpowers actively sought to expand their spheres of influence worldwide. South Asia was affected by this rivalry quite early when Pakistan entered into military pacts with the West in the mid-1950s. On the other hand, the Soviet Union gained influence on India via development assistance, sale of arms and common interest between them to contain Chinese influence in the region. Following the Helsinki Agreement of 1975 which gave recognition to the status quo in Europe, superpower interest in the Third World increased significantly (Dacyl, 1990: 31). South Asia assumed immense strategic importance in superpower competition after the Communist coup in Afghanistan in 1978 followed by Soviet intervention in 1979. With well over a billion people living in the region, and India and Pakistan laced with well-equipped and modern armed forces, and India known to possess nuclear capability and Pakistan strongly suspected of being close to achieving it, it is no wonder that this region of the world has very much been in the grip of hectic political activity with linkages far beyond its traditional geographical limitations.

The diaspora dimension

In her article on resolution of ethnic conflicts, Gabriele Winai-Ström (1993: 344–9) examines two alternative hypotheses, firstly that refugee movements result in increased conflict, and secondly that refugee movements improve the potential for resolution of such conflict. It is not clear how the concept of conflict is handled in the study. The findings of her research support the latter hypotheses: that political refugees who settle in Western Europe help improve the potential for resolution of such conflicts. The examples are of the Swedish government and non-governmental organizations playing the role of mediators between these groups and the governments from which they have fled, and thus helping the peace process and the restoration of democracy in the country of origin.

It is doubtful if such success is generally applicable to cases where a refugee group is associated with a movement striving for secession from an established state. The contrary seems to be more correct. Refugees or activists who settle down abroad become part of the diaspora. It is these elements of the diaspora who maintain a passionate interest in the separatist project and who organize other members of their ethnic group for linking up with the separatist movement. The classic example is the large Irish diasporas in North America and Australia, which have been influenced by activists to support the struggle in Northern Ireland for union with the Irish Republic. The large group of Kurdish refugees from Turkey which arrived in Europe in the 1980s has been playing a prominent role in support of the separatist Kurdish movement in Turkey. Turkish Kurds who had settled in Europe in the 1960s normally did not attach so much importance to their sub-national ethnic identity and considered themselves part of the Turkish nation.

Similarly large South Asian diaspora communities have been settled for a long time in Europe, North America and South-East Asia. These were politicized when activists arrived from the home countries carrying with them accounts of bad treatment. By the early 1980s the revolution in communications had made possible for diaspora groups to maintain intimate and up-to-date contact with the political movement in the home country. Particularly the free flow of audio and video cassette-tapes made propaganda dramatic and entertaining. The South Asian diaspora communities began to play a crucial role in drawing international attention and support towards the separatist struggles of their groups. Both legitimate as well as illegitimate methods were employed. For example they not only sought contacts with international human rights agencies and lobbied governments but also procured weapons from the illegal weapon markets through donations from group members as well as through illicit trade in drugs. On the other hand, movements which lacked the support of diaspora communities were seriously handicapped in their struggle against the state. Thus the resource endowment of separatist movements varied considerably depending on the availability or absence of the support of a diaspora community.

The role of violence in ethnic conflict and separatist struggles

In the final analysis, the ability of the state and of the separatist movements to combat each other is dependent upon their ability to sustain violent action. Most important to note is that separatist movements tend to acquire a lasting and unbending character only when the state resorts to massive repression against them. For it is from the experience of repression that alienated cultural groups acquire a lasting memory of hatred and vengeance against the state, providing them with a cause strong enough to justify their own acts of terrorism. Naked and brutal violence against minorities is the ultimate form of the politics of ethnicity. It is essentially a racist phenomenon. Although racism is an ideology which the state employs explicitly with a view to allocating unequal and differential roles to different ethnic groups while ethnicity is discrimination practised in contravention of democratic and universal values that the state upholds formally, the difference between them is one of form, not of essence. The explicit or implicit practice of discrimination and victimization in which violence has been introduced as a major means of quelling protest and agitation causes such deep cleavages between those dominating the state and those struggling for separation that no amount of appeasement later can truly heal the injury (Arendt, 1970: 46–56).

A sinister angle of this scenario is that the initiation of violence in an ongoing conflict may not have authorization from either a government or a separatist organization; intelligence services may act on their own without sanction from proper authority and indulge in terrorist activities against alleged secessionists. Equally, an extremist group within the separatist movement may itself introduce violence with a view to accelerating the level of conflict to a point where peaceful compromise becomes less likely. Lastly, exploitation of ethnic differences between rival groups may be a strategy that a government may employ to ensure its own survival. This may mean illicit co-operation between the state and a terrorist organization against a common foe.

Ted Gurr (1971: 13–14) explains the psychological underpinnings of violent action as a growing sense of relative deprivation among people against the political system. The sense of relative deprivation develops when there is a perceived discrepancy between the value expectations of people and their value capabilities. Value expectations refer to what people believe they are rightfully entitled to, and value capabilities refer to what people believe they can achieve. Societal conditions that intensify expectations without simultaneously increasing capabilities intensify discontent. Similarly, societal conditions which decrease the average position of people without decreasing their value expectations intensify discontent. Hence, the greater the intensity of discontent, the more likely is violence. Collective discontent tends to be politicized and then expressed in violent action against political objects and actors. Collective violence usually has a political object in mind. Political violence is of the greatest magnitude if both a regime and those who oppose it exercise approximately the same degrees of political control and command similar high levels of institutional support in the society.

Applying Gurr's notion of similar degrees of political control and levels of institutional support in society to separatist struggles, it can be asserted that in a situation where a separatist movement is well equipped militarily, enjoys some amount of popular support and can also employ political clout regionally and internationally, it will be able to mount and sustain the separatist challenge against the state more forcefully. The modern state is normally well equipped to crush internal challenges but rather ineffective in controlling external sources of support to such movements. On the other hand, a movement relying fundamentally on external help is vulnerable to easy collapse if its internal support and fighting capability is weak. In the case where a separatist movement is not backed by powerful internal or external backers, its ability to sustain a protracted political struggle, particularly of the violent type, is seriously limited. In such cases the state can crush that movement rather easily. In any case, shifts and changes in tactics and strategy occur on both sides as they assess the balance of power. In the final analysis, however, the external and internal balance of power, as well as the weight of public opinion and international sympathies, decides the outcomes of such conflicts, although the advantages available to the state in such conflicts are overwhelming.

References

Ahmed, V. and Amjad, R. (1984) *The Management of Pakistan's Economy 1947–82*, Karachi: Oxford University Press.

Alavi, H. (1973) 'The state in post-colonial societies: Pakistan and Bangladesh' in K. Gough and H.P. Sharma (eds), *Imperialism and Revolution in South Asia*, New York: Monthly Review Press.

Alavi, H. (1989) 'Politics of ethnicity in India and Pakistan' in H. Alavi and J. Harriss, *Sociology of Developing Societies: South Asia*, London: Macmillan.

Apter, D.E. (1968) *Some Conceptual Approaches to the Study of Modernization*, Englewood Cliffs: Prentice-Hall, Inc.

Arendt, H. (1970) *On Violence*, New York and London: Harvest/HBJ.

Banerjee, S. (1984) *India's Simmering Revolution: The Naxalite Uprising*, London: Zed Books.

Bardhan, P. (1984) *The Political Economy of Development in India*, Oxford: Basil Blackwell.

Blomquist, H. (1988) *The Soft State: Housing Reform and State Capacity in Urban India*, Uppsala: Uppsala University.

Brzoska, M. (1986) 'Other countries: the smaller arms producers' in M. Brzoska and T. Ohlson (eds), *Arms Trade in the Third World*, Stockholm: SIPRI.

Buzan, B. (1991) *People, States and Fear*, London: Harvester Wheatsheaf.

Buzan, B. and Rizvi, G. (1986) *South Asian Insecurity and the Great Powers*, London: Macmillan.

Clapham, C. (1985) *Third World Politics*, London and Sydney: Croom Helm.

Crow, B. (1990) 'The state in Bangladesh: the extension of a weak state' in S.K. Mitra (ed.), *The Post-Colonial State in Asia: Dialectics of Politics and Culture*, New York: Harvester Wheatsheaf.

Dacyl, J.W. (1990) 'A time for perestroika (restructuring) in the international refugee regime?', *Journal of Refugee Studies*, vol. 3, no. 1.

Demokrati och Makt i Sverige (report prepared by Yvonne Hirdman, Johan P. Olsen, Inga Persson, Olof Petersson and Anders Westholm) (1990), Stockholm: SOU.

Frankel, F.R. (1978) *India's Political Economy, 1947–1977: The Gradual Revolution*, Princeton: Princeton University Press.

Gellner, E. (1964) *Thought and Change*, London: Weidenfeld and Nicolson.

Ghosh, P.S. (1989) *Cooperation and Conflict in South Asia*, New Delhi: Manohar Publications.

Gilmartin, D. (1989) *Empire and Islam: Punjab and the Making of Pakistan*, Delhi: Oxford University Press.

Gunaratna, R. (1990) *Sri Lanka a Lost Revolution: The Inside Story of the JVP*, Colombo: Institute of Fundamental Studies.

Gurr, T.D. (1971) *Why Men Rebel*, Princeton: Princeton University Press.

Hasan, Z. (1989) 'Introduction: state and identity in modern India' in Z. Hasan, S.N. Jha and R. Khan (eds), *The State, Political Processes, and Identity*, New Delhi: Sage Publications.

Hettne, B. (1993) 'Dynamics of ethnic conflict' in H. Lindholm (ed.), *Ethnicity and Nationalism: Formation of Identity and Dynamics of Conflict in the 1990s*, Göteborg: Nordnes.

Hiro, D. (1976) *Inside India Today*, London: Routledge & Kegan Paul.

Johal, S. (1989) *Conflict and Integration in Indo-Pakistan Relations*, Berkeley: University of California.

Khan, R. (1989) 'The total state and the Indian political system' in Z. Hasan, S.N. Jha and R. Khan, *The State, Political Processes, and Identity: Reflections on Modern India*, New Delhi: Sage Publications.

Kohli, A. (1989) *The State and Poverty in India: The Politics of Reform*, Cambridge: Cambridge University Press.

Martinussen, J. (1980) *Staten i perifere og post-koloniale samfund: Indien og Pakistan*, Århus: Forlaget Politica.

Midgal, J.S. (1988) *Strong Societies and Weak States*, Princeton: Princeton University Press.

Mitra, S.R. (1990) 'Between transaction and transcendence: the state and the institutionalisation of power in India' in S.K. Mitra (ed.), *The Post-Colonial State in Asia: Dialectics of Politics and Culture*, New York: Harvester Wheatsheaf.

Moore Jr, B. (1966) *Social Origins of Dictatorship and Democracy: Lord and Peasant in the Making of the Modern World*, Harmondsworth: Penguin University Books.

Moore, M. (1985) *The State and Peasant Politics in Sri Lanka*, Cambridge: Cambridge University Press.

Moore, M. (1990) 'Sri Lanka: the contradictions of the social democratic state' in S.K. Mitra (ed.), *The Post-Colonial State in Asia: Dialectics of Politics and Culture*, New York: Harvester Wheatsheaf.

Mukherji, P.N. (1992) 'Class and ethnic movements in India: in search of a pertinent paradigm for democracy and nation-building in the Third World' in L. Rudebeck (ed.), *When Democracy Makes Sense*, Uppsala: AKUT.

Myrdal, G. (1968) *Asian Drama*, vol. I, New York: Pantheon.

Rudolph, L.I. and Rudolph, S.H. (1987) *In Pursuit of Lakshmi: The Political Economy of India*, Chicago and London: University of Chicago.

Sayeed, K.B. (1980) *Politics in Pakistan: The Nature and Direction of Change*, New York: Praeger Publishers.

Smith, A.D. (1983) *State and Nation in the Third World*, London: Wheatsheaf Books.

Wilson, A.J. (1974) *Politics in Sri Lanka 1947–1973*, London: Macmillan.

Winai-Ström, G. (1993) 'Resolution of ethnic conflicts' in H. Lindholm (ed.), *Ethnicity and Nationalism: Formation of Identity and Dynamics of Conflict in the 1990s*, Göteborg: Nordnes.

Wulf, H. (1986) 'India: the unfulfilled quest for self-sufficiency' in M. Brzoska and T. Ohlson (eds), *Arms Trade in the Third World*, Stockholm: SIPRI.

4

A Theory of Ethnic Conflict and Separatism in Multicultural Post-Colonial States

This chapter summarizes the discussion in Chapters 1–3 and proposes a medium-range theory to explain ethnic conflict and separatism in societies where state–society congruence is weak. Multicultural post-colonial states are typically cases of incongruence between state and society.

States are abstractions of processes and institutions meant to systematize the production and distribution of material wealth and to safeguard society against crime, internal disruption and external aggression. States are also legal and cultural entities usually accorded recognition by other states. As power is unequally distributed in all societies, but concentrated particularly in the state organs, a power élite is inevitably at the helm of state affairs. Because of its control over information — access to media, control of bureaucracy and institutions of higher education and so on — it has many advantages in determining overall policy and allocation of resources and the distribution of material gain and other rewards.

As modern states are the accepted unit for the production and reproduction of society they also become the framework for the survival of each society. The society itself comprises various smaller units such as the individual, family, tribe, caste group, religious community, linguistic groups and nationalities and so on. However, in the contemporary world each society in a routine sense functions within the precincts of the state. In exceptional cases the state may be entirely artificial with no firm linkage in the society so that it disintegrates sooner or later. Such disintegration of the state would not mean the dissolution of that society, although it may cease to exist in that form and parts of it may be annexed by other states. In the long run such bits and parts of a larger social whole may be integrated into other social wholes and be assimilated by them. Thus even society in the sense of a culturally coherent unit of humankind is only relatively permanent.

More common, however, is that the linkage between the state and its various constituent units varies. Some are closer to the state than others in reality in all senses of the word. The chances of survival and stability of the state improve markedly if a significant majority of the people identify themselves with the state. As cultural (that is to say, ethnic) diversity is common in most modern states, if the cultural majority is well represented in the state it enhances the stability of the state. On the other hand, if a cultural minority dominates, state stability may have to be maintained through force. The ethnic connection between the state and society in modern society is stabilized through the majoritarian principle: democracy is rule of the majority. In principle such majority is not ethnic but political. In reality, however, the periodic divisions of society into a political majority and minority is easier if the majority cultural group (or several big ones) is well represented in the state. Even if a state is not democratic the majoritarian principle now pervades state formation universally. Thus the state is relatively more stable if the bigger ethnic group(s) is well represented in the state. Its stability improves further if the minorities are not alienated from the state. However, social and economic inequalities are produced in some measure in all societies and, therefore, tension is inherent in all states: during periods of stress and crisis this can take the form of conflict. In poor, developing societies such tension is more or less constant as inequalities are pervasive and overwhelming.

An important function of the state is, therefore, to promote linkages within society. Thus the educational system, mass media and distribution of material wealth and welfare are some of the means the state uses to improve linkage, in other words to create legitimacy (Easton, 1965: 278–90). Part of the function of state institutions is to ingrain emotional attachment among the people with the state and its symbols. Thus people identify with the state even if they are poor, neglected and deprived. A certain level of false consciousness therefore binds people to the state. Were it not so, rebellions and revolutions would have been routine in world history, and killing and dying for the state a rarity. Since even the most inefficient and apparently weak states can survive for long periods of time, the significance of false consciousness in the state–society relationship can be presumed to be intrinsic to it (Engels, 1970: 461–583; Gramsci, 1976: 210–12; Marx and Engels, 1976: 59).

Unlike the Western states with democratic traditions of long historical standing and continuity, which have acquired a strong cultural interface with the larger society and devised common rules on the distribution of wealth and other rewards (unequally) under advanced capitalism, the multicultural post-colonial states inherit not only a weak interface between the modern state and the ancient, complex society but also a weak economic base (for example, an agrarian economy) to respond to the increasing volume of demands which modernization and development inevitably generate. They therefore have to rely more strongly on ideological, political and cultural activities calculated to consolidate a stable support base for themselves in the larger society and thereby enhance their control over it. Modernization and development, along with the ideological, political and cultural inputs to establish a stable support base in society for the state and the dominant classes, can be described as the main ingredients of the nation–state project.

However, the nation–state project is not only a combination of material interests and calculations about maintaining a certain type of class and social hierarchy but also a normative vision comprising political ideals and present and future societal goals. Some states adopt universal models of nation-building; others choose particularistic ones. In any case, ideology can facilitate integration and gradual assimilation, or it can furnish grounds for forced assimilation or exclusion and expulsion; in extreme cases for genocide. Such ideological choice is reflective of élite preferences and calculations and is modified in practice as different governments and regimes acting in the name of the state relate to society and the external world. If modernization and development initiatives do not suffice and social restlessness is on the increase, even democratic states begin to emphasize the ideological and cultural aspects of the nation–state project because of the need to maintain a close linkage with society. How this happens and in what proportion can be gauged only in the historical context.

Following Ted Gurr (1971), it is assumed that a perceived discrepancy between value expectations and value capabilities results in a sense of relative deprivation. In this connection, uneven development during rapid modernization in particular accentuates the sense of relative deprivation. Change and transformation can have disturbing impact on cultural identity, and élites and intelligentsia of unranked cultural groups (Horowitz, 1985), removed from the state élite in some ethnic sense, can develop interests not compatible with the nation–state project. The emotionally charged nature of ethnicity and its multidimensionality renders it easily manipulable and thus vulnerable to political manoeuvre.

In these circumstances, while the state and its various ideological organs try to promote an official ethnic identity, i.e. an official national identity, group leaders of disgruntled unranked cultural groups — the élite, intellectuals and intelligentsia — strive to push forward an alternative cultural-political discourse the purpose of which is to dissuade group members from identifying with the state-promoted national identity. Rational communication between the state and such a group or groups becomes difficult because, while accusing one another of unreasonable or unfair conduct (related to sharing of power and resources), they invoke different principles of staking their own claims. Thus if the state proceeds from the territorial principle to define the nation, the separatist leadership may invoke primordial ties and vice versa. Similarly, between two or more cultural groups of comparable strength embroiled in ethnic conflict regarding preferential or exclusive rights to the same territory, different principles may be invoked to justify such a claim and the position taken can be subjective and arbitrary. Objective standards for assessing the veracity of claims and counter-claims may become necessary but may be spurned by the concerned parties or one of them, depending on the balance of power obtaining internally and externally.

Grievances can be said to be rational and objective if a group has been excluded explicitly from the potential nation, or if routine discrimination, exploitation and persecution are practised against it by the state. Such a group in an objective sense can be said to share not only a relative sense of deprivation but also an absolute and objective sense of deprivation. The abject poor, officially or socially degraded ethnic groups and minority sects would comprise such a category. It is possible that improvement in their standards of living may also generate a sense of relative deprivation as they may no longer accept their lowly positions and may become achievers in the modern sense of the autonomous rational individual. Or through participation in the modern industrial sector individuals belonging to ranked groups may establish new identities such as those of class. As part of a class the sense of relative deprivation would be expressed in rational terms of exploitation of the labour power and other inequalities.

Such collective grievances and sense of relative deprivation, however, need to be distinguished from that expressed on behalf of multi-class, socially stratified, unranked (Horowitz, 1985) cultural groups claiming to be nations. If expressed on behalf of groups not excluded explicitly or denied a legitimate share of economic gains and political power, or who may in an objective sense have considerably improved their standard of living, the perceived or alleged sense of deprivation can contain a large degree of distortion resulting from manipulation of emotional symbols, prejudices and other negative forms of politics. Assertive élites (Brass, 1974; 1991) and emerging intelligentsia (Gellner, 1964; 1983; Smith, 1983; 1986) are typically the percipients of relative deprivation, bearers of rising expectations and the constructors of separatist identity.

Whatever the merits of an ethnically charged argument, the litany formulated by the leadership of an unranked multi-class cultural group typically rejects universal solutions in favour of exclusive or preferential group rights; hence the subjective rationality of ethnic discourse: for example, rejecting not the principle of exploitation in terms of class relationships but only of alleged exploitation by the state or some other group. If a sizeable intelligentsia exists in a largely illiterate and/or poorly informed and unemployed population, the uncritical dissemination of separatist ideas and attitudes among group members is considerably facilitated. On the other hand, if the intelligentsia is negligible and a traditional élite presides over a mass of poor peasants, the separatist project is slower to evolve. This difference results from the fact that separatist nationalism is about creating a powerful propaganda against the state in the internal and external arena, and this task can be accomplished best by a literate stratum occupying the space between the élite and the mass of society.

The catalogue of grievances put forth by such a group or groups against the state does not necessarily consist of false accusations or erroneous facts and figures purported to give proof of bad treatment by government officials representing the state. There may be substantial truth in such allegations. However, fundamental to the emerging ethnic conflict between the state and the leadership of an unranked cultural group claiming to be a nation is that the latter no longer shares an interest in the nation-state project, and develops an argument based on subjective rationality to legitimize its own urge for power and influence (Breuilly, 1982). In other words, it formulates a separate nationalism and seeks to forge a nation out of group members. When originating among a cultural group or groups concentrated along international boundaries as a political movement explicitly or implicitly suggesting secession, it provokes a powerful reaction from the state, because no state is willing to secede territory.

Two factors are particularly important in assessing why multicultural post-colonial states may, despite no deliberate decision or policy to that effect, be guilty of bad treatment of a disgruntled group. The first is structural: on the one hand, the historical legacies of peripheral capitalism and uneven development are compounded by centralization of power and scarce resources which occurs with the growing momentum of modernization. On the other hand, there is weak interface, particularly in the realm of cultural congruence, between the state and its constituent societal units. Consequently the modernizing state tends to educate more people than it can employ, or provide appropriate jobs for, elsewhere in the economy. More people are dislocated from the subsistence economy, rendered rootless, compelled to seek work in the towns and cities, but end up in some marginal relationship with the rest of society. Such shattering impact is felt more strongly by cultural groups removed from the centre, where the élite and upper classes of the dominant cultural group(s) usually reside. Consequently the post-colonial state's ability to respond to the material and emotional needs of its variegated constituent units is severely constrained. The second is fear. States may violate autonomy arrangements with a cultural group which is perceived to be susceptible to external influence. In unstable regions such as South Asia, holding on to territory is perceived to be imperative as a means of enhancing security. On this point the state can hope to receive broad support from mainstream society against the alleged secessionists because the security concerns of the state are very often shared by people who identify their own safety with the survival of the state.

The state can try a wide range of measures to enhance its control over the disgruntled group. Divisive strategy and tactics may be tried to split the leadership of the disgruntled group or to exploit subgroup differences (for example sectarian differences within a religious community or dialectal differences within a language group). Other means can range from constitutional accommodations of separatism through autonomy formulae and forms of democratic representation to the other extreme of authoritarian integration and forced assimilation. In extreme cases genocide and mass expulsion of suspect groups may be tried to forestall perceived separatist threats.

In any event, granting independence to a part of its population and giving up territory is not normal behaviour for states, particularly those which have not yet developed into functioning industrial economies and where high regional instability deriving from rivalries with neighbours and external interference and influence of big powers and worldwide hostile ideological movements prevails. For developed states which have expanded their productive base on a world scale, seceding territory may not be such a serious loss, but for developing states threatened by external enemies the territory they hold is a part of their strength and power, and necessary to the goals of development.

The theory

Assuming that survival is paramount and overriding in the nation-state project (the various economic, social, cultural, political, ideological and military inputs of the state to consolidate a support base in society by creating a coherent nation) of modern states, and the loss of territory is perceived to be detrimental to such survival, multicultural post-colonial states which almost invariably have a weak interface with the larger society, especially with their culturally distinct constituent units, would use all means available to hold on to territory under their control since secession of territory is perceived to be crucially inimical to survival. Such perceptions are modified in the context of regional and global balance of power. A drastic failure of the nation-state project would be successful secession of territory.

On the other hand, the leadership and intelligentsia of an assertive unranked cultural group staking claim to nation are likely to strive for maximum control over territory and resources and seek exit from the state with a view to establishing a separate state of their own. A drastic failure of the separatist project would be no or poor response from group members or no concessions from the state in the form of autonomy.

If both sides assume uncompromising positions and a failure of the political process occurs, an outbreak of armed and violent conflict is likely and the stage is set for a confrontation between the warring parties.

Things tend to get out of control once massive force has been introduced in the conflict and external actors are involved. By deliberately introducing or escalating violence, a separatist organization or some faction within it, or state security agencies and other secretive organs, can subvert peaceful resolution of the conflict. More crucially, if a separatist movement can solicit economic, military and other types of help from external suppliers it can mount a sustainable armed resistance to the state and may, therefore, spurn peaceful resolution of the conflict. The outcome of such protracted violent confrontation is quite uncertain, although the state normally has the upper hand in such situations and usually can hold on to territory under its control because it can assert its sovereign rights over it (which, of course, is disputed by the separatists) and use the overwhelming force at its disposal to punish internal resistance.

Under the circumstances, agreeing to some sort of autonomy, short of secession, may be acceptable to the state as it does not entail dramatic loss of power and security is not perceived to be radically jeopardized. On the other hand, the separatist project may aim at secession, and the separatists may resort to agitations and violent action to compel the state to concede its demands. However, the option of substantial and real autonomy within a federal system would not be a complete failure of the separatist project if the state withdraws in a substantive sense and grants genuine autonomy to it. It is within the parameters of autonomy that the conflicting entities are likely to agree. Accordingly the nation–state project and the separatist project are likely to be modified in the process of give and take. As regards the conflicting claims of two or more cultural groups of comparable strength located in the same territory to rights over it, the solution is likely to be mutual recognition of each other's share in power and resources. Zero-sum solutions are not likely to succeed in a world where pluralism, equality and democracy have become universal values.

However, real and lasting stability and consolidation in the Third World are not likely as long as outstanding inequalities prevail within developing states as well as in the international system, and the weaknesses of the developing states are exploited by the industrialized world. Regional peace and co-operation among neighbouring states and democratic consensus within them can nevertheless reduce the tensions and promote peaceful change.

References

Brass, P.R. (1974) *Language, Religion and Politics in North India*, Cambridge: Cambridge University Press.

Brass, P.R. (1991) *Ethnicity and Nationalism: Theory and Practice*, New Delhi: Sage Publications.

Breuilly, J. (1982) *Nationalism and the State*, Manchester: Manchester University Press.

Easton, D. (1965) *A System Analysis of Political Life*, New York: John Wiley and Sons.

Engels, F. (1970) 'The origin of the family, private property and the state' in *Marx and Engels: Selected Works*, Moscow: Progress Publishers.

Gellner, E. (1964) *Thought and Change*, London: Weidenfeld & Nicolson.

Gellner, E. (1983) *Nations and Nationalism*, Oxford: Basil Blackwell Ltd.

Gramsci, A. (1976) *Selections from the Prison Notebooks*, London: Lawrence and Wishart.
Horowitz, D.L. (1985) *Ethnic Groups in Conflict*, Berkeley and Los Angeles: University of California Press.
Marx, K. and Engels, F. (1976) *Collected Works*, vol. 5, Moscow: Progress Publishers.
Smith, A.D. (1983) *State and Nation in the Third World*, London: Wheatsheaf Books.
Smith, A.D. (1986) *The Ethnic Origins of Nations*, Oxford: Basil Blackwell Ltd.

5

Cultural and Political Heritage of the Indian Subcontinent

The earliest people to inhabit the Indian subcontinent are believed to have been Proto-Australoids. The Indus Valley civilization, which reached its zenith around 2000 BC, is presumed to have been founded by a Proto-Australoid people maintaining regular contact with Mediterranean culture and mixing with its peoples (Wolpert, 1982). Trade and cultural links between the Indus Valley civilization and the contemporary Sumerian civilization were well established. Migration to this region from other parts of the world began early in prehistoric times. Among the early arrivals were the Dravidian peoples. The Dravidians were followed by the Aryan tribes that began pouring into the Indian subcontinent between 1500 and 1000 BC. They gradually established their hold over the northern, western and central parts of the Indian subcontinent. The Dravidians were defeated and driven southwards. In the eastern regions Mongoloid peoples had been settled from time immemorial. Aryan and Dravidian peoples also crossed over to Sri Lanka. Similarly the Maldives received people from the mainland. From about 1000 BC the Indo-Aryans had vanquished all significant opposition and become the dominant and most numerous group in northern India.

Hinduism and the caste system

Hinduism evolved very gradually out of folklore, legends and mythology of predominantly Aryan tribes evolving from primitive society to more settled and advanced culture. This evolution from prehistory to antique civilization of the Indo-Aryans took place through interaction and racial intermixing with the other peoples in South Asia. Consequently pre-Aryan beliefs and customs found their way into Vedic scriptures, the religious books of the Aryans. Among Hindu gods and deities were to be found both Aryan and pre-Aryan figures (Chennakesavan, 1980: 2–3; Kosambi, 1975: 102–7). This peculiarity lent Hinduism a flexibility which enabled it to admit a rich variety of cults and popular folk beliefs into its beliefs, practices and rituals as well as to tolerate other religions and beliefs.

On the other hand, the flexibility in religious beliefs and tolerance towards others was counterbalanced by the subsequent evolution of rigid social ranking and stratification through *varna* (class or social estate), which in Western usage came to be called as the caste system (Smith, 1963: 25–7). The Aryans, having subdued the other peoples, now evolved the myth of racial purity. The Brahmin priests were supposed to be of the purest Aryan stock. They were followed by the warrior and princely caste of Kshatriyas. Both these castes constituted the nobility. Below them were the ordinary members of society called Vaiyshas. These three *Varnas* were considered clean and accorded the status of twice-born. The dark-skinned Dasas, presumably of mixed Aryan–Dravidian race, were placed at the bottom of the caste system and named Sudras. Outside the pale of caste society altogether were the so-called Untouchables (Wolpert, 1982: 41–2). In this category were placed the defeated Dravidians, Australoids and other minor ethnic groups. However the notion of a fixed and total caste society that froze all inter-mixing in Hindu society is somewhat misleading. New castes were founded or existing ones modified as various new tribes and ethnic groups came in contact with Aryan society and were gradually assimilated into it. The south Indian Dravidian peoples as a whole were classified as Sudras or below, according to Brahminic ideology. More importantly, the fact remained that Hinduism remained ideologically an ethnic religion (Sarma, 1953: 3). Proselytizing has therefore never been a Hindu concern. On the contrary, those at the bottom of the social order have historically been attracted to religions and reform movements offering them better treatment and status (Gopal, 1976: 1–12).

The Hindu social order was challenged several times from within. Rivalry between the two main property-owning noble castes, the Brahmin priests and the ruling Kshatriya princes, for power and influence in society marks the ancient period. The most profound challenges to Brahminic supremacy were posed by two Kshatriya princes, Sidhartha Gautama and Vardhamana Mahavira, the founders of Buddhism and Jainism respectively, during the sixth century BC. Both these religions rejected Brahmin supremacy and were critical of caste oppression. Buddhism, with its emphasis on collective welfare and social service as the means of achieving nirvana (salvation), quite rapidly won over a growing body of adherents. During the third century the Emperor Ashoka abandoned Hinduism in its favour. This boosted Buddhism's fortunes considerably. It spread to central Asia, Sri Lanka, China, and South-East Asia owing to the indefatigable efforts of its monks. However, a later Hindu revival in the second century AD proved even more dramatic. Typically Hinduism sought to absorb Buddhism into its fold by subdivision and doctrinal revision. The Buddha was acknowledged as a true sage and given an honorific station within Hinduism. Buddhism, however, continued to have a substantial separate following in different parts of the Indian subcontinent until much later. After the advent of Islam in India most of its adherents converted to the new faith; others relapsed into Hinduism. At the beginning of the twentieth century Buddhism almost ceased to have a following in mainstream Indian society. In 1956, however, some half a million so-called Untouchables led by Dr Ambedkar embraced Buddhism in a mass ceremony. Conversions to Buddhism have gradually increased thereafter. On the other hand, Jainism, which prescribed asceticism and self-abnegation in the extreme, flourished as a separate religious order in some parts of India during the ancient period but gradually most of its followers returned to the Hindu fold. A tiny Jain community has survived into present times. According to the 1981 Indian census 2.6 million Jains were to be found in India. Most of them live in the Indian state of Gujarat and are traders by caste and profession.

Several other tribes and ethnic groups originating in West Asia and central Europe also entered the South Asian region from the north-west after the early Aryans had settled and become a part of indigenous society. These latecomers gradually adopted the Hindu religion, although their own tribal traditions were not abandoned altogether. Among them the Scythians and Huns were the more numerous. The ruling families and militant sections were granted Kshatriya status and named Rajputs, but most of the lay soldiers and peasants remained on the peripheries of caste society, occupying rather lowly positions.

The Muslim arrival in South Asia

During the time of the second pious caliph, Umar (634–644), Arab traders reached the western coast of India and established links with local traders. In 712 an Arab army invaded Sindh, and captured Sindh and southern Punjab. However, it was the Turco-Afghans who from the eleventh century onwards launched successive waves of invasions on the subcontinent. By the early thirteenth century the important city of Delhi had fallen to the Muslims. Thereafter the invading Muslims from West and Central Asia had to defeat some Muslim sovereign established in northern India in order to establish their own authority. For the next 600 years Muslim dynasties dominated the Indian subcontinent.

More importantly, the Muslims brought with them a religion whose legal system and social norms were quite distinct from Hinduism. Thus rather than Hinduism assimilating Islam, as had been the fate of Buddhism and Jainism, Islam, with its proselytizing zeal and the additional advantage of state power to back it, retained its separate existence. However, during the long Muslim period conversions to Islam took place mostly among the later arrivals such as the Scythian and Hun tribes (Jats, Gujjars, Rajputs and others) of north-western India and among the lower castes of northern and north-eastern India. The Muslim community consisted of two separate groups, an upper crust consisting of the foreign-born and their descendants, called *ashraf*, and the local converts. The former kept their social distance from the latter and there was little sense of community among the two groups. Consequently Islam remained a minority religion. At the time of the arrival of the British only one in four Indians was a Muslim.

The political order during the medieval period

A segmentary, decentralized socio-political order with a Muslim ruler at the pinnacle and a loose descending power hierarchy constituted by lesser Hindu and Muslim princes, chiefs, caste leaders and tribal headmen presided over the mass of peasants, craftspeople, artisans, menials and others in northern India during the medieval period (Ahmed, 1987: 67–8). Most Muslims were Sunnis who followed the Hanafi rites of orthodox Islam. The Islamic Sharia was recognized as the supreme law of the land and the large body of Muslim theologians, called *ulama*, acted as its professional experts. However, the sultans ruled virtually as despots, and strict adherence to Sharia was observed only by a few puritans. Similarly among the common people customary and tribal practices and usages were widely observed.

Although the entrance of Islam in the subcontinent as the religion of the ruling class imposed several disabilities on Hindu society, it did not fundamentally alter its internal shape. Brahmins and other upper-class Hindus continued to maintain their superior station; their property was not confiscated as long as they remained loyal and helped the sultan during war (Antonova, Bongard-Levin and Kotovsky, 1979: 211). Destruction and desecration of Hindu temples did take place, however. But as Richard Eaton (1993) points out, very often only temples representing the king were destroyed. Such destruction was symbolic as it signified the change of ruler. It also contained the collected treasure of the king and was the main attractive target from that angle too. Destroying royal temples was an established political tradition from the Hindu period and not a Muslim innovation. On the other hand, there were also Muslim rulers and notables who adopted more enlightened policy towards Hindu religion and culture, including the building and maintenance of temples. The Emperor Akbar (d. 1605) even tried to construct a common Indian identity. He founded a new syncretic creed, Din-e-Ilahi, which combined principles from Islam, Hinduism and other great religions. It proved to be too radical for those times and perished with the demise of its founder. More importantly, mixed populations consisting of Hindus, Muslims and others were to be found in all the Indian states irrespective of whether the ruler was a Hindu or a Muslim.

Popular movements

During this period, a number of popular movements combining selective Hindu and Islamic ideas with universalist ideas also emerged among Hindus and

Muslims. Among them the most famous was the Bhakti movement. It started as a reform process among Hindus in south India in the eighth century, but gradually spread from the south to north, becoming a forum for people from both the upper and lower castes who were dissatisfied with established Hinduism. Later the Bhaktis opened their movement to Muslims too. Consequently sections of Muslim society were also attracted to its fold. Its most famous exponent was Kabir (1440–1518), a low-caste Muslim weaver (Antonova, Bongard-Levin and Kotovsky, 1979, vol. 1: 225–7). Generally, at the mass level, cultural assimilation between Hindus, Muslims, Sikhs and others proceeded on its own momentum. The common people from all the religions took part in traditional festivals and local customs. Among the peasantry Hindu deities and Muslim saints were often commonly held in high esteem.

The economic basis of the pre-colonial state

The economy remained largely dependent on an agricultural surplus which was extracted by various tiers of the nobility, with the central government claiming a share. Ownership of land in principle remained with the state. The emperor appointed incumbents to different positions who were assigned a share in the agricultural product. Gradually hereditary ownership also evolved. Trade and large-scale production developed in different regions, and linkages with the outside world were well established. For example hundreds of thousands of master weavers in Bengal, particularly at Dhaka in present-day Bangladesh, produced high-quality muslin which was eagerly sought in European markets.

But most of the wealth produced indigenously was frittered away by the upper classes in warfare, pleasurable pursuits and other wasteful activities. Primitive accumulation of capital on a large scale did not occur, although traders and bankers of considerable means did establish their warehouses and trading networks over several regions. The Mughul state appropriated the wealth of deceased merchants and officials and thus precluded the evolution of a capitalist economy and a modern bourgeoisie (Moore, 1966: 322–3). The Indic civilization remained gripped by a pre-modern world vision based on scholasticism and reverence for tradition and custom.

The colonial state and societal transformation

The European powers that came to India were equipped with better weapons and naval power and gradually annexed bits and parts of the Indian mainland, entering from the coastal areas and gradually moving into the hinterland. In this power game the British proved to be the most successful and by the beginning of the nineteenth century they had virtually eliminated the other European powers as serious competitors and rivals. By the mid nineteenth century Britain had achieved at home a thorough industrial transformation. By deliberate policy, production of some outstanding export items of India such as cotton and silk cloth was discouraged and inevitably ruination of master weavers, artisans and traders followed (Mukherjee, 1974: 300–12). Thereafter India, in the subordinate position of an appendage of the imperialist economy, experienced rapid change and large-scale social mobility. Modern means of communication such as railways and all-weather road networks were flung over the Indian subcontinent. These served as the scaffold upon which the premises of modern India were raised.

Several new coastal cities such as Calcutta, Bombay and Madras located in Hindu-majority regions became the centres of modern change and transformation under the British. On the other hand, the older cities of northern India, which were linked to land-route trade, declined in importance. Such change however still left the overwhelming majority of people dependent on a subsistence economy. Cultural transformation was most noticeable in the evolution of a modern-educated élite and a somewhat larger intelligentsia.

The colonial system of political control

In 1858 the government of the English East India Company was dissolved and India was incorporated into the British Empire. The British Indian Empire rested on two systems of political control. Areas directly annexed by Britain became British India and were put under a strong centre with the Viceroy as the chief executive. In the provinces the central government was represented by an all-powerful governor. All the key posts in the administration were held by the British. The modern bureaucratic state system based on rational–legal routines was augmented by a system of political control based on a hierarchical structure of collaboration into which the local élites were co-opted. Representative institutions were introduced gradually, and although elections were instituted universal adult franchise was never granted. Only some 12 per cent of the population at most was enfranchised during the British period.

Apart from directly administered British India, a large number of princely states headed by feudal despots also existed. These were under British protection through treaty. In internal matters the princes were allowed autonomy, including the right to make laws and collect taxes. However, external relations and defence were organized via the British. Small states like Nepal, Bhutan and Sikkim along the Himalayan foothills never came under direct British suzerainty although colonial overlordship was a fact for them too. In the thick inaccessible forests of the north-eastern regions of the subcontinent bordering Burma were to be found several hill tribes. These defied integration into the mainstream colonial system, although their economic and political autonomy increasingly diminished under impact of the expansive colonial order. Also, the tribes of the north-west living along the border with Afghanistan retained internal self-rule in the so-called tribal belt, although these areas also fell into the British sphere of control. Most importantly, after 1857 the subcontinent escaped further external invasions. The empire provided the political framework for internal stability and consolidation.

European religio-cultural offensive and indigenous responses

A system of modern education gradually evolved. It consisted of schools for the élite based on English-medium education, and the ordinary government and municipal schools where education was imparted in the native languages. English-educated natives were gradually recruited into the state bureaucracy and shortly before the colonial withdrawal had been promoted into senior positions. While Queen Victoria's proclamation of 1858 prescribed a secular state, the fact that the British were the ruling power provided ample opportunities to the various Christian churches of Europe to propagate their creeds among the indigenous people. The shock of being subordinated by European powers initially generated despair and serious cultural disorientation. Among élite sections of society, particularly in Punjab, there were some conversions to Christianity. However, this pessimism was followed by a hectic introspection leading to a revival of idealized Hinduism, Islam, Buddhism, Sikhism and other religions (Bhatia, 1987: 114–20; Farquhar, 1967). In this enterprise European scholars played a significant role in fostering a renewed faith in ancient roots.

In terms of cultural revival, both modernist as well as fundamentalist versions appeared. Thus Raja Ram Mohan Roy's (1772–1833) Brahmo Samaj belonged to the modernist type of Hindu response. On the other hand the Arya Samaj was puritan-reformist, while the Hindu Mahasabha and the Rashtriya Swayamsevak Sangh (RSS) were militant forms of orthodox Hindu nationalism. Some of the communal Hindus were members of the all-India Congress. Among Muslims, Sir Syed Ahmed Khan attempted to reconcile Islam with nature and reason. The militant Wahabi movement of the early nineteenth century and the Deoband seminary founded in northern India in 1867 represented Islamic puritanism. The leading élite party, the All-India Muslim League, was communal and employed religion to define nation. Other religio-political parties that later appeared among Muslims were the Jamiat-Ulama-e-Hind, the Ahrars and Khaksars, the Jamaat-e-Islami, the Jamiat-Ulama-e-Islam — all puritanical in their orientations but divided on doctrine and political line. The Ahmadiyya sect broke off from mainstream Muslim society and established itself independently. Among Sikhs the Akali Dal and Sikh Sabha represented Sikh religious and communal interests. Several heterodox Sikh sects also emerged during this period (Bhatia, 1987:

121–202). These communal organizations acted as ideological spearheads against each other and against secular organizations and parties, including the Communist Party. Some of these communal organizations were creations of British design and were meant to create mischief when required.

The social and political role of communal organizations

Bipin Chandra (1989: 1) remarks: 'Simply put, communalism is the belief that because a group of people follow a particular religion they have, as a result, common social, political and economic interests.' He observes further: 'Communalism was not a remnent of the past — a hangover from the medieval period. . . . It was a *modern ideology* that incorporated some aspects and elements of the *past ideologies and institutions and historical background* to form a new ideological and political discourse or mix' (1989: 6).

Although the communal religio–cultural organizations were eclipsed by the two main élite parties, the All-India National Congress (founded 1885) and the Muslim League (founded 1906), their political clout was by no means insignificant. The two élite parties, to varying degrees, made use of the communal organizations to win popular support for their politics. Although Congress was steadfast in its secular–territorial nationalist ideology, many leading members of the Congress party were members of communal organizations and they freely employed religious discourse and symbolism to win political support (Taylor, 1979: 263). When the Muslim League embarked upon its Pakistan project it openly relied on the religious forces to promote it. Similarly the Akali Dal possessed a strong religious character and its leadership rested with religious-oriented politicians. In other words, religious culture inevitably circumscribed politics even when the élite leaders employed secular terminology to negotiate power sharing with one another.

Hindu–Muslim élite competition

Separatism appeared in the modern period among the Muslim élite and intelligentsia as a combination of cultural tension, unequal development of communities and regions, and competition for jobs, as well as a result of British policy to divide and rule. After 1858 the British adopted a policy of co-opting native notables into the colonial power hierarchy. It was, however, the upper-caste Hindus who benefited most from the new opportunities because they had taken to Western education much earlier than the Muslims. The language controversy of the 1880s in the United Provinces (UP; renamed in Hindi as Uttar Pradesh or UP) was the first manifestation of the disturbing impact of uneven development. During the Mughul period (1526–1827) Persian and, later, Urdu were employed as the official languages. Upper-class Muslims who were conversant in these languages naturally benefited the most in terms of employment during the Mughul period. The British continued to employ Persian and Urdu, although English was introduced as the state language on the superior level. Consequently Muslims, who formed only between 13 and 15 per cent of the population of UP, continued to acquire government jobs greatly in excess of their population ratio. A Hindu-led Hindi language revival began to surface in the 1880s, which demanded the replacement of Urdu (written in the Persian script) by Hindi (written in the Devanagri script). The government initially prevaricated but finally Hindi was adopted as the official provincial language. This change hit the Muslim intelligentsia severely. Thus their share in the highest government ranks declined from 64 per cent in 1857 to 35 per cent by 1913. It was, however, still more than double their population strength in UP (Alavi, 1989: 229).

In 1886 Sir Syed, a leading Muslim modernist, founded the Muslim Educational Conference. It was followed by the establishment of the Aligarh College, where Muslim students from all over the subcontinent came to receive a modern education based on the British university model. In terms of politics, Sir Syed decided upon a strategy to solicit British support for Muslim upper-class interests, in return for which the Muslims were to keep away from nationalist politics. Sir Syed therefore took an active role in persuading the Muslims to keep away from the All-India National Congress (1885) which he dubbed a Hindu organization. Although Congress proclaimed a secular nationalist ideology, it was undoubtedly dominated by upper-caste Hindus. By the early twentieth century Congress had been radicalized and had begun demanding greater share for Indians in the management of the country's affairs, something which perturbed the colonial government. With the rise of Mahatma Gandhi as its leader, Congress entered the era of mass politics. Gandhi introduced religious ideas and imagery, deriving largely though not exclusively from the Hindu heritage, into his non-violent methods of political agitation.

A series of administrative and constitutional changes effected by the government in the early twentieth century were to hasten Hindu–Muslim political estrangement. The first was the decision taken in 1905 by the Viceroy, Lord Curzon, to divide the huge and heavily populated province of Bengal into two separate provinces. Although the Muslim élite of Bengal was initially ambivalent on the partition of Bengal, it was persuaded by the government to support it. The Bengali Hindus and the Congress Party began to dub the partition as a devious plot to 'vivisect the motherland'. A massive campaign was launched throughout India against the partition (Qureshi, 1979: 26–8). This included even terrorist attacks against the British and Muslims. In 1911 the government gave in to the growing agitation against the partition and annulled it. The Muslim reaction was one of dismay and deep disappointment.

The second was the introduction of separate electorates. In October 1906 a deputation of top Muslim leaders headed by Sir Agha Khan, the head of the Ismaili Shias, presented a petition consisting of a number of demands on behalf of the Muslim community to the Viceroy, Lord Minto, at Simla. The statement had been approved beforehand by the government, which was anxious to steer Muslim notables away from the Congress. Among the demands presented to the Viceroy the most important was for the creation of a system of separate electorates and provisions for fixed quotas and weightage for Muslims in municipal councils, legislative assemblies and government services. In the Morley–Minto Reforms of 1909 these demands were conceded. While it recognized the great difficulty in finding a suitable system of representation for a society constituted by a plethora of castes, tribes, sects, ethnic groups and religious communities, the pernicious effects of the system of separate electorates on Indian national consciousness were foreseen in the Montagu–Chelmsford Report of 1918, which stated:

> We regard any system of communal representation . . . as a very serious hindrance to the development of the self-government principle. . . . Any general extension of the communal system . . . would only encourage still further demands, and would in our deliberate opinion be fatal to that development of representation upon a national basis in which alone a system of responsible government can possibly be rooted. (*Constitutional History*, 1983: 545–6)

The Muslim League and the 1937 elections

In December 1906 leading Muslims from all over India had gathered in Dhaka on the invitation of Nawab Salimullah and founded the All-India Muslim League. Up until 1936 the Muslim League avoided mass mobilization and other forms of popular agitation and instead concentrated on the question of Muslim share in jobs and representation. The Government of India Act of 1935 greatly extended the elected basis of government at the provincial level. Elections were to be held under it in early 1937. The Congress was at that time the only truly grass-roots all-India party. The Muslim League entered the election campaign on the sole claim that it represented the Muslim community of India and sought a mandate to continue playing that role. However, given the strong provincial content of the 1935 Act, the regional parties in the Muslim majority provinces opposed the attempts of the Muslim League to establish itself in their provinces. The result was a disastrous defeat, as shown in Table 1.

Out of 485 Muslim seats the Muslim League won only 108 seats. The Muslim League did well in Hindu-majority provinces, but was routed in all the Muslim-majority provinces except Bengal. On the other hand, out of a total of 1585 general seats the Congress won 711. However, it contested 58 reserved Muslim seats but could win only 26 of them. Most reserved Muslim seats were won by

Table 1   1937 provincial election returns for the Muslim League

Province	Total Muslim seats	Seats won by Muslim League
Madras	28	11
Bombay	29	20
Bengal	117	40
UP	64	27
Punjab	84	1
Assam	34	9
NWFP	36	–
Orissa	4	–
Sindh	35	–
Bihar	39	–
CP	14	–

Source: Allana (1977: 149).

regional parties. The 1937 elections clearly indicated one important political fact: that Congress was certain to dominate the centre in the subcontinent.

Congress ministries and the Muslim élite's apprehensions

Congress founded ministries in six provinces where it had a majority. It later brought two more provinces under its command. On the other hand, the problem for Congress was that Muslims were largely alienated from it. Out of a total of 58 Muslim seats that it contested, it won only 26 of them. Thus a need to win over the Muslims was felt acutely by the party leadership. Accordingly a mass contact campaign among Muslims was launched in March 1937. However, during this period it made several blunders which were to antagonize the Muslims. For example, it reneged on a pledge given prior to elections to the UP Muslim League to form a coalition government. Now, after scoring a sweeping victory, it insisted that Muslims elected on the Muslim League ticket had to resign from it before they could be considered for appointment in the cabinet.

Scholars of the Indian freedom movement are generally agreed that the coming into power of Congress ministries was a turning point in élite Muslim perceptions of the political situation (Seervai, 1989: 1922). Henceforth the Muslim League was to embark upon a campaign to rouse Muslim fears of a permanent domination in a united India by Congress and the Hindus. Another clumsy move was the adoption of 'Bande Matram' as the national anthem by the Congress governments. This song was considered by Muslims as anti-Muslim. The Muslim League counter-attacked with a rabid communal campaign of vilifying Congress as a harbinger of a Hindu Raj. The general feeling created among Muslims was that Islam was in danger. In 1939 Britain committed India to the Second World War without consulting Indian leaders. Upon this the Congress ministries resigned in protest. The Muslim League celebrated it as a Day of Deliverance.

The rise of the Muslim League

The idea of a Muslim state was first authoritatively presented by a Punjabi of Kashmiri extraction, Sir Muhammad Iqbal (d. 1938), in his presidential address to the annual secession of the Muslim League held in Delhi in 1930. Iqbal based his argument on the so-called Two-Nation Theory, according to which India consisted of two separate and distinct nations — Hindus and Muslims. In 1933 another Punjabi, Chowdhari Rahmat Ali, coined the name Pakistan by taking the first letters of Punjab, Afghania (the North-West Frontier Province), Kashmir, and added 'istan' to include Sindh and Baluchistan. 'Pak' means pure or chaste in Urdu. Rahmat Ali envisaged his Muslim state and nation to be pervaded by an Islamic identity. In the early 1930s nobody took much notice of the idea of a Muslim state.

However, at the beginning of 1940 the Muslim League had succeeded in convincing the Muslim leaders of Punjab, Bengal and Sindh that without its help they would not be able to withstand the Congress's push into their provinces. In its annual session of 1933 Congress had under Jawaharlal Nehru's influence adopted a hostile position on traditional big landlordism, and therefore the powerful Muslim landowners of Punjab and Sindh feared its success. Consequently the provincial Muslim leaders acknowledged the Muslim League as their representative in central Indian affairs and in return the Muslim League promised not to interfere in the internal politics of these provinces (Jalal, 1985). The first major manifestation of Muslim unity was the historic Lahore Resolution of 23 March 1940 which stated:

> Resolved that it is the considered view of this session of the All-India Muslim League that no constitutional plan would be workable in this country or acceptable to Muslims unless it is designed on the following principle, viz., that geographically contiguous units are demarcated into regions which should be grouped to constitute 'independent states' in which the constituted units shall be autonomous and sovereign. (Allana, 1977: 226–7)

In 1942 the Allies were doing badly in the Second World War. On 14 July 1942 Congress passed a resolution demanding the immediate end of British rule. It also sanctioned the launching of a country-wide civil disobedience movement. On 9 August all Congress leaders were arrested and it was declared unlawful. It was not until 1944 that Gandhi and other major Congress leaders were released. On the other hand, the Muslim League urged the Muslims not to participate in the movement. Thereupon between 1943 and 1944 the British installed Muslim

League or pro-Muslim-League ministries in the Muslim majority provinces. Suddenly the writ of the Muslim League was running high in the provinces in which it had been roundly defeated in 1936. From 1943 onwards the landlords of Punjab, Sindh and NWFP started joining the Muslim League. With this crucial class co-opted, the Muslim League embarked upon a mass contact campaign in these provinces.

Communalized election campaign of the Muslim League

The 1945–46 election campaign was conducted by the Muslim League with a patently communal strategy to which was added skilfully the question of class oppression. The peculiar development of capitalism during the colonial period had acquired (because of cultural and other factors) a communal appearance. Thus in the Muslim majority provinces trade and commerce were dominated by Hindus while most Muslims were agriculturalists, many of whom were debt-ridden. On the other hand, most of the big landowners were also Muslims. For example in Punjab and Sindh the modern middle class was predominantly Hindu. The indebted landowners and peasantry of Sindh and Punjab were convinced by the Muslim League that the debt burden incurred to Hindu money-lenders would be cancelled if they supported the Pakistan idea. The rather large, emerging Punjabi intelligentsia hoped to find greater employment opportunities if the more advanced Hindus and Sikhs were driven out. It is to be noted, however, that the common impression that Muslims were grossly under-represented in government services did not conform to the situation of the 1940s. As a tradition, Muslims were employed in large numbers in the important police service in many parts of India. For example in UP, where Muslims made up less than 15 per cent of the total population, some 50 per cent of the police were Muslims. In the late 1930s the Muslim-dominated provincial governments in the Muslim majority provinces began to encourage the employment of Muslim intelligentsia in government services. As a result in the police force Muslims became the majority. Thus in Punjab and Sindh at least 70 per cent of the police force was Muslim. In Bengal too Muslims predominated in the police force (Sayeed, 1978: 154).

To the *ulama* and *pirs* (religious mystagogues) wild promises were made of restoring the glory of Islam in Pakistan and making it conform to the Sharia. Anti-Hindu and anti-Sikh rhetoric was freely employed. On the one hand, in order to maximize Muslim support the Muslim League employed the overarching definition of a Muslim used by the colonial census authorities: anyone who declared himself or herself a Muslim was entered accordingly in the records. Thus support for Pakistan was sought from Sunnis, Shias and all their various subsects as well as from the controversial Ahmadiyya sect. On the other hand, in

Table 2   1945 Central Legislative
Assembly election

Congress	57
Muslim League	30
Independents	5
Akali Sikhs	2
Europeans	8
Total	102

Source: Qureshi (1979).

Table 3   1946 provincial election returns for the Muslim League

Province	Total Muslim seats	Seats won by Muslim League
Madras	29	29
Bombay	30	30
Bengal	119	113
UP	66	55
Punjab	86	79
Bihar	40	34
CP	14	13
NWFP	38	17
Assam	34	31
Orissa	4	4
Sindh	35	35

Source: Allana (1977).

the more formal messages to the world community the Muslim League leader, Mohamed Ali Jinnah, emphasized that Pakistan was to be a modern democracy in which Islamic ideals of social justice were to serve as inspiration (Jinnah, 1976: 231–3; 456; 463). Congress also employed negative slogans but these were directed more against the leadership of the Muslim League than against the Muslim community.

The 1945–46 election results

The 1945–46 elections were held in two stages: in December 1945 members of the Central Legislative Assembly were elected, and in early 1946 members to the provincial assemblies were elected. The election campaign was conducted from two clearly opposite platforms: Congress stood for a united India and claimed to represent all Indians, while the Muslim League demanded Pakistan and claimed to speak for the Muslim nation. In the Central Legislative Assembly elections Congress won all general seats while the Muslim League secured all Muslim seats. The final figures in the elections are shown in Tables 2 and 3.

Out of a total of 495 seats reserved for Muslims, the Muslim League obtained 440. Out of a total of 1585 seats in the provincial assemblies Congress captured 905 seats. The Congress and the Nationalist Muslims (those supporting Indian unity in contrast to Muslim Nationalists supporting Pakistan) secured only 52 Muslim seats. The elections clearly showed that Congress commanded the over-whelming support of non-Muslim voters while the claim of the Muslim League that it was supported by the Muslim voters was also confirmed beyond doubt.

Britain prepares to quit

The principle of self-government had been conceded by the British in the Montagu Declaration of 20 August 1917. The next milestone in the direction of self-rule was Lord Irwin's Statement on Dominion Status of 31 October 1929. The outbreak of the Second World War greatly weakened British resolve to hold on to India. The Cripps Mission of 1942 offered complete independence to India after the war. Thus after the end of the War freedom and independence were imminent.

British policy on self-government had lent legitimacy to the Congress and Muslim League as the two rival representative nationalist groupings in India. As they were the two major all-India élite parties, such recognition was not unreason-able, although it meant that powerful regional parties were sidelined in the process. In this connection the opposition to the Pakistan idea and the Muslim League in the overwhelmingly Muslim North-West Frontier Province (NWFP) from the Khudai Khidmatgars (also known as the Red Shirts) led by Abdul Ghaffar Khan was the most significant. Ghaffar Khan remained steadfastly aligned to Congress and was an ardent supporter of the unity of India (Jansson, 1981).

The failure of the Cabinet Mission Plan

Among influential conservative members of the British India Office, suspicion and hostility towards Congress had always been entertained, and encouraging Muslims to take a separatist course in the freedom struggle had been a consistent strategy of British policy-makers. However, the postwar Labour government under Clement Attlee was sympathetically disposed towards Congress, particularly Nehru who shared its Fabian ideals. Accordingly a high-power mission led by the Secretary of State for India, Lord Pethick-Lawrence, and including Sir Stafford Cripps and Mr A.V. Alexander was sent to India to find out ways and means of keeping India united upon colonial withdrawal. The Cabinet Mission arrived in India on 23 March 1946. When the discussions began with the Indian leaders the Sikh Akali Dal also entered the negotiations. Congress stood for a federal structure with a strong centre. Jinnah argued in favour of a separate Muslim state consisting of the Muslim majority provinces. Alternatively he proposed a loose federation with maximum powers vested in the provinces. Further, at the centre he demanded fifty–fifty representation in government, even though the Muslims constituted somewhere between one-third and one-quarter of the total population of India. On the other hand, the Akali Dal demanded the creation of Khalistan in Sikh-majority areas of Punjab. The Cabinet Mission Plan of 16 May 1946 rejected both the ideas of Pakistan and Khalistan. Instead it proposed a loose union of India, with most of the powers vested in the provinces. Only foreign affairs, defence and communications were to be vested in the centre and it was to have the powers to raise the necessary finances for these subjects. The provinces were to be free to form groups. Moreover every province could by a majority vote of its legislature call for a reconsideration of the terms of the constitution after an initial period of ten years and at ten-year intervals thereafter. A constituent assembly was to be elected for the whole union. Each province was to be allotted seats to the constituent assembly in proportion to its population. The provincial quota was to be divided among the main communities of Hindus, Muslims and Sikhs in proportion to their population (Qureshi, 1979: 255–8). Moreover, the Mission emphasized the importance of setting up an interim government. Although both Congress and Muslim League had serious objections to the Plan, they were nevertheless persuaded to accept it by the government.

However, on 10 July Nehru committed perhaps his greatest political blunder when during a press conference in Bombay he stated that Congress would enter the Constituent Assembly 'completely unfettered by agreements and free to meet all situations as they arise' (quoted in Azad, 1959: 155). This greatly perturbed the Muslim League, as the future status of the minorities was made uncertain by Nehru's rash statement. Therefore some days later it decided to withdraw its support to the Cabinet Mission Plan. Now Jinnah threatened to resort to direct action to achieve Pakistan. The government, however, decided to let Congress form the interim government on the basis of its electoral victory during the 1945–46 elections. This infuriated Jinnah, who gave the call for Direct Action on 16 August 1946.

Direct action

Although rivalry between Congress and the Muslim League was pivotal to the Partition of India, the full significance and shattering impact of communal riots on mass psychology in terms of brutalization of social relations has not been properly assessed in this context. Sporadic clashes between Hindu–Sikh and Muslim gangs had been taking place since the 1946 elections in various parts of north-western India, but communal harmony was largely preserved.

A dramatic escalation in communal discord took place when, on Jinnah's call for a Direct Action Day on 16 August 1946, the Muslim League Chief Minister of Bengal, Hussain Shaheed Suhrawardy, ordered his hooligans and gangsters to attack a run-down Hindu locality. Some 4000 people were massacred, some 15,000 more were injured and 100,000 rendered homeless (Brown, 1985: 326). Most of the victims were Hindus.

Suddenly communal carnage broke out in Punjab, Bengal, Bihar, Sindh and the North-West Frontier Province. The pogroms in Punjab and NWFP were particularly gruesome. The British became spectators to a human tragedy they had largely brought about by their divide-and-rule policy, but which they no longer felt any real responsibility to stop.

Interim government

In the meanwhile an interim government was formed, with Jawaharlal Nehru as vice-president, while the Viceroy remained its chief executive. It took office on 24 August 1946. Efforts were renewed to convince the Muslim League to join it. The Muslim League made its entrance into the cabinet conditional on the recognition of its status as the sole representative of the Indian Muslims. This was agreed and on 15 October the Muslim League decided to join the cabinet. On 25 October the cabinet was reconstituted and a government consisting of Congress, Muslim League and the religious minorities including the Sikhs was formed. It appeared to give a chance to the efforts to keep India united. The Muslim League was allotted five cabinet positions, including the crucial finance portfolio. However, mutual suspicions and animosities among the members of the interim government proved too strong.

In this regard particular mention should be made of the budget proposal prepared by the finance minister, Nawabzada Liaqat Ali Khan, Jinnah's second-in-command in the Muslim League. The budget was deliberately prepared to hit hard against industrial and commercial interests — classes which were supportive of Congress. Sardar Vallabhbhai Patel in particular objected to such a biased budget. Some Congress members of the cabinet even described it bluntly as a communal budget. Thus in the absence of mutual trust and loyalty the working of the interim government was severely impaired. Nehru demanded that the Muslim League should withdraw from the government. Ultimately the Muslim League complied with the demand. Maulana Abul Kalam Azad (1959: 176), the most famous Muslim leader of the Congress, who never accepted the idea of Partition, was later to blame his Congress colleagues obliquely for not adopting a strategy of accommodation which would have kept the Muslim League in the government and thereby Partition could have been avoided. It seems that towards the very end of the freedom struggle Nehru and several other Congress leaders had grudgingly become reconciled to the fact of Partition. Working in co-operation with the

Muslim League in a united India was deemed very problematic, as the League was considered a party representing reactionary interests such as the landlords and communal-minded Muslim *ulama* and divines. Nehru looked forward to modernizing India along a mixed economy based on socialist principles and progressive ideas.

Religious, sectarian and ethnic minorities outside mainstream Hindu and Muslim societies

Christians, Parsis and other smaller minorities were marginalized during the freedom struggle as they were dispersed in society and, therefore, had little choice but to accept future citizenship of the state in which their ancestral homes were located. The so-called Untouchables had earlier on demanded separate electorates for themselves (Dobbin, 1970: 113–15). Gandhi, however, was able to argue successfully that the Untouchables were part of the Hindu social order and not therefore a separate religious community. In his reformist approach to the caste system Gandhi asserted that the Untouchables should be treated as Harijans, that is, children of God, and not degraded or persecuted. Such an approach, along with promises of equitable treatment in an independent democratic India, made the leader of the Untouchables, Dr Ambedkar, accept a place for his people within the Indian polity (Hiro, 1982: 6–7). On the other hand, Dravidian separatism was quite strong in south India before Partition. Congress managed to convince many influential Dravidian leaders to join the fold of the Congress, and thus that separatist threat was also thwarted. Communal electorate had also been extended to the Sikhs in 1921 under the Montagu–Chelmsford reform. They too were successfully persuaded by Congress to join India. On the other hand, the Muslim League was successful in winning Shia and Ahmadiyya support for Pakistan.

Mountbatten divides and quits

The earlier policy of the Attlee government of finding ways and means of keeping India united was abandoned once the Cabinet Mission Plan failed and communal frenzy flared up enveloping different parts of the subcontinent. Moreover, since the Constituent Assembly could not proceed with its task of framing the constitution, the British government accepted the inevitability of Partition. In March 1947 Louis Mountbatten arrived in India as the last Viceroy of India. By that time communal violence had reached frightening proportions. An impending human disaster could be sensed by all those who wielded authority. However, instead of trying to regain control over the situation Mountbatten seemed to have resigned himself to the inevitability of a holocaust. Rather than trying to bring things under control he expended his energies in making the leaders of Congress and

Muslim League speed up the negotiation process leading to Partition. It is an intriguing fact that the original plan to leave India by June 1948 was abandoned by Mountbatten in favour of mid-August 1947. The radio announcement to divide India came on 3 June. First Mountbatten spoke, followed by Nehru, Jinnah and Baldev Singh, the Sikh leader. Less than three months was left before the scheduled withdrawal. The new timetable left little room for an orderly transfer of populations; hence the loss of property and life on a huge scale (Seervai, 1989: 142).

The problem of princely states

The relationship between Britain and the princely states was regulated under the doctrine of paramountcy, which stipulated that in case of a dispute between two or more princely states, or between the states and the government of India, the ultimate decision would lie with the Crown. Britain as the paramount power was obligated to provide protection against internal rebellion. In external relations and defence the states had no autonomous role (Gupta, 1966: 69–71).

As to the future status of several hundred princely states upon British withdrawal, there was no clear government policy. Strictly speaking, the lapse of paramountcy entitled the princes (the legal sovereigns) to remain independent, but they were dissuaded from such a course by the British and advised to join either India or Pakistan. In most cases the question of accession was not problematic. In some cases, however, it was.

The trauma of partition

Under the Indian Independence Act of 1947 of the British Parliament, two dominion states, to be known as India and Pakistan, were to come into being upon British withdrawal in mid-August 1947. The borders drawn between India and Pakistan, however, did not follow any consistent principle. The religious basis of division could not be applied neatly because Hindus and Muslims were to be found in all parts of the subcontinent and the Sikhs were spread over many parts of Punjab. Punjab and Bengal were divided on a religious basis, the western areas of Punjab and the eastern areas of Bengal being allotted to Pakistan. In the summer and autumn of 1947 somewhere between half and one million Hindus, Muslims and Sikhs lost their lives and many times more were maimed, crippled, abducted and driven out from the homes and lands of their forefathers. Some 11 million people crossed the borders of West Pakistan and India in either direction (Brown, 1985: 327). Organized Muslim, Hindu and Sikh armed gangs prowled the land during those fateful months. The riots were particularly gruesome in Punjab, composed of sizeable Muslim (51 per cent), Hindu (33 per cent) and Sikh (14 per cent) communities. In *Stern Reckoning*, an authoritative compilation of evidence on the Partition riots and violence, the author, G.D. Khosla (1989: 3), a former chief justice of the Punjab High Court, made the following observation:

> The great upheaval which shook India from one end to the other during period of fifteen months . . . was an event of unprecedented magnitude and horror. History has not known a fratricidal war of such dimensions in which human hatred and bestial passions were degraded to the levels witnessed during the dark epoch when religious frenzy, taking the shape of a hideous monster, stalked through cities, towns and countryside, taking a toll of half a million innocent lives. . . . To be a Hindu, Sikh or a Muslim became a crime punishable with death.

It is important to note that almost all Muslims from East Punjab crossed over to Pakistan and almost entirely all Hindus and Sikhs moved in the other direction. The first major postwar experiment in ethnic cleansing, therefore, took place in Punjab. Substantial numbers of Muslims crossed West Bengal to come and settle in East Pakistan, and Hindus left East Bengal for India, but on both sides many stayed on. On the whole less than 2 per cent of the Muslim population from other provinces and regions of India migrated to Pakistan in 1947. Later more followed but until 1954, when large-scale migration was stopped by Pakistan, only some 3 per cent of such migrants had settled in Pakistan.

It is amazing that provinces and regions such as Orissa, central India and south India in which Muslims constituted a small minority there were almost no communal clashes. The non-violent traditions in the popular culture seemed to have dissuaded the Hindu masses from attacking the Muslim minority settled among them for centuries. Some 30 million Muslims stayed on in India (Brown, 1985: 328).

The creation of Pakistan did not resolve the Hindu–Muslim problem in a lasting or just sense. Rather it gave a devious twist to future Hindu–Muslim relationships and took the form of hostile rivalry between India and Pakistan. Moreover the future well-being of the 30 million Muslims left behind in India was dependent upon India remaining a democratic and secular state. More importantly, the role of religious nationalism in the post-independence period was to prove pernicious to the development of a rational and democratic political consciousness in the subcontinent. It continues to haunt the politics of India, Pakistan and Bangladesh in a negative manner and should be considered an unfortunate and reactionary legacy from the recent colonial past.

References

Ahmed, I. (1987) *The Concept of an Islamic State: An Analysis of the Ideological Controversy in Pakistan*, London: Frances Pinter.

Alavi, H. and Harriss, J. (1989) *Sociology of Developing Societies: South Asia*, London: Macmillan.

Allana, G. (ed.) (1977) *Pakistan Movement: Historic Documents*, Lahore: Islamic Book Service.

Altekar, A.S. (1962) *State and Government in Ancient India*, Delhi: Motilal Banarsidass.

Antonova, K., Bongard-Levin, G. and Kotovsky, G. (1979) *A History of India*, Book 1, Moscow: Progress Publishers.

Azad, M.A.K. (1959) *India Wins Freedom*, Bombay: Orient Longmans.

Bhatia, S. (1987) *Social Change and Politics in Punjab: 1898–1910*, New Delhi: Enkay Publishers PVT Ltd.

Brown, J.M. (1985) *Modern India: The Origins of an Asian Democracy*, Delhi: Oxford University Press.

Chandra, B. (1989) *Communalism in Modern India*, New Delhi: Vikas Publishing House Pvt Ltd.

Char, S.V.D. (ed.) (1983) *Readings in the Constitutional History of India 1757–1947*, Delhi: Oxford University Press.

Chennakesavan, S. (1980) *A Critical Study of Hinduism*, Delhi: Motilal Banarsidass.

Dobbin, C.E. (1970) *Basic Documents in the Development of Modern India and Pakistan, 1835–1947*, London: Van Nostrand Reinhold Company.

Eaton, R.H. (1993) 'Indo Muslim state formation, temple destruction, and the historiography of holy warrior', unpublished paper presented at the Conference: State Formation and Institution Building in South Asia, held at Sunnersta Herrgård, Uppsala.

Farquhar, J.N. (1967) *Modern Religious Movements in India*, Delhi: Munshiram Manoharlal.

Gopal, R. (1976) *Indian Muslims: A Political History (1858–1947)*, Book Traders: Lahore.

Gupta, S. (1966) *Kashmir: A Study in India–Pakistan Relations*, Bombay: Asia Publishing House.

Hiro, D. (1982) *The Untouchables of India*, London: Minority Rights Group.

Jalal, A. (1985) *The Sole Spokesman*, Cambridge: Cambridge University Press.

Jansson, E. (1981) *India, Pakistan or Pakhtunistan?*, Uppsala: Acta Universitatis Upsaliensis.

Jinnah, M.A. (1976) *Speeches and Writings of Mr Jinnah*, vol. 2, Lahore: Sh. Muhammad Ashraf.

Khosla, G.D. (1989) *Stern Reckoning*, Delhi: Oxford University Press.

Kosambi, D.D. (1975) *An Introduction to the Study of Indian History*, Bombay: Popular Prakash.

Moore Jr, B. (1966) *Social Origins of Dictatorship and Democracy*, Harmondsworth: Penguin University Books.

Mukherjee, R. (1974) *The Rise and Fall of the East India Company*, New York and London: Monthly Review Press.

Qureshi, I.A. (1979) *The Struggle for Pakistan*, Karachi: The University of Karachi.

Sarma, D.S. (1953) 'The nature and history of Hinduism' in K.W. Morgan, *The Religion of Hindus*, New York: The Ronald Press.

Sayeed, K.B. (1978) *Pakistan: The Formative Phase 1857–1948*, Karachi: Oxford University Press.

Seervai, H.M. (1989) *Partition of India: Legend and Reality*, Bombay: Emmanem Publications.

Smith, D.E. (1963) *India as a Secular State*, Princeton: Princeton University Press.

Taylor, D. (1979) 'Political Identity in South Asia' in D. Taylor and M. Jupp (eds), *Political Identity in South Asia*, London: Curzon Press.

Thapar, R. (1979) *Ancient Indian Social History: Some Interpretations*, New Delhi: Orient Longmans Limited.

Wolpert, S. (1982) *A New History of India*, New York and Oxford: Oxford University Press.

6

India

On 15 August 1947 India achieved independence. It was the primary successor state to British colonialism on the Indian subcontinent. Except for territories allotted to Pakistan, all others directly administered by Britain or which were under its control through local arrangements were awarded to India. The several hundred princely states which came within Indian territory could in principle remain independent but were advised by both the British government and the Congress Party to join India. Most of them signed the Instrument of Accession and joined India. Hyderabad state, ruled by a Muslim but 89 per cent Hindu and totally surrounded by Indian territory, declared itself independent but was militarily annexed by India in September 1948. Junagarh and Manavadar, two small states on the Kathiawar Peninsula, were ruled by Muslims but their populations were overwhelmingly Hindu. The rulers decided to join Pakistan even though their states lay well within Indian territory. Pakistan accepted such a procedure. India did not accept their accession to Pakistan because it did not conform to the basis of partition: Hindu majority areas going to India and Muslim majority areas going to Pakistan (Fyzee, 1991: 331). Uprisings took place in the two states and in October–November 1947 Indian troops moved in. In January 1948 Pakistan raised the question of annexation of these states by India in the UN Security Council. A plebiscite arranged by India showed that the people of these states wanted to join India. The government of Pakistan, however, refused to recognize the validity of the plebiscite (Gankovsky and Gordon-Polonskaya, 1972: 165).

Initially the various princely states retained their autonomy, but were later dissolved and merged into the Indian federation. In 1961 India took over militarily the Portuguese colony of Goa on the west coast. In 1975 the tiny Himalayan kingdom of Sikkim was annexed and made the twenty-second state within the Indian Union. The case of the former Jammu and Kashmir State is treated in depth separately in this chapter.

Table 4   Religions of India, no. (millions) and percentage

Hindus	550.0	82.6
Muslims	75.5	11.4
Christians	16.2	2.4
Sikhs	13.0	2.0
Buddhists	4.7	0.7
Jains	3.2	0.5
Others	2.8	0.4

Indian society and polity

According to the Census of India of 1981 the total population of the country was 685,185,000. Its total area was stated as 3,287,000 sq. km. It included the total territory of undivided Jammu and Kashmir state. The principal religions are shown in Table 4. The backward castes of Hindus, called scheduled castes, made up about 100 million or 15 per cent of the population, and the tribal population scattered in different parts of the country, including the aboriginal groups (called Adivasis), accounted for about 60 million people, or 8 per cent of the Indian population. Thus the intermediate castes, called in Indian parlance the 'other backward castes', including the various peasant, pastoral and artisan castes, and the upper-caste Hindus together constituted 59 per cent while the scheduled castes and scheduled tribes made up 23 per cent of the Indian population. It is doubtful if the scheduled castes and tribes consider themselves Hindus (Juergensmeyer, 1988: 1–7; Oommen, 1990: 48; Rudolph and Rudolph, 1987: 37). The annual growth rate of population was 2.1 per cent. The rate of literacy was 36 per cent. The Indian population was estimated to be 796.60 million in 1988 (*Statistical Outline of India*, 1989–90). The principal languages are shown in Table 5. Sanskrit, the classical language of Hinduism, was spoken by only 2900 persons. Besides the main languages, there were many other languages spoken by small tribes and regional groups.

Cultural premisses of the Indian polity

India's well-known political scientist Rajini Kothari (1970: 28) remarks:

> Modern India, in its political aspects, is a product of a variety of influences spread over a long period of time. Three historical strands stand out distinctly as substantial influences. The first is Hinduism, the solid bedrock and unifying framework of Indian society. The second is the British impact of rational-legal authority wielded by a central power that managed to consolidate the whole subcontinent under it. Although operating mainly in the legal and administrative spheres, the British *Raj* also affected fundamental political beliefs and relationships. The third is the reconstructive nationalism of the pre-independence era,

Table 5   Principal languages of India,
millions of speakers

Assamese	9.0[1]
Bengali	51.5
Gujarati	33.2
Hindi	264.2
Kannada	26.9
Kashmiri	3.2
Malayalam	26.0
Marathi	49.6
Oriya	22.9
Punjabi	18.6
Sindhi	1.9
Tamil	44.7
Telugu	54.2
Urdu	35.3

[1] In Assam no census was conducted in
1981 and the figure refers to 1971.

generated in response to the impact of a new world order as transmitted through the colonial power, and developed as a means to political independence and social reform in the context of a slowly expanding framework of democratic institutions.

Notwithstanding the ideological implications of describing Hinduism as the 'bedrock and unifying framework of Indian society' Kothari correctly identifies the central role it has played in modern mainstream Indian national identity formation. For upper-caste Hindus Hindu religion and civilization are rooted in India and are inseparable from it.

T.K. Oommen (1990: 47), assesses the relationship between Hinduism and the Indian polity somewhat differently:

> The political mainstream of India, the Congress Party in its various incarnations, considers peripheral political parties such as the National Conference of Kashmir, the CPI (M) of West Bengal, the Akali Dal of Punjab, the Telugu Desam of Andra Pradesh and the Dravidian parties of Tamil Nadu, as inauspicious omens for the nation-state. Similarly, the twice-born Hindus, inhabiting the Indo-Gangetic plain, the cultural mainstream, look upon the emergence of peripheral cultural nationalism with disapproval and disdain. In each of these contexts the mainstreamers are insiders and the peripherals are outsiders.

The territorial–democratic nation-state project and organizing ideology

In spite of the Hindu cultural factor the Indian central élite organized in the Congress Party decided to base the national identity on a secular territorial basis. This was consistent with the ideology of the anti-colonial freedom movement it had led.

As a multi-class party, Congress had developed during the freedom struggle the tradition of accommodating different shades of nationalist opinion and conflicting interests. Thus competition between these different groups and interests occurred within the party, but such tension was subsumed under the larger consensus on the goal of attaining self-rule and ultimately independence for a united India.

Three strands of thinking on nation-building existed among the Congress High Command. The first concerned a Western—secular approach personified by Nehru, which envisaged integration, and in the longer run assimilation, of the diverse cultural elements into a grand Indian nation. The scientific state, consisting of a strong centre, was to serve as the vehicle for the dissemination of a secular rational political culture. The second was an idyllic approach deriving from philosophical Hinduism which Gandhi stood for. In the Gandhian model, a pluralist society based on spiritual rather than material development could bring about national integration. The third involved a Hindu nationalist approach which shifted between moderate orthodoxy and militancy. It was represented by the party boss, Vallabhbhai Patel, and the majority of Congress cadres. It assumed an interdependent and mutually reinforcing relationship between Hinduism and the Indian nation. It can be asserted that, despite the three different strands, the trauma of Partition made the central élite overly sensitive to the question of unity. Herein can be detected from the start the tendency of overreaction by the Indian state to all signs of separatism among non-Hindus (Chaube, 1989: 298—9; Navlakha, 1991: 2951—2).

The Nehruvian model became official organizing ideology, but deviations began to creep into the conduct of the state from the 1970s onwards (Rudolph and Rudolph, 1987: 83—4). The Gandhian model was never considered a practical formula for establishing a modern industrial state. Rather it was elevated to the position of high morality to which state and society were expected to approximate in conduct. Gandhian morality, particularly the emphasis on non-violence and peaceful reform and agitation, has therefore been invoked frequently in Indian politics by both politicians as well as important private individuals as a means of critiquing the violent state. On the other hand, the more regular Hindu character has gradually been pre-empting the ideological space, but more in a de facto manner. The state has been increasingly exploiting Hindu cultural and emotional symbols to maintain social and political order (Chandoke, 1989: 14—16). As the societal crisis worsened and deepened in the 1980s a galloping rabid Hindu nationalism emerged in mainstream Indian politics.

The Indian Constitution

The high point of the Nehruvian model was the enshrinement of universal values and norms in the Indian Constitution which was adopted by the Constituent

Assembly on 26 November 1949 and came into force on 26 January 1950. Although many features of the Government of India Act of 1935 were retained in the new document, its declarations on human rights and freedoms were quite radical. The working committee which produced the Indian Constitution represented a truly broad-based consensus. Although Congress had an overwhelming majority in the Constituent Assembly, it went out of the way to include religious minorities and non-Congress members of the Assembly in the working committee (Kothari, 1970: 105–6). It was headed by Dr Ambedkar, the leader of the so-called Untouchables (renamed Harijans or 'children of God' by Mahatma Gandhi, but who themselves prefer the designation Dalits). The original document did not explicitly define India as a secular state. The Forty-second Amendment from 1976 describes India as a 'Sovereign Socialist Secular Democratic Republic'. A universal basis of nationhood deriving from territorial criteria was prescribed.

A number of fundamental rights are listed. These include the right to freedom of speech, expression, assembly, association, occupation, property and religion under law. These rights can be suspended during emergency situations, however (Guha, 1976: 57–65; Gokhale, 1976: 66–80). Article 44 envisages the adoption of a 'uniform civil code throughout the territory of India'. Article 46 states: 'The State shall promote with special care the educational and economic interests of the weaker sections of people, and, in particular, of the Scheduled Castes and Scheduled Tribes, and shall protect them from social injustice and all forms of exploitation.'

The Constitution specifies a parliamentary form of government for the Union of India, within a federal structure. The different provinces are called 'States' in the constitution: thus Punjab State, Gujarat State, Kashmir State and so on. The formal head of the Union is the president but executive power is vested in the prime minister and a council of ministers. The federal parliament is composed of two chambers; an upper house, the Raj Sabha, which, for all but twelve of its 238 members, is elected by the states, and a lower house, the Lok Sabha, currently consisting of 530 members directly elected by the people on the basis of universal adult franchise. The Constitution prescribes three separate legislative lists: a Union list, a State list and a concurrent list on which both the Union and State governments can legislate. In case of clash between Union and State legislation the former is to prevail. The State's legislative powers are limited to the maintenance of law and order, local government, education, public health, agrarian relations, forestry, and property laws and taxes (Hiro, 1976: 48).

Strong centre

In financial and legislative matters the Constitution is heavily biased in favour of Union authority. Through the process of central grants and loans the centre exercises considerable influence on the States. More importantly, the federal parliament can alter the boundaries of the States and even amalgamate them. This power can make India function virtually as a unitary state, but it also provides scope for the central government to respond flexibly to demands for provincial and regional autonomy raised by emergent linguistic and cultural groups (Mukherji, 1992: 24). In the mid-1950s most of the existing provinces were reorganized on a linguistic basis. Later more States have been created in response to emergent groups claiming to be nationalities.

President's Rule

Under Articles 352–360 the central government can during an emergency take over the administration of a state and impose President's Rule. If the centre feels that the security of India or a part of it is threatened by external aggression or internal disturbance, Parliament can confer on the Union President the power of the legislature of the state to enact laws. Between 1977 and 1984 President's Rule had been imposed 70 times in different parts of India (Bhattacharya, 1989: 183). There are several laws which can be put into effect to curb civil liberties. The Preventive Detention Act (1950), the Maintenance of Internal Security Act (1971) and the Defence of India Rules (1971) have frequently been invoked during periods of social and political unrest.

Hindi as national language

The Constitution declared Hindi, the major Indo-European language of northern India written in the Devanagri script, as the official language of the Indian Union, but English was to continue as official language for the next 15 years. However, opposition to Hindi from the Dravidian south has meant that English continues to be the language of communication between the centre and the states and between the states. A Hindi promotion office exists in Delhi whose chief purpose is to translate government communications into Hindi and to popularize the usage of Hindi. At some future date Hindi is expected to replace English. As education is a State subject, different approaches obtain on the question of teaching of language. In the south, Hindi is taught as an optional subject at school, but in the northern States it is a compulsory subject. In a general sense a three-language formula in education is followed: English, Hindi and the State language are offered to students.

The central élite and hegemony of civilian rule

A civilian central élite consisting of both politicians and senior bureaucrats has been at the helm of government affairs. This central élite is quite homogeneous in

religious and caste composition. Upper-class northern Indian Hindus of the superior castes, particularly Brahmins (who otherwise make up some 4 per cent of the
Hindu population), predominate in this rather large central élite. Among them a
much smaller core of secular-minded Nehruites have been exercising enormous
influence on the state, particularly in the field of development planning (Frankel,
1978: 114–19; Kohli, 1989: 61–4). This Nehruvian élite initiated from above all
the important socio-economic reforms, such as abolition of untouchability and religious discrimination of any kind by making them penal offences. These and other
similar measures were undertaken 'far in advance of any manifest political aspirations or organised movement of the poor or the socially oppressed or their ideological allies' (Ray, 1989: 138).

As regards the armed forces, India possesses the fourth largest army in the
world. Hindus make up the vast majority of the Indian military, but Sikhs, who
are less than 2 per cent of the total population, constitute 7.5 per cent of all ranks
(Akbar, 1985: 172). Their ratio in the officer corps is even higher. The military has
not been involved directly in domestic politics, but has increasingly been employed
in several armed actions against alleged terrorists and secessionists and anti-state
elements. The much-feared military intelligence Research and Analysis Wing
(RAW), has played a major role in such operations. On the whole, a vast expansion of the civil and military bureaucratic apparatuses occurred as India began its
experiment in nation and state-building within a capitalist social-democratic framework.

The political process

Although a multi-party system conforming to periodic elections has functioned
since independence the Indian political process has been dominated by the omni-
present Congress Party. An elaborate Congress party machinery evolved both at
the centre and in the States. The leadership in the upper and middle echelons of
Congress consisted almost invariably of the propertied classes and upper castes.
However, for remaining in power Congress has needed the support of the poor,
the low castes and religious minorities.

The political forces competing for influence over state power with the omnipre-
sent Congress can be grouped into four main clusters: (*a*) the bourgeois parties of
left and right leanings that differ in inessential terms from Congress, while Congress as a huge clearing house for the propertied classes has enjoyed the advantage
of containing within itself all their individual nuances; (*b*) those parties professing
loyalty to Marxism-Leninism; (*c*) the Hindu communal parties; and (*d*) the various
political parties and movements representing religious and ethnic minorities, often
confined to particular regions and provinces. Some of these regional parties have a
strong electoral support and have been in power at the State level for long periods

of time, while the State Congress parties have been in the opposition. On the other hand, Congress has been ousted from power at the centre only twice, for short periods of time — during 1977–79 and again in 1989–91. Such absence from the centre has not meant a fundamental break in the ideological basis of the state, as the central governments during these periods consisted mostly of former Congressites.

The class and social bases of Indian post-colonial democracy

The Indian industrial bourgeoisie based in Bombay, Calcutta and other major cities acquired quite substantial financial assets before independence and supported the Congress-led freedom movement. After independence such support continued for Nehru's idea of democracy and rapid industrialization. The Indian state in return invested heavily in infrastructure and furnished other assistance to the central big bourgeoisie (Hiro, 1976: 58–60). The thrust towards industrialization, however, was balanced with support to the landowning classes, which were assisted through subsidies and loans for modernizing agricultural production. The vast majority of the industrial workers and poor peasants, rural labourers and the low castes lack influence even when the élite has enacted a number of progressive reforms. From the mid-1960s onwards the crisis of modernization under peripheral capitalism began to emerge, and the political system was increasingly subjected to abuse and manipulation by the ruling élite anxious to hold on to power by all means. Aswini K. Ray (1989: 144) describes India as a 'post-colonial democracy'. Such a democracy 'is likely to keep a numerically large section of the population outside its clientelist network, whose dissent and dissatisfaction needs to be managed more efficiently and when necessary, repressed more effectively'.

It is in the sphere of liberal middle-class literary, artistic and academic freedoms that Indian democracy has been remarkably generous. This feature stands out in the higher educational system which is based on rational and scientific premises. It has encouraged critical inquiry and created strong social science and humanities élite institutions. Pressure from communal Hindu organizations and parties has been growing in recent years to ascribe a Hindu cultural dimension to the educational system, however (Shukla, 1991: 239–45).

The emergence of Hindu nationalism as a major force in Indian politics

Until the end of the 1960s, at least on the central level, Hindu nationalism was removed from the official conduct of the state. Privately, however, some Congress ministers and party strongmen maintained links with Hindu communal organizations. The Hindu Mahasabha (founded 1907), Rashtriya Swayamsevak Sangh (RSS, founded 1925) and Jana Sangh (founded 1951) represented various cultural and militant forms of Hindu fundamentalism. After 1971, when India won a military victory over Pakistan, Mrs Gandhi's personality cult began to be cultivated by sycophants and party functionaries. Slogans such as 'India is Indira and Indira is India' entered the Congress parlance. A crisis of governability began to plague Congress in the early 1970s as corruption and authoritarian measures began to be associated with the government of Prime Minister Indira Gandhi (Kohli, 1990: 3–32). Popular mass agitations broke out throughout the length and breadth of the country in 1974. In 1975 Mrs Gandhi imposed a state of emergency suspending many of the normal parliamentary practices and civil liberties.

During 1975–77 when the state of emergency was in operation Hindu fundamentalists made significant political gains by joining the democratic opposition against the government. On 5 April 1980 some of them came together and founded the Bharatiya Janata Party (BJP). Mrs Gandhi also shifted away from the previous Congress strategy of seeking the support of India's social and religious minorities such as the Dalits and Muslims. Henceforth appeasing Hindu sensibilities to win votes became a routine (Frykenberg, 1993: 244–5). However, it was the BJP, RSS and the Vishwa Hindu Parishad (VHP), an ostensibly cultural and social movement, which became the main forces of Hindu fundamentalism in the 1980s.

A martial discourse based on the *Mahabharata* epic and other heroic tales was carefully cultivated so as to instil militancy and a sense of collective nationalism. The central idea the Hindu fundamentalists promoted was that of Hindutva or Hindu nation (Hellman, 1993). The argument was that only Hindus were trustworthy and loyal citizens of India; further, that Nehruvian secularism had been harmful to Hindus but favoured the religious minorities who had been pampered by the state (Gupta, 1991: 573). In particular hostility was directed against the Muslims, but later also against Sikhs when the Khalistan movement emerged on the political horizon. On the other hand, some sections of the Hindu nationalist movement argued in favour of reform that would allow Dalits to be integrated into the Hindutva. On the whole, however, the Hindu fundamentalist movement remained dominated by traditional sections of the upper castes.

The Indian state and ethnic minorities

India is a modern secular state, but Indian society is steeped in religious culture and identity. A distinction between mainstream Hindu society and others is valid in political analysis.

Scheduled castes and tribes

In 1955 the national Parliament passed the Untouchability (Offences) Act, which criminalized the practice of untouchability. Also by an act of parliament quotas were fixed for the scheduled castes (Dalits) and tribes (Adivasis) in government services, central and provincial legislatures and educational institutions. Consequently some 22 per cent of jobs were reserved for them. It applied to Hindus, Sikhs, Buddhists and Jains — all those rooted in the Hindu religious tradition. Muslims and Christians of scheduled caste and tribal background were technically excluded from availing such quotas. The reservation of seats has, however, been a slow process of upward mobility for the Dalits and Adivasis. Because of their degraded status and extreme poverty, Dalit and Adivasi families are discouraged from sending their children to school. Consequently there is a lack of qualified persons among them and, therefore, the actual percentage of posts filled by Dalits and Adivasis is less than the 22 per cent quota (interviews with Caroline, Chatterji, Mullick, Munda, 1994). Moreover, even when such measures have brought some concrete relief to these subordinate groups, social taboos are still widely held in society and acts of brutality are perpetrated frequently by caste Hindus against the Dalits and the Adivasis. It has been noted that upwardly mobile Dalits are more frequently attacked than those who remain at the bottom (Alavi, 1989: 233–4).

In recent years the Dalits and Adivasis have been making significant advances in the political sphere. A Dalit party, the Bahujan Samaj Party (party of the majority society), won a large number of seats in the UP State parliament in November 1993 and in coalition with the socialist Samajwadi Party, supported by Muslims and the Yadav caste of poor peasants, formed the government under Mulayam Singh Yadav, the Samajwadi Party leader. This appears to be a radical break with the traditional pattern of the upper castes retaining power through Congress, BJP or other established parties (Hardtmann, 1994).

On the other hand, the various Australoid peoples and other smaller groups living in the jungles and hill regions have been facing the intrusion of mainstream society as a result of population growth and industrialization. The liberalization of the economy in the 1980s has meant that the natural resources of these regions have been exposed to Indian and international capital. Consequently displacement of large numbers of people from their traditional abodes and habitats has been taking place (interview with Munda, Mullick, 1994). Processes of Sanskritization, whereby some of them acquire a Hindu cultural overlayer, have been observed, while other groups have resisted such assimilation (Andersen, 1990). In general the indigenous peoples have lacked resources and power to defend and promote their interests.

Christians

Christianity arrived in India quite early. It is believed that St Thomas established the first Christian community in Kerala in southern India. Later conversions followed during the colonial period. Christians constitute 2.6 per cent of the Indian population. Although most of them are converts from the poorer sections and lower castes, 3.5 per cent of élite positions are held by Christians (Saxena, 1989: 192). This follows from the much higher percentage of literacy among Christians who have benefited from the presence of mission schools and colleges, and the fact that Christians have found it easier to adjust to secularism and, therefore, are integrated into the political process. Among Hindu communalists apprehensions about conversions to Christianity have been expressed from time to time, but as a whole the Christians have not been involved in any political confrontation with the Hindu majority.

The Muslim minority

According to the 1981 Census of India, the 75.5 million Muslims were the largest religious minority in the country and comprised 11.4 per cent of the total population. However, except for the State of Jammu and Kashmir where Muslims make up 65 per cent of the population (in the Kashmir Valley they make up an overwhelming majority of 97 per cent), they are a minority in all Indian states. Only in the district of Mallapuram in Kerala in southern India do Muslims constitute a majority. In some towns and cities of UP Muslims form a significant part of the population. There is an urban bias in the composition of the Indian Muslim population: although less than 12 per cent of the Indian population, Muslims make up some 30 per cent of the population in towns and cities (Saxena, 1989: 156). Some 90 per cent of the Indian Muslims are Sunnis.

The predicaments of the Indian Muslim population

The creation of Pakistan as a separate Muslim state was a devastating blow to the overall position of Muslims who stayed behind in India. It greatly angered the Hindus, for whom the whole subcontinent was an indivisible cultural whole wherein were located their ancient roots. Moreover, Muslim entrepreneurs and the intelligentsia of northern India migrated to Pakistan, leaving a largely poor and uneducated Muslim population behind. Consequently Muslims were severely handicapped in competing for the opportunities that development brought about. At the beginning of 1981, out of a total of 3883 Indian Administrative Service Officers only 116 were Muslims. In the Indian Police Service there were 50 Muslims out of a total of 1753. In other lower-grade services the same under-representation was to be found. Employment in the private sector was much worse (Saxena, 1989: 168–70; Akbar, 1985: 310). Such under-representation does not make sense in terms of Muslim incompetence alone;

discrimination in practice surely exacerbates the overall inability of Muslims to seek employment.

Muslim ownership in the production sector is limited to small-scale production. Since the mid-1970s many Muslim craftspeople have been able to make substantial gains from business and employment opportunities in the Arab countries. It has been suggested that increasing anti-Muslim violence in the 1980s has been concentrated in those town and cities which have undergone economic development and where Muslims have fared well. The police sent to control the situation are known to have joined the attacks on Muslims (Hussain, 1989: 282–7).

In recent years Hindu nationalists have sought to highlight the alleged wrongs done against the Hindu community and its religion by the Muslims between the thirteenth and nineteenth centuries. The classic allegation is that in 1528 the founder of the Mughul empire, Zahiruddin Babur, had a mosque built at Ayodhya in northern India on the exact spot where the god Rama is believed to have been born thousands of year ago. Such a claim has been rejected by more serious Indian historians. Some even doubt the historical existence of Rama (Panikkar, 1991: 22–33; Thapar, 1991: 141–60). At any rate, a campaign to dismantle the mosque began in real earnest in 1986. On the other hand Muslims organized themselves to defend the Babri mosque. Prime Minister Rajiv Gandhi tried to placate the inflamed feelings on both sides by, on the one hand, allowing the Hindus to pray inside the mosque, and, on the other hand, recognizing Urdu as the second official language of UP.

The Hindu fundamentalists, however, intensified their campaign for the destruction of the mosque. It culminated in hundreds of thousands of fanatics from different parts of the country coming to Ayodhya in early December 1992. They easily overpowered the small police force and climbed on to the mosque and demolished it in a few hours. Brutal mob attacks on Muslims occurred all over India. Suddenly India was in the midst of perhaps the most serious communal conflict between Hindus and Muslims since the Partition. The Hindu fundamentalists intend to destroy some 3000 other such mosques allegedly built on Hindu temples and holy places.

Muslim assertiveness and Indian society

There is a widespread belief in India that the Muslim population is increasing more rapidly than others because of early marriage. The press has been reporting that big sums of money have been spent by Arab countries to help spread Islam in India (Mathew, 1989: 297). Substantial economic aid is given to Muslim religious organizations for the building of study centres, Koran schools and the upkeep of mosques. Particularly in Kashmir financial support to religious organizations has meant the strengthening of communal identity (Jha, 1991: 35).

Muslim support for secular parties

As regards participation in the Indian political system the Indian Muslims have generally supported secular parties, and until the mid-1970s they formed a vote bank for the Congress Party. However, in the absence of a broad modern middle class and intelligentsia, the ability to participate actively effectively in the secular political process has been weak. The result has been that *ulama* and conservative lay élite Muslims became the leaders and spokesmen of the Muslims. Consequently the conservative Muslim élite was able to extract concessions from the Indian government which in the longer run tended to hinder the integration of the Muslims in the modern secular nation-building. Among them the most crucial was the preservation of the Muslim Personal Law in its traditional form. Thus while the Indian government made some radical modernist changes in Hindu religious affairs, such as conferring the right to Dalits to enter Hindu temples, passage of the Hindu Marriage Act, and several other laws which aimed at the democratization of Hindu society (Smith, 1963: 241–3; 277–91), the Muslims were permitted to practise their own Personal Law, which was highly unfair to women.

The Shah Bano case

In 1985 this problem was highlighted in the well-known Shah Bano divorce case. Shah Bano, a middle-aged Muslim woman, was divorced by her husband, M.A. Khan. Being without any economic means to support herself, she filed a petition in the Madhya Pradesh High Court for a claim to financial support from her former husband. According to Indian law, she was entitled to financial support in such a situation. The court ruled in her favour but her ex-spouse made the plea that in Islam no such permanent financial responsibility devolved upon the man beyond the limited period of *idat* (the period of probation of three months following divorce so as to establish whether pregnancy had occurred prior to dissolution of marriage). Mr Khan appealed in the Indian Supreme Court against the judgement, but his pleas were rejected. Meanwhile the case assumed great political importance, as the Muslim community led by the *ulama* and other conservative leaders including Syed Shahabuddin, the President of the influential All-India Muslim Majlis-e-Mushawarat (Muslim consultative assembly), took to the streets and protested vehemently against the alleged intrusion into the internal domain of Muslim social life by the Indian state.

Many modern Muslims, including academics, lawyers, jurists, Members of Parliament, women activists and political workers, came out boldly in favour of the judgement. Arguments were put forth by both sides of Muslim opinion, but the conservative forces greatly outnumbered the modernists. The whole episode turned into a great manifestation of Islamic traditionalism. Unwilling to antagonize the large Muslim vote-bank, Prime Minister Rajiv Gandhi went along with the traditional standpoint, and a special law exempting Muslims from the general divorce law was passed (*Shah Bano Case*, 1986).

The Dravidian south

During the early twentieth century an anti-Brahmin movement emerged in south India. Brahmins, who associated themselves ethnically with the Aryan north, were overly represented in the government services, something which was resented by the emerging Dravidian intelligentsia, particularly the Tamils. Dravidian opposition to northern India domination was quite strong during the 1950s and lingered on into the 1960s. After independence it crystallized around the opposition to the imposition of Hindi as national language. Widespread demonstrations and agitations broke out and some deaths also occurred. However, with the creation of the four Dravidian linguistic states in 1956 the separatist movement petered out (Barnett, 1976). The south has been relatively calm in the 1970s and 1980s, although Tamil and Telugu nationalisms continue to be strong regional forces (Mahmud, 1989: 208–38).

The hill peoples of the north-east

In the mountains and forests of north-east India a number of tribal peoples, who are either converts to Christianity or followers of Buddhism, have been involved in separatist clashes with the Indian state since the 1950s although they initially chose to remain within India (Chaube, 1989: 298–9). The Nagas of the northeast fought a bitter but abortive armed struggle in the 1950s for independence from India. In 1963 India conceded autonomy to Nagaland by making it a state within the Indian Union. Demands for maximum autonomy of the other hill peoples were also initially resisted with force by the state. However, in the 1970s the principle of autonomy was also extended to other hill people and three new States of Meghalaya, Manipur and Tripura were created. Mizoram was made Union territory (Maxwell, 1980).

Other minorities

The position of minor groups such as Buddhists, Jains and Parsees (ethnic Persians, followers of Zoroaster) and others varies but on the whole secularism has worked in their favour. In 1956 Dr Ambedkar and several thousand of his followers converted to Buddhism. More conversions followed among the Dalits, and in recent years these have gained momentum.

The separatist challenges of the 1980s on the north-western flank of India

The first major manifestation of ethnic tension in the 1980s took place in the north-eastern State of Assam in 1983. The local Assamese carried out a bloodbath of Bengali refugees, mostly Muslims who had fled the 1971 civil war in East Pakistan. Mrs Gandhi despatched her security forces too late and some 3000 people were killed (Hussain, 1989: 283). It was, however, on the north-west border with Pakistan that the Indian state was to face the greatest challenges to its territorial integrity.

Sikh separatism

The present boundaries of the Punjab state were demarcated in 1966. According to the Census of India of 1981, the total population of Punjab was 16,789,000. Sikhs constituted 60.75 per cent, Hindus 36.93 per cent, the rest were Christians and some Muslims. Punjabi, written in the Gurmukhi script, is the official language of the state. Most people are Punjabi-speaking, but in the urban centres many speak Hindi. The total area of Punjab is 50,400 sq. km. Thus Punjab is one of the smaller states in the Indian Union, in terms both of population and of size. In 1986–87 Punjab, after Goa and the capital territory of Delhi, had the highest per capita income of Rupees 4719 (*Statistical Outline of India*, 1989–90). Its success in improved agricultural production through employment of modern technology is considered phenomenal. The growth rate of industrial development, mostly agro-based but also small-scale manufacturing, is also remarkable. A dynamic capitalist economy has been consolidated (Gill, 1992a). Why Punjab has been plagued by ethnic strife and separatism is, therefore, apparently puzzling. In order to understand the current Punjab problem we need first to put its history in perspective, particularly the role of Sikhism in modern Punjab history.

The social and cultural origins of Sikhism

Sikhism was founded in the Punjab in the late fifteenth century by a Khatri (i.e. one of the Kshatriya caste), Nanak Chand (1469–1539). Influenced by the Bhakti, the northern Indian Sant tradition and Islam, particularly its Sufi traditions, Guru Nanak, as he came to be called, rejected the caste system and stressed the worship of one God. He upbraided the contemporary Muslim as well as Hindu religious and political establishments for their corrupt ways and urged true worship of the timeless God (Cunningham, 1918: 41–3; Macauliffe, 1909: 37–65). He advised his disciples to participate actively in societal affairs with a view to achieving salvation through hard work and piety rather than by hermetic withdrawal and solitary meditation. To provide a practical example of collective

welfare, Nanak founded a system of free community kitchens, and was able to per-
suade his followers, who came largely, though not exclusively, from Hindu ranks,
to eat together and thus reject untouchability (Singh, 1986: 49).

However this anti-caste measure does not seem to have extended to all sectors of
social life: Nanak and his nine successors — all Khatris by caste — contracted
marriage for themselves and their children within the caste boundary (Ahmed,
1990: 104). However, notwithstanding the practical continuation of traditional
Hindu distinctions, Sikhism, with its strong emphasis on human equality, made
headway largely among the agricultural and artisan castes of Punjab, castes otherwise assigned a lowly station in the Hindu social order. Among them the Jats were
the most numerous. These strata were thereby able to achieve upward mobility.

Before his death Guru Nanak nominated one of his trusted disciples, Angad
(1504–52), as his successor guru. This was resented by some of his followers,
who instead proclaimed Nanak's eldest son, Sri Chand, as their guru and
founded the Udasi sect. The succession of most of the later gurus was also challenged by contenders and pretenders. The Sikh gurus claimed to be neither the
incarnation of God, as was the case of Hindu gods, nor prophets receiving direct
revelation from God, as in the Islamic tradition. They made the modest claim of
being exemplary spiritual guides who were not to be worshipped or considered
infallible (Cunningham, 1918: 45, 69). However, their followers gradually hal-
lowed much of their spoken words and deeds, thus creating a Sikh dogma and
orthodoxy.

Sikhism remained a peaceful reformist sect during the time of the first four
gurus, almost indistinguishable from other reformist brotherhoods. The Emperor
Akbar, known for his tolerant views, was impressed by the learning of the fifth
guru, Arjun (1563–1606), and honoured him with expensive presents and grants
in land and revenue. Gradually Sikh power based on peasant and petty trader
support began to emerge in north-western India, and was looked on with concern
by the later Mughul emperors, who ordered military action against some of the
later Sikh gurus.

Militant Sikhism

The tenth and last guru of orthodox Sikhs, Gobind Rai (1666–1708), abandoned
the conciliatory policy which had characterized the attitude of his predecessors. He
maintained a regular army, well-trained and disciplined. Most of his soldiers came
from the poorer sections of the peasantry and artisan castes. The Sikhs began to
collect revenue and other taxes in areas under their control, and Sikh power
became a dominant force in the politics of northern India. Gobind Rai fought
many battles against both Muslim and Hindu chiefs. His campaigns, it seems,
were not viewed necessarily as religious crusades by the Punjab populace: many

Muslim notables opposed to Mughul supremacy sided with him, and Muslim and Hindu soldiers were to be found in substantial numbers in the Sikh armies.

The creation of the Khalsa

In 1699 Guru Gobind Rai summoned his followers to collect at Anandpur in northern Punjab. At this gathering he decided to organize the Sikhs along distinctive lines and instituted the system of baptism. Five men, a Brahmin, a Kshatriya and three men from the Sudra castes, were chosen to drink out of one bowl to signify their initiation into the fraternity of the Khalsa (literally, the pure). They were given one family name: Singh, which means a lion. The baptism meant that they had given up their previous professions and become soldiers of the Khalsa, abandoning all other social ties except that of the Khalsa, and giving up rites and rituals not sanctioned by the Sikh faith. Further, five emblems were introduced: hair and the beard were to be worn unshorn all the time (*kes*); a comb was to be carried (*kangha*); a knee-length pair of breeches was to be worn all the time (*kach*); a steel bracelet was to be worn on the right hand (*kara*); and a sabre was to be carried all the time (*kirpan*). These five identity markers and some other related practices were instituted as part of purist Sikh identity (Singh, 1963: 82–4). Gobind Singh declared further that there was to be no other guru after him. The Sikh holy book, the Granth Sahib (also known as Adi Granth), was to be the ever-present guru from which the Sikhs were to seek guidance. It was in this way that the line of living gurus came to an end. In 1708 Guru Gobind Singh died from stabbing wounds inflicted by two Muslim assassins.

The Khalsa Sikhs became the orthodox majority. They began to be referred to as the *kesedhari* Khalsa (i.e. those who wear their hair unshorn). Gradually the Khalsa also subdivided into various theological configurations as new interpretations and rival claims to leadership were put forward by the devout. The militant Khalsa creed from quite early times appeared particularly attractive to the vast Jat peasantry of middle and eastern Punjab, who were accorded Sudra low-caste status in the Hindu system (Singh, 1963: 89). Large numbers of Jats in western Punjab had gone over to Islam some centuries earlier. Under the Khalsa movement the Jats of central and eastern areas emerged as the new power in Punjab. Thereafter the Sikh religion came to be identified more strongly with the Khalsa and the Punjabi Jat, although sizeable numbers of Khalsa Sikhs were not Jats, and not all Sikhs subscribed to the five emblems. The latter became known as the *Sahajdharis* (i.e. those who take time to adopt). On the other hand, several breakaway sects founded earlier by rival claimants to guruhood continued to exist.

New sects were founded by reformers and dissidents rejecting Gobind Singh's teaching. Some of these sects reclined into Hinduism, either becoming one of its many cults or simply merging into its mainstream. As regards the relationship between Hinduism and Sikhism, historically the lines between them were never drawn so distinctly and many people continued to subscribe to a popular religion combining Hindu and Sikh beliefs. Also, among some Punjabi Hindus raising one son as a Sikh was an established tradition. In fact intermarriage between Hindus and Sikhs of the same caste was quite common, particularly in West Punjab. These traditions continued into the present times (Akbar, 1985: 131–3). The exceptions were Jat Sikhs, who rarely married into Hindu Jat families.

The Golden Temple: spiritual and temporal centre of Sikhism

Some permanent centres of Sikh faith and influence were established early in its history. The most important among these is the Golden Temple established at Amritsar by the fourth guru, Ramdas. It contains, among other things, the Akal Takht (i.e. the throne of the Immortal) established by the sixth guru, Hargobind, who wore two swords signifying a linkage between spiritual and temporal authority (*The Truth*, 1985–86: 36). Five high priests preside over the Akal Takht and constitute the highest moral authority. Current separatist ideas among Sikhs emphasize the creation of a state where the supreme authority of the Akal Takht can be realized, indicating the possibility of the subordination of secular government to the ruling of high priests in a future Khalistan.

Rise of the Khalsa as the new military–feudal class of Punjab

During the eighteenth century the Mughul Empire was delivered severe blows by a series of attacks led by Persian and Afghan invaders. First came the Persian Nadir Shah (in 1738 and 1739) who laid waste Punjab and the areas around the capital, Delhi. A series of invasions followed under the Afghan Ahmed Shah Abdali (1747–48, 1748–49, 1751–52, 1756–57, 1759, 1762, 1764, 1766 and 1769) that played havoc with the social order of contemporary Punjab and northern India. Muslims, Hindus and Sikhs all became victims of the genocide that followed Afghan victory. At any rate, no Mughul administrative or military structure worth the name survived the repeated onslaughts. In these circumstances, the Sikh Khalsa who had taken to the forest emerged as a strong force in Punjab. With their mobile military formations intact and with the old order a shambles they could now emerge as the strongest military force in Punjab. The pinnacle of Sikh power was the establishment of the Kingdom of Punjab under Ranjit Singh in 1799. Thus, the Sikh rise from a minor sect to the ruling community of Punjab was consummated in the creation of an independent kingdom.

Punjab under Ranjit Singh (1799–1839)

In 1801 Ranjit Singh proclaimed himself Maharaja (supreme king) and began a long reign of expansion and consolidation. After crushing all opposition, Ranjit Singh embarked upon a policy of reconciliation. Accordingly, Muslim and Hindu Punjabis were included in his council of ministers and advisers. Muslims and Hindus along with Sikhs were to be found at all levels within the army, including positions of command. Over the years Ranjit Singh earned the reputation as a just and wise ruler. Many reforms were introduced, including free medicine and separate courts for the three main communities of Punjab (Singh, 1985: 48–50). However, notwithstanding an emphasis on Punjabi cultural identity, the Sikh kingdom retained Persian as the official language of the state (Chaudhry, 1977: ii).

At that time, the British were expanding rapidly in northern India. Ranjit Singh died in 1839. A struggle for the throne erupted among different claimants to the throne. The British thereupon took full advantage of the situation and invaded Punjab. Several battles were fought between the British and the Sikh armies. Finally in 1849 Punjab was occupied by the British army.

Punjab under the British

The British wanted to safeguard their Indian empire from Afghan raiders and the Czarist Russian empire beyond. Accordingly, many Sikh chieftains were won over through bribery and confirmation of their proprietary rights over estates and princely states. A part of the semi-desert region of West Punjab was converted into rich agricultural land through a vast network of irrigation canals and waterworks. Cultivation of cotton was encouraged as it was in great demand from the British textile industry. Population from the overpopulated East Punjab was settled in the canal colonies. Thousands of Sikhs were among the new settlers (Bhatia, 1987: 83–9; Singh, 1966: 116–18).

Despite these new opportunities, however, northern and eastern Punjab continued to suffer from overpopulation, scarcity of good agricultural land and fragmentation of land-holdings. In the past such pressing circumstances had forced Punjabis from these regions to seek employment in the armies of both native rulers and invaders. British policy supported this trend: Sikhs, Punjabi Muslims and Hindu Rajputs considered 'martial races' by colonialism were encouraged to seek employment in the British Indian army. Sikhs who joined the army were encouraged to maintain the outward symbols of the Sikh faith (Chopra, 1989: 74–7). Thus orthodox Sikhism was in a way consolidated via the army requirements.

The Sikh diaspora

Towards the end of the nineteenth century Sikhs from the overpopulated areas of East Punjab had begun to emigrate to other parts of the world in search of work. As one of the main communities serving in the British Indian army, they had acquired considerable experience of the outside world. They went to China, South-East Asia, East Africa, the USA, Canada and other places where British colonialism had its connections. However, for those wishing to enter North America considerable difficulties were created by the US and Canadian governments. In 1910 the Canadian government passed a law which virtually banned the entry of South Asians (Leigh, 1922: 17). The immigrants protested against such discrimination but their pleas were ignored. Consequently, in March 1913 the more daring of these people decided to form a revolutionary organization called the Ghadar Party with the view to returning to India to start a revolution that would expel the British from India. However, the plot was foiled by British intelligence. Many Ghadarites were arrested on their way to India. Others were rounded up in Canada and from the west coast of the USA. The few who did manage to reach India were able to stir up parts of the Punjab countryside. They were betrayed, however, and the movement fizzled out. Many of these revolutionaries were executed while others were given long sentences and sent to the Andaman Islands (Josh, 1977; Leigh, 1922: 17–21). Substantial numbers of Sikh youths inspired by the Ghadarite spirit joined the various anti-colonial organizations. Among these were the Congress and Communist parties.

During the 1950s and 1960s a second wave of Sikhs were to join the diaspora. Thousands of Sikhs, mainly from the Jullundhar district of East Punjab, reached the industrial cities of Britain, as work was plentiful in industry after the Second World War. This was to serve as the basis for further outflows from India during the 1960s and early 1970s. At present some 1 million Sikhs live outside India and some 3 million live outside Punjab in other parts of India (Helweg, 1989: 307).

The growth of communal identities in Punjab

As mentioned earlier, Persian was the court language of Ranjit Singh, the only genuinely Punjabi ruler to have founded an independent Punjabi kingdom in the last thousand years. The British replaced Persian with Urdu as the medium of instruction in schools and as official language at subordinate level. Some British officers argued in favour of Punjabi but were overruled as Punjabi was considered merely a dialect of Urdu (Chaudhry, 1977). In the late nineteenth century, nationalism was on the rise in India, and this affected Punjab too. Here, besides the all-embracing nationalism of the All-India National Congress, nationalism also took the shape of religious revival among the three major communities of Muslims, Hindus and

Sikhs. It started as a defensive reaction to the hectic missionary activities of Christian missionaries in Punjab. In 1873 a revivalist Sikh organization, the Sikh Sabha, was founded at Amritsar. In 1902 the Chief Khalsa Diwan was established. Both organizations were dominated by rich landed classes (Singh, 1986: 58–9).

However, soon afterwards the religious revival took also the form of an acrimonious religious debate among Muslim, Hindu and Sikh priests and intellectuals. The fear of being absorbed into Hinduism has confronted Sikh puritans throughout their short history. In early twentieth century a controversy emanated among Hindu and Sikh zealots over the status of Sikhism. While certain Hindu leaders tried to prove that the Sikhs were merely a Hindu sect, the Khalsa Sikhs asserted that they were a completely different religious community. Confusion was added to the argument when some non-Khalsa Sikhs themselves declared that they were Hindus (Kapur, 1986: 46–7). These developments prompted the Khalsa Sikhs to revitalize their communal institutions. Moreover from the Census of 1931 onwards the communalization of identity in Punjab could be noticed in the returns on mother tongue. Although Punjabi was spoken at home by people of the three communities, élite Muslims began to identify themselves with Urdu, while Hindus began to associate themselves with Hindi, and Sikhs with Punjabi (Brass, 1974: 291–2).

The emergence of the Akali Dal

In 1920 the Akali Dal was established with the specific purpose of promoting Sikh communal interests and cultural identity. The initiative came when a movement was started to recover Sikh temples and holy places from the British-appointed priests called *mahants*. The *mahants* were in many cases known for not complying with the standards of piety upheld by the orthodox; some *mahants*, in fact, were not even Sikhs but Hindus. The colonial administration initially backed the *mahants*, and considerable force was used against the Sikh protesters. The agitation dragged on for five years during which many Sikhs died, offering only passive resistance (Mukherji, 1985: 71–118). Finally in 1925 the government changed its policy and handed over the temples to the Sikh community.

The government passed a Sikh Gurdwara Act, which placed the management of the Sikh shrines and temples under an elected Sikh body called Shiromai Gurdwara Prabandhak Committee (SGPC). The SGPC took over considerable financial assets attached to the shrines. Thereafter elections to the SGPC became an important event in internal Sikh politics. The Akali Dal gradually took the shape of a political party. Its linkage to the SGPC was organic and it developed a style of politics which was heavily immersed in religious symbolism and discourse. In the post-independence period it became a major platform for the articulation of Sikh populist demands (Singh, 1986).

Partition of India and the division of Punjab

In the 1940s the demand for a separate Muslim homeland raised by the Muslim League gathered momentum in Punjab. A section of the Sikh community floated the idea of a separate state: Sikhistan/Khalistan (Kumar and Sieberer, 1991: 140). But since the Sikhs made up only 14 per cent of the Punjab population, and, except for some areas in eastern Punjab, were spread out thinly all over the province, their ability to press for their separate state was limited. The Sikhs therefore were wooed by both Congress and the Muslim League. The Muslim League leadership offered the Sikhs autonomy and even right to maintain their army in Sikh-majority areas (Chopra, 1984b: 81). But since Pakistan was going to be a state of the 'Muslim Nation' the Sikhs were wary of Muslim League overtures. On the other hand, the Congress president, Jawaharlal Nehru, assured the Sikh leaders that their religion and separate identity would be respected in democratic India (Kumar and Sieberer, 1991: 146). The Sikh leadership organized in the Akali Dal therefore decided to hitch their future to secular India.

But the problem that agonized the Sikh leaders most was the fate of Punjab. Was this Muslim majority province going to go to Pakistan? For the Sikhs such a prospect was completely unacceptable. Of all the communities in Punjab the Sikhs were the most deeply rooted in its soil. Sikh identity — ethnic, religious, historical and cultural — was inseparable from Punjab. They were therefore totally opposed to any constitutional scheme that gave the entire Punjab to Pakistan. But, realizing that they might not be able to stop completely such an eventuality, they demanded that Punjab should be divided on religious grounds: the Muslim majority areas of West Punjab going to Pakistan and the Hindu—Sikh majority areas of East Punjab being given to India. The Congress backed this Sikh demand. Additionally, communal riots in Punjab were initiated deliberately first by Sikh communal leaders who wanted to create place for all Sikhs who were expected to leave West Pakistan. According to Paul Brass (1974: 319—20), Sikh communal leaders had already at that time begun to aim at the concentration of Sikhs in East Punjab and had started terrorist activities to force the Muslims to flee. In any case, Punjab was divided on a religious basis. Consequently, in the wake of the communal violence which broke out in Punjab, Sikhs and Hindus left West Punjab for India and Muslims left East Punjab for Pakistan. Several hundred Sikh holy places were left behind in Pakistan including the birthplace of the founder of the Sikh faith, Guru Nanak.

Sikhs in independent India

In the pre-partition Punjab Sikhs were largely a rural people. There was also a trading section among Sikhs. In northern Punjab it comprised Khatris known as

Bhapas, elsewhere it was mainly the Arora trading caste that was involved in trading and shopkeeping. The majority of Sikhs belonged to the largest agricultural caste of Punjab, the Jats, who made up some 50–60 per cent of the total Sikh population (Jeffrey, 1986: 48). The second largest group consisted of the artisan castes, among whom the carpenters referred to as Ramgarhias (an honorific title acquired by their ancestors earlier in Sikh history for heroic performance in the resistance struggles) were the most influential. At the bottom of the social scale were the converts from Untouchable stock known as Mazhabis.

After partition the Jat Sikh refugees from West Punjab settled in the East Punjab rural areas where they were allotted land against claims of land left behind in Pakistan. Also, as Jats they could easily assimilate among the East Punjab Jats who bore similar sub-caste names as these refugees. However several hundred thousand Sikhs were relocated elsewhere in India. West Punjabi Hindus and Sikh Bhapas, being often town-dwellers, were inclined to look for urban areas of settlement. They headed towards the towns of East Punjab and beyond, particularly the capital, Delhi. The artisan and menial castes among Sikhs were distributed both in the rural and in the urban areas. The overall pattern remained the same as earlier: Sikhs were concentrated more in the villages and rural settlements while Hindus predominated in the towns and cities (Brass, 1974: 300).

Many Sikhs moved beyond Punjab in search of work. They were particularly successful in the transport sector, where Sikh truck and bus owners and drivers became a dominant group. Most Sikhs continued to seek employment in the army. Gradually Sikh entrepreneurs were to emerge in the top bracket of Indian producers and traders. By the 1980s some 3 million Sikhs were estimated to be settled outside Punjab in other parts of India. As mentioned earlier, migration to Britain started in the 1950s among Sikhs, particularly from the Jullundhar district (Ballard, 1983: 119–35). It continued into the 1960s and early 1970s.

The Punjabi Suba agitation

The pre-Partition Punjab was a huge administrative unit created by the British which included large non-Punjabi-speaking areas. The ratio of the three main religious groups of Muslims, Hindus and Sikhs was: Muslims 51 per cent, Hindus 33 per cent and Sikhs 14 per cent. Pakistan received the larger part of pre-independence Punjab. Many non Punjabi-speaking areas continued to be part of the post-independence Indian Punjab. In East Punjab, Hindus now constituted some 64 per cent and Sikhs 33 per cent and Muslims around 2 per cent. The Sikh princely states of Patiala, Nabha, Jind, Faridkot, Kapurthala, Malerkotla, Kalsia and Nalagarh in East Punjab were merged on 5 May 1948 and named Patiala and East Punjab Union (PEPSU). The Union home minister Sardar Patel declared this merger as the creation of the Sikh Homeland (Singh, 1989: 101). However, in 1956 PEPSU was merged with Punjab.

In 1949 the Punjab government had recognized both Punjabi and Hindi as the regional languages of the province, but Akali Sikhs wanted the redrawing of Punjab borders on a linguistic basis. They wanted not only Punjabi as the sole language of the state but also that it should be written in the Gurmukhi script (created by the second guru, Angad) and not in the Devanagri script used by Hindi. On the other hand, the Hindu communalists led by the Jana Sangh (founded 1951) advised the Punjabi Hindus to declare Hindi as their mother tongue. Consequently Hindi was entered as the mother tongue of most Hindus in the 1951 Census. It is important to note that some leading Punjabi Hindu members of the Congress also supported the Hindu communalists (Gill and Singhal, 1984: 603–8).

Initially the Indian government was opposed to the reorganization of the administrative structure of India on a linguistic basis. However, there was widespread opposition to the centre from the regional forces on this question. Consequently, the States Reorganization Commission set up in 1953 to demarcate State (i.e. province) boundaries accepted linguistic criteria as the basis of establishing new provinces. Several new States had come into being on such a basis in different parts of India. However, when it came to Punjab the Commission refused to concede the Sikh demand for an exclusive Punjabi-speaking State. It was feared that the creation of a Sikh-dominated Punjab might exacerbate intercommunal relations between Sikhs and Hindus. This suspicion was based on the fact that the Sikh leader Master Tara Singh, a Khatri refugee from the Rawalpindi district of North Punjab, articulated his demand for a Punjabi State in religious terms, and had consequently been opposed by the powerful Hindu communal lobby in Punjab, which wanted to have Hindi declared as the official language of Punjab. The Commission took the position that Hindi and Punjabi were not sufficiently distinct from each other to justify separation on a linguistic basis. It therefore recommended the retention of both Punjabi and Hindi as the official languages of the province (Brass, 1974: 320).

In 1955 the Akali Sikhs led by Master Tara Singh began to agitate for a separate Punjabi Suba (province). These essentially peaceful agitations continued into the first half of the 1960s. Thousands of Sikhs courted arrest, many were subjected to police brutality, and some even took recourse to the Gandhian tactic of fast-unto-death, although in only one case did it lead to a death. The Punjabi Suba agitation, however, was not supported by all Sikh castes and classes. The Mazhabi Sikhs were opposed to the creation of a Punjabi Suba, because they feared domination by upper-caste Sikhs in such a province (Nayar, 1966: 334). Furthermore, the Congress Sikhs, led by Pratap Singh Kairon, showed little enthusiasm for the Punjabi Suba idea.

In September 1965 war broke out between India and Pakistan which was fought essentially along the Punjab border. The Sikhs, who had bitter memories of the Partition riots, offered enthusiastic support to the Indian war effort. Akali leaders came out forcefully against Pakistan in their speeches and sermons. Furthermore, the leadership of the Akali Dal had since 1962 passed into the hands of a new leader, Fateh Singh, a Jat by caste. Fateh Singh dropped the religious overtones of the Punjabi Suba demand and instead projected it as a secular demand based purely on language (Brass, 1974: 322–6). In the changed atmosphere of the Punjab politics in the post-1965 war era a basis for compromise between the central government and the Sikh nationalists came about. The new prime minister of India, Mrs Indira Gandhi, accepted the Sikh demand, and the Punjabi Suba was finally established in 1966. The Hindi-speaking districts were separated to form the State of Harayana. Some parts of old Punjab were allotted to Himachal Pradesh. Although there were some Sikh grievances about the demarcation of territory, they now made up the majority, but only a narrow one. Between 58 and 61 per cent of the population of the new Punjab declared itself Sikh. At any rate, the Sikhs were now in a majority, and Punjabi written in the Gurmukhi script had become the sole official language of Punjab State.

Caste divisions among Sikhs and electoral politics of Punjab

The creation of the Punjabi Suba greatly enhanced the prestige of the Akali Dal, but it did not lead to a dramatic increase in its popular support. This followed from the peculiar caste and class composition of the Sikh community and the political divisions in Punjab. As mentioned earlier, a radical anti-colonial tradition among Sikh had led to many of them joining the Congress Party during the freedom movement. The more revolutionary sections were attracted to the Communist Movement in pre-Partition Punjab. These political loyalties continued to claim the support of Sikh voters, and thus the Akali Dal remained one of the prominent parties competing for their support in elections. In the peculiar political milieu of Punjab, utilization of religion and caste links was widely practised by all the major parties. The core voters of the Akalis were the agricultural caste of Jats who constituted some two-thirds of the Sikh population. But Jat society, comprising a vast number of independent peasant-proprietors, was ridden with factionalism as a result of disputes over property, social influence and contending ambitions to influence and power. Jats were known for their independent manners and a propensity to violence. The peculiar structure of property holding consisting of large numbers of independent owners only aggravated the sense of rivalry and conflict (Pettigrew, 1975: 121–4). Consequently the Akalis were supported only by sections of Jats.

Furthermore, after the Jat takeover of the Akali Dal under Fateh Singh, the

Table 6   Punjab election results, 1952–80 (seats won)

	1952	1957	1962	1967	1969	1972	1977	1980
Congress	60	71	49	48	38	66	17	63
Akali Dal	31	–	19	24	43	24	58	37
AD (Master)[1]	–	–	–	2	–	–	–	–
Jana Sangh	0	5	4	9	8	0	–	–
BJP	–	–	–	–	–	–	–	1
Janata	–	–	–	–	–	–	25	0
CPI	6	3	9	5	4	10	7	9
CPI (M)	–	–	–	3	2	1	8	5
Others	13	7	5	13	9	3	2	2
Total	110	86	86	104	104	104	117	117

[1] Akali Dal led by Master Tara Singh

Source: Jeffrey (1986: 112).

Table 7   Punjab elections, 1952–80 (percentage of valid votes)

	1952	1957	1962	1967	1969	1972	1977	1980
Congress	35	48	44	37	39	43	34	45
Akali Dal	15	–	12	21	30	28	31	27
AD (Master)[1]	–	–	–	5	–	–	–	–
Jana Sangh	5	9	10	9	9	5	–	–
BJP	–	–	–	–	–	–	–	6
Janata	–	–	–	–	–	–	15	3[2]
CPI	5	14	7	5	5	7	7	7
CPI (M)				3	3	3	4	4
Other parties	15	5	10	4	5	1	–	1
Independents	25	24	17	16	9	13	9	7

[1] Akali Dal led by Master Tara Singh
[2] Combined votes for three groups

Source: Jeffrey (1986: 112).

business and trading caste Sikhs often supported breakaway factions of the Akalis. Similarly Sikh artisan castes rarely voted for the Akalis. They tended to support the Congress. The Untouchable converts (Mazhabi Sikhs) almost never voted for the Akalis, since Jat society looked down upon them even when canonical Sikhism predicated to the contrary. Consequently, apart from the 1977 anti-Congress wave in which Mrs Gandhi and the Congress were swept out of power in the national elections, the Akalis had been used to getting less than one-third of Sikh votes. Most of the time Congress had been in power. More interestingly, both Congress and Akali Dal entered into coalitions between themselves and with other parties. Tables 6 and 7 show how seats and percentages of votes were distributed in the elections held between 1952 and 1980.

Contradictions of agricultural modernization and development in Punjab

At the time of independence, India faced a gigantic problem of feeding her teeming millions. The traditional food grain production systems proved patently inadequate in meeting the needs of the people. India therefore initially had to rely on import of wheat and other cereals and on food aid. The idea of a modernization of agriculture through structural changes in production methods was promoted by the World Bank and other related international development agencies as the proper strategy for developing countries to resolve their chronic food shortage problem as a vital element in their development programmes (Rudolph and Rudolph, 1987: 319–22). The possibility of attaining self-sufficiency in food supply found eager support among Indian planners and the government. Already land reforms had been undertaken with a view to eliminating the old-style land-lordism.

Punjab was considered as the most appropriate region for experimentation in the Green Revolution, as this development strategy came to be called. A good supply of water, the egalitarian nature of land holdings resulting from land reforms and changes brought about by a major reshuffle in ownership as a result of Partition, and the general reputation of the Punjabi farmer as a progressive and hardworking peasant, were considered the special merits of Punjab (Jeffrey, 1986: 28–32). In addition the Indian planners considered Punjab more suitable for agricultural production than for the setting-up of heavy industry. The close proximity of Punjab to the Pakistani border seems to have dissuaded the Indian planners from considering it useful as a venue for heavy industry (Wallace, 1990: 264). However, agro-industry and middle-range production increased rapidly. Most such industry was owned by Hindus.

Consolidation of Sikh power and the emergence of a rich farmer élite

The Sikhs were as a whole, however, clearly the chief beneficiaries of economic development and political gain in Punjab. They were favoured not only by the Akali Dal but also by Congress, which had a substantial support among Sikhs, in the allocation of jobs. In the administrative, police, educational and revenue departments Sikhs were represented in much greater numbers than their ratio in the Punjab population. Some 80 per cent of all types of administrative posts were held by Sikhs (Malik, 1989: 23–9). Even in the central government superior services, both civil and military, Sikhs are represented in much greater proportion than their percentage of the total Indian population. Thus at the beginning of the 1980s an overall 8 per cent of central government employees were Sikhs (Akbar, 1985: 172).

By the early 1970s Punjab had been converted into one of the most prosperous states of India. In terms of an even spread of wealth over a wide segment of society, Punjab advanced the most. Metalled roads, brick houses, expansion of school and university education, modern hospitals, and other indicators of increasing welfare typified the Punjab countryside (Jeffrey, 1986: 26–8). Generous government loans and subsidies were available and many Sikhs borrowed beyond their means to partake in the new opportunities. However, an important role in this transformation which the Punjab peasants brought about was also played by remittances from Sikh immigrants in Europe (overwhelmingly in Britain), North America, South-East Asia and the Gulf region (Sharma, 1981: 279). These sizeable and prosperous Sikh diaspora communities later came to play an important role in internationalizing the separatist conflict in Punjab during the 1980s.

A rich class of modern Sikh farmers had been consolidated in the process. The Akali Dal became the stronghold of the landowning Jat capitalist farmers (Chopra, 1984b: 108–10). However, it continued to rely on religious causes for mobilizing popular support, although the aims and objectives underlying such strategy became increasingly materialistic and mundane in compliance with vested Sikh interest. As a result Akali popularity began to dwindle, particularly among the poorer sections of the Jats who, lacking capital and influence, could not benefit from the capital-intensive Green Revolution technology. Consequently the marginal and poor farmers began to sell their land and either join the landless labour or seek opportunities elsewhere. Thus in 1961 the landless agricultural labour constituted 17 per cent of Punjab's rural population. It increased by 1981 to 38.26 per cent (Gujral, 1985: 45). Moreover, during the great boom of the 1960s a dearth of cheap labour had occurred. By the mid-1970s the import of cheap labour from outside Punjab began to hurt the interests of Punjab's own poor, mostly Sikh and Hindu scheduled castes who, despite all-round prosperity, remained a large group (Dhami, 1981: 296–7: Gujral, 1985: 45).

The Sikh intelligentsia

More crucial to note is that a large intelligentsia evolved in Punjab from among the more humble sections of society. Lower middle-class Sikhs benefited from the expansion in education. The prosperity of the 1960s enabled many Sikh peasants to buy their children a college education. Once uprooted from their humble backgrounds these BA degree-holders did not want to return to agriculture or take up low-paid jobs (Gill and Gill, 1990: 2507). Frustration naturally emerged among these new achievement-oriented elements. The situation was complicated further by the fact that by the early 1980s the debt burden, incurred during the early phase of the Green Revolution by many middle and poor peasants, became increasingly heavy as the market for their goods did not continue to maintain the upward trend and in fact began to fluctuate rather disturbingly.

This intelligentsia was culturally strongly linked to traditional religion and mores, and so became rather easily attracted to the religious revival which had been going on among the various centres of Sikh learning in the Punjab country-side. These centres had started receiving large donations from the prosperous farmers and as a result could intensify the revival of religious identity which rapid modernization seemed to threaten.

The Anandpur Sahib Resolution

The Akalis were never so effective as to make themselves the sole spokespeople of the Sikh community. In fact a serious challenge was mounted to Akali pretensions to represent Sikh religious interests by the Sikh Chief Minister from the Congress Party, Giani Zail Singh (later Home Minister and President of India), who during his term in 1972–77 tried to wrest support of religiously minded Sikhs from the Akalis. He went out of the way to appease the religious sentiments of his community. His conduct of government was marked by an increasing adherence to Sikh rituals. All this made the Akalis look constantly for issues that could improve their standing in Sikh society and in election results.

Consequently in 1973 the Akali leadership came out with the first version of the historic Anandpur Resolution in which various economic, political and religious concessions from the government were demanded (Akbar, 1985: 178–81). Among the economic demands were better prices for Punjab's agricultural products on the internal Indian market and a greater share of the water resources. Also, it was demanded that the ceiling on ownership of agricultural land should be raised to 30 acres instead of 17.50 acres. On the other hand an anti-trader and anti-industrialist (both dominated by Hindus) bias was quite clear, because it demanded that: 'all key industries should be brought under the public sector' (quoted in Tully and Jacob, 1985: 47). Also, employment of Sikhs into the army was to continue on the basis of merit. Expected cuts in such employment on the basis of parity for other provinces were not acceptable to Sikhs. The political demands concentrated on the provision of substantial provincial autonomy and limitations on the constant interference in Punjab politics by the centre directly and through its provincial branch. More specifically the central government was to limit its jurisdiction to defence, foreign relations, currency and general communications (Tully and Jacob, 1985: 46–51). Among the religious rights were demands for conferring the status of holy city on Amritsar, the relay of Sikh religious sermons on government radio channels, the integration of Sikh preaching sects on an all-India basis, and improvement of relations with Pakistan so as to enable Sikh pilgrims to visit their shrines in Pakistan on a more regular basis, and a set of other such pleas — all couched in vague terms.

These demands reflected the interests of the landowning upper crust of Sikh society, but were given as usual a populist religious flavour. On the question of autonomy the resolution took a maximalist position which was impossible for Mrs Gandhi to accept. In fact over the years she had increasingly been interfering in provincial matters and had established a highly personalized and centralized type of control system over Indian politics. Consequently the central government dubbed the Resolution as a secessionist document (Tully and Jacob, 1985: 50). It is interesting to note that several versions of the 'Anandpur Sahib Resolution' were later put forth by different Sikh factions.

The Punjab conflict of the 1980s

The propagation of the Anandpur Sahib Resolution improved Akali Dal's standing among Sikhs and the Akali Dal cashed in on its new-found popularity in the Punjab elections of 1977. It coincided well with the growing frustration among the people of India with the strongly centrist and authoritarian policies of Mrs Gandhi. As a countrywide movement developed, defections started taking place from the government, and the Congress Party also split. The main section, however, remained loyal to Mrs Gandhi. It began to be referred to as Congress-I (that is, the main faction led by Mrs Gandhi). In the general elections of 1977 Congress-I was badly defeated. The main victor on the all-India level was the broad coalition of several right-wing, centre and left-wing parties called the Janata alliance. In Punjab the Akali Dal and the Hindu-communal party, the Jana Sangh, won most seats. These two traditional communal rivals formed a coalition government during the brief Janata period (1977–79).

The rise of Sant Jarnail Singh Bhindranwale

In 1975, the Akali Dal had actively participated in the anti-Emergency movement against the government of Mrs Gandhi. Some 45,000 Sikhs courted arrest. Following election defeat Mrs Gandhi had nearly decided to retire from politics, but was persuaded by her nearest advisers to try a comeback. The choice fell on Punjab as the starting point for such a campaign. Acting on the advice of her younger son Sanjay Gandhi (who perished in a plane crash in 1980) and the defeated Congress chief minister of Punjab, Giani Zail Singh, she began to look for a Sikh leader who could help her against the Akalis. The choice fell upon Sant Jarnail Singh Bhindranwale (1947–84), a religious preacher and agitator opposed to the upper-class Sikh gentry organized in the Akali Dal. Bhindranwale, who belonged to a poor peasant family of the Jat caste, was encouraged to challenge the Akalis.

Initially Bhindranwale was unsuccessful against the Akalis, but in 1978 he emerged as a hero when his group clashed with the minor breakaway sect of

Nirankari Sikhs. Thirteen of his group and three Nirankaris were killed. There-after his popularity and influence increased rapidly both in Sikh society and in the Punjab administration where Sikhs were in the majority. In his puritanical sermons Bhindranwale urged Sikhs to abandon drinking and immorality and to return to a strict Khalsa way of life. Among his followers a diverse range of people began to gather. Many unemployed BA degree-holders and some Naxalites who had survived the police terror of the late 1960s and early 1970s became his devout disciples. Moreover his anti-landlord rhetoric won him support from the subordinate non-agricultural castes (Jeffrey, 1986: 175–9). At the same time, some other extremist Sikh groups were formed, but the largest following was that of Bhindranwale.

Events leading to the attack on the Golden Temple

In 1980 Mrs Gandhi was back in power. Punjab also was under a Congress-I government. She now saw in Bhindranwale a greater menace than the Akalis. The Congress press began to portray him as a dangerous and disruptive fanatic. This led to a confrontation between Bhindranwale and Congress on the one hand, and between Sikh and Hindu extremists on the other. Political assassinations began to loom large on the Punjab horizon. Bhindranwale was accused by the government of being behind some of the terrorist acts against Hindus, Sikhs opposed to him, free-thinking Sikh scholars and political activists and the Niran-karis (Oberoi, 1993: 257–8). He was arrested, but later discharged. This time it was pressure from the Akalis that made the government release Bhindranwale. The Akalis wanted to be in line with the popular mood among Sikhs and adopted a friendly attitude towards Bhindranwale. On the other hand, Hindu extremists in the neighbouring state of Harayana began to attack Sikhs living there. However, despite a drastic increase in the illegal circulation of firearms in Punjab and politi-cal terrorism, communal violence between Sikhs and Hindus did not break out on a large scale. The two communities continued to live side by side in the towns and villages of Punjab.

On 12 June 1982, Bhindranwale and several hundred of his heavily armed fol-lowers, fearing government action, entered the Golden Temple in search of sanc-tuary. Among them was included a disgraced former hero of the Bangladesh War, Major General Shahbeg Singh. Shahbeg had been dismissed just prior to retire-ment on charges of corruption. Similarly there were other Sikh notables who had felt humiliated at the way they had been treated during the Asian Games held in Delhi earlier in 1982. Sikh agitators had threatened to internationalize their griev-ances by going to the sports stadiums with black banners. No matter what their position and rank, Sikhs were stopped and checked by police, and many were not allowed to proceed towards the venue of the Games (Tully and Jacob, 1985:

84–92). A feeling of hurt and anger pervaded among them and some joined the Bhindranwale camp.

Surrounded by several thousand Sikhs, Bhindranwale intensified his campaign against the government and began propagating the idea of a separate homeland. Simultaneously Sikh leaders based in North America and Britain gave the call for an independent Sikh state: Khalistan. An explosive situation began to develop, but for almost two years the government did nothing decisive to contain it. On 6 October 1983 the Congress-I government in Punjab was dismissed and President's Rule was proclaimed. According to Tavleen Singh (statement on videotape: *Bleeding Punjab*), a noted Sikh woman journalist, until the end of 1983 there was no significant supply of arms in the Golden Temple precincts. These were allegedly smuggled in with government connivance. It was calculated to provoke an armed clash with the Sikh militants, defeat them, and thereby win the sympathy of Hindu public opinion which had increasingly been influenced by the propaganda of anti-Congress Hindu nationalists that the Congress had pampered the minorities and neglected the Hindus. Tangible benefits were to accrue from such a strategy in the form of a victory in the national elections due at the end of 1984. Whatever the truth, it was not until 2 June 1984, two years after the original occupation, that Mrs Gandhi took the drastic step of ordering the Indian army to Amritsar to prepare for a manoeuvre to oust Bhindranwale and his supporters from the Golden Temple. This she did notwithstanding warnings from many informed observers of the Punjab scene to desist from such a fatal temptation. Among them was the famous Sikh historian and writer Khushwant Singh (statement on videotape: *Bleeding Punjab*).

Exchange of fire between the army and the militants began on the night of 3 June, but it was on the night of 5–6 June that the Indian army, under the command of a Sikh officer, Major General Kuldip Singh Brar, stormed the Golden Temple. Operation Blue Star, launched with the help of tanks and armoured vehicles, proved no easy success. The Sikh militants entrenched inside the precincts of the temple complex gave a tough battle. They were, however, overwhelmed by the superior force of the army, which took control of the Golden Temple by the morning of 7 June. Bhindranwale, Shahbeg Singh and several hundred other Sikhs were slain. Casualties among the troops also ran into hundreds. The library inside the Golden Temple, containing the most sacred of Sikh relics and documents, was burnt (Aurora, 1984: 90–104). Another tragic aspect of this showdown was that the launching of Operation Blue Star coincided with a Sikh festival. Many Sikh pilgrims, including women, children and old people were inside the Temple when the army action began. Many of them were killed or injured as a consequence.

The assault on the Golden Temple caused an uproar among Sikhs all over the world. Sikh troops mutinied at many places. Many Sikh officers in the armed forces and the civil administration resigned their offices in protest. Revenge for this desecration of the holiest Sikh shrine was pledged by many in the community (Tully and Jacob, 1985: 192–217).

The external factor

The earliest publicity for the idea of Khalistan was given in the 1970s by diaspora Sikhs settled in North America and Britain. The *White Paper on the Punjab Agitation* released by the government of India on 10 July 1984 claimed to provide evidence of subversive activities of pro-Khalistan Sikhs. Among the prominent actors mentioned are Dr Jagjit Singh Chauhan and Ganga Singh Dhillon. The former was based in the United Kingdom and the latter in the USA. Both were accused of being in contact with American members of Congress and senior Pakistani officials. Among the Sikh organizations actively supporting the Khalistan scheme were the National Council of Khalistan, Dal Khalsa, Babbar Khalsa and Akhand Kirtani Jatha. The basic assertion was that the Khalistan movement was a conspiracy of foreign powers and their handful of Sikh agents, the majority of the Sikh community being loyal and patriotic. The Indian government and press have maintained throughout the Punjab crisis that Pakistan was providing bases, training and other help to Sikh separatists. The highest level of Pakistan involvement was alleged during the Zia period (1977–88), but it continued later on (Rizvi, 1990: 18–19; *Arms Supply from Pakistan*, 1992?; *Terrorist Revelations*, 1992?).

Assassination of Indira Gandhi; massacre of Sikhs and human rights violations

On 31 October 1984, two of Indira Gandhi's Sikh bodyguards shot her dead in the compound of her Delhi residence. The assassination provoked Hindu outrage against the Sikhs on a massive scale. Outside Punjab, Sikhs were hunted down, stabbed and shot and their homes burnt. Children, women or the old received no quarter. The mayhem was especially gruesome in the capital, Delhi. The number of those dying in Delhi alone was estimated at several thousands. The police and other branches of the civil administration did nothing for three days to stop the violence.

An independent inquiry committee of private citizens established clear proof of Congress involvement in the Delhi riots. Similarly another independent citizens' report on Punjab showed that the police had let loose a reign of terror, torturing and killing Sikh suspects, and raping their women (*Report of the Citizens' Commission*, 1985; *Truth About Delhi Riots*, 1985; *Oppression in Punjab*, 1985). These allegations were confirmed by Amnesty International and the Minority Rights Group, both based in London. Up until now, in spite of repeated demands, the people identified and accused in the various reports of being behind the Delhi riots have not been tried in a court of law.

The Punjab Accord, but lack of progress

Notwithstanding the great rise in terrorism in Punjab, a settlement was reached by the central government with a Sikh religious dignitary, Sant Harchand Singh Longowal. The Punjab Accord, as it came to be called, was signed on 24 July 1985. The central government conceded many Akali demands, including the right of people to seek employment in the army on merit rather than fixed quotas, setting up a commission to look into the question of sharing of river waters, and, more importantly, Chandigarh, the joint capital of Punjab and Haryana, was to be handed over exclusively to Punjab by 26 January 1986. Also India was to be made a true federal republic with greater autonomy for the States (*Punjab Settlement*, 1985). On 20 August 1985 Longowal was assassinated by unknown assailants.

A few weeks later in September elections were held to the Punjab Assembly. The Akalis won 73 seats out of 117 and formed a ministry under Surjit Singh Barnala. Both Congress and extremist Sikhs were rejected by the Sikh voters. However, the government reneged on the commitments, largely because of opposition from Haryana and sensitivity to Hindu votes. The Accord has therefore turned into a dead letter. On 26 January 1986 a militant Sikh faction called the Panthic Committee proclaimed from the Akal Takht the creation of Khalistan as its ultimate goal (Oberoi, 1993: 269–70). Similar pronouncements were made by the militants on later occasions. In May 1987 the Akali government was dismissed, apparently for its failure to contain terrorism. Punjab was placed under President's Rule.

Protraction of Punjab conflict 1988–92

During May 1988 the Indian authorities launched Operation Black Thunder to flush out some militants who were entrenched inside the Golden Temple. This time a prolonged siege and sniper fire were employed to dislodge the militants. While 36 militants were killed during the operation, the rest surrendered after a few weeks. In the 1989 elections to the Lok Sabha (Union lower house of Parliament), an Akali faction led by Simranjit Singh Mann won six out of 13 seats in Punjab. Two more were won by allies of the Mann group. Mann had been demanding the right of national self-determination for the Sikhs, and interpreted his success as affirmation of Sikh support for self-determination. On 26 December 1990 various Sikh parties and religious organizations, including the Akali Dal factions and SGPC, passed a resolution at Gurdwara Fatehgarh Sahib demanding self-determination for Sikhs. Mann has in subsequent statements made a distinction between his notion of self-determination and complete secession in the form of an independent state demanded by the extremists. What that means is rather ambiguous (Akhtar, 1991–92: 14). There are confusing statements made by other Akali leaders also.

Violence in Punjab escalated in 1990 and continued into 1991. The non-Congress central governments of V.P. Singh (1989–90) and Chander Shekhar (1990–91) also failed to bring the Punjab situation under control. Some 35,000 persons are estimated to have died by the end of 1991. This includes persons killed by militants, militants killed by the state agencies and innocent people killed both by the militants and by the security forces in Punjab as well as those killed outside Punjab, including the victims of the November 1984 riots in Delhi and elsewhere (Gill, 1992b: 187). Bomb blasts, random shootings, kidnappings of political opponents and industrialists and extortion of huge ransoms from them became frequent occurrences during this period. Many innocent Hindus have been killed in the dastardly terrorist attacks. Gangs of criminals, including disguised policemen, were reported to be prowling the province in the pursuit of illegal gains and other crimes.

Restoration of the political process

The Indian government called for elections to the Punjab State Assembly on 19 February 1992. After seven years, elections were again being held (the last time had been in 1985; in 1989 only elections to Lok Sabha were held). The turn-out was, however, very low, only 20 per cent, as the various Akali factions called for a boycott and the militants threatened physical elimination of those who participated in the election. The elections were held nevertheless and the Congress-I secured twelve of the 13 Lok Sabha seats and 87 of the 117 seats in the Punjab Assembly. Sardar Beant Singh, a Jat Singh belonging to the Congress, formed the ministry. The new government decided to give a free hand to the police and security forces to strike at the militants.

Select target elimination and relative peace in 1993

The police and security forces claimed great success with the strategy of systematic pursuit of select militant leaders and activists. Random shooting down of suspects, which had been followed in the previous years, proved counter-productive. This policy seems to have succeeded in bringing down the level of violence. The revival of the political process encouraged some of the moderate Akali factions to re-enter the political arena quietly. A general improvement in the Punjab situation was reported by the famous Sikh historian Khushwant Singh in the *Times of India* of 27 and 28 October 1992.

About 2100 militants, including 28 frontline activists, were reported killed in 1992. The government claimed to have arrested 1500 Sikh militants, and another 600 were reported to have surrendered. Among them was the chief organizer of the international unit of the Babbar Khalsa, Gurdeep Singh Sivia. The militants, however, remained active in some areas. A total of 1510 civilians, including 250 police personnel, died at the hands of militants during 1992. It meant a decrease from 1991 by 40 per cent in the killings of civilians and 48 per cent in the deaths of security forces (*Times of India*, 2 January 1993). During 1993 low-level militant activities continued, but the government seemed to have gained the upper hand. The Beant Singh government persisted with the policy of concentrating on militants while seeking to bring moderate Sikhs back into the political process. However, durable peace in Punjab is far from established.

The concept and ideology of Khalistan

The earliest ideas about a separate Sikh state in the post-independence period were put forth by Sirdar Kapur Singh, a senior civil servant who had been dismissed from service on corruption charges. His book *Sachi Sakhi*, in Punjabi, is his account of an unsuccessful attempt on his part to convince the Indian government to give him a fair chance to prove his innocence. He alleges that the corruption charges were framed against him by the prejudiced Indian administration because he was a devout Sikh. Kapur Singh began to propagate the idea of Khalistan in the 1960s and continued to do so until his death in 1986. However, it was the movement for a Sikh-majority Punjabi province which kept Sikh nationalists occupied during the 1950s and 1960s, and not until the 1970s was this idea raised seriously again in India.

Sant Jarnail Singh Bhindranwale (1947–84)

The speeches of the supreme leader of militant Sikhs, Sant Jarnail Singh Bhindranwale, are available in several audio-cassette and video-cassette tapes which are easily available in Europe. The recurring theme in his speeches is that India is a Hindu state ruled by Brahmins. Bhindranwale mentions several instances with exact dates, names of places and people which provide, according to him, evidence of unfair treatment of Sikhs by the Punjab and central governments. Particularly, police brutality perpetrated against orthodox Sikhs and the leniency extended to Hindus receives great emphasis. He urges Sikhs not to initiate violence but also never to let violence against them go unchallenged and unpunished. This, he asserts, is the essence of the teachings of the Sikh gurus and the Sikh traditions of resistance to tyranny.

Particularly emphasized is the militant role of Guru Gobind Singh. The Sikhs are advised to acquire firearms and motorcycles with a view to fighting for their rights. The speeches are full of religious symbolism and Bhindranwale strongly predicates a return to Sikh orthodoxy. Speaking in rustic Punjabi, he employs persuasion as well as threats to communicate his message. It seems he is determined to give the impression that he runs his own government. It is important to note that Sant Jarnail Singh Bhindranwale never directly demanded the establishment of Khalistan, although he preached the inevitability of the Sikh freedom from India.

Interviews with Sikh spokesmen

I conducted interviews during 1986–87 with various spokesmen of the Khalistan Council, a sort of umbrella organization comprising different militant groups based in Europe and North America. These spokesmen belonged to different organizations. The theme uniting them was their accusation that India was a sham secular democracy and that in fact it was a Hindu communal state functioning in the interest of the upper castes. Apart from this common complaint, and the conviction that Khalistan should be based on Sikh moral values and historical legacy, the proponents of the Khalistan idea differ from each other on their conception of an ideal Khalistan. Guru Gobind Singh was acclaimed as the ideal political leader, as both military–political leader and a champion of the peasantry and lower castes against feudal oppression.

Dr Jagjit Singh Chauhan — the London-based and for some years the self-styled President of Khalistan — preferred a Punjabi state on the pattern of Ranjit Singh. It was to be based on an economic system which was to respect private property. Industry which caused pollution was to be disallowed. Agro-industries were to be promoted. However, the right to a share in agricultural property of girls was to be banned as it conflicted with 'Sikh tradition'. Dr Chauhan hoped to succeed with his Khalistan scheme through a popular uprising in India and support of friendly Western powers. Davinder Singh Parmar, who appeared on British television as the holder of the potential portfolio of Defence Minister in future Khalistan, also emphasized the golden period of Ranjit Singh and the historical rights of Sikhs to be given back Punjab, which had been taken away from them by the British in 1849. Both Dr Chauhan and Parmar admitted that the Khalistan idea was not popular among Sikhs until the Indian army invaded the Golden Temple.

The editor of the *Sikh Messenger*, Indarjit Singh, complained that the Indian government was creating all types of obstacles for Sikh entrepreneurs to establish themselves in Punjab. Gurmej Singh Gill, holding the potential portfolio of Prime Minister, emphasized the importance of the Sikh values of tolerance. However, only those creeds that were based on a belief in God were to be allowed in Khalistan. Secularism and Western democracy were not to be accepted as they tended to weaken the religious basis of society and divide people. Man Mohan Singh Khalsa of the Dal Khalsa group laid stress on the imposition of true Khalsa values. Gurdeep Singh of the Babbar Khalsa emphasized the militant character of Khalsa ideology. He admitted that the Babar Khalsa had eliminated many people in Punjab, but according to him they were all guilty of crimes against Sikhs. Lachman Singh Anjala, member of the Khalistan Council in North America, and Dr Chanan Singh Chan from Sheffield, Britain, visited Stockholm in the summer of 1987. They drew attention to the anti-feudal struggle of Guru Gobind Singh. According to them Khalistan was to be a revolutionary state which was to abolish caste and big landlordism. All the proponents of the Khalistan idea rejected untouchability and emphasized the equal social status of women in Sikhism.

The Khalistan Charter

In December 1987 the monthly *Khalistan News* (published in the UK by the Khalistan Council) started serializing the 'Instrument of Charter of Khalistan', a sort of declaration of the main ideological and constitutional framework of the proposed future state of Khalistan. The December 1987 and January 1988 issues provide a definition of the Sikh nation: a community sharing common belief in orthodox Sikhism. From this premiss is derived the conclusion that, just as Hindus were given India and Muslims Pakistan, Sikhs should have their own separate state. The February 1988 issue announces the social, economic, political and foreign policy of Khalistan. Thus, while different interest groups will have the right of representation, there will be no room for political parties or trade unions in Khalistan. Religion and state will not be separated, rather, all aspects of life will be regulated according to divine commands as preserved in the Sikh faith. The economy is to be based on free enterprise. Considering that in 1988 the Cold War was very much on, the author/s of the Charter make this intriguing, though somewhat odd, announcement that Khalistan will 'offer to contribute with manpower for service with the North Atlantic Treaty Organisation'.

The Khalistan movement a foreign conspiracy

There are, of course, many Sikhs who find the Khalistan project incompatible with Sikh interests and religious traditions. Harbans Singh Ruprah, a businessman in Britain, claimed that the Khalistan movement was engineered from abroad. The USA, the UK and Germany were party to a conspiracy to destabilize India because it was emerging as a major economic power in the Third World. Moreover, India's arch-enemy Pakistan was openly supporting the Khalistan movement. Similar views have been expressed by many other Sikh scholars and intellectuals with whom I have had the opportunity to talk.

Kashmiri separatism

The princely State of Jammu and Kashmir owes its origins to the treaties reached in 1846 between the victorious British power and a general of the defeated Sikh army of Punjab, Gulab Singh Dogra, a Rajput Hindu ruler of Jammu, whereby the latter paid Rupees 7.5 million for annexing Kashmir Valley and other adjoining territories previously a part of the Sikh kingdom of Punjab under Ranjit Singh. The total area of the undivided pre-Partition Jammu and Kashmir State in 1947 was 222,236 sq. km. There was an overall Muslim majority of 78 per cent, although the ruler was a Hindu of the Rajput Dogra sub-caste. Since 1949, the State has been divided into two parts: two-thirds is under Indian control. According to the Indian Census of 1981 it had a total population of 5.9 million. It includes the Kashmir Valley, Jammu and the vast but desolate Ladakh region. One-third of the former Jammu and Kashmir is under Pakistani control. It is known as Azad Kashmir (Free Kashmir). The Pakistani official statistics for 1981 give 2.5 million as the total population of Azad Kashmir. In addition, Gilgit and Baltistan (which were not technically part of the former Jammu and Kashmir State but paid a tribute to it) with 1 million inhabitants are under direct Pakistani administration (Akhtar, 1991: 5). It is important to note that the majority of Azad Kashmiris are not Kashmiri-speaking. Many speak some dialect of Punjabi.

India considers the whole of Jammu and Kashmir State an integral part of its territory and thus lays claim to the part in Pakistani possession (Subrahmanyam, 1990). Pakistan maintains that it is liberated, independent territory upon which a sovereign Azad (independent) Kashmir government has jurisdiction. It considers the Indian Kashmir occupied territory. Pakistan would like the future of the whole of Jammu and Kashmir State to be decided in accordance with UN resolutions pertaining to it, which require that the people on both sides of the former Jammu and Kashmir State be given an opportunity to choose through a universal plebiscite (Haque, 1992: 72). However, the people are to choose between joining either India or Pakistan. A third option of the State choosing to be independent is rejected by both India and Pakistan (Wirsing, 1993: 142). India maintains that neither the option of independence nor that of holding a plebiscite is relevant any more because an elected Jammu and Kashmir Constituent Assembly ratified accession to India in 1952 and that after 1972, when the Simla Agreement was signed between India and Pakistan, the Kashmir problem was no longer a matter for international mediation (Subrahmanyam, 1990: 170–80).

The Kashmir problem can be considered a classic outcome of the vagaries of colonial withdrawal. Technically the lapse of paramountcy upon British withdrawal meant that the princely states could declare themselves independent. However, the British government made it clear that there was no other choice before them except to join either India or Pakistan in accordance with the religious majority obtaining in them. On the other hand, the legal right to sign the Accession Bill was vested in the ruler, who was expected to take into consideration the wishes of his people. Such vague guidelines left it entirely to the discretion of the rulers to choose their relationship with India and Pakistan. Consequently power politics, security concerns, national prestige and political opportunism, in addition to invo-cations of the principle of self-determination as recognized by the UN, constitute the various facets of this seemingly intractable dispute between the two states. It is important to recall that the UN literature on the principle or right to self-determi-nation includes both a positive meaning (right of a people to choose freely their political destiny) and a negative meaning (non-interference of outside powers in the internal affairs of a nation-state). While Pakistan invokes its 'positive' features (in the limited sense of freedom of the peoples of Jammu and Kashmir only to choose between India or Pakistan), India emphasizes the negative ones.

Indian Kashmir

The Kashmir under Indian jurisdiction can be divided into three main geographi-cal regions: the Kashmir Valley, Jammu and Ladakh. Urdu has been adopted as an official language although it is not the mother-tongue of any indigenous group. The Kashmir Valley contains a Muslim majority of more than 97 per cent. The main language in the Valley is Kashmiri. The 3 per cent minority population of Kashmir Valley consists of the Kashmiri Pundits (Brahmins), who despite several centuries of Muslim domination clung on to their ancient faith. In 1941 Jammu had a 61.3 per cent Muslim population which declined drastically when Muslims fled to Pakistan during Partition. According to the 1981 Census there were 62 per cent Hindus and 33.8 per cent Muslims in the Jammu region. Dogri and Punjabi are the main languages of Jammu. The third region is the sparsely populated Ladakh. It had a total population of only 68,380, of which Buddhists were in a slight majority and the rest were Muslims. A number of Tibetan languages are spoken in Ladakh. An overall 65 per cent of the Indian Jammu and Kashmir popu-lation was Muslim in 1981, predominantly of the Sunni persuasion, 28 per cent was Hindu, 2 per cent Sikh and 1 per cent Buddhist.

Official statistics report a dramatic improvement in the standard of living in Jammu and Kashmir state between 1977 and 1984. During 1977–78, 33.4 per cent of the population lived under the poverty line. In 1983–84 it had declined to a mere 16.3 per cent. The per capita income for 1986–87 was Rupees 3344, while in 1971–72 it was only Rupees 588. Therefore, according to Indian figures, Kashmir was one of the more prosperous states within the Indian Union (*Statis-tical Outline of India*, 1989–90).

The Muslims of Kashmir Valley have in recent years been drawn into a conflict with the Indian state. Therefore, unless indicated, the discussion below of the

Kashmir problem refers to the history and events pertaining to the Kashmir Valley.

The cultural heritage of Kashmir

Hinduism was the main religion of the Kashmir Valley before Emperor Ashoka introduced Buddhism into the region. For several centuries Buddhism was the chief religion of Kashmir. Later there was a Hindu revival. In the early sixth century AD the Huns became the dominant power in Kashmir. It was a period in which Kashmir suffered immense cruelty. By AD 530 Kashmir was free again. Gradually a Saivaite branch of Hinduism evolved in Kashmir through a fusion of Hindu and Buddhist outlooks. The most famous of Hindu kings of Kashmir was Lalitaditya (AD 697–738), who led his armies into Bengal in the east, Konkan in the south, Turkestan in the north-west and Tibet in the north-east. About 1339 Kashmir came under Muslim rule when a local strongman, Rainchan Shah, a Buddhist, converted to Islam and took the name Sadruddin (Gupta, 1966: 18–19).

Although Sufism played an important role in the conversion of Kashmiris to Islam, the use of force was also extensive. The most famous Sufi to visit Kashmir was Ali Hamadani, who arrived from Iran in 1381. Legend says that he was accompanied by 700 Sufis, who set up a network of proselytizing activities. However, S.S.A. Rizvi (1991: 32–3) asserts that Hamadani stayed for only three years during which he ordered the use of force to convert Brahmins and had some temples demolished. Many later Sufis also 'found new avenues for promoting their commercial interests and ransacked Hindu temples in order to enrich themselves and their local followers' (1991: 33). During the reign of Sultan Sikandar (1389–1413), who was a disciple of Hamadani's son, Mir Muhammad, many ancient temples were demolished and considerable force was used to convert Hindus to Islam. Hindus had three choices: exile, conversion to Islam or death. Hindu books of learning were thrown into the Dal Lake and thousands of Brahmins were slaughtered (Gupta, 1966: 19). A later indigenous Sufi movement challenged the followers of Hamadani. It was headed by holy men, known as *Rishis*. The *Rishis* attempted a synthesis between Sufi teachings and Saivaite Hindu ideas and were more successful in converting poor and neglected Hindus to Islam (Rizvi, 1991: 34–5).

In 1417 the famous Zainul Abedin became the ruler of Kashmir. Under him Kashmir flourished in all senses of the word. Hindu temples were rebuilt, Brahmins who had gone into exile were called back. He built bridges, offered concessions to the cultivators and patronized the fine arts. Zainul Abedin died in 1470. Later the Chaks took over power in Kashmir. Under them Sunni Muslims and Hindus were persecuted. In 1586 the Mughuls occupied Kashmir. By the early eighteenth century the Mughul state was exhausted. The Afghans captured Kashmir and ruled between 1752 and 1819. It was another period of great cruelty in Kashmir's history. Hindus and Shia Muslims were killed in large numbers. In 1819 the ruler of Punjab, Ranjit Singh, occupied Kashmir. During Sikh rule Muslims were the object of extreme persecution (Choudhary, 1991: 8; Gupta, 1966: 19).

Ranjit Singh died in 1839. In the wars which ensued between the British and the successors of Ranjit Singh, a former minister of the late Maharaja, the Dogra Rajput ruler of Jammu, Gulab Singh, sided with the former. In lieu of his services the British sold the Jammu and Kashmir region for Rupees 7.5 million to Gulab Singh in 1846 (Cunningham, 1918: 403–5). Thus Jammu and Kashmir state became one of the several hundred vassal states of the British Indian empire. Dogra rule lasted until 1947 when Hari Singh signed the Accession Bill and joined India.

The ruling élite during the last dynasty consisted of the Dogras of Jammu, the tiny but influential intellectual élite consisting of Kashmiri Brahmins, and some Muslim notables. Although some improvements did take place under the Dogras, the pace of change was very slow. The Kashmiri Muslims remained abjectly poor, working mostly as poor peasants. It was common for impoverished Kashmiris to forsake their homeland in search of work in the adjoining plains of Punjab and northern India. The early twentieth century witnessed the birth of social and political currents in India which rapidly enveloped far-flung areas and regions, including Kashmir.

Beginnings of political activity

In 1931 the first major protest movement against Dogra despotism emerged in the Valley. Kashmiri Muslims, inspired by the *ulama*, came out agitating against what they perceived was iniquitous Hindu rule. The Maharaja ordered severe action against the agitators, which resulted in some deaths (Navlakha, 1991: 2952). Communal tension rose throughout the state. A positive development was that the Maharaja agreed to permit the formation of political organizations. In 1932 the All-Jammu and Kashmir Muslim Conference was formed under the leadership of Sheikh Abdullah. Only a handful of Kashmiri Muslims had by the 1920s acquired degrees in higher education. One such Muslim was Sheikh Abdullah (1905–82), who started his career as a science teacher but later became famous as the leader of Kashmir Muslims.

In 1934 a legislative assembly, based on a narrowly restricted franchise, was established in Kashmir (Singh, 1982: 13). Meanwhile British India was fermenting with nationalistic and patriotic movements. The mass movement during this period was essentially under the influence of the Congress. To the Congress's strategy of non-violent agitation had been added a radical vision of socio-economic change and secularism under the influence of Jawaharlal Nehru. It was this combination which made a profound impact on the emerging Kashmiri leadership. Consequently Abdullah's perceptions of Kashmir's struggle began to change from a Muslim—Hindu tangle to a conflict between the Kashmiri people and the decadent feudal class ruling over them (Singh, 1982: 50). Sheikh Abdullah was charmed by Nehru (a Kashmiri Brahmin by origin), and the two shared a vision of a united India where all citizens were to be enabled to develop and improve their life conditions without discrimination of religion or race. However, this vision was not shared by all in the Muslim Conference and a split occurred in 1939. A majority led by Abdullah renamed their organization as the National Conference. Socialist and Marxist Muslims, Hindus and others joined the National Conference (Navlakha, 1991: 2957). A minority led by Chaudhari Ghulam Abbas continued to work for Muslim interests in Kashmir.

Abdullah rejected the Muslim League's Two-Nation theory and its demand for a separate Muslim state. He advocated a radical land reform in Kashmir on the lines suggested by Nehru for a future Congress government in free India. In 1944 the National Conference adopted a social charter called New Kashmir. It envisaged equality of citizens irrespective of 'religion, race, nationality of birth'. Right to work for all and equal rights for men and women were to be granted. Landlordism was to be abolished and peasants were to become owners of the land they worked. Similarly workers were to be provided with a comprehensive social security system. Concentration of private property was to be broken up (Gupta, 1966: 55—7). In May 1946 the National Conference launched the 'Quit Kashmir' movement, a non-violent agitation which aimed at dislodging Dogra rule. Abdullah was arrested on 20 May and a wave of arrests and repression followed. Among mainstream politicians Nehru came out strongly in favour of Abdullah and courted arrest. Abdullah was, however, arrested and put in prison by the Kashmir government (Teng, 1990: 28—9). In January 1947 elections (based roughly on 8 per cent of the adult population) were held to the Kashmir Assembly. The National Conference boycotted the elections, but the Muslim Conference contested and won 16 of the 21 Muslim seats. There was, however, no doubt that the National Conference was the more popular of the two parties (Navlakha, 1991: 2953).

Accession to India

Neither India nor Pakistan found the Radcliffe Award, according to which their international boundaries were demarcated, satisfactory. The allocation of portions of the Muslim-majority district of Gurdaspur in Punjab to India furnished India with a dirt track, rather than a proper road, connecting it to Kashmir. All other main roads connected Kashmir to areas and towns which became part of Pakistan (Wolpert, 1982: 353). The Kashmir government offered to sign standstill agreements with both India and Pakistan. Pakistan signed such an agreement on 15 August, but India neither rejected the offer nor accepted it (Teng, 1990: 33). Meanwhile communal riots were raging in Punjab, and quickly spread to Kashmir. The Muslim Conference instigated a massacre of Hindus and Sikhs in the Muslim-majority Poonch region of Kashmir state. On the other hand anti-Muslim riots on a large scale broke out in Jammu. The Maharaja ordered his troops to quell the rebellion. Muslims were killed in the thousands, and more than half a million fled to Pakistan. On the other hand, armed Muslim tribesmen from the NWFP entered the Valley, apparently looking for revenge and hoping to liberate Kashmir from Dogra rule (Akhtar, 1991: 5).

The major column of armed men entered Kashmir from Pakistan on 21–2 October 1947. They were nearly successful in capturing the airport of the capital, Srinagar, but in this dramatic moment of success the tribesmen fell prey to an ancient vice common among them: looting, plunder, and rape (Choudhary, 1991: 22–4). Whatever their initial reaction, the Kashmiris now turned against these intruders. Some died fighting the intruders and were remembered as martyrs by the Kashmiris (Akbar, 1991: 109–10; Gupta, 1967: 111–14). Confronted by the prospect of losing his state to the invaders, Maharaja Hari Singh on 24 October requested help from India. A senior civil servant, V.P. Menon, arrived in Srinagar and told the Maharaja that Indian troops would be sent to his succour only if he acceded to India. It is widely believed that the Maharaja wanted to declare himself independent, but given the grave situation reluctantly agreed to join India (Choudhary, 1991: 24; Teng, 1990: 29–37). Thus on 26 October 1947 Maharaja Hari Singh signed the Accession Bill in favour of India.

However, the accession was only provisional. Clause 7 of the Accession Act stated that the Maharaja was not committed to accept the future constitution of India. Article 8 affirmed that Kashmir retained its sovereignty (Akbar, 1991: 135). Only three subjects were surrendered to India: defence, external affairs and communications. With such a paper in hand India air-lifted soldiers *en masse* into Kashmir. Under pressure from India the Maharaja released Abdullah from jail and made him chief emergency officer. Abdullah condemned the raids into Kashmir from Pakistan and asserted the sovereign right of the people of Kashmir to decide their future freely. On 25 March 1948 Sheikh Abdullah became the prime minister of Jammu and Kashmir. It was not, however, by any means certain that after communal rioting Sheikh Abdullah retained his leading position among Kashmiri Muslims. He needed express guarantees from the Indian government to convince his essentially Muslim constituency that joining India was better for them rather than becoming a part of Muslim Pakistan.

These guarantees principally required the recognition of Kashmir's autonomy (Navlakha, 1991: 2953).

On 1 January 1948 the Indian government decided to take the Kashmir dispute to the United Nations (a decision it was to regret ever after). India alleged that regular Pakistani troops were fighting in Kashmir and that they should be expelled. In subsequent debates, India assured the UN that the accession of Kashmir was only provisional and the ultimate status of Kashmir was to be determined through a free and universal plebiscite. However, both India and Pakistan took the position that the Kashmiris could choose to join either India or Pakistan. The idea of a separate Kashmir state was overruled by both sides. The Security Council Resolution on the Kashmir problem which laid down the terms for the settlement was passed on 21 April 1948. The core of the resolution was that a plebiscite would be held under UN supervision when peace had been established. An essential element of the establishment of peace was that Pakistan was to see to it that the tribesmen and Pakistani nationals vacated the territories of the state. Thereafter the Indian government was to withdraw its own troops gradually in stages until only a minimum required for maintenance of law and order remained (Haque, 1992: 74; full text of the resolution given in Subrahmanyam, 1990: 142–6). On the plebiscite, Article B.7 stated: 'The Government of India should undertake that there will be established in Jammu and Kashmir a Plebiscite Administration to hold a plebiscite as soon as possible on the question of accession of the State to India or Pakistan.' A UN Commission composed of Czechoslovakia, Argentina, Belgium, Colombia and the United States was set up to look into the Kashmir problem.

The resolution recognized India's legal presence in Kashmir resulting from the signing of the Accession Bill. Pakistan was to withdraw from the territories of the State before the plebiscite could be held. However, armed clashes between India and Pakistan continued and their troops remained in the state. Gradually attitudes hardened on both sides. Finally a ceasefire was arranged by the United Nations which came into effect on 1 January 1949. By that time less than one-third of the Kashmir state had come under Pakistani control. In July 1949 agreement was reached on the ceasefire line and United Nations observers were stationed on both sides of the line of control to monitor it. In subsequent years Pakistan was to reiterate its demand for a plebiscite while India was to overrule it on the plea that Pakistani forces were occupying parts of the state and therefore the holding of an impartial plebiscite was out of the question (Choudhary, 1991: 40–2). After Pakistan entered the military alliances of the Central Treaty Organization (CENTO) and the South East Asia Treaty Organization (SEATO), the Kashmir dispute began to be treated by the superpowers in terms of Cold War interests. While the USA generally, though not consistently, supported the Pakistani position, the Soviet Union tended to sympathize with India (Haque, 1992: 85).

Article 370

Meanwhile the Maharaja and Sheikh Abdullah had agreed that Kashmir should unite with India, but that its special status to maximum autonomy should be preserved. This position was accepted by India. Consequently on 17 October 1949 the Indian government granted through Article 306A special status, in accordance with Clause 7 of the Accession Act, to Jammu and Kashmir. It is interesting to note that it was a leading Muslim freedom fighter, Maulana Hasrat Mohani, who interrupted the proceedings of the Indian Constituent Assembly and raised objections against the exceptional status conferred upon Kashmir. Continuing his speech Mohani expressed the hope 'that in due course even Jammu and Kashmir will become ripe for the same sort of integration as has taken place in the case of other states' (quoted in Akbar, 1991: 136). Later Article 306A was incorporated as Article 370 in the final text of the Constitution of India. Article 370 was, however, described as a temporary provision and the president of India could declare it partially or wholly inoperative provided the State Assembly recommended such a course of action (*Constitution of India*, 1992: 213).

Sheikh Abdullah in power

In October 1950, the general council of the National Conference formally demanded that a constituent assembly be elected to frame a constitution for Kashmir and to decide the issue of accession to India. Elections were held in Kashmir in 1951. The National Conference won all the 75 seats, of which 73 were elected unopposed. Rigging of elections by the ruling party and cliques was alleged by the opposition. It is interesting to note that all subsequent elections in the state have been dubbed unfair by both the pro-Pakistani forces in the Kashmir Valley and the Hindu lobby of Jammu (Navlakha, 1991: 2957; Singh, 1982: 63–8; Teng, 1990: 86–7). On the other hand, the Indian government considered the 1951 election result a vindication of its stand that Kashmiris did not want to join Pakistan. In Pakistan allegations were made that high-handed methods had been used to keep out the opposition from contesting elections. In July 1952 Sheikh Abdullah and Jawaharlal Nehru signed the Delhi Agreement, which reaffirmed Kashmir's maximum autonomy within the Indian Union. On 11 August 1952 Abdullah explained the implications of Article 370: 'In actual effect, the temporary nature of this [Article 370] arises merely from the fact that the power to finalize the constitutional relationship between the state and the Union of India has been specifically vested in the Jammu and Kashmir Constituent Assembly' (quoted in Burke, 1973: 44).

Reforms under Abdullah's leadership and opposition from Jammu and Ladakh

The National Conference government under Sheikh Abdullah embarked upon an ambitious plan to develop his poverty-stricken State. Top priority was given to education, and radical land reforms were introduced. Landed estates were abolished without compensation, the ceiling on landownership was fixed at 23 acres and the reclaimed land was transferred to landless peasant-tillers (Akhtar, 1991: 11–12; Graham, 1990: 36). The land reform greatly hurt the landlords of Jammu and Ladakh, while thousands of Muslim peasants were the main beneficiaries. It is important to note that the National Conference government could put through such radical legislation because the Kashmir Valley, where it had total support, alone constituted a majority of the state's population. In practice, this single-region support base led to the establishment of a one-party democracy in Kashmir. According to Balraj Puri (1991: 15–20; 1992: 2020–1), himself from Jammu and a noted commentator on the Kashmir problem, the inability of Abdullah and other leaders of the National Conference to recognize the distinct identity of Jammu and accommodate its regional aspirations within the State has exacerbated the Kashmir problem. It has been viewed as a Muslim–Hindu (Kashmir Valley–Jammu) problem, whereas it is in reality a question of regional identity and interests within the Kashmir State.

In Jammu and Ladakh the landowning class turned against what they perceived was a biased Muslim government from the Kashmir Valley. Consequently the Jammu-based landlord lobby and Hindu communalists joined ranks and founded the Praja Parishad (Navlakha, 1991: 2958). Its sole purpose was to destroy Abdullah's political credibility. On the other hand, the powerful landowning Buddhist lamas demanded a radical alteration in the relationship between Ladakh and the rest of the Kashmir State: either special status within Kashmir or its separation from Kashmir and its amalgamation into East Punjab or Jammu or a reunion with Tibet (Akhtar, 1991: 28).

The 1953 coup

The leader of the Jana Sangh (founded 1951), S.M. Mookherjee, had made opposition to Article 370 his main propaganda weapon against Nehru in mainstream Indian politics. He demanded that Kashmir should be integrated into the Indian Union on the same basis as other States. Mookherjee was able to win the support of the Sikh Akali leader of East Punjab, Master Tara Singh, who nurtured many grievances against Muslims for the partition of Punjab. Moreover, both hated Nehru and secularism (Akbar, 1991: 143). Within the Congress Party a strong lobby was present which wanted the central government to control Kashmir more firmly. Similar views were shared by many in the Indian bureaucracy and intelligence services. The loyalty of Abdullah was doubted, and he was accused of conniving with the Americans in a bid to secure their help in making Kashmir an independent State (Akbar, 1991: 145–7). Another lobby at the centre suspected Abdullah of pro-Communist sympathies (Navlakha, 1991: 2957).

On the other hand, a sort of ambivalence always marked Abdullah's attitude towards the question of union with India. His public utterances on this issue were confused and contradictory. Within the National Conference, however, a group emerged which stood for greater integration with India. Given these complications, by the end of 1952 a virulent anti-Abdullah campaign had been set in motion in the Hindu-dominated Jammu region by an alliance which included the Jana Sangha, Rashtriya Swayamsevak Sangh (RSS), the Jammu Praja Parishad — all Hindu communal parties — and the Jammu faction of the Sikh Akali Dal. Abdullah's deputy prime minister, Bakshi Ghulam Mohammad, led the revolt from within the National Conference. In the early morning of 8 August 1953 Sheikh Abdullah was removed from office and arrested 'on charges of corruption, malpractice, disruptionism, and dangerous foreign contacts' (Gupta, 1966: 264). This high-handed act provoked rioting and demonstrations in the Kashmir Valley. Thus began an ordeal of long spells of detention with brief spurts of freedom for Abdullah. Between 1953 and 1975 Abdullah was imprisoned nine times and spent all together fifteen years in jail. During this period the Indian government promoted its yes-men in Kashmir, and, although elections were regularly held, intimidation and coercion of those opposed to increasing Indian influence in Kashmir was widely practised (Engineer, 1991a: 9; Hiro, 1976: 213–18).

A constitution for Kashmir

The Kashmir Constituent Assembly ratified the Accession to India on 6 February 1954. Out of a total membership of 75, a majority of 64 voted in favour of accession. From the Indian point of view accession was thus ratified by the Kashmir Constituent Assembly in accordance with the Delhi Agreement of 11 August 1952. The government of Pakistan protested strongly, however, pointing out that such ratification was not consistent with the UN requirements. The Security Council also regarded the move as invalid (Akhtar, 1991: 12; Choudhary, 1991: 51). The Kashmir Constituent Assembly adopted a constitution for the state in January 1957. It was the only State of the Indian Union with a constitution of its own. The head of government of Kashmir was designated as prime minister instead of chief minister as in other Indian States. On the other hand, the constitution declared that the State was an integral part of India. Further, that the territories of the State were those that existed on 15 August 1947, which meant that claims were laid on the Pakistani Azad Kashmir.

Muslim assertiveness and changing Indian positions

A strong pro-Pakistani lobby had always existed among Kashmiri Muslims. The decision of the Indian government never to hold a plebiscite was indicative of a fear that the Muslim majority might vote against it. An Islamic basis for agitation arrived when a holy relic, a hair believed to belong to Prophet Muhammad, disappeared from the Hazratbal shrine at Srinagar on 26 December 1963. Disturbances spread quickly and the situation seemed threatening. Rioting continued into early 1964. Fortunately for the Indians, the hair was found, confirmed by experts, and restored. This way a major showdown was averted (Akbar, 1991: 157–64). This show of strength by Muslims, however, perturbed the non-Muslims, and in Jammu and Ladakh voices were raised demanding greater integration with India.

However, military reverses suffered by India at the hands of the Chinese in 1962 seemed to have convinced Prime Minister Nehru that, in order to face future threats from China, reduction of tension on its western border with Pakistan was imperative. For doing that, it was realized that the resolution of the Kashmir dispute with Pakistan had to be accomplished. Negotiations began between the two countries but ended inconclusively (Johal, 1989: 116–17). In 1964 Sheikh Abdullah had been released from jail. President Ayub Khan of Pakistan invited Abdullah to visit Pakistan. Nehru was also anxious to probe further the possibilities of a solution of the Kashmir conflict. On 23 May Abdullah left for Pakistan. The mission was cut short, however, when Nehru died suddenly on 27 May 1964.

Thereafter, a change in Indian thinking on Kashmir seemed to have occurred and greater and faster integration was pursued. Articles 356 and 357 of the Indian Constitution were extended to Kashmir, whereby the President of India and the Indian Parliament could directly assume the authority in a State if its legislative machinery was not functioning satisfactorily. In 1965 the Kashmir Assembly adopted the sixth amendment whereby the President of India now appointed a governor, as in other Indian States, and the office of prime minister was replaced with that of chief minister as was the regular practice in other States. Moreover in 1965 it was decided to establish a branch of the Congress Party in Kashmir. The National Conference was no longer to be allowed to dominate Kashmir politics exclusively. The strategy of putting Kashmir directly under Congress control was consummated finally in 1967 when the strongly pro-integration Chief Minister of Jammu and Kashmir, Ghulam Muhammad Sadiq, decided to dissolve the National Conference and merge it into Congress (Akhtar, 1991: 12–13).

Pakistan's Operation Gibraltar

A change in Pakistani foreign policy began to occur during the early 1960s. The architect of the new approach was Foreign Minister Zulfikar Ali Bhutto, who sought a friendly equation with China. As a friendly gesture some territory in the northern areas was surrendered to China and a treaty was signed which stated that there were no border disputes between the two countries. India protested because it alleged that the land surrendered to China was a part of Kashmir. On the Kashmir issue Bhutto was an advocate of direct action. Consequently Foreign Minister Bhutto, Foreign Secretary Aziz Ahmed and Major General Akhtar Husain Malik prepared Operation Gibraltar, which was to lead to the liberation of Kashmir (Akbar, 1991: 170). In August 1965 Pakistan dispatched armed men into the Indian Kashmir in the hope of provoking a popular rebellion. However, once again Kashmiris showed little enthusiasm for the Pakistani initiative. Pakistani regular forces crossed the line of control at Chamb and seemed to be succeeding in their military advance. At this point Indian troops crossed the international border near Lahore on 6 September 1965 and the conflict escalated into a full-scale border war which raged for more than a fortnight. A ceasefire ordered by the UN Security Council brought hostilities to an end on 23 September.

Once peace had been restored, diplomatic initiatives were on the way to bring the two adversaries to the negotiating table. The Soviet Union invited President Ayub Khan and Prime Minister Lal Bahadur Shastri to Tashkent. The two met in 1966. An agreement to seek peaceful resolution of conflicts was reached between the two countries. However, no progress was made on the Kashmir question.

The Simla Agreement

In 1971, another war took place between India and Pakistan, this time over the East Pakistan situation. The Indian army intervened on behalf of the East Pakistani resistance and meted out a crushing defeat on Pakistan. Some 94,000 Pakistani soldiers were taken as prisoners of war. As is usual after such events, trouble-shooting diplomatic activity soon followed. In the summer of 1972 President Bhutto and Prime Minister Indira Gandhi met at the Indian hill station of Simla. Besides the POWs held, India also occupied some 12,893 sq. km of Pakistani territory on the western border. The discussions resulted in the Simla Agreement. Both sides affirmed to work together towards the creation of durable peace and harmony between them, to cease carrying out hostile propaganda against each other and to promote understanding between each other through exchanges in the field of culture and science (*Simla Agreement*, 1972). More crucially, Article 1 (ii) stated:

> That the two countries are resolved to settle their differences by peaceful means through bilateral negotiations or by any other peaceful means mutually agreed

upon between them. Pending the final settlement of any of the problems between the two countries, neither side shall unilaterally alter the situation and both shall prevent the organisation, assistance or encouragement of any acts detrimental to the maintenance of peaceful and harmonious relations.

Article 4 (ii) stated:

In Jammu and Kashmir, the line of control resulting from the ceasefire of December 17, 1971 shall be respected by both sides without prejudice to the recognised position of either side. Neither side shall seek to alter it unilaterally, irrespective of mutual differences and legal interpretations. Both sides further undertake to refrain from the threat or the use of force in violation of this Line.

Article 6 stated: 'the representatives of the two sides will meet to discuss further the modalities and arrangements for the establishment of durable peace and normalisation of relations, including . . . a final settlement of Jammu and Kashmir.'

Interpretations of the agreement

Pakistan recovered its 94,000 prisoners and its occupied territory, but no real progress on Kashmir could be made. Both sides interpreted the Simla Agreement in a manner advantageous to them: India insisted that the principle of bilateralism meant that the Kashmir problem was no longer an international issue and that the line of control had become the international border, while Pakistan insisted that the Simla Agreement recognized that the Kashmir problem had yet to be resolved. Both were apparently right.

Return of Abdullah

The defeat suffered by Pakistan at the hands of the Indian army and the secession of its eastern wing seemed to have convinced Sheikh Abdullah that the balance of power in the subcontinent had tilted decisively in favour of India. He therefore opened negotiations with Indira Gandhi in 1973 to seek a mutually acceptable solution. After a series of talks, finally on 24 February 1975 the Kashmir Accord was signed between the Indian government and Sheikh Abdullah. The Indian government reaffirmed that Article 370 was the basis of the special relationship between India and Kashmir, but refused to rescind laws enacted by the Union Government on Kashmir during Abdullah's terms in prison between 1953 and 1975. In return Abdullah recognized the validity of the accession by the Kashmir State Assembly in 1954 (at a time when Abdullah was in prison), but revived the National Conference as a separate political party (Akhtar, 1991: 13–14). In the historic 1977 elections (in which the Congress was defeated badly all over India and for the first time a non-Congress government under the Janata Alliance came into power) the National Conference campaigned on the basis of two slogans, autonomy and Kashmiri nationalism, and won 47 seats out of a total of 75. Congress secured 11 and the Janata Party 13.

Towards armed conflict in the 1980s

In 1980 Mrs Gandhi returned to power at the centre. Once again the levers on Kashmir were tightened. The new electoral strategy which Congress adopted on a countrywide basis aimed at widening the Hindu support base. In the context of Kashmir it meant that Mrs Gandhi began to extend greater patronage to the Hindu lobby in Jammu. In typical fashion a campaign was launched once again against Abdullah. His government was maligned for corruption and price raising. In response Abdullah revived the controversy over accession and talked about independence.

The Resettlement Bill

In 1980 Abdullah introduced the Resettlement Bill in the Kashmir Parliament. It was meant to provide a legal framework for the return and settlement of Kashmiris who had fled the state and taken refuge in Pakistan and elsewhere during the riots and violence of 1947–49. It was bitterly opposed by the centre and projected by the Indian media as a security risk. It was feared that many people whose loyalty lay with Pakistan and spies and agents could return to Kashmir (Akhtar, 1991: 16). Despite stiff opposition the Kashmir Assembly passed the bill by majority vote on 30 March 1982. However, when it was sent for assent to the governor B.K. Nehru (the governor is an appointee and representative of the central government), it was refused.

Sheikh Abdullah died on 8 September 1982 after a long period of ill health. Before his death he had nominated his elder son, Dr Farooq Abdullah, as his successor. Mrs Gandhi supported Farooq Abdullah's appointment as chief minister. In his inaugural address to the Kashmir Assembly Farooq stressed his Kashmiri identity and simultaneously declared Kashmir's bonds with India unbreakable. However, Farooq would not budge on his support for the Resettlement Bill, notwithstanding Mrs Gandhi's fierce opposition. On 4 October 1982 the Bill was again adopted by both houses of the Kashmir Parliament, and Governor B.K. Nehru had to give his assent (Akhtar, 1991: 16). Many pro–Islamic and pro–Pakistani organizations and parties that hitherto had opposed the National Conference expressed admiration for Farooq Abdullah's defiant stand.

The election of 1983

In June 1983 State elections were held in Kashmir. According to Pran Chopra (1991: 30): 'A thoroughly communal campaign run by Indira Gandhi in the State in 1983 was followed in 1984 by a cynical dismissal of the State Government, one of the worst examples of its kind anywhere in India'. Initially Farooq sought an alliance with the Congress but the deal could not be worked out. On the other hand, some leading pro-Pakistan politicians who were traditional rivals of the National Conference, such as the influential religious figure Mir Waiz Maulvi Farooq, offered help to Farooq Abdullah which the latter accepted. The election result gave the National Conference a majority of 47 seats, of which eight were from Jammu. Congress won 26 seats.

The dismissal and return of Farooq Abdullah

During 1983–84 Farooq Abdullah took a leading part in co-ordinating efforts of non-Congress chief ministers of different Indian States to organize a joint front against the central government headed by Mrs Gandhi. In the meantime pro-Pakistan activities were increasing in the Valley. Demonstrations and agitations against India became frequent. Farooq condemned the activities of the pro-Pakistani agitators, branding them as anti-state elements. The situation worsened dramatically when on 3 February 1983 an Indian diplomat, M.H. Mahatre, was kidnapped in London by a group claiming to be the Kashmir Liberation Army. In exchange for Mahatre the KLA demanded the release of the leader of the Jammu Kashmir Liberation Front (JKLF), Maqbool Butt, who was in jail in India on terrorist charges. However, before anything could be worked out Mahatre was found dead in Birmingham. Maqbool Butt was hanged on 3 February 1984 (Akhtar, 1991: 17).

The next few months saw the rapid deterioration of the situation in neighbouring East Punjab, culminating in the attack by the Indian army on the Golden Temple in June 1984. In Kashmir Sikhs attacked Hindu temples. Farooq Abdullah was sacked and replaced by his brother-in-law G.M. Shah. After Mrs Gandhi's assassination there were widespread violent and brutal attacks on Sikhs in Jammu. In the fast-deteriorating situation the leading communal Hindu organizations and parties such as the Bharatia Janata Party (BJP), RSS and the Vishwa Hindu Parishad (VHP) intensified their campaign for the abrogation of Article 370 and Kashmir's integration with the rest of India. In Kashmir the effect of such a campaign was the accentuation of the Islamic identity.

The fall of the G.M. Shah government

Despite the growing unrest and civil disobedience, the G.M. Shah government remained in power. However, events in northern India were to make this impossible. In February 1986 the infamous Ramjanambhoomi–Babri Masjid controversy took a dramatic turn when Hindus were allowed by the government to worship inside Babri mosque at Ayodhya. The Muslims of India reacted angrily to the decision. In Kashmir, the Islamic factor had been on the ascent after the Iranian Revolution and particularly after General Zia began to support Afghan guerrillas fighting the Soviet army. The Ayodhya incident, therefore, galvanized the Islamic forces in Kashmir to more daring protests and agitations against India. G.M. Shah was dismissed and the centre imposed Governor's Rule. This is a provision applicable only to Jammu and Kashmir State whereby the governor in an emergency situation can suspend the ordinary machinery of government including the legislature and assume direct administrative control. However, it can be prolonged at most for six months. Thereafter only President's Rule can be imposed, which means that the State comes directly under the control of the Union Government.

Election of 1987 and Farooq Abdullah's political blunder

Elections in Indian Jammu and Kashmir have always attracted considerable political attention, not only within the different regions of the State but also in Delhi and in Islamabad. Since 1967 Congress had been directly participating in the State elections. Congress had been pressurizing Farooq for some years to agree to form a coalition government. In 1986 the Rajiv–Farooq accord was finally signed. A virulent communal election campaign was launched during the State elections held in March 1987, both by the Hindu nationalist party, the BJP, which had recently established itself in Jammu, and by the Muslim United Front, consisting of several Muslim political parties. However, the National Conference succeeded in securing 38 seats while Congress won 24. The Muslim United Front could win only four seats. As usual, the opposition alleged massive rigging. Table 8 gives a breakdown of the elections held to the State assembly between 1951 and 1987.

At any rate, the formation of a National Conference–Congress coalition government with Farooq Abdullah as chief minister proved to be highly inopportune. By that time anti-India feelings were running high in the Valley. Farooq's willingness to bow before pressure from the centre was seen as an act of capitulation (Mahmud, 1989: 19). Strikes and demonstrations multiplied. Pro-Pakistani slogans began to appear everywhere. The agitators exploited all social and cultural occasions to demonstrate their opposition to India. It was clear that such activity was being carried out by organized cadres. The Indian government alleged Pakistani involvement.

Economic bases of growing unrest in Kashmir

Although political grievances and Islamic revivalism predominate in the Kashmir situation, economic factors have also been an important dimension of the problem.

Table 8   Jammu and Kashmir Assembly elections, 1951–87

	1951	1957	1962	1967	1972	1977	1983	1987
National Conference	75	68	69	8	[1]	47	47	38
Congress	–	–	–	61	57	11	26	28
Jana Sangh	–	–	–	4	3	–	–	–
Praja Parishad	–	5	3	–	–	–	–	–
Janata Party	–	–	–	–	–	13	–	–
BJP	–	–	–	–	–	–	–	2
Muslim United Front	–	–	–	–	–	–	–	4
People's Conference	–	–	–	–	–	–	1	–
Jamaat-e-Islami	–	–	–	–	5	1	–	–
Harijan Mandal	–	1	–	–	–	–	–	–
Panthars Party	–	–	–	–	–	–	1	–
Independents	–	1	2	2	9	4	1	4
Total	75	75	75[2]	75	75[2]	76	76	76

[1] No National Conference candidates.
[2] Elections not held for one seat.

Source: Akhtar (1991: 23).

However, like the situation in Punjab the problem is not one of absolute deprivation, but the typical one of uneven development: achievements in the educational sphere greatly outstrip employment opportunities. Before 1947, the state of Jammu and Kashmir was one of the poorest princely States in the Indian subcontinent. The progressive educational policy adopted by Abdullah enabled many poor students to study at the universities free of charge. The old feudal-type landownership structure was smashed and a large number of peasant proprietors came into being. Additionally, the Indian government subsidized many items of daily consumption in Kashmir. Such developments, however, could not escape a regional–communal dimension being put on them by critics: the most dramatic improvements accrued to impoverished Muslims of the Valley while the privileges of the Hindu and Buddhist landowners of Jammu and Ladakh were curtailed.

At any rate, modernization had produced, as in neighbouring Indian Punjab, a sizable intelligentsia. The main sources of employment for educated Kashmiris were the government services and public corporations. There being two sets of administration, central and provincial (that is, State administration), according to Saifuddin Soz (1991: 39–40), Hindus accounted for 83.66 per cent of senior positions in the central government bureaucracy in the State, while Muslims held only 13 per cent. The Muslim share in gazetted services was less than 6 per cent. In the nationalized banking sector Muslim representation was as low as 1.5 per cent. In the much larger State bureaucracy (that is, the provincial administration) there were more Muslims, but Hindus were represented slightly in excess of their ratio of the total population of Jammu and Kashmir (Engineer, 1991b: 262–79).

By 1986–87 the number of educated unemployed young people was 100,000. After the troubles started some 300,000 were without a job. Their numbers have swelled as the conflict drags on. As regards development and industrialization, of the total all-India national investment in public sector enterprises between 1947 and 1987, Jammu and Kashmir's share was only 0.03 per cent. Similarly the ratio of grants and loans from the central government remained unfavourable. For example, the adjoining State of Himachal Pradesh, in many ways similar to Kashmir in physical traits, had been receiving 90 per cent as grants and 10 per cent as loans from the central government. However, Kashmir had been given 70 per cent as loans and 30 per cent as grants. The allegation of neglect by the central government is questioned by S.N. Wakhaloo (1991: 38–44), who asserts that the centre has been more than fair to Kashmir. He draws attention to the achievements in modern road and railway line construction, the great increase in hydro-electric power production, building of a watch-making factory, establishment of a telephone industry and a modern airport at Srinagar besides the general improvement in education.

Whatever calculations are made regarding development or neglect, much of Kashmir's earnings was based on tourism. Around it a handicrafts industry had blossomed, but industrialization in general was negligible. In recent years the development of hydro-electric power from the abundant water resources in Kashmir has been given priority by the Indian government. An agreement was signed between the Swedish and Indian governments in October 1989 whereby the former was to provide development grants of Swedish Kronors 700 million for the Uri Hydro-electric Power Project to be built some 70 km from Srinagar. When completed it will have a full capacity to generate 480 megawatts of electricity. It is expected to meet the needs of the State as well as produce a surplus for export. The construction is expected to include substantial investments in infrastructure such as roads and land development (*India Uri Project*, 1994).

Escalation in violence

Low-key use of force and terror had been going on in the Indian Kashmir since the early 1970s in exchanges mainly between the JKLF and the Indian police and security forces. In 1988, two bombs exploded in the capital Srinagar. Their effect on the otherwise tense and charged political situation was dramatic. Suddenly the level of confrontation between the Indian state and the Kashmiri separatists rose sharply. The JKLF and another militant organization, the People's League, were behind these blasts (Akhtar, 1991: 47). The JKLF leader Amanullah Khan was to remark: 'Our armed struggle started on July 31, 1988 by blasting three buildings belonging to the Government of India in Srinagar' (quoted in Noorani, 1991: 123). The Indian reaction was one of dismay and shock. Farooq Abdullah declared a war against the secessionists and alleged that Pakistan was supporting them. However, more bomb blasts followed, and anti-Indian slogans appeared everywhere. The separatists seemed to have gained the initiative. Thus, when elections to the Indian Lok Sabha were held in Kashmir in 1989, the Kashmiri Muslims virtually boycotted them. Only some 5 per cent of the electorate voted in the Valley (Akbar, 1991: 214).

At the centre, Rajiv Gandhi lost the 1989 elections and the Janata Dal, an alliance of several right, left and centre parties, came into power under the leadership of V.P. Singh. The new government was confronted by a major crisis in Kashmir when on 8 December 1989 Dr Rubiyya Sayeed, the daughter of the Indian Home Minister, Mufti Muhammad Sayeed, a Kashmiri, was kidnapped by JKLF militants. The militants demanded that in return for her release five of their activists in government custody should be set free. Farooq Abdullah, who at that time was in power, objected to any such deal being worked out with the kidnappers (Akbar, 1991: 217). The government, however, gave in to the blackmail and released the JKLF militants. No sooner had Dr Sayeed been released than the same government embarked upon a tough line. A much-hated bureaucrat, Jagmohan, who had earlier served in Kashmir, was sent back as governor. Farooq Abdullah resigned in protest; he was later to leave for the USA, apparently for medical treatment. By the end of 1993 Farooq had not returned to Kashmiri politics.

It is noteworthy that until then, despite mounting provocations and a rapidly deteriorating situation, the central government continued to exercise restraint, and repression was not employed on a massive scale. All this was to change dramatically. Governor's Rule was imposed, and Jagmohan let loose a reign of terror. On 19 January 1990 the most extensive house-to-house search by paramilitary forces began in the capital Srinagar. However, the effect of such repression on the people proved to be very different from what the government hoped to achieve. Suddenly the whole of Srinagar was in a mood of total defiance. Men, women and children came out in the streets to express their anger (Akbar, 1991: 218–19). The crowds were fired upon by the police and paramilitary forces. In Pakistan, Prime Minister Benazir Bhutto openly expressed sympathy for the Kashmiris. The mosques in Srinagar began to give calls for liberation. Amid this situation the spiritual leader, Mir Waiz Maulvi Farooq, known for his strong pro-Pakistani sympathies, was shot dead by unknown assailants on 21 May. This brought hundreds of thousands of Kashmiris out in the mourning procession. The administration panicked and the paramilitary forces opened fire, killing 57 mourners. The six-month Governor's Rule was followed by the imposition of President's Rule.

State terrorism versus separatist terrorism 1990–92

The world press and international and Indian human rights organizations have published several reports listing harrowing details of rape, pillaging and mass murder perpetrated by the Indian security forces. Use of torture against suspected terrorists has been extensive. Also, acts of terror committed by the militants are widespread. This is confirmed by Indian as well as international fact-finding missions and human rights organizations (*India's Kashmir War*, 1990; *Kashmir Bleeds: Report on Kashmir Situation*, 1990; *Kashmir Under Siege*, 1990; *Human Rights in India*, 1991; *Kashmir: A Land Ruled by the Gun*, 1991; Gopsill, 1993). Amnesty International was refused permission to visit Kashmir. It has, however, continuously monitored the situation and published several urgent appeals against human rights violations in the state.

It is noteworthy that Kashmiri women have been participating actively in the resistance movement. It has been noted, however, that such participation has been accompanied by the fundamentalists forcing the women to adhere strictly to traditional Islamic restrictions like covering their bodies and concealing their faces behind a veil (*Kashmir: A Land Ruled by the Gun*, 1991). On the other hand, most of the 200,000 Hindu community, consisting mainly of the Kashmiri pundits, has fled the Kashmir Valley. Most have headed for Jammu but some reached Delhi and were put up in camps. According to M.J. Akbar (1991: 219), a former member of the Indian Parliament and a noted commentator on Kashmir, the exodus of Hindus was masterminded by Jagmohan and RAW so that the communal angle to the conflict was accentuated. Jagmohan was removed in May 1990 and replaced by Jagdish Saxena, a former head of RAW. This change did not bring about any significant reduction in repression and brutality practised by the state.

There is evidence to suggest, however, that the militants have also employed terror against the Kashmiri pundits. Some 32 pundits had been murdered by the end of 1990 (*Kashmir 1991*: 9), among them Tikalal Tapru, a senior advocate, M.K. Ganju, a retired session judge, and Lassa Koul, director of the Sri Nagar television (Akbar, 1991: 220). Especially targeted are Muslims, Kashmiris as well as those from other parts of India, who do not go along with the anti-India line of the militants. Among those killed have been Professor Mushirul Haque, Vice-Chancellor of Kashmir University, and his secretary, Abdul Ghani, Maulana Masoodi, the veteran hero of the National Conference freedom movement and Mir Mustafa, an independent member of the Kashmir Assembly. The various organizations have also been involved in acts of terror against one another. Two Swedish engineers working on the Uri Hydro-electric Power Project were kidnapped in 1991 by the Muslim Janbaaz Force group, but later released. Some Israelis were also kidnapped but later released.

According to Pakistani sources some 300,000 Indian troops had been deployed in Kashmir by 1991. Tim Gopsill (1993) gives the estimated number of Indian troops as 400,000. Pakistani estimates in 1993 were in the vicinity of 500,000. According to JKLF sources some 50,000 militants were active in Kashmir in 1991. On the other hand India alleged that between January 1990 and October 1992 the Kashmiri militants had killed 1585 innocent men and women. Among them were 981 Muslims, 218 Hindus, 23 Sikhs and 363 security forces personnel. Among those killed, twelve were political leaders and 510 government officials (*Pakistan Abetting Terrorism*, 1993?). The total number of people killed in Kashmir is estimated by India to be some 7000 while JKLF figures put them in the vicinity of 25,000. Some 30,000 are thought to be in detention (Khan, 1992).

Support for the militants is widespread in the larger society. Many Muslim officials of the state government, including the police, were believed to be sympathetic to the militants. Consequently the Muslim population of Kashmir has been totally alienated from India (Tarkunde, 1990). Forest and mountainous terrain along the line of control between India and Pakistan render the borders porous, allowing easy movement to both sides. Throughout 1992 troubles in Kashmir remained at a high intensity level. The militants claimed great success in their missions while India claimed to have brought the situation under control and crushed the rebellion.

T.N. Kaul, a Kashmiri pundit who served as India's Foreign Secretary and as Ambassador to the USA and USSR, wrote in the *Hindustan Times* of 23 September 1992:

> India . . . will have to give real autonomy to all States including Kashmir. Although Kashmir does enjoy a large degree of autonomy under the Indian Constitution, larger than any other State in India or elsewhere, Delhi has whittled it down by playing party politics in Kashmir and encouraging one faction after another to rule there. Although India has poured more money per capita in Kashmir than in any other State, this has gone mainly into the pockets of corrupt politicians and their supporters. What is more, Delhi has tried to impose its own administrators in key positions in Kashmir instead of trusting local people. . . . India . . . must further strengthen her secular democracy and give real autonomy to the States.

In the same article, Kaul chides Pakistan for supporting terrorism in Kashmir and persisting with its divisive Two-Nation theory. He wondered what would be the implications of the application of such a theory for the 100 million Muslims who live in India. Furthermore, the author draws attention to the discrimination and mistreatment meted out to the religious minorities and the female population in Pakistan, and contrasts it with secular democracy practised by India.

The Kashmiri diaspora

Several hundred thousand Azad Kashmiris have settled in Britain since the 1950s and 1960s. The Azad Kashmiris had always been ardent supporters of Kashmir's separation from India and its union with Pakistan. More recently the idea of a separate independent Kashmir, comprising territories that formed part of the pre-1947 Jammu and Kashmir State, has gained ground among the new generation in both Britain and Azad Kashmir. Financial support to the militant groups is forthcoming from this diaspora community. The author was able to talk to a cross-section of Azad Kashmiris in the UK during 1991. They seemed to be supportive of one or other of the Kashmiri groups based in that country.

Pakistani involvement

Although Pakistan officially denies providing military assistance to the militants, the evidence is overwhelming that Pakistan's contributions to the training, indoctrination, arming and cross-border movement of Kashmiri Muslim insurgents have been very substantial (Wirsing, 1993: 148; *Pakistan Abetting Terrorism*, 1993?; *Tribune*, 4 February 1993). Coverage of the Kashmir problem by the international news media has also confirmed extensive Pakistani involvement. At any rate, the only route for supply of arms to the militants is through Pakistan. The Indian press has particularly pointed out the Pakistani ISI as masterminding the Kashmir operation. The Pakistani fundamentalist party, the Jamaat-e-Islami, has been organizing its own training camps for Kashmiri recruits. Pakistan is reported to have shifted its support from the JKLF to the Islamic groups because the latter stand for merger of Kashmir with Pakistan. The Pakistan government has shown great nervousness over the growing attraction of an independent Jammu and Kashmir state among people of Azad Kashmir (Ballard, 1991: 513–15). Attempts by Kashmiri protesters to cross the line of control from the Pakistani Kashmir into the Indian part have been disallowed by the Pakistan government (Wirsing, 1993: 151).

International Islamic guerrilla involvement

Although no co-ordinated international Islamic guerrilla movement exists officially, the rudiments of one were laid when a resistance movement was set up in Pakistan to liberate Afghanistan from communist rule. The US and British secret services played the key role in setting up the resistance while the ISI executed most of the operations. Muslim guerrillas from several Muslim countries took part in the campaign, which they saw as a holy war. After the successful completion of the Afghan operation some of the guerrillas were reported to have joined the struggle in Kashmir. This participation, however, seems to have been of a limited character. The Indian authorities have claimed to have captured an Afghan (*Indian Express*, 3 January 1993). However, the level of international Muslim guerrilla participation has not been ascertained yet.

Political groups active in Pakistani Kashmir

The larger militant groups active in Indian Kashmir, such as the JKLF and the various Islamic outfits, have their affiliates on the Pakistani side too. The Pakistani authorities have watched with great vigilance the activities of these groups. Among them the Kashmir Democratic Forum (KDF) is one group based in the Pakistani Azad Kashmir. Although its following is small it has branches in several Western European countries, with its headquarters in Switzerland. It is opposed to the Two-Nation Theory approach of Pakistan and seeks a negotiated solution to the Kashmir problem. Like the JKLF it proposes that Kashmir should come under UN supervision for a period of five to seven years, after which a referendum should be held to give the people a chance to decide their future (*Indian Express*, 25 December 1992).

The occupation of Hazratbal mosque by the militants in October 1993

Things did not change fundamentally in Kashmir during 1993. Among the most dramatic happenings was the occupation of the Hazratbal mosque by Kashmiri militants on 15 October 1993. Various organizations such as the JKLF, the Ikhwan-ul-Muslameen, Al-Jehad, Allah Tigers, Jamayat-ul-Mujahideen and the Hizbul Mujahideen collaborated in this venture. The plan, it seems, was to provoke India to attack this shrine, which is believed to house a hair of the Prophet Muhammad, and thus provoke a religious confrontation. However, the Indian government did not repeat the fatal mistake of assaulting a holy place as it did in the case of the Golden Temple in Amritsar in 1984. Rather it ordered a siege, and negotiations were opened with the militants inside the mosque. On 16 November the militants started coming out and surrendering. The Indian government claimed to have arrested two Pakistani and some Afghan nationals among them (*Times of India*, 19 October 1993).

Pakistan's failure to muster support from Muslim states

It is noteworthy that Pakistan has not been very successful in securing the support of the other Muslim states. While radical nationalist Muslim states like Iraq and Syria have been unwilling to support the Pakistani position, the Islamic fundamentalist states such as Saudi Arabia have tended to sympathize with Pakistan (Singh,

1991: 129–33). However, there are exceptions too. Libya has tended to be pro-Pakistan, while Iran has in recent years been reluctant to support Pakistan. Thus, when Pakistan tried to secure support in the General Assembly of the United Nations for sending a fact-finding committee to Kashmir, it failed to materialize because when the matter was put before a meeting of the Organization of the Islamic Countries in New York on 23 November 1993 support for it was lacking even from the Muslim states. It was therefore dropped.

Kashmir and the West

No clear-cut or common policy has been adopted by the Western states on the Kashmir issue. During the Cold War the USA tended to support the demand for a plebiscite. Now, when the bipolar balance of power does not exist any more, the latest concern of US strategic planning is the containment of Islamic fundamentalism. Thus the USA may be unwilling to extend support to the creation of a Kashmir state dominated by Islamic fundamentalists. Thus on 14 November 1990 the US Ambassador to Pakistan, Robert B. Oakley, stated: 'US government no longer urges a plebiscite on Kashmir as contained in UN resolutions of 1948 and 1949' (quoted in Akhtar, 1991: 62). Consequently Pakistan has been warned several times for alleged backing to the Kashmiri militants. Some individuals from the State Department, however, do from time to time express sympathy for the Kashmiri nationalists.

On the other hand, there is some speculation in Indian and Pakistani political circles that the USA may want the creation of an independent Kashmir state which could be induced to seek US military protection against India and Pakistan. In such a situation, it could be used as a forward base against China, India, Iran and Pakistan: all four problematic to US interests because of their known nuclear capability or suspected interests in acquiring it. Another theory circulating is that Pakistan is soliciting US support on the Kashmir question in exchange for abandoning its nuclear weapons programme. In the absence of a counterweight the USA now has unrivalled influence in the world. It remains to be seen if it will bring to bear its influence on the Kashmir question in a responsible manner.

Ideology, and militant groups active in Indian Kashmir

There are a number of militant Muslim groups active in the Indian Kashmir. Although the best known is the JKLF, the combined strength of the fundamentalists is greater. There are both Sunni and Shia fundamentalist groups, but the former dominate the Islamic movement.

The Jammu Kashmir Liberation Front (JKLF)

The largest single group fighting for Kashmiri independence is the JKLF, which was founded in 1966 and has been active in the Indian Kashmir. The JKLF gained international publicity when its cadres hijacked an Indian Airlines domestic flight and made it land in Lahore in 1971. Since then JKLF has been involved in various other militant operations against the Indian authorities. It stands for an independent Kashmir state, but considers India the main enemy of Kashmiri freedom. After the execution of its president, Maqbool Butt, in 1984, Amanullah Khan, who hails from the Pakistani Azad Kashmir, now heads the organization. JKLF has broad support in the Kashmir Valley, in the Pakistani Azad Kashmir and among the several hundred thousand citizens of Azad Kashmir settled in Britain. It has been very active in Western Europe and North America, lobbying support from governments and politicians. Several documents detailing the alleged atrocities committed by the Indian security forces in Kashmir have been released by it. The JKLF has pledged to create a democratic state in Kashmir in which the minorities will be treated as equal citizens.

Interview with Raja Zafar Khan of JKLF

An interview, summarized as follows, was recorded in London in June 1991 with the London-based spokesman of the Diplomatic Affairs of the JKLF, Raja Zafar Khan, who has represented JKLF at the UN and in various other international forums.

The people of Jammu and Kashmir constitute a separate nation whose roots lie in a distinct nation that evolved over thousands of years. JKLF considers all the territories of the former Jammu and Kashmir State an indivisible whole and wants the right of self-determination to be given to the Kashmiri nation consisting of all the people living there. The Kashmiri people never ceased to oppose the forcible annexation of Kashmir by India, but until 1990 their voice was not heard. Suddenly dictatorships crumbled in Eastern Europe. The effect on Kashmir of this new wave of freedom movements was profound. In April 1990 more than a million people marched in Srinagar. The Indian authorities responded with random shootings. Many people were killed and hundreds were injured. The Indian government has branded the freedom struggle in Kashmir as a terrorist Islamic fundamentalist movement. This is very wrong. JKLF stands for tolerance and democracy. Many Kashmiri Hindus support the liberation cause, but are frightened to express their support publicly. JKLF also wants Pakistan to vacate Kashmir.

A proper utilization of the vast and abundant natural resources of Jammu and Kashmir can make it a very prosperous state. Kashmir is the Switzerland of Asia and there are many opportunities awaiting future investors.

Amanullah Khan

Arguing that both India and Pakistan are unlawfully occupying Jammu and Kashmir state, the JKLF chairman, Amanullah Khan, speaking at a round table discussion, organized under the auspices of the Socialist Group of the European Parliament at Brussels in October 1993, proposed that the UN should directly take charge of Jammu and Kashmir State:

> One way to solve the issue . . . would be to re-unite the divided Kashmir after simultaneous and complete withdrawal from the State of all Indian and Pakistani armed forces and civil personnel and the whole Jammu Kashmir State (as it existed on August 14, 1947) be given under the control of the United Nations for 5 to 10 years. . . . At the end of this period people of the entire State be opportune to determine [a faulty construction; probably should read as 'At the end of this period the people of the entire State be given the opportunity to determine': author's comments], through democratic means (under French system of elections), under UN supervision and without any kind of external pressure or influence, whether the whole State should become a fully independent country or become a permanent part of India or Pakistan.

Other groups

The other groups active in Indian Kashmir are more candidly pro-Pakistan and Islam-oriented. They would prefer Kashmir to join Pakistan and be made an Islamic society in a thorough sense. Among them the Muslim Conference, People's League, Mahaz-e-Azadi and Jamaat-e-Islami, a namesake and counterpart of the Pakistani fundamentalist party, combine peaceful with extra-constitutional means of agitation. Since 1972 the latter has been taking part in elections, but has generally failed to make any impression. A number of underground militant groups also exist. Among them are the Hizbul Mujahideen, Hizbul Islam, Muslim Student Federation, Allah Tigers, Islami Student League, Islami Jamiat-i-Tulba, Muslim Janbaz Force, Al-Badr and Al-Jehad (Akhtar, 1991: 53).

The United Jihad Council (UJC)

In September 1990, six major militant groups formed the United Jihad Council. Those outfits that joined this apex body were the Hizbul Mujahideen, Muslim Janbaaz Force, Tehrik-i-Jehad-i-Islami, Al-Umar Mujahideen, Hizbullah and Operation Balakot. JKLF also in principle joined the Council with the intention of building a more co-ordinated fighting strategy against India. Such participation in an overtly Islamic-oriented council by JKLF is pointed to by the Indian government as proof that in reality the JKLF is also a communal organization.

References

Ahmed, I. (1990) 'Sikh separatism in India and the concept of Khalistan' in K.R. Haellquist (ed.), *NIAS Report 1990*, Copenhagen: Nordic Institute of Asian Studies.

Akbar, M.J. (1985) *India: The Siege Within*, Harmondsworth: Penguin Books.

Akbar, M.J. (1991) *Kashmir: Behind the Vale*, New Delhi: Viking.

Akhtar, S. (1991) 'Uprising in Indian-held Kashmir', *Regional Studies*, vol. IX, no. 2, Islamabad: Institute of Regional Studies.

Akhtar, S. (1991–92) 'Punjab at the crossroads', *Regional Studies*, vol. X, no. 1.

Alavi, H. (1989) 'Politics of ethnicity in India and Pakistan' in H. Alavi and J. Harriss (eds), *Sociology of 'Developing Societies': South Asia*, London: Macmillan.

Andersen, P.B. (1990) 'Theoretical reflections on Santal and Hindu elements in the Santal Karam ritual', unpublished paper presented at the Seventh Annual Conference of the Nordic Association of South East Asian Studies, held at Klintholm Haven.

Arms Supply from Pakistan and Narco-Terrorist Links (1992?) (no date of publication given), Government of India.

Aurora, J.S. (1984) 'Assault on the Golden Temple: 5–6 June 1984' in A. Kaur *et al.* (eds), *The Punjab Story*, New Delhi: Roli Books International.

Ballard, R. (1983) 'The context and consequences of migration: Jullundhar and Mirpur compared', *New Community*, vol. XI.

Ballard, R. (1991) 'Kashmir crisis: view from Mirpur', *Economic and Political Weekly*, vol. XXVI, nos 9 and 10, 2–9 March, Bombay.

Barnett, M.R. (1976) *The Politics of Cultural Nationalism in South India*, Princeton: Princeton University Press.

Bhatia, S. (1987) *Social Change and Politics in Punjab: 1898–1910*, New Delhi: Enkay Publishers PVT Ltd.

Bhattacharya, M. (1989) 'Bureaucracy and politics in India' in Z. Hasan, S.N. Jha and R. Khan (eds), *The State, Political Processes, and Identity: Reflections on Modern India*, New Delhi/Newbury Park/London: Sage Publications.

Brass, P.R. (1974) *Language, Religion and Politics in North India*, Cambridge: Cambridge University Press.

Burke, S.M. (1973) *Pakistan's Foreign Policy*, London: Oxford University Press.

Chandoke, N. (1989) 'Religion, culture and the state' in M. Shakir (ed.), *Religion, State and Politics in India*, Delhi: Ajanta Books.

Chaube, S.K. (1989) 'Ethnicity, regionalism and the problem of national identity in India' in Z. Hasan, S.N. Jha and R. Khan (eds), *The State, Political Processes, and Identity: Reflections on Modern India*, New Delhi/ Newbury Park/London: Sage Publications.

Chaudhry, N.A. (1977) *Development of Urdu as Official Language in the Punjab (1849–1974)*, Lahore: Government of the Punjab.

Chopra, P. (1991) 'The cycle of blunders' in A. Engineer (ed.), *Secular Crown on Fire: The Kashmir Problem*, Delhi: Ajanta Publications.

Chopra, V.D. (1984a) 'Rise of Sikh fundamentalism' in V.D. Chopra, R.K. Misra and N. Singh (eds), *Agony of Punjab*, New Delhi: Patriot Publishers.

Chopra, V.D. (1984b) 'From Azad Punjab to Khalistan' in V.D. Chopra, R.K. Misra and N. Singh (eds), *Agony of Punjab*, New Delhi: Patriot Publishers.

Choudhary, S. (1991) *What Is the Kashmir Problem?*, Luton: Jammu Kashmir Liberation Front.

The Constitution of India (1992) New Delhi: Universal Book Traders.

Cunningham, J.D. (1918) *A History of the Sikhs*, London: Humphrey Milford/Oxford University Press.

Dhami, M.S. (1981) 'Caste, class and politics in the rural Punjab: a study of two villages in Sangrur District' in P. Wallace and S. Chopra, *Political Dynamics of Punjab*, Amritsar: Guru Nanak Dev University.

Engineer, A.A. (1991a) 'Introduction' in A. Engineer (ed.), *Secular Crown on Fire: The Kashmir Problem*, Delhi: Ajanta Publications.

Engineer, A.A. (1991b) 'Appendix III' in A. Engineer (ed.), *Secular Crown on Fire: The Kashmir Problem*, Delhi: Ajanta Publications.

Frankel, F.R. (1978) *India's Political Economy, 1947–1977: The Gradual Revolution*, Princeton: Princeton University Press.

Frykenberg, R.C. (1993) 'Hindu fundamentalism and the structural stability of India' in M.E. Marty and R.C. Appleby (eds), *Fundamentalisms and the State: Remaking Polities, Economics, and Militance*, Chicago and London: University of Chicago Press.

Fyzee, A.A.A. (1991) 'Accession of Kashmir is not final' in A.A. Engineer (ed.), *Secular Crown on Fire: The Kashmir Problem*, Delhi: Ajanta Publications.

Gankovsky, Y.V. and Gordon-Polonskaya, L.R. (1972) *A History of Pakistan (1847–1958)*, Lahore: People's Publishing House.

Gill, K.K. and Gill, S.S. (1990) 'Agricultural development and industrialisation in Punjab: some issues related to the Pepsi model', *Economic and Political Weekly*, 10 November.

Gill, S.S. (1992a) 'Development experience of a fast growing region in a slow growing backward economy: recent socio-economic changes in the Punjab', conference paper presented at the Indian Institute of Advanced Studies, Shimla.

Gill, S.S. (1992b) 'Punjab crisis and the political process', *Economic and Political Weekly*, vol. XXVII, no. 5, 1 February.

Gill, S.S. and Singhal, K.C. (1984) *Economic and Political Weekly*, vol. XIX, no. 14, 7 April.

Gokhale, P.G. (1976) 'The preamble, the directive principles and the fundamental rights: Parliament's role in conflict resolution' in S.L. Shakdher (ed.), *The Constitution and the Parliament in India*, New Delhi: National Publishing House.

Gopsill, T. (1993) *'Heaven on Fire'*, a fact-finding report prepared on behalf of the British Parliamentary Human Rights Group.

Graham, B.D. (1990) *Hindu Nationalism and Indian Politics: The Origins and Developments of the Bharatiya Jana Sangh*, Cambridge: Cambridge University Press.

Guha, A.C. (1976) 'The Preamble, the fundamental rights and the directive principles' in S.L. Shakdher (ed.), *The Constitution and the Parliament in India*, New Delhi: National Publishing House.

Gujral, I.K. (1985) 'The economic dimension' in A. Singh (ed.), *Punjab in Indian Politics: Issues and Trends*, Delhi: Ajanta Publications.

Gupta, D. (1991) 'Communalism and fundamentalism: some notes on the nature of ethnic politics in India', *Economic and Political Weekly*, vol. VI, nos 11 and 12.

Gupta, S. (1966) *Kashmir: A Study in India–Pakistan Relations*, Bombay: Asia Publishing House.

Haque, M. (1992) 'U.S. role in the Kashmir dispute: a survey', *Regional Studies*, vol. X, no. 4.

Hardtmann, E. (1994) 'Partiets valtriumf vände upp-och-ned på indisk politik: Kanshi Rams mål att lågkastiga får makten i hela Indien', *Sydasien*, nr 3.

Hellman, E. (1993) *Political Hinduism: The Challenge of the Viśva Hindu Parisad*, Uppsala: Uppsala University.

Helweg, R.W. (1989) 'Sikh politics in India: the emigrant factor' in N.G. Barrier and V.A. Dusenbery (eds), *The Sikh Diaspora: Migration and the Experience Beyond Punjab*, Delhi: Chanakya Publications.

Hiro, D. (1976) *Inside India Today*, London: Routledge & Kegan Paul.

Human Rights in India: Kashmir Under Siege (1991), New York and Washington, DC: Asia Watch Report.

Hussain, M. (1989) 'The Muslim question in India', *Journal of Contemporary Asia*, vol. 19, no. 3.

India: Uri Hydroelectric Power Project, Report no. 9 (12 April 1994), Stockholm.

Indian Express (newspaper), 25 December 1992; 3 January 1993.

India's Kashmir War (1990), Delhi Committee for Initiative on Kashmir.

Jeffrey, R. (1986) *What's Happening to India?*, London: Macmillan.

Jha, P.S. (1991) 'Frustrated middle class' in A.A. Engineer (ed.), *Secular Crown on Fire: The Kashmir Problem*, Delhi: Ajanta Publications.

Johal, S. (1989) *Conflict and Integration in Indo-Pakistan Relations*, Berkeley: University of California.

Josh, S.S. (1977) *Hindustan Gadar Party: A Short History*, New Delhi: People's Publishing House.

Juergensmeyer, M. (1988) *Religious Rebels in the Punjab: The Social Vision of Untouchables*, Delhi: Ajanta Publications.

Kapur, R. (1986) *Sikh Separatism: The Politics of Faith*, London: Allen and Unwin.

Kashmir 1991, a report by Physicians for Human Rights (UK).

Kashmir: A Land Ruled by the Gun, 1991, Delhi: Committee for Initiative on Kashmir.

Kashmir Bleeds (1990), Srinagar: The Human Rights Commission.

Kashmir Under Siege (1990), report by the Punjab Human Rights Organisation.

Kaul, T.N. (1992) *Hindustan Times*, 23 September.

Khalistan News (December 1987–January 1988), Kent: Khalistan Council.

Khan, A. (1993) 'Underlying causes of Kashmir dispute (and reasons for its remaining unresolved)', paper presented at a round table discussion on Kashmir, held under the auspices of the Socialist Group, European Parliament, held in Brussels, 18–19 October.

Khan, R.Z. (1992) 'The Kashmir question and struggle for identity', paper presented at a Seminar on Kashmir, University of Sweden, 11 and 12 April.

Kohli, A. (1989) *The State and Poverty in India: The Politics of Reform*, Cambridge: Cambridge University Press.

Kohli, A. (1990) *Democracy and Discontent: India's Growing Crisis of Governability*, Cambridge: Cambridge University Press.

Kothari, R. (1970) *Politics in India*, New Delhi: Orient Longman.

Kumar, R.N. and Sieberer, G. (1991) *The Sikh Struggle: Origin, Evolution and Present Phase*, Delhi: Chanakya Publications.

Leigh, M.S. (1922) *The Punjab and the War*, Lahore: Government Printing Press.

Macauliffe, M.A. (1909) *The Sikh Religion*, vol. 1, Oxford: Clarendon Press.

Mahmud, K. (1989) *Indian Political Scene, 1989: Main Contenders for Power*, Islamabad: Institute for Regional Studies.

Malik, Y.K. (1989) 'Democracy, the Akali Party and the Sikhs in Indian politics' in D. Vajpeyi and Y.K. Malik (eds), *Religious and Ethnic Minority Politics in South Asia*, New Delhi: Manohar.

Mathew, G. (1989) 'Politicisation of religion: conversions to Islam in Tamil Nadu' in M. Shakir (ed.), *Religion, State and Politics in India*, Delhi: Ajanta Books.

Maxwell, N. (1980) 'India, the Nagas and the north-east', *Minority Rights Group Report* no. 17, London: Minority Rights Group Ltd.

Mukherji, P.N. (1985) 'Akalis and violence' in A. Singh (ed.), *Punjab in Indian Politics: Issues and Trends*, Delhi: Ajanta Publications.

Mukherji, P.N. (1992) 'Class and ethnic movements in India: in search of a pertinent paradigm for democracy and nation-building in the Third World' in L. Rudebeck (ed.), *When Democracy Makes Sense*, Uppsala: AKUT.

Navlakha, G. (1991) 'Bharat's Kashmir War', *Economic and Political Weekly*, vol. XXVI, no. 51, 21 December.

Nayar, B.R. (1966) *Minority Politics in the Punjab*, Princeton: Princeton University Press.

Noorani, A.G. (1991) 'Benazir's surrender to generals' in A.A. Engineer (ed.), *Secular Crown on Fire: The Kashmir Problem*, Delhi: Ajanta Publications.

Oberoi, H. (1993) 'Sikh fundamentalism: translating history into theory' in M.E. Marty and R.C. Appleby (eds), *Fundamentalisms and the State: Remaking Polities, Economics, and Militance*, Chicago and London: University of Chicago Press.

Oommen, T.K. (1990) *State and Society in India: Studies in Nation-building*, New Delhi/Newbury Park/London: Sage Publications.

Oppression in Punjab (1985), Birmingham: Hind Mazdoor Kisan Panchayat.

Pakistan Abetting Terrorism in Jammu and Kashmir (1993?), Government of India publication, no date or place of publication indicated.

Panikkar, K.N. (1991) 'A historical overview' in S. Gopal (ed.), *Anatomy of a Confrontation: The Babri Masjid—Ramjanmabhumi Issue*, New Delhi: Viking.

Pettigrew, J. (1975) *Robber Noblemen*, London: Routledge and Kegan Paul.

Punjab Settlement, July 24, 1985, Delhi: Government of India.

Puri, B. (1991) 'The challenge of Kashmir' in A.A. Engineer (ed.), *Secular Crown on Fire: The Kashmir Problem*, Delhi: Ajanta Publications.

Puri, B. (1992) 'Ominous portents from Kashmir', *Economic and Political Weekly*, vol. XXVII, no. 38, 19 September.

Ray, A.K. (1989) 'Towards the concept of a post-colonial democracy: a schematic view' in Z. Hasan, S.N. Jha and R. Khan (eds), *The State, Political Processes, and Identity: Reflections on Modern India*, New Delhi/Newbury Park/London: Sage Publications.

Report of the Citizens' Commission (on Delhi riots, 31 October to 4 November) (1985), Delhi: Citizens' Commission.

Rizvi, H.A. (1990) 'Pakistan—India relations in the eighties', *Regional Studies*, vol. XIII, no. 3.

Rizvi, S.A.A. (1991) 'Islamic proselytisation: seventh to sixteenth centuries' in G.A. Oddie (ed.), *Religion in South Asia*, New Delhi: Manohar.

Rudolph, L.I. and Rudolph, S.H. (1987) *In Pursuit of Lakshmi: The Political Economy of India*, Chicago and London: University of Chicago.

Saxena, N.C. (1989) 'Public employment and educational backwardness among the Muslims of India' in M. Shakir (ed.), *Religion, State and Politics in India*, Delhi: Ajanta Books.

Shah Bano Case (1986), ed. B.R. Agarwala, New Delhi: Arnold-Heinemann.

Sharma, T.R. (1981) 'Political implications of the Green Revolution' in P. Wallace and S. Chopra, *Political Dynamics of Punjab*, Amritsar: Guru Nanak Dev University.

Shukla, S.C. (1991) 'Ethnocentrism and education: an Asian perspective', *Journal of Education Planning and Administration*, vol. V, no. 3, July 1991.

Simla Agreement (1972), 2 July.

Singh, B. (1982) *State Politics in India: Explorations in Political Processes in Jammu and Kashmir*, New Delhi: Macmillan India Ltd.

Singh, G. (1986) *Religion and Politics in the Punjab*, New Delhi: Deep & Deep Publications.

Singh, G. (1989) *History of Sikh Struggles*, vol. 1, *1946–1966*, New Delhi: Atlantic Publishers & Distributors.

Singh, K. (1963) *A History of the Sikhs*, vol. 1, *1469–1839*, Princeton: Princeton University Press.

Singh, K. (1966) *A History of the Sikhs*, vol. 2, *1839–1964*, Princeton: Princeton University Press.

Singh, K. (1985) *Ranjit Singh: Maharajah of the Punjab 1780–1839*, New Delhi: Orient Longman.

Singh, M. (1991) 'Arabs and Kashmir' in A.A. Engineer (ed.), *Secular Crown on Fire: The Kashmir Problem*, Delhi: Ajanta Publications.

Singh, S.K. (1982) *Sachi Sakhi* (in Punjabi), Vancouver: Modern Printing House.

Smith, D.E. (1963) *India as a Secular State*, Princeton: Princeton University Press.

Soz, S. (1991) 'An ostrich-like attitude towards Kashmir won't do' in A.A. Engineer (ed.), *Secular Crown on Fire: The Kashmir Problem*, Delhi: Ajanta Publications.

Statistical Outline of India 1989–90, Bombay: Tata Services Ltd.

Subrahmanyam, K. (1990) 'Kashmir', *Strategic Analysis*, vol. XIII, no. II, May.

Tarkunde, V.M. (1990) 'Kashmir: the truth', a letter by retired Justice V.M. Tarkunde, *Indian Express*, 8 April.

Teng, M.K. (1990) *Kashmir Article 370*, New Delhi: Anmol Publications.

Terrorist Revelations — the Pakistani Connection (1992?) (no date of publication given), Government of India.

Thapar, R. (1991) 'A historical perspective on the story of Rama' in S. Gopal (ed.), *Anatomy of a Confrontation: The Babri Masjid–Ramjanmabhumi Issue*, New Delhi: Viking.

Times of India, 27, 28 October 1992; 2 January 1993; 19 October 1993.

Tribune (Indian newspaper), 4 February 1993.

Truth About Delhi Riots (1985), Delhi: Citizens for Democracy.

The Truth: An International Magazine on Sikhism, vol. 2, December 1985 and April 1986, nos 3 and 4, Quebec.

Tully, M. and Jacob, S. (1985) *Amritsar: Mrs Gandhi's Last Battle*, London: Jonathan Cape.

Wakhaloo, S.N. (1991) 'The centre has been more than fair to Kashmir' in A.A. Engineer (ed.), *Secular Crown on Fire: The Kashmir Problem*, Delhi: Ajanta Publications.

Wallace, P. (1990) 'Sikh minority attitudes in India's federal system' in J.T. O'Connell, M. Israel, W.G. Oxtoby, W.H. McLeod and J.S. Grewal (eds), *Sikh History and Religion in the Twentieth Century*, New Delhi: Manohar.

White Paper on the Punjab Agitation, 10 July, 1984, New Delhi: Government of India.

Wirsing, R.G. (1993) 'Kashmir conflict: the new phase' in C.H. Kennedy (ed.), *Pakistan 1992*, Bouldner: Westview Press.

Wolpert, S. (1982) *A New History of India*, New York: Oxford University Press.

Audio and video cassette tapes

Khushwant Singh, journalist, writer and Sikh historian (videotape: *Bleeding Punjab in Search of Peace*).
Tavleen Singh, journalist (videotape: *Bleeding Punjab in Search of Peace*).
Sant Jarnail Singh Bhindranwale audio (1–13) and video (1–3) cassette tapes.

Interviews in the UK, July 1986

Dr Jagjit Singh Chauhan
Gurmej Singh Gill
Manmoham Singh Khalsa
Davinder Singh Parmar
Harbans Singh Ruprah
Gurdeep Singh
Indarjit Singh

Interviews in Stockholm, June 1987

Lachman Singh Anjala
Dr Chanan Singh Chan

Interview in London, June 1991

Raja Zafar Khan, JKLF

Interviews in Stockholm, October 1994

E. Ezhil Caroline, Dalit Women's Organization of South India
Saral K. Chatterji, Director, the Christian Institute for the Study of Religion and Society (CISRS), New Delhi
Samar Bosu Mullick, Consultant on Tribal Studies for CISRS, Ranchi University, Bihar
Ram Dayal Munda, President, the Indian Confederation of Indigenous and Tribal Peoples, Ranchi, Bihar

7

Pakistan

On 14 August 1947 Pakistan emerged as an independent Muslim state in the Indian subcontinent through the separation of the Muslim-majority north-western and north-eastern zones from the rest of India and their amalgamation into a single state. In between the two wings of Pakistan were 15,000 km of Indian territory. West Pakistan comprised the western portions of the former Punjab province, the North-West Frontier Province (NWFP) and the tribal areas, the whole of the Sindh province, British Baluchistan, and the princely States of Bahawalpur, Khairpur, Makran, Las-Bela, Chitral, Dir, Swat, Amb and Phulra (Gankovsky and Gordon-Polonskaya, 1972: 97–8). The ruler of Bahawalpur toyed with the idea of declaring independence but was dissuaded from doing so. On the other hand, Kalat state in Baluchistan declared independence but was annexed militarily in April 1948. East Pakistan received the eastern portions of the Bengal province and the Sylhet district of Assam. In 1956 Pakistan was transformed from a dominion of the British empire into a republic. It heralded the end of the era of princely States.

Altogether Pakistan received 23 per cent of the territory and 19 per cent of the population of colonial India. West Pakistan had a population of 33.70 million, East Pakistan 42 million. In December 1971 East Pakistan seceded from Pakistan to become the independent state of Bangladesh. In this chapter a discussion of East Pakistan is excluded as it is covered in the next chapter on Bangladesh.

Pakistani society and polity

According to the 1981 Census of Pakistan, the total population of the country was 84,253,644 and total territory 796,095 sq. km, excluding Azad Kashmir. Christians (largely to be found in Punjab and Karachi) and Hindus (almost all to be found in Sindh province) are the main religious minorities of Pakistan. The annual population growth rate was 3.1 per cent, the highest in South Asia, and the overall rate of literacy was 23.3 per cent in 1981. Pakistan's population in 1988 was estimated at 105.50 million (*Pakistan's Statistical Yearbook*, 1989).

Table 9   Religions of Pakistan, no. and percentage

Muslims (Sunnis and Shias)	81,450,057	96.7
Christians	1,310,426	1.6
Hindus	1,276,116	1.5
Ahmadis	104,244	0.1
Parsis	7,007	
Sikhs	2,146	0.1
Buddhists	2,639	
Others (Parsis, Sikhs, Buddhists, etc.)	101,009	

Table 10   Percentage of main languages in Pakistan

Baluchi	3.01
Brauhi (or Brohi)	1.20
Hindko	2.43
Pukhto (or Pushto)	13.14
Punjabi	48.17
Saraiki	9.83
Sindhi	11.77
Urdu	7.60
Others	2.81

Cultural premisses of the Pakistani polity

Because the religious bond between Indian Muslims served as the rationale for the creation of Pakistan, it was common faith in Islam rather than historical right to territory which has primarily fashioned Pakistani identity. Consequently, religious minorities were marginalized gradually, and nearly excluded from the nation-state project during the period of General Muhammad Zia-ul-Haq. Although figures are not available on sectarian divisions, around 85 per cent of Muslims are estimated to be Sunnis. Pakistani Sunnis are divided into various subsects. The second largest group among Muslims is the Shias, including the main Ithna Ashari as well as the minor Ismaili and Bohra groups. According to the Demographic Research Institute of Karachi University, Shias make up 12–15 per cent of the Muslim population. Shias themselves claim to be more than 30 per cent, while Sunni sources put the Shias at only 6 per cent of the Muslim population (Qureshi, 1989: 109). The Ithna Ashari are to be found in all parts of Pakistan. Small but influential Ismaili and Bohra communities are located in Karachi and parts of Sindh. Ismailis are also to be found in Gilgit in the northern mountainous areas. A minor and obscure sect of Zikris is to be found along the Makran coast in Baluchistan. The Ahmadiyya themselves claim to be Muslims, but are classified since 1974 by an act of the National Assembly of Pakistan as non-Muslims.

The confessional nation-state project and organizing ideology

The Islamic antecedents of the state — the Two-Nation theory, the 1945–46 rabidly communalist election campaign conducted by the Muslim League and the bloody division of colonial India — have in the post-independence period served as the backdrop and compulsive reference for the discussion on the nation-state project. Three different interpretations of the relationship between Islam, state and nation were present among the Muslim League leaders who received power and authority in Pakistan. The first was the contradictory position of the supreme leader of the Pakistan movement Mohamed Ali Jinnah who, on the one hand, advocated a separation between religion and the state and advanced the idea of a Pakistani nation consisting of all citizens in his oft-quoted 11 August 1947 address to the Pakistan Constituent Assembly, but who, on the other hand, had played the pivotal role in ascribing credibility and legitimacy to the religious basis of nationhood and on that basis brought about Partition. The secular position of Jinnah never received much attention in Pakistani *real-politik* as the Islamic dimension became a central feature of the political discourse. Rather, secularism and Jinnah's speech became the slogan of marginal elements — liberal and left-leaning politicians, academics and oppressed minorities — hoping in vain to give the ruling élite a bad conscience for its drift towards greater theocratization of state and society.

The second interpretation was a middle position held by most of the top leaders of the Muslim League, with Liaqat Ali Khan (first prime minister after independence) in the lead, who spoke in favour of an Islamic democracy. It has remained consistently the position of the modern-educated state élite and mainstream politicians, but has defied translation into a coherent constitutional and legal formula. The third was a candidly theocratic position upheld by the large body of the *ulama* (Muslim theologians) and *pirs* (religious mystagogues) who had been co-opted by the Muslim League into its election campaign for the 1945–46 elections (for detailed treatment of the three positions see Ahmed, 1987).

In the years immediately after independence the religious experts were eclipsed by the modernist élite, but gradually they gained political clout and influence and started pre-empting the ideological space. In a political sense, this could occur because of the opportunism and machinations of politicians, who began exploiting Islam for conducting negative politics. Governments in power would resort to some Islamic principle to denounce the opposition's demands for elections and regional autonomy as secessionist; centrist politicians out of power could equally invoke Islam to assail the government for alleged un-Islamic conduct. The third position was also strengthened because many Pakistanis were sincerely convinced that the classical Islamic political heritage was superior to the Western democratic model.

A strong slant towards theocratization of the polity occurred in 1974 when the controversial Ahmadiyya sect was declared non-Muslim. It was a Machiavellian move by Prime Minister Zulfikar Ali Bhutto to win support in Punjab from the *ulama* and other religious forces. Ironically it only emboldened the *ulama* to demand greater Islamization, and culminated in the fall of Bhutto in 1977. Under General Zia-ul-Haq (1977–88) the creation of a chaste Islamic nation and polity was extended to direct state patronage, and discriminatory legislation against women and non-Muslims was enacted.

Constitutional development

The Government of India Act of 1935, amended by the Indian Independence Act of 1947, continued to serve as the constitutional framework for distribution of powers between centre and provinces until 1956. It took nine years for the various political and regional factions present in the Pakistan Constituent Assembly to agree a constitution that satisfied the requirements of being Islamic, federal and a parliamentary democracy (Binder, 1961). No national elections were held under the 1956 constitution, however. On the other hand, governments changed quickly and political instability reigned supreme. In October 1958 senior bureaucrats and army bosses staged a bloodless coup. The commander-in-chief of the Pakistan Army, General Mohammad Ayub Khan, imposed martial law, abrogated the constitution and himself became the Chief Martial Law Administrator and President (Choudhary, 1969: 134–6).

Ayub Khan, however, sought democratic legitimacy for his rule and upon the recommendations of the Constitutional Commission, headed by Pakistan's chief justice, gave the country a new constitution in 1962. The main distinguishing feature of the 1962 constitution was that it prescribed a presidential type of government. The president was to be elected indirectly under a system of basic democracy consisting of an electoral college of 80,000 directly elected members. During Ayub's period some reformist and progressive Islamic laws in the sphere of marriage and divorce were adopted, but this process could not be extended to other domains of social life because of the strong opposition to such policy from the *ulama* and *pirs*. When Ayub fell from power in 1969 the 1962 constitution was also rejected. The 1973 constitution was adopted by an elected National Assembly. It reverted to the parliamentary system of government and elections were to be held directly on adult suffrage.

All three constitutions declared a commitment to the Islamization of the legal system of Pakistan and required the president of the republic to be a Muslim. The 1973 constitution went further and required the prime minister also to be a Muslim. On the other hand, a commitment to respect human rights within 'Islamic limits' was present in the three constitutions (Gankovsky and

Moskalenko, 1978). The 1973 constitution is currently applicable with several modifications introduced in it during the Zia period.

Strong centre

All three constitutions repose strategic administrative and financial powers in the central government. The 1973 constitution, however, reflected a greater recognition of the federal principle, but in practice it has been flouted by the all-powerful centre. Since December 1971 Pakistan consists of four provinces: Baluchistan, NWFP, Punjab and Sindh. In recent years, a demand to reorganize the administrative structure of Pakistan radically has come from several quarters. The proposal is to split the various provinces into several smaller ones. Thus far the centre has ignored such pleas.

Urdu as national language

Besides the Islamic factor, another symbol of Pakistani nationalism is the Urdu language, although it is the mother-tongue of only a tiny minority of migrants from northern and central India who settled in Pakistan after Partition. Historically Urdu was associated with upper-class Muslim culture of northern and central India and of Hyderabad Deccan. Elsewhere Urdu was cultivated by the educated sections of Muslim society. In Punjab, from where the British recruited most of their soldiers, it had been the medium of education in all government schools established during the colonial period (Chaudhry, 1977).

The declaration of Urdu as national language was opposed most strongly by the Bengalis and Sindhis, whose languages were in official use in their provinces before independence. In 1954 both Urdu and Bengali were recognized as national languages by the Pakistan Constituent Assembly. The declaration of Urdu as national language, however, was a symbolic gesture of the central élite. In practice English was retained as the official language. It continues to be used as the official language of the state and of the provinces.

The central élite and domination of the oligarchy

The Muslim League, which received power from the British at the time of independence, was a motley collection of Muslim politicians including the regional leaders, who shortly prior to Partition had come together with the sole objective of avoiding domination of Congress in a united India. The death of the founder of Pakistan, Quaid-i-Azam Mohamed Ali Jinnah, on 11 September 1948 weakened the Muslim League profoundly. Defections and splits rendered it ineffective and the civilian political process disintegrated. Consequently Pakistan has experienced long spells of military–bureaucratic rule during which the political process was either completely suspended or tolerated with various qualifications and restrictions. As a result elected governments, whenever they have existed, have held on to power at the discretion of what Hamza Alavi has described as the all-powerful 'military–bureaucratic oligarchy'. Mohammad Waseem (1989: 141) defines the Pakistani state as a 'bureaucratic polity' which has sought economic development and modernization through its involuted paternalism. Hassan Gardezi and Jamil Rashid (1983) describe Pakistan as a 'Praetorian State'. This is the subtitle of the book of which they are the editors, but strangely enough the concept of praetorianism is not discussed anywhere in the book. The various articles included in it, however, substantiate the general notion of praetorianism presented by Huntington (1968: 196–8) as a society without effective institutions and in which corruption is rampant among those who are entrusted with guarding it (that is, the military). Different implications follow from these various formulations, but what is commonly emphasized is that bureaucratic fiats, in the shape of ordinances and martial law edicts, have almost invariably superseded constitutional provisions and parliamentary practice and procedures.

However, some significant changes have occurred since independence in the ethnic composition and structure of the oligarchy. Initially, Urdu-speaking Muslims, called Mohajirs (refugees), were over-represented in the powerful civil service of Pakistan (Ali, 1992: 184). After 1951, when Pakistan's first prime minister, Liaqat Ali Khan, a Mohajir, was assassinated, Punjabi bureaucrats greatly strengthened their hold over the state while Mohajir influence began to dwindle. After General Ayub Khan came to power in 1958 the Punjabi–Pukhtun military–bureaucratic oligarchy acquired virtually veto powers, albeit in a de facto manner. Later when General Muhammad Zia-ul-Haq captured power in July 1977 the predominantly Punjabi army eclipsed the bureaucracy, which was constrained to play second fiddle.

It is important to remember that despite such changes in the ethnic composition of the state machinery a substantial Mohajir presence in the superior services continues, but at a diminishing rate. In the 1980s Punjab had 56 per cent representation which corresponded roughly to its population strength in the federal government secretariat. Rural Sindh had 3 per cent although its population share was 14 per cent. Urban Sindh, that is, Karachi and Hyderabad, had 25 per cent representation consisting mainly of Mohajirs and Punjabis domiciled in urban Sindh, whereas the population of these two cities was only 10 per cent of the total population of Pakistan (Kardar, 1992: 319).

As regards the army, it is estimated that 85 per cent is of Punjabi origin (Ali, 1992: 185). This figure was frequently mentioned by Sindhi intellectuals whom the author met in 1990. It is disputed by Hanif Ramay and Fakhar Zaman (both interviewed in 1990), two leading Punjabi politicians and intellectuals, who assert that the Pukhtun ratio of the army exceeds 30 per cent. Khalid bin Sayeed (1980: 71) breaks down the composition of the army in the 1960s as 65 per cent Punjabi and 35 per cent Pukhtun. However, in another place in the same book he asserts that Pukhtun representation in the armed forces by the late 1970s was between 15 and 20 per cent (Sayeed, 1980: 121). The exact ethnic composition of the military remains a secret.

It is important to note that Sindhis and Baluchs have from the beginning been nearly absent in the army and still remain grossly under-represented. According to a senior Pakistani bureaucrat, in the year 1990 some 65,528 persons from Sindh applied for non-commissioned posts in the army. Of these 54,857 qualified, of whom 70 per cent were Urdu-speaking and 30 per cent were Sindhi-speaking. As regards commissioned posts, 294 applied from Sindh and Baluchistan. Of these only 14 qualified, of whom nine were Urdu-speaking and five were either Sindhi or Baluchi–Brauhi speakers.

The political process

Because of long spells of dictatorship the system of political parties has not strongly established itself in Pakistan. The Muslim League disintegrated quickly after independence. Its various fractions and rumps, however, have been revived from time to time. It was the Pakistan People's Party (PPP) founded in 1967 by Zulfikar Ali Bhutto that attained the character of an all-Pakistan party (that is, after 1971; before that it was the major party in West Pakistan). Currently Pakistan is dominated in the centre by two major political groupings, the PPP led by Benazir Bhutto and a revived Muslim League led by Nawaz Sharif.

The political opposition competing for power with the oligarchy are: (a) all-Pakistan moderate Muslim parties which are sometimes in power and other times out of it; (b) religious parties with their sectarian and subsectarian affiliations; (c) regional nationalist and ethnic parties; and (d) Marxist parties and groups which are rather marginal in Pakistani politics. Both regional and sectarian types of separatism have been evolving in Pakistan as the state centre came increasingly to be dominated by Punjabi–Pukhtun nationalities and Sunni theological overtones during the period of General Muhammad Zia-ul-Haq (1977–88).

Class and social bases of authoritarian rule

The powerful landed classes were the main beneficiary in the creation of Pakistan and subsequently furnished a solid base for conservative and reactionary politics. Moreover, Pakistan lacked an industrial base at the time of independence. Its establishment was undertaken largely by migrant Muslim entrepreneurs belonging to the ethnic minorities of Sunni Memons, Shia Ismailis and Bohras as well as the

Punjabi caste of Sunni Chinioti sheikhs — groups with experience in commerce and industrial production acquired in the recent colonial period. This nascent bourgeoisie had little interest in democracy. Rather it relied on the authoritarian state to expand and consolidate its position. As regards the middle class, it was not only small but also culturally biased in favour of some sort of an Islamic polity. The tiny working class, consisting mainly of railway and textile workers and the peasantry, were lacking influence and effective organization. Additionally, the powerful body of *ulama* and *pirs* whom the Muslim League had mobilized for popularizing the Pakistan idea lent a theocratic dimension to authoritarianism. Thus the objective material and intellectual basis for democracy was rather lean. Subsequent socio-economic development and change did not suffice to transform this socio-cultural structure in a modernist or democratic direction.

The drift towards a theocratic type of Islamic society was consummated during the regime of General Zia-ul-Haq. In particular the educational system was subjected to severe revision and distortion. Critical inquiry in historical and social science research was discouraged and pseudo-science and mythology were bestowed respectability (Hoodbhoy, 1985: 190–3; Waseem, 1989: 399–400). There was also a deliberate attempt to divest Pakistani identity of its cultural and historical roots in the Indic civilization and instead link it to Middle Eastern Islamic tradition (Hoodbhoy and Nayyar, 1985: 174–6).

The confessional state, deviant sects, religious minorities and women

Because Pakistan was declared explicitly and categorically a confessional state during the period of General Zia, the creation of an exemplary Islamic polity has inevitably required the Islamization of state and society. Such a task has not been unproblematic, since Pakistan comprises several Muslim sects and subsects and religious minorities which are resistant to such regimentation. At the present historical phase tension between various Sunni subsects is not of much political significance although it tends to erupt into violent clashes every now and then.

The Sunni–Shia rift

The Shias of India were somewhat wary of the idea of Pakistan as it portended domination by the Sunni majority. However, Mohamed Ali Jinnah and many other leading members of the Muslim League were Shias. They were able to placate Shia fears by promises of basing Pakistan on a non-sectarian Islam.

In contemporary Pakistan, Shias are dispersed in society at all levels and in all regions. Among big landowners, industrialists, bankers and the civil and military apparatuses Shias are prominently represented. Recruitment from some Shia localities in Punjab is quite substantial in the army (interview, Naqi, 1990). Moreover, at the élite level there is considerable assimilation among Sunnis and Shias. On the mass level Shia–Sunni theological differences have always tended to rupture into ugly brawls and violence. This problem has worsened in recent years.

After General Zia-ul-Haq came to power in 1977 Pakistan acquired clearly fundamentalist Sunni overtones, reflecting the influence of the teachings of Maulana Abul Ala Maududi (d. 1979), Pakistan's well-known Islamic ideologue. On the other hand, the Shia of Pakistan were emboldened by the coming to power of Khomeini in neighbouring Iran in early 1979. Thus assertive and at times aggressive Shia behaviour in Pakistan could be noted. A growing tendency among many *pirs* who claimed descent from Muhammad to patronize the cult of Ali and adopt other Shiaite cultural symbols complicated the sectarian scene. A Shia political party, the Tahrik Nifas-e-Jafaria, was founded in 1979. The first clash between the state and the Shias took place when the latter refused to pay to the state the alms tax, *zakat*, and the land tax, *ushr*, which Zia had introduced in 1980. As a Sunni-oriented government it did not qualify to receive Islamic levies from Shias, who argued that they paid these taxes to their own clergy. The government initially dismissed Shia protests, but when they led to demonstrations and agitation the government agreed to exempt Shias from offical collection of *zakat* and *ushr* (Qureshi, 1989: 126–33).

The power politics of the Gulf region also impinged upon the sectarian tension in Pakistan. Shia Iran and its Sunni Arab rivals have been involved since several decades in a power struggle to establish hegemony in the Gulf region. The Iranian Revolution added an ideological dimension to the power game. Most notably it meant a fierce competition between Iran and Saudi Arabia to try to lead the Muslim world. However, Iran and Saudi Arabia — fundamentalist and very rich — nevertheless represent two opposite and mutually hostile types of doctrines, which are peripheral to mainstream Sunni Islam. Shiaism is heterodox, while Wahabism is an extremist type of Sunnism which is vehemently critical of the cult of saints prevalent among traditional Sunni societies.

At any rate, with more than a million Pakistanis working in the Gulf region and the Pakistani armed forces involved in the defence and security arrangements of Saudi Arabia and several other minor Arab emirates, both Iran and Saudi Arabia have considered it important to cultivate support in Pakistan. The Iraqi regime, notwithstanding its secular pretensions, has also sought to cultivate a lobby among Sunni *ulama*. In the 1980s, on the one hand, the Iranian–Saudi ideological and power competition, and, on the other hand, the Iranian–Iraqi war intensified the efforts of these actors to seek greater support in Pakistani society. Consequently in the late 1980s large sums of money, leaflets, books, audio and video cassette-tapes poured into Pakistan, projecting one or other point of view. Such propaganda offensives have been backed by the inflow of weapons of a quite sophisticated nature. The result has been the formation of militias bearing such belligerent names as the Sipah-i-Sahaba (the militia devoted to the Companions of the Prophet, a Sunni outfit) and the Sipah-i-ahl al-bayt (the militia devoted to the Family of the Prophet, a Shia outfit). These and several other such outfits indulge frequently in terrorist attacks against one another. Pakistan is currently serving as the battleground of Middle Eastern proxy wars, albeit so far on a small scale (Khan, 1994: 27–37).

However, as Shias are not concentrated in large numbers in any part of Pakistan, there is no likelihood of the emergence of a strong secessionist movement among them. The Shia political party, the Tahrik Nifas-e-Jafaria, has not been able to make any impression in the elections. Some Sunni *ulama* have been demanding that Pakistan should constitutionally be declared a Sunni state. Others have even demanded that the various categories of Shias should be declared non-Muslims. Similarly there are demands to declare the Zikris of Baluchistan non-Muslims. Such extremist demands, however, do not command much attention at present from the state.

The Ahmadiyya

The Ahmadiyya sect owes its origins to the preachings of Mirza Ghulam Ahmad (1835–1908), who was born at Qadian in the Punjab in a Sunni landowning family. He began his religious career as a keen Sunni debater who combated both Christian missionaries and Hindu reformers with clever doctrinal arguments which won him acclaim from other Muslims (Kennedy, 1989: 71–101). However, soon Mirza staked a claim to being a prophet and made heterodox statements on doctrine. Moreover, he took political positions which were openly pro–British and thus acquired the reputation among the orthodox *ulama* of an impostor and a British stooge.

The Ahmadiyya mission was formally declared in 1901, and at the request of Mirza himself was shown as a separate sect in the Census records (*Report of Court of Inquiry*, 1954: 10). During the colonial period the Ahmadis received government protection and were recruited in the civil administration and army. The conversions to the Ahmadiyya faith occurred mostly in Punjab. Their influence elsewhere in South Asia remained marginal. The Ahmadiyya, like the Shia, had been co-opted by the Muslim League in the 1940s campaign for Pakistan. According to Wali Khan (1987: 29–30), it was Sir Zafrulla Khan, a leading loyalist Ahmadi, who, on the instructions of the viceroy, Lord Linlithgow, prepared the memorandum on the concept of two dominion states — India and Pakistan — in the second week of March 1940 and communicated it to the Muslim

League. It based its 23 March 1940 Lahore Resolution on lines suggested in the memorandum.

In any case, Sir Zafrulla was made Pakistan's first foreign minister by Jinnah. During the early post-independence period a disproportionately large number of Ahmadis were holding senior positions in the civil service and armed forces. The head of the community, Mirza Bashir-ud-din, and some other senior Ahmadis made statements to the effect that Ahmadi influence on the state would be employed to spread their faith in Pakistan, particularly in Baluchistan (*Report of Court of Inquiry*, 1954: 199–200). Such utterances provoked a reaction among the *ulama* of Punjab, among whom the anti-Ahmadiyya sentiment was strongly entrenched. Things came to a head in 1953 when violent agitation broke out in Punjab against the Ahmadis. Many Ahmadis were killed and looting of their property was widespread. There was a strong indication of the complicity of the Muslim-League-led Punjab government in the riots (*Report of the Court of Inquiry*, 1954: 261–4). As the agitation grew out of control and loss of life and property spread outside Punjab the central government called in the army and imposed martial law. The agitation was crushed with great force. Subsequently several leading *ulama* were tried in martial law courts: some were found guilty and harsh penalties including the death sentence were passed on some of their leaders. However, later a general reprieve was announced and they were released from prison.

The Ahmadiyya issue receded into the background for some years, although it never ceased to be discussed and debated among the Islamic groups. The issue was brought back to life in 1974 when the National Assembly of Pakistan, dominated by the Pakistan People's Party of Zulfikar Bhutto, passed a law declaring Ahmadis non-Muslims. In 1984 the Zia regime imposed further restrictions on the Ahmadis, who were forbidden to use Islamic nomenclature in their religious and social life. Violent attacks against Ahmadis revived and many Ahmadis were injured or killed. Some recanted their faith, others resorted to dissimulation while some, including their present spiritual leader, fled to the West. The Ahmadiyya are today an officially persecuted community in Pakistan.

Christians

Conversions to Christianity took place in the areas which comprise present-day Pakistan largely after the British had annexed Punjab and Sindh in the 1840s. Most conversions took place from among the untouchable Hindu castes, although some élite families also embraced it. When Partition occurred, the Christians who belonged to the Pakistani areas accepted the new state as their homeland. In fact some of their local leaders in Punjab co-operated with the Muslim League during the campaign for Pakistan. That their religious rights would be threatened in

Pakistan was not clearly anticipated by them, as Jinnah and other modernist Muslim League leaders had in their public utterances dissociated themselves from traditional theocracy (Babar, 1993: 85).

In independent Pakistan, Christians, as a poor and low-status group, continued to work in menial professions. Some acquired a modern education through the efforts of the missions and were employed as teachers, nurses and other staff in schools and hospitals. Ironically, upper middle-class Muslim families sent their children to the prestigious English-medium schools and colleges run by Europeans, but indigenous Christians were treated with routine contempt by the larger society. However, until Zulfikar Ali Bhutto came to power, the Christian community had not been affected adversely by specific state policy. The policy of nationalization of important sectors of the economy begun by Bhutto also included the taking over of some of the missionary-owned educational institutions in Punjab. Such policy was by no means inspired by anti-Christian sentiments. Rather it fitted into the radical populism of the Bhutto regime.

However, as these schools and colleges were practically the only places where Christians could find employment, they opposed such nationalization. Demonstrations and protest marches were organized against the takeovers. The protesters were beaten up and fired upon by police and some casualties occurred. Staff were forcibly evicted from their homes and the property owned by the missions was confiscated. Thereafter the Christians were not heard of again in mainstream politics until General Zia-ul-Haq embarked upon his Islamization policy, and in 1985 the system of separate electorates was reintroduced in Pakistan (it had been inherited from the colonial period and was abolished formally in 1956 when the first constitution came into force). General Zia, in compliance with traditional Islamic law, wanted to separate the primary Muslim-Pakistani nation (that is a nation entitled to equal rights) from the non-Muslims. This reform was welcomed by some Christian leaders and the Catholic Church as it assured the minorities representation while in the general electorates they tended to be ignored. However, the more radical sections of the Catholic and Protestant communities expressed their opposition to it, alleging that separate electorates excluded them from the Pakistani nation and gave constitutional sanction for discrimination and segregation (Khan, 1993: 99–102).

The apprehensions of the radicals seem to have been borne out by subsequent experience. In the late 1980s several acts of violence were carried out by fanatical sections of Muslim society against Christians. At least one murder and many cases of burning of churches and Christian property were reported in the early 1990s (*Saavan*, October 1992, January 1993). Under the Blasphemy Ordinance of 1986 a Christian, Gul Masih, was sentenced to death by a Pakistani lower court in October 1992 for allegedly having made abusive remarks about Prophet Muhammad (*'Blasphemy' Episode*, 1992).

Hindus

In Sindh some half a million Hindus remained after Partition. Very few Hindus were to be found elsewhere in West Pakistan. After the riots in the earliest years after independence Sindhi Hindus preferred to lie low and avoid political attention as their religious links with India placed them in a vulnerable position in Pakistan. Communal attacks against Hindus began to occur in the mid-1980s as the overall ethnic crisis in Sindh deteriorated. Following the destruction of the Babri mosque at Ayodhya and the brutal killings of Muslims which accompanied it, a fierce reaction took place in Pakistan. Destruction of property and temples took place all over Pakistan, and Hindus were killed and injured in hundreds, mainly in Sindh but also in Baluchistan (several reports in *Herald*, January 1993).

Although the government officially urged the people to exercise restraint, some ministers were responsible for whipping up mass hysteria through crass demagogy and other such antics. Mobs of angry protesters marched on Hindu temples and destroyed them. Ironically, most temples in Punjab were no longer in use as places of worship simply because there were no Hindus around to use them. Poor, homeless Muslim refugee families had been residing in some of them from 1947. The net result of the mob fury was that these people were rendered homeless.

Other minorities

As regards the minor religious minorities such as the Parsees, Sikhs and Buddhists, they are also affected adversely by the increasing theocratization of Pakistan. In the Gilgit and Chitral regions are to be found Ithna Ashari Shias, Ismaili Shias and Sunnis. Here the competition between Iran, the Ismaili mission with its spiritual leader, Prince Agha Khan (based in Europe), and the Zia government backed by the Saudis, to increase their membership and influence led to several clashes in the 1980s. The tiny community of some 4000 of the Kalash Kafirs of the Chitral Valley have in particular been subjected to aggressive conversion onslaughts during the Zia regime (Ahmed, A.S., 1988: 23–8). Some *ulama* demand that all non-Muslims should be declared Dhimmis (protected minorities) and made to pay the Islamic poll tax, *jizya*. This drastic demand has not received serious attention from the state thus far.

Women

Very few Muslim women had attended school or college before independence. The various governments that came to power in Pakistan before the Zia regime had gradually expanded educational facilities for women. Consequently some were working as doctors, nurses, teachers and in various other capacities. Some improvement in the marriage status had also occurred after the promulgation of the Muslim Family Law Ordinance of 1961.

However, under General Zia efforts were made to reverse this trend. Although neither the Muslim Family Law Ordinance of 1961 was withdrawn nor disenfranchisement of women took place, several other hostile measures were undertaken. Thus in 1984 a new Law of Evidence was adopted which reduced the worth of the evidence of a female witness to half the worth of a male witness in a court of law (Ahmed, 1987: 221). A campaign to eliminate obscenity and pornography was also announced. It took however the form of a campaign against general emancipation and equal rights of women. Leading Muslim theologians hostile to female emancipation were brought on the national television to justify various restrictions on women (Khawar and Shaheed, 1987: 77–96).

The Pakistani state and separatism of linguistic nationalities

Pakistan's historical and cultural existence as an entity dates only from 1947. Muslim unity during the struggle for Pakistan was based on a negative approach to power sharing with Congress. In the post-independence period this unity was severely strained when the question arose about power sharing among the various linguistic units of Pakistan. The installation of authoritarian rule at the centre brought forth separatist challenges which aimed beyond autonomy, at secession from the state.

Punjabi centrism

Punjab constituted more than 57 per cent of the total population of Pakistan in 1981. Punjabis possessed a historical head start in terms of a preponderant representation in the state at all levels of authority. Culturally, Urdu and Muslim nationalism, the two main symbols of Pakistani nationhood, were strongly entrenched among the Punjabi élite and intelligentsia from before Partition. The post-independence development and modernization has benefited Punjab immensely. Punjabi industrialists figured prominently among the top 22 industrial houses of Pakistan in the mid-1960s. Some of them advanced in the ranking, and by the 1980s the control of the 'prestigious Federation of Pakistan Chamber of Commerce and Industry, which is based at Karachi, passed into Punjabi hands, the crowing symbol of the new Punjabi domination' (Alavi, 1990: 29). Thus in the 1980s 'most of the businesses have been taken away from the Memon/Ismaili/Gujrati community and are today in the Chiniotis and other Punjabis in the city' (Ali, 1992: 185).

The modernization of agriculture under the Green Revolution strategy, which began in the early 1960s in West Punjab, brought handsome profits to the land-lords and the upper crust of the peasantry. Sections of the uprooted poor peasan-try and other subordinate classes could, however, find openings elsewhere, first during industrial expansion in Punjab and Karachi; later, from the mid-1970s onwards and into the 1980s, many emigrated to the Gulf region where work was available in plenty. Several thousands headed towards Europe and North America. In 1984 Pakistan's legally registered foreign workers were 1.3 million (the real number was definitely much higher because many were living abroad illegally or were not entered into the records). Of these 85 per cent were Punjabis and Pukhtuns, Punjabis forming the overwhelming majority. The same year US$2.85 billion were remitted by these workers. It constitutes the equivalent of 82 per cent of Pakistan's total export earnings or some 10 per cent of the gross national product (Kennedy, 1985: 42). More strategically, the modernization and expansion of the Pakistan armed forces has also benefited Punjab and NWFP. In 1974 there were 324,000 personnel in the armed services. By 1982 the number stood at 478,000. The defence budget in 1974 was US$713 million. By 1981 it had risen to US$1,857 (Jones, 1985: 73). Such expenditure brought increasing benefits to the predominantly Punjabi and Pukhtun personnel in the armed forces.

Notwithstanding Punjab's overall gains in development, the typical problems of dissolution of subsistence agriculture and share-cropping, and levels of educational production exceeding employment opportunities, did not leave Punjab unscarred. Not all could find employment elsewhere. Large numbers joined the army of the unemployed. Consequently, both during the radical movement unleashed by Zulfikar Ali Bhutto in the late 1960s and during the 1980s anti-Zia agitations, the poor and unemployed young people in Punjab played an active role.

Punjab and the Saraiki issue

The Saraiki-speaking people (14.9 per cent) in Punjab are located mainly between southern Punjab and northern Sindh, but one Saraiki-speaking area, Dera Ismail Khan, belongs to NWFP. It touches the borders of Baluchistan. A large number of Punjabi-speaking Muslim refugees from East Punjab were settled in the Saraiki-speaking belt, especially in the towns. On the other hand, Saraiki-speaking tribes have historically been moving into Sindh and currently form a majority of the population in northern Sindh, where many people tend to be bilingual. In recent years the Saraiki élite and intelligentsia (educated in the Urdu medium like the rest of Punjab) have been claiming the status of a nationality on the basis of their language. C. Shackle (1976: 1–9) points out several varieties of Saraiki, some of which are close to Punjabi while others are closer to Sindhi and other languages of the adjacent regions. Orthodox Saraiki Marxist-nationalists maintain that Saraiki is not a dialect of Punjabi but a separate tongue altogether, and that on such a basis the Saraiki-speaking people constitute a separate nationality (Jafery, 1986: 57–70). Further, they emphasize their indigenous roots and assert that they have not been part of traditional Punjab or Sindh. Their main demand is the creation of a separate Saraiki province. This demand has been rejected by the centre.

When the author took up this question in 1990 with some Punjabi intellectuals and academics the opinion was divided on whether Saraiki was merely a dialect of Punjabi or a separate language altogether. The president of the Punjab PPP, Fakhar Zaman, thought that Saraiki was one among many other dialects of Punjabi. Hanif Ramay, a former PPP chief minister of Punjab, had a similar standpoint. Both also thought that it was the feudal landowners of the Saraiki belt who were behind the separatist movement. Professor Hamid Hasan Kizilbash, a political scientist, thought, however, that the creation of a separate Saraiki province would weaken the hold of the landowners in the longer run as the modernization processes will be hastened with the creation of a new administrative structure. The former student and now labour leader Rao Tariq Latif, who had lived in the Saraiki areas, was of the view that Saraiki was a separate and distinct language. Thus far the Saraiki national question remains of low intensity, mainly debated among intellectuals and political activists. Saraiki leaders have opposed bitterly suggestions made by some politicians about Biharis from Bangladesh being settled among them. It remains to be seen what policy the centre will adopt on the emerging Saraiki issue.

Pukhtun separatism

The NWFP has 15.1 per cent of the total population, including that of the Federally Administered Tribal Areas (FATA). Ethnic Pukhtuns constitute the predominant group in NWFP. Pukhtuns are to be found in large numbers across the border in Afghanistan, where they constitute the majority ethnic group. In the elections held in NWFP in 1946 the Frontier Congress won 30 seats, including 19 Muslim seats while the Muslim League secured only 17. Yet the province was allotted to Pakistan after a referendum which allowed only two options: the province could either join India or Pakistan. The Frontier Congress wanted a third option, namely the creation of an independent state of Pukhtunistan. This demand was overruled by the British. The Frontier Congress therefore boycotted the referendum. Thus out of a total electorate of 572,798 only 292,118 cast their votes. Votes cast for Pakistan were 289,244 and for India 2874. This meant that 50.5 per cent of the electorate voted for Pakistan (Jansson, 1981: 222). It is important to remember that although the NWFP was overwhelmingly Muslim and consisted mainly of ethnic Pukhtuns — 91.1 per cent according to the Census of India of 1941 — there were two major linguistic divisions among them. A majority spoke

Pukhto or Pushto and were related to tribes and clans across the border in Afghanistan, and a significant minority spoke Hindko or Saraiki — languages which are closer to Punjabi. In two of NWFP's six districts, Hazara and DI Khan, Hindko and Saraiki were the major languages and the support for the Muslim League was overwhelming.

The issue of Pukhtunistan figured prominently in Pakistani politics in the 1950s. The Red Shirts leader Abdul Ghaffar Khan and some of his close associates were kept in detention. The Pukhtunistan issue received diplomatic support from Afghanistan and some sympathy from India. However, the economic and political opportunities which opened for the Pukhtuns in Pakistan in the 1960s weaned them away from separatism. Under the so-called One-Unit scheme the different West Pakistani provinces and territories were amalgamated into a single province which was named as the Province of West Pakistan. It opened opportunities for a free flow of labour in all directions, and Pukhtuns from the poverty-stricken regions of NWFP began to come in large numbers to the industrial city of Karachi. This trend continued to grow over the years. Moreover, there was a sizeable Pukhtun presence in the bureaucracy and army at all levels, including top policy-making positions. The Pukhtuns moved into industrial production during the 1960s and by the 1970s at least three Pukhtun industrial houses were to be found among the top 30 (Sayeed, 1980: 121–2).

More importantly, Pukhtun politicians and parties were integrated into mainstream politics during the 1970 general elections. This trend has continued, and currently the Pukhtun parties are fully integrated into Pakistani politics. Consequently the Pukhtunistan issue has quietly slipped into oblivion. The power conflict going on currently in Afghanistan between the Tajik president, Rabbani, and the Pukhtun prime minister, Gulbadin Hikmatyar, has attracted the support of the Pukhtuns in Pakistan for the latter. This may have a destabilizing impact on the northern Pakistani province.

Baluch separatism

Baluchistan is the biggest province in terms of area. It is, however, also the most sparsely populated, constituting only 5.1 per cent of the total Pakistani population. Baluchistan consists of three major ethnic groups: Baluch, Brauhi and Pukhtuns. A sizeable number of Punjabis and Mohajirs have also been settled in the capital, Quetta, for more than half a century. The Baluch and Brauhi have traditionally been considered one political group — Baluch — although they speak very different languages: Baluchi is Indo-Iranian and Brauhi a Dravidian language. Baluchi tribes also live in southern Iran and some nomadic Baluch are found in Afghanistan.

British Baluchistan acceded to Pakistan in 1947 through the decision of the Shahi Jirga, a consultative assembly whose members were nominated by the government. The ruler of Kalat State, the Khan of Kalat, however, declared himself independent on 15 August 1947. On 1 April 1948 the Pakistan army was sent into Kalat. Thereupon the Khan signed the accession document. His younger brother, Prince Abdul Karim, however, declared a revolt against Pakistan. Some skirmishes took place but finally the rebels were defeated (Harrison, 1981: 22–3). The second round of Baluchi confrontation with Pakistan took place during the early years of the Ayub regime (1958–69). Although it consisted mainly of skirmishes between the Pakistan army and Baluch guerrillas, over the allotment of agricultural land to army officers in the Pat Feeder area, the problem was a more fundamental one of resisting modernization promoted by the state as it threatened the iron hold of the tribal chiefs, called *sardars*, over their tribes. Thus the building of roads and opening of schools by the government were condemned as ways and means of establishing Punjabi control over Baluchistan (Ahmad, 1975: 31)

The third confrontation lasted four years (1973–77) and involved at its height more than 80,000 Pakistani troops and at least 35,000 Baluch guerillas. It erupted when the elected government of Baluchistan was dismissed by Zulfikar Ali Bhutto on 12 February 1973 under the pretext that it had exceeded its constitutional authority and that it had been involved in a conspiracy to begin an armed rebellion. Bhutto obtained US$200 million in emergency military and financial aid from Iran to crush the rebels (Harrison, 1981: 36). Iran even dispatched 30 Huey Cobra helicopters to assist the Pakistani military. On the other hand Baluch fighters found sanctuary in Afghanistan from where they launched surprise attacks on the army. According to one estimate some 5300 Baluch were killed or wounded. The army casualties were 3300 (Khan 1983: 71). In July 1977, when General Zia captured power, the imprisoned Baluchi leaders, Ghaus Baksh Bizenjo, Ataullah Mengal and Khair Bakhsh Marri, were freed. In 1978 6000 more Baluch prisoners were set free and a general amnesty for those who had fled to Afghanistan was announced. The Baluch insurgence thereafter petered out. Currently ethnic tension between the Baluchi–Brauhi majority and the 25.7 per cent Pukhtun minority is emerging in Baluchistan.

Sindh

According to the 1981 Census, Sindh was the second biggest province of Pakistan in terms of its population of 19,029,000. Sindhi speakers made up 52 per cent, Urdu speakers, known as Mohajirs, who migrated to Pakistan from India, constituted 22.64 per cent, Punjabis 7.69 per cent, Pukhtuns 3.06 per cent and Baluchs 4.51 per cent. Other languages spoken were Saraiki, 2.29 per cent, Brauhi, 1.08

per cent, and several other minor languages such as Khuchi, Gujrati and Memoni. Well over a million Hindus were living in Sindh. Elsewhere in Pakistan Hindus had almost ceased to exist.

Thus Sindh is the most linguistically, religiously and ethnically diverse province of Pakistan. More importantly, Pakistan's main industrial city, Karachi, is also the only major seaport of the country. Its importance for the Pakistani economy and security is therefore immense.

Cultural and political heritage of Sindh

The first Muslim armed incursion into India took place during the Umayyad period (660–750). An Arab army landed in 712 on the western coast of India near present-day Karachi with the intention of chastising the Hindu ruler of Sindh, Raja Dahir, who had allegedly been harassing Arab merchant vessels returning with their cargoes from Sri Lanka and beyond in the East. Dahir was defeated and many of his subjects embraced Islam. Sindh and southern Punjab were conquered by the Arabs and remained attached to the caliphate based in Damascus and later Baghdad. The lapse of Arab rule in the eleventh century was followed by two Sindhi dynasties, Soomro and Sama, who together ruled for some 500 years. These were followed by the central Asian Arghuns and Tarkhans. The Mughul Emperor Akbar tried to impose a more centralized control over Sindh but the native clans and tribes successfully resisted such incursion. Finally the separate status of Sindh was recognized by the Mughuls, and a native Kalhoro dynasty came to power (Ahmed, 1992: 158–9). It was succeeded by the Talpurs, a Baluch tribe settled in Sindh. The Talpurs were defeated by the British in 1843.

Although the majority of Sindhis became Muslims, both through conquest and through the work of Muslim sufis, more than 29 per cent remained Hindus. Sindhi Hindus in large numbers adhered to the Nanakpanthi sect, which was profoundly influenced by the reformatory ideas of the founder of the Sikh movement in Punjab, Guru Nanak (1469–1539). Until the beginning of the twentieth century, Muslim–Hindu interaction was relatively peaceful in Sindh. Pre-colonial Sindh was essentially a tribal society with a predominantly agricultural and pastoral economy. The few large towns such as Hyderabad and Shikarpur served as commercial centres. The Hindu merchant caste of Bhai-bands constituted the urban middle class of wealthy merchants. Government functionaries at the middle and lower levels came mainly from the Hindu caste of Amils. On the other hand, political and military power rested essentially with the Muslim tribal chiefs and landowners, and Sindh was ruled despotically; there was no question of general democratic rights and freedoms (Khuhro, 1981: 170). From the eighteenth century onwards Sindh came under increasing pressure from Afghanistan and Iran. In the early nineteenth century the Sikh kingdom of Punjab had made inroads into Sindh. At the time of British conquest Sindh was divided into the three princely states of Hyderabad, Khairpur and Mirpur, ruled by Talpur chiefs.

Sindh under the British

The British conquered Sindh in 1843. This altered Sindh's socio-economic structure decisively, shattering its relative isolation from the rest of India. Between 1843 and 1847 the British ruled Sindh as a single province. In 1847 it was amalgamated into the Bombay Presidency. However, Sindh remained dominated by big Muslim landowners known as Waderas. Even by South Asian standards Sindhi Waderas were notorious for leading a life of indulgence and waste on a pattern reminiscent of the decadent stages of Western feudalism. The peasant, known as Hari, was at the complete mercy of the Wadera. Bonded labour was widely prevalent, tying large sections of the dependent peasantry and artisan castes to tyrannical Waderas (Gankovsky and Gordon-Polonskaya, 1972: 141). Sindhi nationalist historians point out the heroic but abortive struggle in the 1940s of the Hurs, the followers of Pir Sibghatullah, against the British. They conducted a guerrilla war against the British, apparently out of a sense of devotion to their *pir* who had prophesied that he would become the new ruler of Sindh (Ahmed, 1992: 161). Notwithstanding such exceptional challenges to British power, landowners generally sided with the colonial authorities.

Modern change crept rather slowly into Sindhi society. The Hindu middle class was the first to take to modern education. Hindu educationists and philanthropists, however, did not restrict admittance to their schools only to Hindus. Many Sindhi Muslims also studied in these institutions. The main beneficiaries of the modern school system, however, were the lower middle-class Hindus. On the other hand, Muslim landowners took no interest in public education. Rather they actively opposed the opening of schools in their localities (Mehkri, 1987: 57–63).

The movement for separation of Sindh from Bombay

It is interesting that the first public opposition to Sindh's union with Bombay was ventilated by a prominent Sindhi Hindu, Harchandrai Vishindas, at the 1913 annual secession of the All-India National Congress at Karachi. Again in 1917 and 1918 the idea of separation was aired by prominent Sindhis, both Hindus and Muslims. The landowning class, however, remained ambivalent on the question of separation from Bombay (Jones, 1977: 34). In those early years both Congress and Muslim League favoured the idea of separation.

However, the emerging consensus in favour of separation turned awry as economic grievances and religious disputes cropped up between Muslims and Hindus. In 1927 communal riots broke out in Larkana in northern Sindh over the alleged abduction and forced conversion of Muslim women and children by Hindus. This incident received wide publicity. Among Muslims a feeling developed that the colonial authorities sided with the Hindus during the riots. The Larkana riots shattered the hitherto successful Muslim—Hindu joint front in favour of Sindh's separation from Bombay (Jones, 1977: 37—40). Thereafter, the Muslims began to press for separation while the Hindus preferred union with Bombay. Congress changed course and began to support the Hindus while the Muslim League remained steadfast in its support for separation of Sindh from Bombay. In 1936 Sindh was separated from Bombay and made a proper province.

The support for the Pakistan demand in Sindh

The penetration of Sindhi agriculture by capitalist practices under British patronage had brought about the indebtedness of Muslim peasants and small cultivators to Hindu moneylenders. According to one estimate, by 1936 only 13 per cent of Sindhi Muslim agriculturalists were free from a debt obligation to the moneylender (Ahmed, P.A., 1988: 74). Consequently the problem of Muslim indebtedness began to figure prominently in Muslim circles. Many prominent Muslims such as Ayub Khuhro, Abdul Majid Sindhi, Abdullah Haroon, Hatim Alavi and others joined the Muslim League, which had previously had no significant following in the province. In 1938 a branch of the Muslim League was formally established in the province. The future leader of Sindhi separatism in Pakistan, G.M. Sayed, joined the Muslim League in 1938. Before that he had been a prominent member of Congress.

The Sindh Muslim League was the first in India to adopt a resolution in October 1938 demanding the right of self-determination for the Muslim majority provinces and their right to establish a federation of autonomous states (Allana, 1977: 193—4). Thereafter a special committee was established under the leadership of G.M. Sayed, which toured Sindh propagating the Pakistan scheme. Many peasants and lower middle-class Muslims were attracted to the idea of Pakistan, as it was seen as a means of getting rid of the Hindu moneylenders.

Sindh joins Pakistan and the expulsion of non-Muslims

According to the 1941 Sindh Census, the total population of the Sindh province (minus Khairpur State) was 4,535,008. There were 3,208,325 Muslims, who constituted 70.7 per cent of the total population. Hindus and the tiny Sikh groups together were 1,326,683 and thus constituted 29.3 per cent of the total population. The moneylending and landowning Hindu classes were only a small section of the Sindhi Hindu community. Most worked as petty shopkeepers or as labourers and tenant-cultivators of Muslim landlords (Khosla, 1989: 238). In March 1943 the

Sindh Assembly passed a resolution demanding the creation of Pakistan. In the 1946 elections the Muslim League won all the 35 seats reserved for Muslims in Sindh. On 26 June 1946 the Sindh Assembly was the first to decide to join the Pakistan Constituent Assembly. The whole of Sindh province was allotted to Pakistan under the Independence Act of 1947.

As communal riots broke out, some 1 million non-Muslim Sindhis fled to India. The communal riots in Sindh, however, were not so bloody and gruesome as in neighbouring Punjab, and some 500,000 Hindus, predominantly from scheduled castes, stayed behind. The general atmosphere of intolerance in Sindh at that time against Hindus and Sikhs can be gauged from two examples (Khosla, 1989: 236).

> Let there be in Pakistan, the separate centre of Islam,
> We shall not in Pakistan have to look at faces of non-Muslims.
> The abode of the Muslim Nation will brighten up only,
> When in Pakistan there remain no idolatrous thorns.
> They [Hindus] whose function is to be slaves have no right to participate in Government,
> Nowhere have they succeeded in governing.
> > Song sung at the Muslim League Conference at Sultankot (Sindh)

> Let the Hindus of Sindh leave Sindh and go elsewhere. Let them go while the going is good and possible, else I warn them that a time is fast coming when in their flight from Sindh, they may not be able to get a horse or an ass or a gari [car] or any other means of transport.
> > Mohammad Ayub Khuhro

Sindh in Pakistani politics

Pakistan chose Karachi as its interim capital. Suddenly it was transformed from a small cosmopolitan second harbour to Bombay to the centre of power of a new state. The change was indeed dramatic. For example, in 1941 the total population of Karachi was only 358,492. Muslims constituted 42.5 per cent and non-Muslims 57.5 per cent of its population. The city centre population consisted largely of Sindhi Hindus, Gujarati-speaking and Kutchi-speaking Hindu and Muslim trading castes and sects, Parsees, Goans, Anglo-Indians and Europeans. Muslims from Punjab and northern India had also started settling in Karachi, as its commercial and military importance increased after the First World War. Some Sindhi Muslim landlords had also built their residences in the wealthier areas of Karachi, but very few common Sindhi Muslims were to be found in Karachi city. It was along the coastal areas of Karachi that Baluch and Sindhi fishing villages and settlements were located.

Mohajirs take over Karachi and dominate urban Sindh

Between 1947 and 1954 more than 1 million Urdu-speaking Muslims, mainly from northern India, migrated to Sindh. By 1954 further large-scale inflow had been severely restricted by the Pakistan government. Initially the Sindhi leaders and public extended generous hospitality to the Mohajirs, but relations were soured soon afterwards. In 1948 Jinnah ordered Karachi to be separated from Sindh and made federal territory. This action was taken without consent of the chief minister of Sindh, Ayub Khuhro, who protested, but was overruled and instead dismissed from office on corruption charges (Jalal, 1990: 88).

Thereafter the Mohajir-dominated central government intensified efforts to bring more Urdu-speaking refugees into Karachi. Riots were instigated in 1948 against Hindus and Sikhs who had stayed on in Karachi. This resulted in another flight of non-Muslims to India. It seems that the Mohajir politicians felt unsure of their political future in a population with which they were affiliated only by religion. If democratic elections were to be held the Mohajirs needed a reliable and stable constituency for their support base. Consequently, concentrating Mohajirs in Karachi and Hyderabad was given priority. Thus, already in 1951, some 50 per cent of the urban population of Sindh was constituted by Mohajirs. Over 80 per cent of the population of Karachi, 66 per cent of Hyderabad, 67 per cent of Mirpur Khas and 67 per cent of Nawabshah comprised Mohajirs (Kardar, 1992: 310). Those coming from the semi-desert regions of Rajasthan were relocated in different parts of the Sindh interior. However, most poor and illiterate Mohajirs were left to fend for themselves. They established shanty towns on the outskirts of Karachi and Hyderabad.

Allotment of evacuee property

The flight of Hindus to India was fully exploited by the upper crust of the Sindhi landed classes. According to one estimate, of the 1,345,000 acres left behind by Hindus, as many as 800,000 acres were appropriated by Sindh landowners (Gankovsky and Gordon-Polonskaya, 1972: 138; Jalal, 1990: 87). On the other hand, most urban property abandoned by the non-Muslims was allotted to the Mohajirs to compensate them for loss of property in India. In practice this paved the way for corruption. Claims filed by the refugees were not properly checked or investigated. In extreme cases of nepotism and favouritism, only an oath declaring loss of property in India was admitted as valid proof. As a consequence substantial urban property was acquired by well-connected Mohajirs. Even hundreds of thousands of acres of agricultural land was allotted to élite Mohajirs. On the other hand, a bill passed a year before Partition by the Sindh Assembly requiring land mortgaged to Hindu moneylenders to be returned to the original owners, mostly small

Sindhi landlords and peasants, was not converted into law upon the instructions of Jinnah (Kardar, 1992: 310).

One-Unit, development and Sindhi grievances

Rapid economic development at all costs was the main objective which the central élite set before itself in the immediate years after independence. Overriding objections and opposition from the nationalist forces of the non-dominant provinces, the various provinces and princely States in West Pakistan were amalgamated under the so-called One-Unit scheme into a single province of West Pakistan on 30 September 1955. This way many hindrances to the free movement of capital and workforce were removed. Additionally, the whole of West Pakistan was now consolidated against the majority province of East Pakistan. Such measures greatly tightened the grip of the central élite on the country. The unification scheme was supported by 'the landed magnates of Sind and the big landlords in several districts of Pakhtunistan [NWFP] and Baluchistan which were in the grip of peasant movements' (Gankovsky and Gordon-Polonskaya, 1972: 209).

However, initially many members of the Sindh Assembly refused to support the amalgamation bill but were cajoled and intimidated into giving assent. G.M. Sayed and the small body of Sindhi nationalists and leftists were put under detention (Gankovsky and Gordon-Polonskaya, 1972: 216–17). This time Ayub Khuhro was back on good terms with the central government. Through his efforts the bill was approved by the Sindh Assembly in December 1954. Out of 109 members, 104 were present, of whom 100 voted in favour of the scheme (Malik, 1988: 55).

The construction of barrages and allotment of land

Plans for establishing a vast irrigation network in Sindh had been worked out already during the British period. The largest river in the subcontinent, the Indus, flowed through the province, and since time immemorial its water had been used for agriculture and riverine trade, but the traditional exploitation of its vast water resources was limited. The British constructed the Sukkur Barrage in the 1930s in northern Sindh. The British seemed to have had a low opinion of Sindhi farmers and therefore cultivators from neighbouring Punjab were settled to work the new lands. Thus several thousand Punjabis settled in Sindh during the 1930s.

Most of the land had been distributed during the colonial era, but 642,460 acres were still available for distribution prior to One-Unit. Between 1955 and 1958 the government allotted non-Sindhis 153,620 acres and Sindhis 123,586 acres in the Sukkur Barrage area (Ahmed, P.A., 1988: 79). The policy of constructing more barrages in Sindh was continued after independence. Foreign aid was forth-coming from the West, and Pakistan embarked on an ambitious plan of indus-trialization and agricultural development. Two more barrages, at Kotri and Guddu, were built on the Indus during the 1950s and 1960s. This rendered several million acres of former desert and semi-desert fit for cultivation. The government of General Ayub Khan showed little regard to Sindhi sensibilities about land rights in the development schemes in Sindh. Thus, when the applica-tions from the public for allotment of land in the Kotri and Guddu barrage devel-opment schemes were processed by the government, the Sindhi applicants were discriminated against. The choicest lands were reserved for military officers and the civil service (for details see Ahmed, P.A., 1988: 79–100). Upon the initiative of the Sindh Hari Committee (a radical peasant organization) more than 100,000 peasants applied to be allotted land in the scheme, but only some 20 per cent of the land was allotted to Haris (Mirza, 1987: 18–21). Most of it was auctioned off. The new owners, who were mostly Punjabis, brought over peasant cultivators from their own areas to work the land. A new Punjabi settlement in interior Sindh took place as a consequence.

The impact of industrialization on Sindhi and Mohajir groups

Before Partition, some Sindhi Hindus had acquired experience of modern indus-trial production. They were now gone. The Waderas had kept away from industry, and therefore no Sindhi entrepreneurial class was available in Pakistan. Sindhis were also absent from the working class as most were still caught up in some form of bonded relationship to the Waderas. Thus in the 1950s and 1960s indigen-ous Sindhis were largely bypassed by the rapid changes taking place in Karachi. As regards the Mohajirs, the upper crust stuck to their stronghold in the bureaucracy. Some moved into medium-range production, and the intelligentsia continued to seek employment as professionals, as functionaries in government service and as white-collar employees in industry. The majority of Mohajirs, however, worked as labourers in industry. The incoming Punjabi and Pukhtuns began to strain the Mohajir hold over Karachi, and the first ethnic clashes in Karachi took place between Pukhtuns and Mohajirs in the mid-1960s.

Zulfikar Ali Bhutto and the rise of Sindhi influence in Pakistani politics

A political route to influence began to emerge for Sindhis when Ayub Khan recruited a top Sindhi landlord, Zulfikar Ali Bhutto, as a minister. After serving in some junior ministries, Bhutto rapidly rose to become the very conspicuous foreign minister of Pakistan. In 1967 he founded the Pakistan People's Party (PPP). It adopted a populist ideology represented by three slogans: 'Socialism Is

Our Economy', 'Democracy Is Our Politics' and 'Islam Is Our Religion'. Bhutto projected himself as a believer in a strong Pakistan and was able to gain support quickly in Punjab among radical intellectuals, the urban lower middle class and the peasantry. In Sindh many landlords and *pirs* joined the PPP (Ahmad, 1976: 49–50). Here Bhutto concentrated on Sindhi grievances such as the question of provincial autonomy which had been usurped through One-Unit. Bhutto's populism catered for all aggrieved classes and cut across ethnic lines. Even sections of Mohajirs joined the PPP.

In the 1970 general elections the PPP won a landslide victory in both Punjab and Sindh. It swept the polls in the Sindhi regions, but did well also in Karachi and Hyderabad. Most Mohajirs, however, supported the Islamic or middle parties (Ahmed, 1992: 143). Bhutto came to power in truncated Pakistan in late 1971 after East Pakistan had seceded and become Bangladesh. The PPP formed the government both at the centre and in the Punjab and Sindh provinces.

The 1972 language riots

Before Partition, education in schools and colleges in Sindh was imparted mainly in the Sindhi language. In the early post-independence years Sindhi continued to be employed in schools in Karachi. The influx of Mohajirs brought the establishment of a number of Urdu-medium institutions. After the creation of One-Unit, the ideological emphasis put on greater national integration around Islam and the Urdu language made education in Sindhi appear dysfunctional to the military–bureaucratic oligarchy. Thus in 1958 Ayub Khan forbade the teaching of Sindhi in Karachi, and in interior Sindh the Mohajirs were exempted from learning Sindhi (Ahmed, 1985: 238). Sindhis could study in their native language only up to the sixth grade. At the higher level most teaching began to be conducted in Urdu. This change slowed down the growth of the Sindhi intelligentsia, which in any case was a relatively small one. Notwithstanding such adverse developments, Sindhi newspapers and magazines continued to be published. This helped to preserve and disseminate a Sindhi cultural identity among the reading public (interview, Lashari, 1990).

In early 1972 Chief Minister Mumtaz Ali Bhutto (first cousin of Z.A. Bhutto) announced that Sindhi would be made the sole official language of Sindh. This provoked a fierce reaction from the Mohajirs, who rioted in Karachi. These protests were ignored and on 7 July 1972 the Sindh Assembly, dominated by the PPP, declared Sindhi the sole official language of the province. The demand of the opposition to make Urdu an additional official language was rejected. In another move, a non-official resolution was moved in the Assembly which required non-Sindhis to learn Sindhi within three months, if they wanted to keep their job in the government (Sayeed, 1980: 154).

Another important reform introduced was the fixing of a favourable quota for the grossly under-represented interior Sindh in educational institutions and government jobs. Thus in federal government services the 19 per cent quota of posts for Sindh was divided as follows: 40 per cent (or 7.6 per cent) for Karachi, Hyderabad and Sukkur and 60 per cent for rural Sindh. However, the quota applied only to superior grade posts and not to all levels (Research Officer, 1989: 187−9). These measures inflamed Mohajir opposition. Bloody clashes between Mohajirs and the PPP took place in Karachi and Hyderabad. Even interior Sindh was disturbed by ethnic violence. It is important to note that during the language riots a demand to separate Karachi from the rest of Sindh and to make it a separate province in its own right was ventilated from Mohajir quarters (Sayeed, 1980: 155). The rising tide of ethnic disturbances finally forced the Sindh government to waive the imposition of Sindhi for the next twelve years. When the twelve-year limit lapsed in 1984, General Zia ignored the law. Thus both Sindhi and Urdu remain currently the official languages of Sindh.

The mega-city of Karachi and the growing economic crisis

Karachi's population began to expand rapidly after independence and continued to grow during the 1950s and 1960s. By the beginning of the 1970s it had begun to acquire the typical characteristics of Third World mega-cities: bad housing, soaring prices of real estate, overcrowding and illegal settlements on the outskirts. These difficulties were compounded when the Soviet Union intervened in Afghanistan and Afghan refugees began to pour into Pakistan in the millions: thousands of them headed towards Karachi. In a few years Afghan colonies sprouted up around Karachi from where illicit trade in weapons, drugs and other types of smuggling was carried out more or less with impunity. As the Pakistan government received massive economic and military aid from the USA during this period, it ignored the criminal activities of the Afghan mafias and their Pakistani associates. Violence and crime multiplied in and around Karachi (Noman, 1988: 188). The contagion quickly spread to other parts of Pakistan. The term 'Kalashnikov culture' began to circulate in Pakistan as a description of the overall dehumanization and brutalization of society. Inevitably Mohajir, Sindhi, Punjabi, Pukhtun, Afghan and Baluch criminal gangs clashed over power, influence and share in illicit drug trafficking and other crime. Gang fights, organized and premeditated attacks by armed militias on each other's strongholds in the shanty towns, created havoc among the hapless populations of these run-down localities (Hussain, 1990: 185−90). Murder, arson, rape and other brutalities were freely practised. The Pakistani authorities proved quite ineffective in bringing the situation under control.

By 1981 Karachi's population was estimated to have exceeded 8 million

3

33

(including those in the shanty towns), but there was no cessation in the inflow of outsiders. An important demographic change occurred in the ethnic composition of Karachi. In 1951, 80 per cent of its population was constituted by Mohajirs. In 1981, Mohajirs made up 54.3 per cent, Punjabis 13.6 per cent and Pukhtuns 8.7 per cent of greater Karachi. The Sindhis continued to remain a small minority of 6.3 per cent (Ali, 1992: 181). In the 1980s thousands of Iranians fleeing from the Islamic Republic of Iran, Sri Lankans from the ethnic war in their own country, and poverty-stricken Indian Muslims and Bangladeshis also crossed the porous Indo–Pakistan border and settled in Karachi. While 60 per cent of Karachi's population lived in areas where clean water, sewerage and other facilities were available, the remaining 40 per cent lived in slums of one sort or another. The Mohajirs were located largely in the core areas, although in several large shanty towns poverty-stricken Mohajirs predominated. In any case, while Karachi contained less than 10 per cent of the total population of Pakistan, one-third of the country's industrial and financial assets were located in it (Zaidi, 1992: 340).

Sindhi and Mohajir separatist movements of the 1980s

By the early 1980s both Sindhi nationalists and Mohajir activists were deeply worried about their position in Sindh. Whereas the Sindhis feared becoming a minority in their own home province if further influx of outsiders was not stopped, the Mohajirs saw a bleak future for themselves if the incoming Punjabis, Pukhtuns, and their close kin, the Afghans, were not kept out of Karachi. The problem was that although the Sindhi nationalist and Mohajir intellectuals faced a growing threat from other entrants into the province they historically harboured mutual suspicion and hostility. Thus attempts to join ranks were foundered by the various contradictions present between the two groups.

Sindhi separatism

Although a Sindhi separatist tendency emerged soon after independence it remained rather impotent in securing mass support. In this connection, Sindhi social structure was a major hindrance. Although sections of the Sindhi landowning classes disapproved of the allotment of land to Punjabi, Pukhtun and Mohajir officers in the development schemes, the more conservative big landowners were wary of the radicalism of the Sindhi Hari Committee and had welcomed the settlement of army officers in Sindh as a check on the Haris (Gankovsky and Gordon-Polonskaya, 1972: 147–9). Under the circumstances the Sindhi nationalists, consisting of a handful of cultural purists like G.M. Sayed and various leftist intellectuals, failed to capture the popular Sindhi imagination during the 1950s and 1960s. The rise of the PPP and the subsequent coming into power of a PPP government in Sindh had led to the fixing of quotas in government services and higher educational institutions for rural Sindh, and had played an important role in facilitating the evolution of a Sindhi intelligentsia. Consequently they began to be recruited into the administration. Especially, Sindhis began to be employed in the strategic police force.

The Sindhi separatist tendency received a major boost in 1977, but from a very different direction. In July the elected government of Z. A. Bhutto was toppled by the army. After a controversial trial Bhutto was executed on 4 April 1979. The decision of the Pakistan Supreme Court clearly indicated an ethnic bias. Of the seven presiding judges a majority of four Punjabis found Bhutto guilty of conspiring in the murder of a political opponent and ordered his execution. The three others, a Sindhi, a Pukhtun and a Parsee from Baluch, did not find the evidence conclusive and dissented from the majority decision.

The execution furnished the Sindhis with much-needed emotional and cultural symbols to articulate grievances against Punjab and the army. Separatist ideas now gained wider currency among the PPP, predominantly Sindhi, cadres. Some clashes between PPP cadres and Punjabi army officers stationed in Sindh took place. The Zia regime invoked martial law and other draconian legal rules and regulations. Mass arrests followed. Floggings and other types of torture were applied against the arrested cadres. Some executions ordered by military courts took place.

Murtaza Bhutto, the elder son of Z.A. Bhutto, pledged to avenge the death of his father. An organization, the Al-Zulfikar, was formed to organize resistance to the Zia regime. Bases were established in neighbouring Afghanistan, and Libya was reportedly providing funds for the Al-Zulfikar. The Pakistani press reported that India was providing training to Al-Zulfikar cadres. In 1981 Al-Zulfikar cadres hijacked a PIA airliner, and an army captain on board the flight was killed before it landed at Kabul, the main operational base of Murtaza Bhutto at that time. Several other operations, including murderous attacks on government functionaries or collaborators of General Zia, were carried out in Pakistan by Al-Zulfikar but it failed to establish a popular base in society. Sporadic actions continued into the 1990s. By 1993 some 20,000 PPP workers had been jailed because of alleged involvement in Al-Zulfikar activities (*Herald*, August 1993).

The Movement for the Restoration of Democracy (MRD), the PPP and G.M. Sayed

Opposition to the Zia dictatorship brought together a wide range of anti-Zia forces, including the PPP. In August 1983 the formation of MRD, an alliance of several parties, was announced. It was to mobilize mass demonstrations and agitations throughout Pakistan. In Sindh the movement was led by the PPP, which also bore the brunt of military repression. Another organization which emerged with great force during this period was the Sindhi Awami Tehrik led by Rasul Baksh Palejo. Ideologically the Sindhi Awami Tehrik drew its inspiration from Maoist ideas of peasant revolution (Noman, 1988: 183). Its support came from a small number of students, workers and peasants. Other groups that took part in the movement were the left-leaning Sindhi Hari Committee (by that time a spent force, having faced severe repression all those years), and those cadres of the Jiye Sindh Group which defied the passivity of their leaders and took part in the agitations. The government retaliated in full fury. Labour unions were banned and trade union activists were rounded up. In particular suspected Al-Zulfikar activists and sympathizers were hunted down all over Pakistan. Torture was employed extensively. Consequently the movement in Sindh as well as elsewhere collapsed under the full weight of state terror. Some 300 Sindhis died in the police and military operations (Kardar, 1992: 313; Khan, 1983: 168–70). The only parts of Sindh which remained passive were the Mohajir strongholds of Karachi and Hyderabad.

In spite of considerable radicalization and mass participation of the Sindhi masses and their rallying around the PPP, its leadership could not develop any clear direction. Mrs Nusrat Bhutto and Benazir Bhutto were put in detention during this period. Those leaders who were outside were deeply divided on the aims of the movement. However, what perturbed the PPP leadership, both those under detention and those leading the struggle, such as Ghulam Mustafa Jatoi, was the separatist swing among PPP cadres. Since its inception the PPP had been a party aiming at attaining greater power at the centre and had acted practically as a counterpoise to the separatists. This characteristic remained unchanged, notwithstanding the vicissitudes confronted by its leaders (who, in any case, have been immediate members of the Bhutto family), after the death of Zulfikar Ali Bhutto.

It is intriguing to note that, while Sindhi feelings against the centre were inflamed to the extreme, the leader of the Jiye Sindh, the arch Sindhi nationalist, G.M. Sayed, remained aloof from the popular upsurge. In his calculations the movement only strengthened the PPP, which Sayed considered a centre-oriented party aiming exclusively at returning to power in a united Pakistan. It was, therefore, a party which was inimical to his goal of secession from Pakistan. Proceeding on such assumptions Sayed cultivated amiable relations with General Zia-ul-Haq — conduct for which he has not been able to give a rational or plausible explanation (*Herald*, February 1992).

Elections without political parties

Having crushed the MRD movement, General Zia arranged a referendum in 1984 on the Islamic character of Pakistan. At that time, leaders of almost all political parties, except those of the pro-Zia Jamaat-e-Islami and the Muslim League led by the biggest Sindhi *pir*, Pir Pagara, were in detention. The people were asked to vote on whether the people endorsed the process of Islamization of laws begun by the government. The government claimed a turnout of 64 per cent, of which 96 per cent were reported to have voted in favour of General Zia's reforms. However, international news agencies such as Reuters, and the Manchester *Guardian* reported the turnout as low as 10 per cent (Bhutto, 1989: 275). Next, in January 1985 Zia called for national elections. However, the participation of political parties was disallowed and candidates had to contest as private individuals. In the absence of political parties, ethnic ties such as those based on *biradari*, sect, tribe and other such particularistic differences became the basis of vote gathering (Mehdi, 1988: 31).

From among the elected members of the National Assembly, Zia appointed a relatively unknown Sindhi, Mohammad Khan Junejo (a disciple of Pir Pagara), as prime minister. However, differences developed between Zia and Junejo, as the latter felt obliged to respond to the wishes of the National Assembly. In May 1988 Zia dismissed Junejo. In August Zia-ul-Haq and US ambassador Arnold Raphael perished in a mysterious plane crash.

Mohajir separatism

On 18 October 1951 Prime Minister Liaqat Ali Khan, the doyen of Mohajirs, was assassinated while addressing a public meeting at Rawalpindi in Punjab. In Mohajir perceptions it was the beginning of the decline of Mohajir influence in Pakistan. The murder remains a mystery to this day. At any rate, it was followed immediately by the Punjabi bureaucrats expanding their control over the state, and in 1960 the capital of Pakistan was shifted from Karachi to Islamabad in northern Punjab. The Mohajirs working for the federal government had to abandon Karachi. On the other hand, following the creation of One-Unit and the rapid industrialization which followed in Karachi, Punjabis and Pukhtuns headed towards it in large numbers (Ali, 1992: 180–3). Furthermore, the governments of Ayub Khan (1958–69), Yahya Khan (1969–71) and Zulfikar Ali Bhutto (1971–77) carried out retrenchments of government officers on charges of corruption. Mohajir bureaucrats figured prominently in these expulsions.

In the crucial 1970 elections, which catapulted the PPP into power, Mohajir votes had been dispersed. Except for some Marxists and the Shia minority among Mohajirs, most voted for the Jamaat-e-Islami or the several other doctrinal Sunni parties. The Muslim League had become a spent force, and at any rate it was no longer controlled by Mohajirs. More crucially, the existing fundamentalist Jamaat-e-Islami and the other doctrinal Sunni parties stood for issues and objectives much broader than the purely ethnic concerns of the Mohajirs. More dramatically, the rise of the PPP and its coming into power in Sindh in 1972, followed by the language riots, created a tremor in Mohajir circles. It is interesting to note that, although Mohajirs had lost control over the political parties, the intellectual and cultural hold over the powerful Karachi press was still very much an exclusive domain of the Mohajirs. In the turbulent years when Z.A. Bhutto was in power the Mohajirs continued to challenge the PPP in Sindh. Thus when in 1977 the combined opposition parties formed the PNA (Pakistan National Alliance) and launched the Nizam-e-Mustafa Movement (Movement for the Establishment of an Islamic State based on the Model of the Pious Caliphate) against Bhutto on allegations of general corruption, misrule and, more immediately, election rigging, the Mohajirs played a prominent role in disrupting law and order in Karachi and Hyderabad.

The Mohajir intelligentsia and ethno-nationalism

At the beginning of the 1980s the Mohajir sense of relative deprivation was clearly reflecting Gurr's notion of perceived discrepancy between the value expectations of people and their value capabilities. Much of the old guard, the erstwhile landowning élite of northern India, was dead and gone or living a retired life. Even General Zia, who had tried his utmost to crush the PPP during the MRD movement, had nevertheless sought to balance his action by choosing a Sindhi, Muhammad Khan Junejo, as the prime minister. Mohajirs felt sidelined by these developments.

The Karachi University was a Mohajir stronghold, and the student union had mostly been dominated by the right-wing Islami Jamiat-e-Tulba, the student wing of the Jamaat-e-Islami, thanks to Mohajir support. An initiative to organize the Mohajirs politically on an exclusive ethnic basis was first taken by a group of young men belonging to the Karachi University. On 11 June 1978 some lower middle-class student activists founded the All-Pakistan Mohajir Student Organization. According to the founder, Altaf Hussain (later the supreme leader of the Mohajirs), he and his friends had to face considerable opposition, including armed assault and other acts of terror, from the rival student organizations, particularly the Islami Jamiat-e-Tulba, during their initial efforts to mobilize the Mohajirs. The organization, however, won over Mohajir support by basing itself exclusively on their specific grievances. Sectarian differences between Sunnis and Shias were put aside and the Mohajirs established themselves as a separate ethnic group in the University (Hussain, 1988: 30–45).

The establishment of the MQM

The Mohajir Quomi (national) Movement (MQM) developed out of the Mohajir student movement. It was formally inaugurated on 18 March 1984. In his autobiography, *Safr-e-Zindagi* ('Life's Journey', 1988), Altaf Hussain, the non-office-holding supreme leader of the MQM, points out proudly his and Chairman Azim Ahmed Tariq's humble origin from among the lower middle class. He alleges not only that the non-Mohajir ruling class was inimical to the MQM but also that upper-class élite Mohajirs refused to associate with the MQM. At any rate, with a clear ethnic stand the MQM quickly expanded its support base. From 1986 onwards MQM leaders began to draw giant public meetings and demonstrations in Karachi and Hyderabad (Ali, 1992: 185). Although the MQM is essentially a party of the Urdu-speaking migrants from India, it worked towards an alliance with the Memons and other minor ethnic groups of Karachi (ethnically related to the erstwhile big bourgeoisie which had taken the lead in industrialization in the 1950s but had gradually been losing out to the Punjabi–Pukhtun industrial houses) who shared an interest in stopping further influx of Punjabi, Pukhtun and Afghan settlers in the city. It is important to point out that the Punjabi intelligentsia was employed in large numbers in the various government and private services in Karachi and was particularly resented by Mohajirs. MQM's strategy of clearly aiming at ethnic grievances proved extremely effective, and it made a clean sweep of the votes in local elections of 1987 (Zaidi, 1992: 340).

The claim to nationality

In a political and ideological sense the most dramatic change which occurred in Mohajir self-perception under the influence of MQM was the assertion of a separate and distinct national identity deriving from north Indian Urdu-oriented culture. Hitherto Mohajir leaders had always emphasized the overarching Muslim identity and belittled all notions of identity deriving from linguistic and regional culture. In the context of Pakistan such an assertion was not entirely arbitrary, as the state had been founded on such a principle. However, now, when the much larger Punjabi and Pukhtun nationalities were fast expanding their hold over the state and were wresting away government jobs from the Mohajirs and Sindhi influence in politics had grown considerably, Muslim nationalism no longer seemed to be an effective argument to make claims on the state. Instead the argument was advanced that Mohajirs constituted the fifth nationality of Pakistan — Baluchs, Pukhtuns, Punjabis and Sindhis being the other four. The claim to fifth nationality created a storm in Sindhi political circles of Sindh as it portended the severance of the Karachi–Hyderabad region from Sindh. Under no circumstance could Sindhis bear the loss of Karachi and Hyderabad (interviews with Mumtaz Bhutto, Hamida Khurho, Faqir Lashari, Hafeez Pirzada, Junaid Sumroo and Mir Thebo, 1990).

Opinion in the intellectual circles of Punjab was also quite hostile to such a claim. The author had the opportunity to discuss the fifth nationality claim with well-known Punjabi intellectuals such as Ahmed Salim, Fakhar Zaman, Hanif Ramay, Professor Azizuddin Ahmed, Professor Khalid Mahmud and many others. They all rejected such a claim as preposterous. On the other hand, the Sindhi sociologist—historian Feroz Ahmed wrote a long article which was published in four instalments in the weekly *Viewpoint* of Lahore (18, 25 August, 1, 8 September 1988) where, after discussing critically the historical, psychological, cultural and political aspects of such a claim, he made a rather positive assessment: 'By basing its appeal on ethnic rights the MQM has avoided playing up Islam, a significant departure from the Mohajir political tradition. In a sense, the MQM could be considered secular. . . . The MQM has been instrumental in cutting the Mohajir's umbilical cord from the Punjabi ruling establishment' (8 September 1988: 28). This perception of a Sindhi nationalist scholar about the MQM reflected the hope of a Sindhi—Mohajir working alliance against the centre. However, later events were not to allow such an alliance to stabilize.

The MQM and escalation in violence

A noteworthy feature of the meteoric rise of MQM was an overall escalation in violence as a means of conducting politics. S. Akbar Zaidi (interview, 1990), a noted commentator and scholar of the Sindh situation, candidly described the MQM as a terrorist organization with unmistakable fascistic tendencies in its ideology and style of politics. A common suspicion was that the MQM was a protégé of the military intelligence, the much-feared Inter Services Intelligence (ISI), which had allegedly been supplying arms to the MQM on the direct orders of General Zia-ul-Haq, who wanted to curb the rise of the PPP at any cost. Others have pointed out the MQM's policy of sharing power with Memon and other older ethnic minorities of Karachi as a link with non-Punjabi big financiers who might have an interest in reducing Punjabi domination in the city.

At any rate it is important to note that Zia-ul-Haq played upon the fears not only of Mohajirs but also of Sindhis of both rightist and leftist leanings who were opposed to the resurgence of the PPP and the Bhutto family's influence in Sindh. Thus co-operation between the Zia government, Jiye Sindh and MQM took place during this period. Altaf Hussain of the MQM and G.M. Sayed met several times to discuss common interests and possibly common action on stopping Punjabi and Pukhtun influx into Karachi and elsewhere in Sindh (Bakhtiar, 1992: 32–3; Hussain, 1988: 61–5).

Separate province or city-state?

The meteoric rise of the MQM as the vehicle of Mohajir aspirations emboldened its leaders to demand the creation of a separate Mohajir Suba (province) including

Karachi and Hyderabad. A pattern later developed for the MQM to put forward clarifications, repudiations and denials about the separation demand, and then allude to separation; the idea of separation itself remained ambiguous, as some versions suggested complete secession and the creation of a city-state. The fear of Mohajir violence drove leaders of the Punjabi and Pukhtun settlers to establish the Punjabi–Pukhtun Itehad (PPI) party. The emergence of PPI further compounded the already entangled nature of ethnic terrorism in the province. Heavy infiltration by the ISI was suspected in the MQM, PPI and even Jiye Sindh (interview with a senior bureaucrat, 1990).

Post-Zia developments in Sindh 1988–93

After the death of General Zia-ul-Haq in August 1988, demands for new elections were raised from many quarters. President Ghulam Ishaq Khan, a senior Pukhtun bureaucrat, announced new elections for November 1988. This time political parties were free to contest in their own name. However, the situation in Sindh suddenly turned explosive when on 30 September a gang opened indiscriminate fire in Hyderabad on unarmed people. Over 250 people, mostly Mohajirs, were slaughtered in the carnage. On 1 October, Mohajir militants mowed down some 60 people, mostly Sindhis, in Karachi (*Herald*, June 1990: 39). Not surprisingly, the election campaign in Sindh acquired a manifest ethnic character. Given the long repression during the Zia period, Benazir enjoyed obvious sympathy in Sindhi society. In Punjab also the PPP continued to attract mass support. Benazir Bhutto tried to tone down the Sindhi aspect of her party, emphasizing belief in a strong Pakistan. On the other hand MQM contested on a patently ethnic basis. On 16 November elections were held to the National Assembly. The PPP won 93 seats in the National Assembly, and thus became the largest party in a 207–member National Assembly. After some wrangling by the oligarchy she was allowed to form the government and on 12 December Benazir secured a vote of confidence in the Parliament and became prime minister.

Sindh under PPP

In the Sindh provincial elections held on 19 November 1988 the gains of the PPP were quite impressive. Out of a total of 100 seats the PPP secured 67. These gains were made in mainly Sindhi majority constituencies. In the Mohajir constituencies MQM candidates carried the day, securing 26 seats, thus becoming the second largest party in the Sindh Assembly. Initially the PPP and MQM reached a 59-point accord about sharing of power and jobs in Sindh. The PPP–MQM coalition government, however, collapsed in early 1990 when the MQM ministers resigned in protest over allegations of non-implementation of the accord. There are some indications that the PPP did not act in a spirit of accommodation and was largely responsible for the dissolution of the coalition.

Thereafter the MQM called for mass demonstrations and agitations. Violent clashes between the PPP and the MQM increased enormously. Both sides committed the most atrocious crimes against each other's cadres. Some 200 workers belonging either to the PPP or the MQM were kidnapped by the opposite side. Of these some 50 remained in captivity over a week. The rest were dropped off at different parts of the city. The MQM called for a strike on 7 February to press for the release of its cadres from PPP custody. On that day within a space of ten hours some 60 people were killed, some because of police firing and others in MQM–PPP clashes. The next day the MQM agreed to hold talks. These were held in the presence of Major General Moid of the Sindh Force, who acted as chief mediator. The result was agreement on exchange of hostages. On 11 February 1990 both sides exchanged their hostages. The Pakistani public was shocked to learn that the 27 injured hostages had been tortured by electric drilling machines, red-hot knives and iron bars during their captivity. The police also recovered badly mutilated dead bodies of five PPP workers from different parts of Karachi (*Herald*, March 1990). Assassinations, random shootings, kidnappings, arson and other gruesome crimes created a reign of terror in Karachi and in other parts of Sindh.

On 27 May 1990 occurred the Pucca Qila massacre in Hyderabad Sindh. A demonstration organized by the MQM was fired upon by the police. Some 60 people died, including at least a dozen women. Next day the MQM struck in Karachi and Hyderabad. Many Sindhis were killed. The government seemed paralysed during this period. While the PPP alleged that the MQM was defying the Benazir Bhutto government with the connivance of the army and ISI, the MQM asserted that the police was dominated by Sindhis and therefore victimized the Mohajirs. Dacoit (armed robber) gangs, which had mushroomed in interior Sindh at the time when the government unleashed its repression during the MRD movement of 1983, had by the late 1980s become regular features of the bizarre Sindh social and political scene. Burglary, abduction and looting spread terror in the province. The Pakistani press and MQM sources alleged an Indian hand in the Sindh crisis. A fact-finding mission of the Human Rights Commission of Pakistan, however, observed in its report (*Sindh Inquiry*, 1990: 61):

> The Mission felt greatly concerned at indications of the involvement of Army intelligence agencies, especially the ISI, in sponsoring and protecting armed organisations responsible for violence in the urban areas of Karachi and Hyderabad. . . . There were also allegations that notorious dacoits had received patronage from these organisations. . . . Following the 1983 Army operation [army action in Sindh during the MRD agitation], the Army indeed had a distinct image of a partisan. It is considered a pro-Punjabi organisation and is viewed as an oppressor by a substantial number of people in Sindh.

Dismissal of the PPP

On 6 August 1990 President Ghulam Ishaq Khan dismissed Benazir from her post as prime minister, accusing her government of massive corruption and inability to control the deteriorating situation in Sindh. The national and provincial assemblies were dissolved and new elections were called for October 1990. The PPP entered the contest in alliance with some other smaller parties. The name given to this new configuration was the Pakistan Democratic Alliance (PDA). The PDA won only 44 seats of the 207 total National Assembly seats. The rival Islamic Jamhoori Itihad (IJI), led by Nawaz Sharif, a Punjabi industrialist, enjoyed the sympathies of the oligarchy. It won 106 seats. Allegations of widespread election rigging by the oligarchy in favour of IJI were levelled by the PPP (Richter, 1993: 33). International observers, however, declared the election relatively fair. Nawaz Sharif became the next prime minister of Pakistan.

Sindh under Jam Sadiq Ali

In Sindh, the PDA (that is PPP) won 46 seats out of a total of 100. The IJI won six, MQM secured 28, two more than its bag of 26 in the 1988 election. Nineteen seats were won by independent candidates and one by Sindhi nationalists. Although the PDA was the biggest party, Jam Sadiq Ali, a Sindhi landlord of some standing and a former PPP member, formed the government with the support of the independents, IJI and MQM. The important point to note is that both PPP and MQM maintained their leading positions as parties representing Sindhi and Mohajir communities respectively. In early 1992 Jam Sadiq Ali died. By that time he had earned the reputation of a cruel persecutor of PPP cadres and activists. On the other hand, the more extremist Sindhi nationalists preaching secession were generally ignored by his government.

Army crackdown on MQM and dacoits

In March 1991 the MQM leader, Altaf Hussain, arrived in the UK, apparently for a medical check-up after having undergone surgery the previous year. He was to set up his base in that country and has not returned to Pakistan since then. It was widely speculated in the Pakistani newspapers that Hussain feared some sort of action against him by the state. The MQM's terror tactics and extremism had annoyed many senior military officers in charge of Sindh and punitive action was expected to follow. Moreover, Altaf Hussain was reported to be paranoid about possible assassination attempts against him by dissatisfied MQM cadres. Although he was surrounded by fanatical devotees who carried out merciless and brutal acts of terror on his instructions, his wrath had been directed not only against those opposed to the MQM but also against dissidents within the movement. Some of these dissidents were powerful in their own right and Altaf dreaded retaliation from such quarters (Ahmed, 1993: 62–4). Under these circumstances he left for Britain from where he began to direct his followers to different actions via telephone and recorded messages on videotapes. Thus terrorism continued to rage in Sindh even when one of the key players in the sinister game removed his direct presence from it.

At the end of May 1992, Home Minister Shujaat Hussain made a statement to the effect that the Indian RAW was directly involved in training and funding Jiye Sindh and Al-Zulfikar cadres (*Jang*, 28 May). Prime Minister Nawaz Sharif reiterated the same allegations at the beginning of June and announced that the UN had been intimated of such interference (*Jang*, 9 June 1992). However, while the central government of Nawaz Sharif and the provincial Sindh government of Jam Sadiq Ali concentrated their efforts on curbing the PPP, both the military corps commander of Karachi, Lieutenant General Naseer Akhtar, and the army chief, General Asif Nawaz, took a different view of the law and order situation in Karachi and the rest of Sindh. Apparently the death of an army officer at the hands of MQM terrorists changed the perceptions of these military commanders (in spite of the fact that ISI was supporting the MQM), who began to view the MQM as the main culprit behind the appalling law and order situation in Karachi.

Thus in May 1992 the army announced a plan to weed out terrorism and dacoit gangs from Sindh. The actual action began a few weeks later in June. Operation Clean-Up began with raids by the army against the MQM strongholds as well as the growing menace of roving dacoits in interior Sindh. The public announcement of the plan had helped the MQM take precautionary measures, but the army nevertheless made spectacular discoveries of MQM prisons, torture chambers and a sizeable cache of arms in the possession of the terrorists. Within the first few weeks most of the top leaders of the MQM had been arrested (*Jang*, 21–29 June 1992). Several cases of murder and other crimes were registered against Altaf Hussain.

All the MQM members of the Pakistan National Assembly and Sindh Assembly resigned in protest. Later, defections from MQM took place and a rival MQM faction called MQM Haqiqi (Genuine MQM) came into being (Jafri, 1992: 25–30). Further splits and defections followed later. Violence and murders committed by different MQM factions against each other appeared as another nasty feature of the Sindh crisis. By the end of 1992 the MQM had been dealt severe blows but was by no means smashed. In the meantime serious rifts were reported to have developed between Altaf Hussain, who stood for extremism, and the formal chairman of the MQM, Azim Ahmed Tariq, who favoured a negotiated settlement of the ethnic conflict. Disputes over the control of party funds and other matters also existed between the two. Consequently a faction within the

MQM began to side with Azim Ahmed Tariq. On 1 May 1993 Azim Ahmed Tariq was murdered by some unknown assailants. His assassination is widely believed to have been an inside job. The leaders of the dissident MQM Haqiqi, who had begun to improve their relations with Azim Ahmed Tariq, directly accused Altaf Hussain of ordering the murder (Bakhtiar, 1993: 64–7).

In the meantime military action in the Sindh interior dealt severe blows to the menace of dacoity. However, some of the gangs escaped detection and arrest because of protection and support forthcoming from powerful landowners, corrupt officials of the police and general administration and from the ISI. During Operation Clean-Up the divisions within the state organs on strategy and policy became manifest — the ISI backing the MQM and the regular army acting against it — indicating the confusion and contradictions within the centre.

Benazir Bhutto again as prime minister

During the latter half of 1992 a rift began to develop between President Ghulam Ishaq Khan and Prime Minister Nawaz Sharif. The latter wanted to rescind the 8th Amendment adopted during the period of General Zia-ul-Haq which gave wide discretionary powers to the president, empowering him to dismiss a sitting prime minister if he felt that the government was not being carried out in consonance with the constitution. Ishaq Khan reacted peremptorily by dismissing Nawaz Sharif from office in April 1993, accusing him of corruption and a range of other irregularities. Benazir Bhutto had been taken into confidence by the man who had dismissed her earlier on similar charges. For her support the President gave several portfolios to PPP members in the central cabinet led by Interim Prime Minister Balkh Sher Mazari. However, Nawaz Sharif appealed against the dismissal in the Pakistan Supreme Court, which, in a rare display of defiance against the president, found in its judgement of 26 April 1993 the accusations of the president unfounded and ordered Nawaz Sharif to be restored as prime minister (Abbas, 1993).

At this stage the army advised both Nawaz Sharif and Ishaq Khan to resign. Moin Qureshi, a top World Bank Pakistani official, was summoned back to Pakistan and made caretaker prime minister until new elections were held. In October 1993 elections were held and out of 195 Muslim seats in a full house of 207 the PPP secured 86 seats while the rival Muslim League led by Nawaz Sharif secured 73 (*Herald Election*, 1993: 21). The MQM boycotted the election to the National Assembly in protest over the military action (it contested the Sindh provincial election, however). Benazir managed to work out a coalition with several other parties and became prime minister in November 1993.

PPP in power in Sindh

In Sindh the PPP made a clean sweep in the Sindhi regions and secured an overall majority of 56 seats out of the total of 100. On the other hand, the MQM maintained its position as the sole representative of Mohajir interests and won 27 seats. The Sindhi secessionists did not directly participate in the elections and instead supported various other nationalist Sindhis in the PPP and other parties. Murtaza Bhutto, who had returned to Pakistan after several years of exile abroad, was elected to the Sindh Assembly as an independent. So also was moderate Sindhi nationalist leader Mumtaz Ali Bhutto. The PPP formed the government under Abdullah Shah.

The MQM continued to threaten the government with violent action, and the demand for creating a separate Mohajir province by separating Karachi and Hyderabad from the rest of Sindh was reiterated with great emphasis. Altaf Hussain, living in Britain, persisted with his extremist message, inciting his supporters to different protest actions against the PPP through speeches recorded via telephone and videotapes. The army has continued patrolling Karachi and other trouble spots in Sindh, and thus Operation Clean-Up has not been actually terminated. In fact the army has won some sort of gratitude from the weary and oppressed Sindhi people. On the whole there has been a decrease in violence but gun battles between the police/army, MQM, PPP/Sindhi militants have been claiming both intended and random victims.

External involvement

The ethnic conflict in Sindh has not attracted any significant international support or interference. Although the Cold War tension was high in South Asia during the 1980s, it left Sindh rather unaffected. G.M. Sayed did try to secure support from India, but was refused officially by Rajiv Gandhi. Indian interference has been alleged by the Pakistan government and the Pakistani press has been reporting the existence of training camps set up by the chief Indian intelligence agency, RAW, for both Jiye Sindh cadres and Al-Zulfikar. It is also alleged in a Pakistani government publication that between 1982 and 1992 India was responsible for 2444 acts of terror, including bomb blasts in Punjab and NWFP, and that 1354 persons were killed and 5088 injured. Further that in the case of Sindh, India recruited its agents particularly from among the Hindu population of the province (Rizvi, 1993). Some senior Pakistani bureaucrats also accuse India of having infiltrated the MQM.

Notwithstanding the barbarity of the crimes committed by the various terrorist organizations, dacoits, mafia gangs, and the various state organs including the police, army, intelligence and security services, the fact is that since powerful external backers were not available to either the MQM or Jiye Sindh, the actual devastation and destruction did not reach comparable proportions to that of the Sikh and Kashmir separatist movements in India or the Tamil movement in Sri Lanka. As far as the Al–Zulfikar movement is concerned, even if it did operate from bases in Afghanistan and received help from India, Libya and other sources, it failed to develop a distinct, separate profile from the PPP. The PPP, as the biggest Sindhi party, remained a pragmatic multi–class organization whose top leaders function within a strategy of a strong and integrated Pakistan. In recent years Al–Zulfikar has practically ceased to exist, as Murtaza Bhutto has returned to Pakistan and has been trying hard to work out a pardon from the state. His election to the Sindh Assembly is proof that the state is willing to consider his rehabilitation.

In any case, the most ardent champions of Sindhi nationalism, those who have themselves declared their intention of creating an independent Sindhu Desh (Land of the River Indus), such as G.M. Sayed, lack the support of a sizeable diaspora community living in the West which could be mobilized to extend monetary support and publicity and to procure arms for them. The Sindhi Hindus and Sikhs driven out of their hearths and homes and dispatched to India during Partition and later have assimilated into mainstream Indian society. They would have little interest in supporting the secessionist movement which now obtains in their erstwhile homeland. As regards the MQM, it also lacks the support of a sizeable and prosperous diaspora community. The Urdu-speaking Muslims of northern India are in no position to help the Mohajirs. Rather they resent the fact that they were abandoned by the élite which migrated to Pakistan. Under the circumstances, the Pakistani state has been able to contain the situation in Sindh at a much smaller cost in men and material.

Sindhi ideological positions

A wide range of opinions obtain among Sindhis on the relationship with Pakistan. Here they are grouped as centrists, moderate nationalists and secessionists.

The PPP's centrism

Mass Sindhi sympathies continue to be claimed by the PPP. As argued earlier, the PPP has thus far given priority to strategies aiming at coming into power at the centre. Its employment of Sindhi grievances has been a part of the strategy of returning to the centre. As long as the PPP can be accommodated in mainstream politics, Sindhi separatism is likely to be defused. Sindhi separatism became intense when General Zia proceeded to smash the PPP. On the other hand, the PPP is by no means a consolidated and democratic organization. It remains a family enterprise heavily dependent on the person of Benazir Bhutto; hence the uncertainty of its future. It is worth remembering that persons with Sindhi nationalist leanings are also to be found in the PPP and have been elected to the National and Sindh Assemblies. Among the cadres also, Sindhi nationalism commands popularity.

Moderate nationalists (interviews)

Mumtaz Ali Bhutto served as the PPP Chief Minister of Sindh during 1972–73. When the author met him in March 1990 he was chairman of the Sindh National Front. His ideas on Sindh and its relationship with Pakistan are culled from an interview recorded with the author in March 1990 and from the *Manifesto of the Sindh National Front* issued in 1989. The main points are as follows:

1   There must be a confederation of 'autonomous and sovereign' provinces as envisaged in the 1940 Pakistan Resolution. The principle of equality should be concretized in terms of equal representation in all central institutions including the executive, legislative, judicial organs and in the armed forces. The office of prime minister should rotate among the provinces.
2   Decentralization of power should be effected so that only defence, foreign affairs, currency and customs remain with the centre. All other powers, including financial powers, must be vested in the provinces.
3   A welfare state based on a fair distribution of wealth and adequate help and assistance to the poor, needy and old should be created.
4   All natural resources of Sindh such as oil, gas, coal, marble, granite, wood and all food products are the property of Sindh and should be utilized for its benefits.
5   No more dams should be built on the river Indus. The water of the Indus should be shared according to international law and rules on rights of riparian owners.
6   The influx of outsiders into Sindh must be stopped.
7   There should be joint electorates on the basis of adult suffrage. Separate electorates should be abolished.
8   Sindhi language and culture must be protected and promoted.
9   Women should be treated as equals and given equal opportunities in public life.

Junaid Soomro, a former member of Sindh Assembly and the Deputy Secretary General of the Sindh National Front, traced the present sufferings of Sindh to the wrong decision of Sindhi Muslim leaders to support the Muslim League's Two-Nation Theory which resulted in the creation of a country based on religious ideology. Abdul Hafeez Pirzada, formerly a federal law minister in the PPP government of the early 1970s, speaking on behalf of the Sindh National Alliance (consisting of several parties), argued that a loose federation of Pakistani provinces was the only acceptable solution for the Sindh National Alliance. Sindhis have historical rights to their ancient homeland. Whereas the claim of the Saraiki-speakers located in southern Punjab to nationality is acceptable, because they have inhabited a specific territory continuously, it is illegitimate when claimed by the Urdu speakers who are recent arrivals in Sindh. Those people who came from India until 1954 and adopted Sindh as their homeland are part and parcel of the Sindhi nation provided they forgo claim to a separate nationality. Sindhis do not want Biharis (stranded in Bangladesh) to come to settle in Sindh. The Sindh National Alliance was opposed to the building of military cantonments in Sindh and to the further influx of outsiders. The present crisis in Sindh had been aggravated by the divisive role played by the Pakistani intelligence services. Mr Pirzada alleged that the intelligence services were working on a sinister plan to uproot all Mohajirs from the interior and relocate them in the Karachi–Hyderabad belt. Dr Hamida Khuhro, daughter of the late Ayub Khuhro, and a noted historian of Sindh in her own right, asserted that the Urdu speakers did not come to settle in Sindh as refugees, but as settlers to the mythical land of Pakistan where they wanted to control everything. Pakistan should not be for a special group but for all Muslims. It should be a loose federation in which the autonomy of Sindh is respected.

Sindhi Awami Tehrik: class struggle and ethno-nationalism

The author tried very hard to interview the leader of the Sindhi Awami Tehrik, Rasul Baksh Palejo, and although contact could be established with him via close associates of the latter, it was not granted. Palejo seeks to combine the national question in Sindh with the social question of peasants' and workers' rights. Palejo takes an anti-Wadera stand and holds the landlords partly responsible for the suffering of Sindh (Noman, 1988: 183).

More interesting is that he identifies the Mohajirs as responsible for Sindh's economic and political deprivation while working on a strategy aiming at enlisting the support of radical leftist Punjabi factions. A sort of a united front of the 'sons of the soil' of Pakistan is to work towards the isolation of the Mohajirs, who are considered alien settlers. Palejo denies that Sindhis want to secede from Pakistan. Their real demand is for the respect of their democratic rights within a federal Pakistan. For his pro-Punjabi leanings Palejo has been branded by G.M. Sayed as an agent of the military intelligence.

G.M. Sayed and secessionism

The veteran Sindhi leader G.M. Sayed (born 1904) is undoubtedly the most senior champion of Sindhi nationalism. After the creation of Pakistan Sayed joined efforts with the Pukhtun leader Abdul Ghaffar Khan to oppose the formation of One-Unit. During the Ayub era Sayed was imprisoned several times. He founded the Jiye Sindh Mahaz (Long Live Sindh Front) in the second half of the 1960s. Sayed was sidelined during the 1970 elections which propelled Bhutto and the PPP into power both at the centre and in Sindh. During the 1983 MRD movement Sayed maintained amiable relations with General Zia. In 1988 the Jiye Sindh joined the Sindh National Alliance along with several other Sindhi nationalist parties and factions with a view to contesting the elections against the PPP. However, the sympathies of the Sindhi masses remained steadfast with Benazir. In the 1990 elections the secessionists were once again rejected by the electorate. In 1993 they did not field candidates directly but supported other moderate nationalists within the PPP and among independents.

Sindhu Desh (Land of the River Indus)

Sayed considers the creation of Pakistan as the most unfortunate event in the modern history of the Indian subcontinent, and his support for it during the freedom struggle his greatest blunder. It is interesting to note that in 1943 Sayed himself invited talented and educated Muslims from northern India (that is, those now called Mohajirs) to come to Sindh to assist the Sindhi people in their development and uplift. However, when Pakistan came into being the Mohajirs behaved like exploiters themselves or functioned as agents of vested interests who employed Islam to legitimate exploitation (1985: 75–6).

In an interview given to the monthly *Herald* of Karachi (August 1989: 183) Sayed mentions his unsuccessful attempts to solicit foreign help: 'We are seeking foreign help for our independence. So far we have failed. I went to Mr Rajiv Gandhi, he did not give me any support. We tried the Russians, but we did not get any help. We even tried to get some sympathy from Afghanistan and from the Americans, but neither helped us.'

In his book *A Case for Sindhu Desh* (1985), Sayed presents his main arguments in favour of the creation of a separate Sindhi state. He blames Jinnah for taking various wrong steps which were harmful to the interests of the 'original peoples of Pakistan'. Among these were the imposition of Urdu as national language and concentration of all powers at the centre dominated by Punjabis; 'The third . . . was the move by Mr Jinnah to send for high Civil Servants from the Muslim minority provinces of India and install them in superior administrative positions in the country' (1985: 11).

Although Sayed is not a Marxist, he is surrounded by many leftists. Thus when defining a nation he employs without reservation the Stalinist definition of nationality and nation. He presents a glorious version of Sindhi nationhood. He asserts that the Sindhi homeland corresponds to a definite geographical area around the

River Indus in which the Sindhi language had been spoken throughout the ages. Different religions and races have contributed to the creation of a Sindhi 'national character' which is based on the cherished memories of Sindhi heroes and folklore. Sindhis are hospitable, non-violent, altruistic, patriotic, tolerant, prefer love to hatred and resist tyranny. Sufi culture and traditions have in particular played an important role in forming the mild Sindhi national character. Sayed contrasts the virtues of Sindhi nationalism with the vices of the Punjabi–Mohajir ruling class. The latter are aggressive, expansionist and intolerant. The Mohajirs settled in Sindh are advised to break links with the Punjabis. Sayed writes 'You [Mohajirs] may retain Urdu as your language at homes. You may even study Urdu as your language in schools, but you must accept Sindhi as a sole national language of Sindhu Desh' (1985: 76).

Main socio-economic and political features of Sindhu Desh

Sayed summarizes his position as follows (1985: 80–5):

1   Independent Sindh Desh will attempt a drastic redistribution of agricultural land from non-Sindhis to Sindhis.
2   Trade, commerce, banks, insurance companies and government agencies will be wrested away from aliens and brought under the 'management and control of Sindhi speaking and permanently settled people in Sindh' (1985: 81).
3   Immigration from outside will be checked. All those lacking permanent domicile and 'resisting absorption in the Sindhi society and all the agents of alien intrigues shall be expelled' (1985: 81).
4   All jobs and employment opportunities shall be reserved for Sindhi nationals.
5   Sindhi shall be the sole national and official language of Sindh. 'Any one who would not know the language, will not be given right of citizenship.'
6   Heavy and basic industries will be given priority in Sindh.
7   Property of Sindhi Hindus and Sikhs grabbed by outsiders will be appropriated and returned to Sindhi Muslims or to those Sindhi Hindus who may choose to return to their motherland.
8   'The institutions of Pirdom and tribal headmenship shall be prohibited by law' (1985: 83). Holders of such titles and government officers will not be allowed to contest elections.
9   A strict separation of religion and state will be instituted constitutionally and in law.
10   All means of production will be nationalized in accordance with the principles of socialism.
11   An equitable land reform will be implemented. A ceiling on 200 acres to be cultivated collectively by four families will apply in the barrage areas.

12   The traditional role of women as housewives is to be abolished and they are
     to be integrated into public life as equals through modern education and
     training.
13   Sindhi culture will be promoted; non-Sindhi names of places will be replaced
     by Sindhi ones, 'an imposing large statue of Raja Dahir Sen [the Hindu ruler
     of Sindh defeated by the Arabs] shall be installed' (1985: 84).
14   'The State of Sindhi Desh shall be established on the basis of Secularism,
     Socialism, Democracy and Nationalism.'
15   Sindhu Desh will work towards greater fraternity with India, Afghanistan
     and Arab states and derive progressive inspiration from the Soviet Union.

Other secessionist factions and groups

Although G.M. Sayed is the best known proponent of Sindhu Desh, there are
various other nationalist and national-Marxist groups active in Sindh. Close to
the extremist line of secession are the Jiye Sindh Tehrik, the Jiye Sindh organization, Jiye Sindh Qaum Parast Party and the Jiye Sindh Taraqqi Pasand Party.
The latter is regarded as the best organized and most militant. Its leader, Dr
Qadir Magsi, and several other cadres are facing trial before an anti-terrorist
court for alleged involvement in the September 1988 carnage of Mohajirs.

Mohajir ideological positions

Unlike the Sindhis, who are organized in different groups and parties and hold
moderate to extremist positions on Sindhi nationalism, the Mohajirs came to be
dominated by the MQM. Some continued to play an active role in the Jamaat-e-
Islami and other parties, but the MQM has managed to stifle all dissent among the
Mohajirs through threats and terror. It is, therefore, essentially the thinking of the
MQM leadership which is relevant in the contemporary Sindh situation.

The most noteworthy change in Mohajir self-perceptions which occurred with
the ascent of the MQM was the shift from an all-inclusive and comprehensive
Muslim nationhood idea, upon which the Mohajirs had previously based their
claims and rights, to an entirely new theory according to which the Mohajirs constituted a separate fifth nationality on the basis of their distinct mother-tongue,
Urdu, and north Indian culture (Hussain, 1988: 79−91). The MQM theoreticians
argued that, just as Punjabis, Pukhtuns, Sindhis and Baluchis were recognized as
nationalities on the basis of language and historical culture and had been allotted
separate provinces, similarly new arrangements had to be made to protect the
interests of the Mohajir nationality. The implications of such an exercise of
national self-definition was some sort of division of Sindh along ethnic lines.

Socio-economic and political programme of the MQM

It is noteworthy that the demand for a separate province is not set forth in Altaf Hussain's book *Safr-e-Zindagi* (1988) although it has been projected in public speeches and other statements. The following are the main demands listed in the book:

1   Domicile in Sindh should only be granted to those persons who have been residing continuously in Sindh for at least the last twenty years, and fake domicile certificates should be rescinded after thorough enquiry.
2   The police force in Sindh should be composed of the permanent residents of Sindh. The existing police force was comprised mostly of non-locals [i.e. mostly Punjabis], brought over under One-Unit. Such a police had no sympathy for the local people and was responsible for many atrocities perpetrated against Mohajirs.
3   The influx of Afghan refugees into Sindh, particularly Karachi, had brought a thriving trade in armament and explosives going on in the Afghan camps. Afghans should be confined to camps near the Afghan border.
4   The rapid population increase in Sindh, particularly Karachi, should be halted by inflow of illegal immigration from the other provinces being forbidden.
5   The continuing encroachment of land and establishment of shanty towns should be stopped.
6   The quota system in Sindh based on the distinction between urban and rural Sindh should be reformed so that its present bias in favour of the rural areas is removed. Both groups should be allocated seats and jobs according to their population, while room for merit should be provided.
7   Employment in industry in Sindh should also go to the permanent residents of Sindh.
8   Since the time of Ayub Khan, Mohajirs have been discriminated against in terms of recruitment to senior services. This should be rectified.
9   Biharis stranded in Bangladesh are Pakistani citizens. They should be allowed to immigrate to Pakistan without further delay.
10   The border with India in Sindh at Khokrapar should be opened immediately so as to facilitate travelling of people with relatives on both sides.
11   Admission to schools and institutions of higher education should be reserved for the local residents.

Azim Ahmed Tariq

In an interview recorded with the author in March 1990 the official chairman of the MQM, Aziz Ahmed Tariq, asserted that the Mohajirs came to Pakistan out of free choice. There was some rioting in UP, but it was at the invitation of Quaid-i-Azam Mohamed Ali Jinnah to Mohajirs to come and administer Pakistan that they left India and came to Pakistan. On the other hand, Jawaharlal Nehru pleaded with the UP Muslims to stay on, but preference was given to the request of the founder of Pakistan. It was primarily among the Mohajir and to some extent in Punjab that an awareness and capability to administer a modern state existed.

The Mohajirs came to Pakistan with an ideology based on equality and freedom of religion and a modern scientific outlook. In Sindh, where most of them settled, they found tribal, Wadera-dominated societies. Thus the basic clash between Mohajirs and Sindhis was between a modern dynamic culture and a stagnant tribal culture. When Mohajirs came to Karachi they lived under miserable conditions. The elders in the community established schools and colleges with their own private means. The Waderas did not want their masses to receive modern education and thus challenge their traditional power. So they diverted the Sindhis against Urdu-medium education and Mohajirs.

In Pakistan, all governments beginning with Ayub Khan have victimized Mohajirs. The Sindhi complaint that they are alienated from political power is baseless. After Zulfikar Ali Bhutto became the prime minister of Pakistan, Sindhis have been co-opted in a power sharing. For example General Zia-ul-Haq controlled the Sindh situation with the help of many influential Sindhis. He appointed a Sindhi, Muhammad Khan Junejo, as prime minister. Later another Sindhi, Ghulam Mustafa Jatoi, served as interim prime minister in 1988, and now Benazir Bhutto is incumbent in that coveted office. The real losers in power sharing are Mohajirs who are neither to be found in important central positions nor do they have a separate province of their own. The language bill of 1972 divided the population of Sindh into two distinct cultural entities. The only solution that can work in Sindh is parity in jobs and employment between Sindhis and Mohajirs. There should be parity on the base level, but at the higher level selection should be by merit.

References

Abbas, Z. (1993) 'Back to the battlefront', *Herald*, June.
Ahmad, A. (1975) 'The national question in Baluchistan' in F. Ahmed (ed.), *Focus on Baluchistan and Pushtoon Question*, Lahore: People's Publishing House.
Ahmad, I. (1976) *Pakistan General Elections 1970*, Lahore: South Asia Institute.
Ahmed, A.S. (1988) *Pakistan Society: Islam, Ethnicity and Leadership in South Asia*, Delhi: Oxford University Press.
Ahmed, F. (1985) 'Pakistan's problems of national integration' in A. Khan (ed.), *Islam, Politics and the State: The Pakistan Experience*, London: Zed Books.
Ahmed, F. (1988) 'The rise of Mohajir separatism I–IV', *Viewpoint*.
Ahmed, F. (1992) 'Pakistan's problem of national integration: the case of Sind' in S.A.

Zaidi (ed.), *Regional Imbalances and the National Question in Pakistan,* Lahore: Vanguard.

Ahmed, I. (1987) *The Concept of an Islamic State: An Analysis of the Ideological Controversy in Pakistan,* London: Frances Pinter.

Ahmed, P.A. (1988) *Kaya Hum Ikhatay Reh Saktay Hein?,* Lahore: Maktab-e-Fikr-o-Danish.

Ahmed, Y. (1993) 'The rise and fall of Altaf Hussain', *Herald,* January.

Alavi, H. (1989) 'Politics of ethnicity in India and Pakistan' in H. Alavi and J. Harriss, *Sociology of 'Developing Societies': South Asia,* London: Macmillan.

Alavi, H. (1990) 'Authoritarianism and legitimation of state power in Pakistan' in S.K. Mitra (ed.), *The Post-Colonial State in Asia: Dialectics of Politics and Culture,* New York: Harvester Wheatsheaf.

Ali, B. (1992) 'Political forces in Sind' in S.A. Zaidi (ed.), *Regional Imbalances and the National Question in Pakistan,* Lahore: Vanguard.

Allana, G. (ed.) (1977) *Pakistan Movement: Historic Documents,* Lahore: Islamic Book Service.

Babar, N. (1993) 'Religious discrimination in the name of the law', *Herald,* January.

Bakhtiar, I. (1992) 'The good, the bad and the ugly', *Herald,* July.

Bakhtiar, I. (1993) 'Apathetic show' and 'A call for all factions', *Herald,* June.

Bhutto, B. (1989) *Daughter of Destiny,* New York: Simon and Schuster.

Bhutto, M.A. (1989) *Manifesto of the Sindh National Front,* Karachi.

Binder, L. (1961) *Religion and Politics in Pakistan,* Berkeley: University of California Press.

The 'Blasphemy' Episode (1992), Lahore: Human Rights Commission of Pakistan.

Chaudhry, N.A. (1977) *Development of Urdu as Official Language in the Punjab (1849–1974),* Lahore: Government of the Punjab.

Choudhary, G.W. (1969) *Constitutional Development in Pakistan,* Lahore: Longman.

Gankovsky, Y.V. and Gordon-Polonskaya, L.R. (1972) *A History of Pakistan (1947–1958),* Lahore: People's Publishing House.

Gankovsky, Y.V. and Moskalenko, V.N. (1978) *The Three Constitutions of Pakistan,* Lahore: People's Publishing House.

Gardezi, H. and Rashid, J. (eds) (1983) *Pakistan: The Roots of Dictatorship: The Political Economy of a Praetorian State,* London: Zed Books.

Harrison, S.S. (1981) *In Afghanistan's Shadow: Baluch Nationalism and Soviet Temptations,* New York and Washington, DC: Carnegie Endowment for International Peace.

Herald (English-language monthly, several issues), Karachi.

Hoodbhoy, P.A. (1985) 'Ideological problems for science in Pakistan' in M.A. Khan (ed.), *Islam, Politics and the State: the Pakistan Experience,* London: Zed Books.

Hoodbhoy, P.A. and Nayyar, A.H. (1985) 'Rewriting the history of Pakistan' in M.A. Khan (ed.), *Islam, Politics and the State: The Pakistan Experience,* London: Zed Books.

Huntington, S.P. (1968) *Political Order in Changing Societies,* New Haven: Yale University Press.

Hussain, A. (1988) *Safr-e-Zindagi,* Lahore: Jang Publishers Press.

Hussain, A. (1990) 'The Karachi riots of December 1986: crisis of state and civil society in Pakistan' in V. Das (ed.), *Mirrors of Violence: Communities, Riots, and Survivors in South Asia,* Delhi: Oxford University Press.

Jafery, Z. (1986) *Saraiki, Sind, Baluchistan: S.S.B. and National Question,* Multan: Melluha Publications.

Jafri, H.M. (1992) 'MQM: a fight to the finish?'; 'Voices from the frontline'; 'Journey into hell' in *Herald*, August.

Jalal, A. (1990) *The State of Martial Law: the Origins of Pakistan's Political Economy of Defence*, Cambridge: Cambridge University Press.

The Daily Jang (Urdu), London.

Jansson, E. (1981) *India, Pakistan or Pakhtunistan?*, Uppsala: Acta Universitatis Upsaliensis.

Jones, A.K. (1977) *Muslim Politics and the Growth of the Muslim League in Sind, 1935–1941*, PhD thesis, Duke University.

Jones, R.W. (1985) 'The military and security in Pakistan' in C. Baxter (ed.), *Zia's Pakistan: Politics in a Frontline State*, Lahore: Vanguard.

Kardar, S. (1992) 'Polarizations in the regions and prospects for integration' in S.A. Zaidi (ed.), *Regional Imbalances and the National Question in Pakistan*, Lahore: Vanguard.

Kennedy, C.H. (1985) 'Rural groups and the Zia regime' in C. Baxter (ed.), *Zia's Pakistan: Politics in a Frontline State*, Lahore: Vanguard.

Kennedy, C.H. (1989) 'Towards the definition of a Muslim in an Islamic state: the case of Ahmadiyya in Pakistan' in D. Vajpeyi and Y.K. Malik (eds), *Religion and Ethnic Minority Politics in South Asia*, New Delhi: Manohar.

Kennedy, C.H. (1992) *Pakistan: 1992*, Boulder: Westview Press.

Khan, A.A. (1993) 'The Christians bearing their Cross', *Herald*, January.

Khan, A.A. (1994) 'The rise of sectarian mafias; blind faith; faction replay', *Herald*, June.

Khan, M.A. (1983) *Generals in Politics: Pakistan 1958–1982*, New Delhi: Vikas Publishing House PVT Ltd.

Khan, W. (1987) *Facts Are Facts: The Untold Story of India's Partition*, New Delhi: Vikas Publishing House Pvt Ltd.

Khawar, M. and Shaheed, F. (1987) *Women of Pakistan: Two Steps Forward, One Step Back?*, Lahore: Vanguard.

Khosla, G.D. (1989) *Stern Reckoning: A Survey of the Events Leading up to and Following the Partition of India*, Delhi: Oxford University Press.

Khuhro, H. (1981) 'Muslim political organization in Sind 1843–1938' in H. Khuhro (ed.), *Sindh: Through the Centuries*, Karachi: Oxford University Press.

Malik, R. (1988) *The Politics of One Unit, 1955–58*, Lahore: University of the Punjab.

Mehdi, S. (1988) *Politics Without Parties: A Report on the 1985 Partyless Election in Pakistan*, Lahore: SAHE.

Mehkri, G.M. (1987) *Sorrows of Sindh*, Hyderabad Sind: Sind Friends Circle.

Mirza, M. (1987) *Aaj Ka Sindh*, Lahore: Progressive Publishers.

Noman, O. (1988) *The Political Economy of Pakistan 1947–85*, London: KPI.

Qureshi, S. (1989) 'The politics of the Shia minority in Pakistan: context and development' in D. Vajpeyi and Y.K. Malik (eds), *Religious and Ethnic Minority Politics in South Asia*, New Delhi: Manohar.

Report of the Court of Inquiry Constituted under Punjab Act II of 1954 to Enquire into the Punjab Disturbances of 1953 (Munir Report) (1954), Lahore: Government Printing Press.

A Research Officer (1989) 'Under-representation of the people of Sind in federal services' in K. Bahadur and U. Singh (eds), *Pakistan: Transition to Democracy*, New Delhi: Patriot Publishers.

Richter, W.L. (1993) 'The 1990 general elections in Pakistan' in C.H. Kennedy, *Pakistan: 1992*, Boulder: Westview Press.

Rizvi, A.H. (1993) *India: A Terrorist State* (document supplied by the Pakistan Embassy in Stockholm).

Saavan (bilingual Urdu–English monthly), Lahore.

Sayed, G.M. (1985) *A Case for Sindhu Desh,* Bombay: Sorath.

Sayeed, K.B. (1980) *Politics in Pakistan: The Nature and Direction of Change,* New York: Praeger.

Shackle, C. (1976) *The Siraiki Language of Central Pakistan: A Reference Grammar,* London: School of Oriental and African Studies.

Sindh Inquiry: Summer 1990, Lahore: Human Rights Commission of Pakistan.

Waseem, M. (1989) *Politics and the State in Pakistan,* Lahore: Progressive.

Zaidi, S.A. (1992) 'Sindhi vs Muhajir contradiction, conflict, compromise' in S.A. Zaidi (ed.), *Regional Imbalances and the National Question in Pakistan,* Lahore: Vanguard.

Interviews March–April 1990

Professor Azizuddin Ahmed (Punjabi)

Mumtaz Ali Bhutto, chief minister of Sindh in 1972 (Sindhi)

Rafiq Khan, PPP activist and political refugee in Sweden (Punjabi)

Dr Hamida Khuhro, academic, Sindhi historian (Sindhi)

Professor Hamid Hasan Kizilbash, political scientist, Punjab University (Punjabi)

Faqir Muhammad Lashari, journalist (Sindhi)

Rao Tariq Latif, labour leader and political activist (Urdu-speaking refugee settled in Lahore, Punjab, and assimilated into Punjabi culture)

Professor Khalid Mahmud (Punjabi-speaking Azad Kashmiri)

Hussain Naqi, journalist (Urdu-speaking refugee settled in Lahore, informed on Shia affairs)

Abdul Hafeez Pirzada, ex-law minister in PPP government (Sindhi)

Hanif Ramay, ex-chief minister of Punjab and PPP leader (Punjabi)

Junaid Bakhsh Soomro, ex-member Sindh Legislative Assembly (Sindhi)

Mir Thebo, Sindhi political activist

S. Akbar Zaidi, Senior Research Officer, Department of Applied Economics, Karachi University (Urdu-speaking refugee)

Fakhar Zaman, poet, writer and politician, president of Punjab PPP in 1990 (Punjabi)

Several senior Pakistani bureaucrats who wish to remain anonymous

8

Bangladesh

On 16 December 1971 East Pakistan broke away from Pakistan and became the sovereign, independent state of Bangladesh. At that time it had a population of over 74 million, squeezed into only 143,999 sq. km.

Bangladeshi society and polity

According to the 1981 Census of Bangladesh the total population of the country was 87,120,000. The religious composition was as given in Table 11. The annual population growth rate was 2.3 per cent. The rate of literacy was 25 per cent. The estimated population of Bangladesh in 1989 was 109.13 million.

Languages

More than 98 per cent of the Bangladesh population is Bengali-speaking. The various tribes and aboriginal groups constitute less than 1 per cent of the population. Some speak local Bengali dialects, others various Tibeto-Burmese languages and two minuscule groups speak Dravidian languages. There are at present some 250,000 Urdu-speaking Bihari Muslims stranded in Bangladesh. They had originally migrated to East Pakistan from the neighbouring Bihar province at the time of Partition in 1947. During the 1971 civil war, which culminated in the creation of Bangladesh, the Biharis tended to collaborate with the Pakistani army. Most expressed the desire to migrate to Pakistan. Consequently, except for those few who have adopted Bangladeshi citizenship, they are considered Pakistani citizens who are to be repatriated to Pakistan. Pakistan, on the other hand, has been reluctant to accept them.

From East Pakistan to Bangladesh

Much to the chagrin of the Bengalis, in February 1948 Prime Minister Liaqat Ali Khan stated in the Pakistan Constituent Assembly that Urdu would be the sole

Table 11 Religion in Bangladesh, 1981, no. and percentage

Muslims	75,487,000	86.6
Hindus	10,570,000	12.1
Buddhists	538,000	⎫
Christians	275,000	⎬ 1.3
Others	250,000	⎭

national language of Pakistan. This was reiterated later in March by Governor-General Mohamed Ali Jinnah in a public speech at Dhaka. Now, Bengali was not only the mother-tongue of more than 55 per cent of Pakistan's population but also a highly developed language which had been in official use for a long time. Jinnah's speech provoked angry demonstrations by Bengali students. The language question was to become the centrepiece of emergent Bengali nationalism. Bengalis expressed their dissatisfaction against West Pakistani domination in the provincial elections held in East Pakistan on 8 March 1954. A United Front consisting of Bengali parties such as the Awami League, the Krishak Sramik Party and the Nizam-e-Islam Party won 223 out of 237 Muslim seats. The ruling Muslim League secured only 10 seats. A United Front government was formed on 3 April 1954. On 19 April 1954 the Constituent Assembly of Pakistan passed a resolution recognizing both Urdu and Bengali as national languages, but stipulating that English would be an official language for another 20 years. However, on 30 May the central government dissolved the East Pakistan Assembly and the government was dismissed, ostensibly for advocating secession (Gankovsky and Gordon-Polonskaya, 1972: 204–5).

In the economic sphere also, Bengali grievances began to mount. The flight of Hindus to India did provide opportunities to the Bengali Muslims to advance into lower and medium range professions and economic activities. However, the top positions in the bureaucracy and army remained in the hands of West Pakistanis. For example Bengalis constituted only 7 per cent of the Pakistan army (Khan, 1983: 18). Similarly, big business and industry located in East Pakistan was owned by the West Pakistan bourgeoisie. The ten-year period 1955–65 saw Pakistan make impressive strides in industrial development, mostly in light consumer products. Undertaken with massive financial and technological assistance from the industrialized West, the development strategy and policy which the state adopted tended to accentuate uneven development between the two wings of the country. Some 70–80 per cent of development aid was allocated to West Pakistan and the remainder to East Pakistan. On the other hand, the resources transferred from East Pakistan to West Pakistan between 1948–49 and 1968–69 were to the tune of Pakistani Rupees 31,120 million. Jute mills were established in East Pakistan, but their owners were West Pakistanis. In 1968–69 the per capita income of East Pakistan was Rupees 291.5 and in West Pakistan Rupees 473.4. Consequently the Bengali majority began increasingly to see itself as a victim of 'internal colonialism' (Ahmed, 1973: 421–5).

The liberation struggle

The Awami League led by Sheikh Mujibur Rahman appeared as the main representative of Bengali separatism in the late 1960s. Several other Bengali radical-nationalists such as the peasant leader Maulana Bhashani also demanded greater autonomy for East Pakistan. Sheikh Mujibur Rahman put forward a six-point programme of East Pakistan autonomy (*Bangladesh Papers*, 1980: 23–33):

1   Pakistan should be a true federation based on the 1940 Lahore Resolution.
2   The federal government should deal only with two subjects, viz.: Defence and Foreign Affairs, and all other residuary subjects should be vested in the federating states.
3   There should be two separate but freely convertible currencies or one currency may be maintained if flight of capital from East to West Pakistan is stopped through constitutional provisions.
4   The powers of taxation and revenue collection should be vested in the federating units.
5   There should be two separate accounts for foreign exchange earnings of the two wings, indigenous products shall move freely between the two wings, and the units should be empowered to directly establish trade and commercial relations with foreign countries.
6   A separate militia or paramilitary force should be set up for the defence of East Pakistan.

The six-point programme went far beyond the ordinary notion of federalism and was virtually a call for converting Pakistan into a confederation. Despite its drastic contents the military government of General Yahya Khan (1969–71) let the Awami League propagate it freely during the December 1970 general elections. To everybody's surprise, not least that of the West Pakistan ruling military–bureaucratic oligarchy, the Awami League made a clean sweep of the polls. It won 160 out of 162 seats for East Pakistan in the 300-member Pakistan National Assembly. In West Pakistan the Pakistan People's Party (PPP) emerged as the main winner with 83 seats in the National Assembly.

By winning an absolute majority the Awami League was, in accordance with parliamentary procedure, entitled to form the government at the centre. However, President Yahya Khan was dissuaded from doing so by his advisers, particularly the main winner in West Pakistan, Zulfikar Ali Bhutto (Khan, 1983: 24–35). Talks between the government and the Awami League leadership took place, but the deadlock could not be broken. In the evening of 25 March 1971 the army launched a military operation against perceived targets of a growing insurgence. Thereafter followed several months of bloodshed and debauchery at the hands of the army. Hindus, students and trade union activists were particular targets of the army (interviews Ahmed, Maniruzzaman, Razzaq, 1990).

Several million Bengalis fled to India. Thousands came back trained to fight the army. The leadership of the Mukti Bahini, the main organization involved in the armed struggle, was in the hands of Awami League leaders who fled to India and established their bases there. Gradually a Bengali resistance began to evolve within the larger society. Within Bangladesh, sections of the leftist forces also launched armed struggle against the Pakistani army. As a result West Pakistani army and civilian personnel, their families and Bengali and Bihari collaborators of the Pakistani authorities were killed in large numbers. Atrocities perpetrated by the militants were also harrowing. Cases of rape, burning and maiming of women and children were reported in the Pakistani and international press. By September–October 1971 tens of thousands of Bengalis had joined the guerrilla army. By November the guerrillas were becoming effective. On 3 December, the Indian army intervened. It was given full support by the people. By 17 December the Pakistan army had surrendered and 94,000 troops were taken prisoners by India. The number of people killed during the army's genocide is estimated to have exceeded several hundred thousand (Ali, 1983: 90–6).

During the civil war most of the politically active *ulama* of East Pakistan either remained aloof from the liberation struggle or sided with the Pakistani state. They perceived in the break-up of Pakistan a loss for Islam. The Biharis collaborated with the Pakistani army because they identified themselves with the unity of Pakistan.

Cultural premisses of the Bangladeshi polity

Two cultural factors are intrinsic to the Bangladeshi national identity. Firstly, the Islamic faith is shared by more than 86 per cent of the population. Bangladeshi Muslims are almost entirely Sunnis. Secondly, a rich artistic and literary tradition is preserved in Bengali, one of the most developed languages of the Indian subcontinent. According to Talukder Maniruzzaman (1982: 215–16), East Bengal has historically been quite distinct from West Bengal. The population of the eastern region, known as Vanga, was predominantly Buddhist and of Mongoloid extraction. It was here that Islam gained most of its converts, largely through the efforts of the various Sufi orders. West Bengal, known as Gauda, was of mixed Aryan stock and predominantly Hindu.

The syncretic–majoritarian nation-state project and organizing ideology

Although the liberation struggle had involved destruction of life and property on a large scale, Sheikh Mujibur Rahman and his nearest colleagues seemed to have had no clear vision of the ideological foundations of an independent Bangladesh. They had invoked secular Bengali nationalism but were not seeking a merger with the adjacent Indian State of West Bengal, where Hindus constituted the vast majority in a population of over 44 million. Therefore, although the struggle against West Pakistan was expressed in terms of linguistic nationalism and legitimized in terms of allegations of exploitation and discrimination by West Pakistan, the religious factor continued to be the actual cut-off point for the territorial realization of self-determination: self-determination over Muslim East Bengal. Consequently, nation-building in the relatively more homogeneous Bangladesh has contained an underlying religious dimension.

The state has been experimenting with a syncretic–majoritarian model of nation-state which seeks to synthesize the Bengali linguistic identity with an Islamic one. There are arguments suggesting that the Bengali language spoken by the Muslims of Bangladesh differs substantially from that of the Hindu Bengalis because of the presence of a rich vocabulary of Persian, Arabic and Urdu words (interview, Hosein, 1990). The promotion of a Bangladeshi cultural identity has been receiving state patronage in various spheres. The mass media and school system have, of course, been involved in such projects. In recent years, a drift towards greater conformity to Islamic symbols and values has been taking place and it seems that the majoritarian–syncretic project is likely to move away from the secular pole.

The Bangladesh Constitution

The 1972 Bangladesh Constitution adopted by the National Assembly of Bangladesh declared the state as a secular, democratic, unitary People's Republic of Bangladesh. A parliamentary democracy, based on a universal adult franchise was adopted as the framework for government. However, the principle of secularism was replaced under the constitutional amendment of 1977 with a clause which stated: 'absolute trust and faith in the Almighty Allah to be the basis of all actions'. Also, whereas in 1972 the usual term 'Bengalee' had been used to describe the citizens of Bangladesh (Iftekharuzzaman and Rahman, 1986: 18–19), in 1977 the citizens of Bangladesh were redefined as 'Bangladeshi'. Article 2A inserted by Act 30 in 1988 declared 'The state religion of the Republic is Islam, but other religions may be practised in peace and harmony in the Republic'.

Bangla as national language

Originally Article 3 had declared 'Bengali' as the official language. In 1988 it was replaced by 'Bangla' as the name of the official language. As mentioned earlier, it was asserted that Bangla had a different vocabulary — deriving from Islamic sources such as Persian, Arabic and Urdu tongues — in comparison to Bengali spoken by Hindus. At any rate, the decision to change the name to Bangla was in consonance with the distinction drawn between Bengalee and Bangladeshi. Thus Bangla and Bangladeshi became the distinguishing symbols of Muslim East Bengali identity.

The central élite and the political process

Notwithstanding its origins in a bloody civil war, Bangladesh did not undergo a social revolution. The Bengali bureaucrats and military officers trained and recruited during the Pakistan period became the upper echelon of the Bangladeshi state machinery. Craig Baxter (1984: 77–8) distinguishes between the freedom fighters and the 'returnees' in the army. The former trace their roots to the liberation struggle against Pakistan and consider themselves the custodians of the radical nationalist spirit. On the other hand, the returnees are those who were stationed in Pakistan during the war and could return only after liberation. The two sections have had their differences, and the rift has subsequently plagued their relationship. It is interesting to note that in 1980 the combined strength of the Bangladesh armed forces was only 77,500 (Hossain, 1983: 24–5). Although subsequently some expansion has taken place it has not been dramatic.

The military coup against Sheikh Mujibur Rahman in 1975 was carried out by radical middle-range officers disappointed with the widespread corruption of the civilian regime. The later coups and counter-coups have also had a high degree of participation of middle-range officers. Additionally, the large body of freedom fighters, some trade unions, particularly that of the union of transport workers, the student community and the urban middle class also enjoy considerable political clout (*Bangladesh*, 1986: 73).

At present, two main moderate political parties compete for power at the centre: the Bangladesh National Party (BNP) led by Prime Minister Mrs Khalida Zia and the Awami League led by Mrs Sheikh Hasina. Right-wing religious parties have in recent years considerably increased their influence on the state. The Marxists are in disarray and lack influence.

The class and social bases of populism

Neither big landlords nor a significant industrial bourgeoisie were inherited by Bangladesh at the time of liberation. Moreover the larger West-Pakistani-owned industries were nationalized. After liberation several indigenous medium-range producers found an opportunity to advance and today constitute the upper bourgeoisie, producing mostly light consumer goods. A powerful factor in the country is the rather large number of rich peasants and capitalist farmers (Asplund, 1977: 99, 120–2; Baxter, 1984: 79–80). The somewhat egalitarian class structure is augmented by the absence of caste among Bangladeshi Muslims. However, the vast majority of the population, consisting of peasants and workers, is abjectly poor and without influence on the political process.

All the regimes that have come to power in Bangladesh have had a populist–nationalist approach to politics in which the Islamic factor has gradually been elevated to a central position by the central élite: both as a means of attaining legitimacy at home and in response to external pressure and perceived threats. In 1973 Sheikh Mujibur Rahman won a massive election victory. Thereafter his popularity began to dwindle because the state failed to manage the egregious socio-economic problems of unemployment, widespread destruction during the liberation struggle and overall dislocation. Global inflation and price-hiking in the aftermath of the 1973 Arab–Israeli war hit Bangladesh badly. A devastating famine ravaged Bangladesh in 1974. Additionally anti-India feelings rose sharply among the middle class, which blamed India for, on the one hand, not seeking an amiable solution with Bangladesh over the sharing of river waters, and, on the other hand, subverting Bangladesh's jute industry through various unfair means.

But worst of all, the government and leaders of the Awami League were suspected of widespread corruption. The leftist forces within the army wanted to carry through a social revolution. Confronted by rising public discontent, Mujib began to invoke Islamic symbols to regain the political initiative and to solicit Arab petro-dollars (Kabir, 1986: 51–3). In 1975 he attempted a constitutional coup against the democratic basis of Bangladesh by introducing a one-party system. This triggered a military coup in August 1975 by young officers, mostly holding the rank of major and below. Sheikh Mujibur Rahman and some of his family members were brutally murdered.

The government of General Ziaur Rahman (1975–81) began to emphasize the Islamic cultural identity of the state in a more concerted manner. The constitutional clause in the preamble of the 1972 constitution explicitly mentioned secularism as one of the ideals of the liberation (Ahmed, 1984: 93). General Ziaur Rahman had it deleted, and instead 'trust and faith in the Almighty Allah' was inserted and Islam was declared as the state religion. The fundamentalist Jamaat-e-Islami, which had been disgraced for collaborating with the Pakistani army, was allowed to re-establish itself. The assumption of a more explicit Islamic identity helped Bangladesh to cultivate closer relations with Saudi Arabia and other Gulf states (Baxter, 1984: 104–5). This brought forth substantial financial support from the Islamic countries, and Bangladeshi workers began to be recruited in the

Gulf region. Relations between India and Bangladesh began to deteriorate while with Pakistan they improved. In retaliation India mounted its assistance to the tribal guerrilla movement in the Chittagong Hill Tracts (CHT).

General Hussain Mohammed Ershad (1982–90) continued more or less the same policy of greater adherence to Islamic discourse and symbolism. Consequently the fundamentalist forces began to reassert themselves, demanding Islamization of the polity. Since 1991 an elected government under Mrs Khalida Zia has been in power. Thus far Bangladesh has not gone so far as to declare Bangladesh an Islamic state. The state does not impose any religious or gender restrictions on the political rights of citizens. It is only in personal matters that Islamic law applies currently, but voices are being raised for a more substantial Islamic overhaul of the legal system.

Ethnic conflict and separatism

Although Bangladesh is the poorest of the four countries included in the present investigation, it has not faced ethnic conflict of the same intensity as the other three largely because of a high degree of homogeneity in terms of religion and language. However, the notion of homogeneity in the Bangladeshi context needs to be put into perspective.

Hindus and other minorities

Bengali Hindus constitute the main religious minority of Bangladesh. They are dispersed throughout the country both in rural and urban areas. In 1947 Hindus made up some 23 per cent of the population of East Pakistan. In 1951 the Hindu percentage of the population had gone down to 22 per cent. By 1961 it had declined to 18.3 per cent. Hindus kept migrating to India because of an increasing sense of insecurity resulting from recurrent communal riots. During the 1971 civil war, the Pakistan army particularly targeted the Hindus in its cleansing operations. This resulted in a massive flight to India. Thus the delayed Census held in 1974 (that for 1971 could not be held because of the civil war) gave the Hindu population as only 13.5 per cent. Thus a decrease of almost 5 per cent from the 1961 figure had occurred because of the civil war. The 1981 Census gives the Hindu population as 12.1 per cent. Therefore the trend of Hindus migrating to India had continued.

The reasons for migrating are not entirely political. In the neighbouring West Bengal state a Marxist regime has been in power for more than a decade. It has carried out many reforms in the interests of the peasants and the poor. Many poor Bangladeshi Hindus cross the border in the hope of a better life under the Marxist government. However, attacks on Hindus increased dramatically after the December 1992 Babri mosque incident in India. Destruction of Hindu temples, arson, looting and brutal acts of rape and killing took place in the wake of the riots in India (*Bangladesh*, 1993). A new wave of migration from Bangladesh is currently on the way.

As regards Christians and other minorities dispersed in the society, very little is known. It is among the hill people of the Chittagong Hill Tracts that separatism has received its strongest expression through the combined impact of economic development and Bengali cultural extension in the region.

The Chittagong Hill Tracts

The Chittagong Hill Tracts (CHT) are situated in one of the most trouble-ridden regions of South Asia. India, Burma and Bangladesh share borders in the region and each state has been facing separatist challenges from the hill peoples located there. The CHT consist traditionally of the Bandarban, Rangamati and Khagrachari districts of Bangladesh. They are surrounded on the east by the Indian state of Mizoram (established in 1976), the Burmese state of Arakan in the south and the Indian state of Tripura in the north and north-west. Bangladesh's chief port and second largest city, Chittagong, is only a few kilometres away. The CHT cover 13,190 sq. km and form around 10 per cent of the total land area of Bangladesh. Slightly over half of the forest area lies in the CHT. Some 25 per cent is classified as reserved. The remainder is designated as 'unclassed state forests' (Bertocci, 1989: 153). The CHT play an important part in the economy of Bangladesh. There were only about 751,000 people or less than 1 per cent of the Bangladesh population living in this region. In 1981 of these some 60 per cent were tribals and the rest Bengalis settled in this area.

The CHT have the largest concentration of Bangladesh's tribal peoples, 49.2 per cent. They are also known locally as Adibashis or indigenous people, although they might have migrated from the adjoining Burmese region only some centuries earlier. The tribals are mostly Buddhists although some tribes are Hindu. Christians and Animists are also to be found. The main source of livelihood of the tribals is subsistence agriculture, mainly shifting swidden cultivation called *jhum* (slash and burn) farming, although plough cultivation has also grown substantially over the years. In 1981 some 17.7 per cent of the tribal adult population was recorded as literate as against 25 per cent for the rest of Bangladesh. The tribals are organized into a system of chieftains. The Bengali population is involved in a number of economic activities, including trade and agriculture. After 1947 the Pakistan government began to settle some landless cultivators in the hill tracts. The government of Bangladesh followed the same policy, although since 1985 the government of Bangladesh is formally committed to stopping further influx. At any rate, the influx of Bengalis was seen by the hill people as colonization. The CHT ethnic conflict and separatist struggle grew out of the increasing Bengali presence and the various developmental initiatives taken in the region by the Bangladesh government.

The tribes living in CHT are the Chakma, Marma, Tripura, Tanchanga, Mura, Uchai, Lushai, Bom, Pankua, Chak, Khiang and Mumis (Bertocci, 1989: 144). The Chakmas are the largest and the dominant group in cultural, educational and economic as well as political terms. Their numbers in 1981 were estimated at around 210,000 or 48 per cent of the tribal population. The Chakmas have their own folklore and mythology as well as religious literature and script. They speak a dialect of Bengali. The second largest group is the Marma, who are pejoratively referred to as Maghs. They were estimated to be some 125,000 or 28 per cent. The third largest group is the Tipperas, who make up 12 per cent of the tribal population. Tipperas live on both sides of the international boundary between Bangladesh and India. The other tribes also have kin in the adjoining areas of India and Burma. Allegiance to kinship groups is stronger than to the states in which these people are placed.

History of the Chittagong Hill Tracts

Historically the CHT hill people remained largely secluded from the plains people. The Mughuls had integrated the plains of Chittagong district into their empire as early as 1713. However, the hills to the east were left out of the imperial system, but were obligated to pay a tribute in the form of a levy on cotton. In 1760 the British took over the Chittagong region from the Mughuls. The new power continued to levy a tax on cotton. Additionally it tried to introduce non-tribespeople as tax collectors, but this innovation was successfully resisted by the local people. Thereafter tribal chiefs took on the function of tax collection on behalf of the British (Bertocci, 1989: 146). In 1787 the British conquered the CHT but left the area in a quasi-independent status. In 1860 it was officially annexed and the District of Chittagong Hill Tracts was established. The CHT forests presented an obvious potential for economic exploitation. As the economic activities, mainly timber and bamboo trade via the rivers, grew, the British encouraged Bengalis to settle in this area. The Bengali settlers gradually came to control the new economy and in the process reduced the tribespeople into a dependent position.

This change created considerable dissatisfaction among the tribes. Consequently the British changed their policy. In 1900 the CHT Regulation was adopted, which empowered the officer in charge of the area to restrict migration to the district from other parts in the region. The CHT Regulation gave the local people a limited measure of self-government. The 1900 Regulation divided the Hill Tracts into three revenue spheres, each headed by a Raja (king). Additionally, the British created a hierarchy by creating privileged landowning classes (Amin, 1988–89:

111). Measures were also undertaken to isolate the CHT from other parts of British India. In 1921 CHT was declared a 'Backward Tract'. The Government of India Act of 1935, which served as the constitutional framework for British India, declared it as a 'Totally Excluded Area'.

The 1947 Partition allotted CHT to Pakistan. This was strongly opposed by the tribespeople who preferred union with India. As a Mongoloid, Buddhist people the tribespeople feared union with a confessional state created in the name of Islam. They raised the Indian flag and their leader, Sneh Kumar Chakma, demanded that CHT should be incorporated into India. However, such protests were of no avail. In any case, from the very onset a mutual suspicion existed between the tribals and the government of Pakistan (Banu, 1991: 240). Thus from 1947 to 1956 Pakistan continued to appoint British deputy commissioners in CHT so as to avoid antagonizing the indigenous people who were opposed to Muslim domination (Bertocci, 1989: 149). However, the modernizing Ayub regime abolished the special status of CHT in 1964. Local officials and locally recruited police were replaced by non-locals. Restrictions on immigration were lifted. Efforts were made to incorporate the tribal people into mainstream Pakistani politics. The government encouraged the spread of education in the CHT. Several schools and a college were opened in the CHT during the early 1960s.

Economic grievances of the tribals

The economic integration of CHT into the Bengali economy also dates from the British period. By the 1860s Bengali moneylenders (of the Hindu Mahajan caste) had begun to replace the tribal chiefs as providers of credit to the hill people. The new lending system soon turned into pure extortion reducing the tribespeople into virtual slavery. On the other hand, the government accelerated trade in forest products while simultaneously introducing measures to conserve the forests. Various tariffs on timber and bamboo products were introduced. Bengalis from the plains who came to control the wood trade made the most of the new opportunities. In 1875 some areas of the CHT were declared as reserved. The traditional slash and burn or swidden system of cultivation known locally as *jhum* was forbidden in the reserved forests. Concerted efforts, including generous grants, were made to induce the tribesmen to abandon swidden cultivation in favour of plough cultivation and to settle down in sedentary villages. However, such attempts met with little success. Gradually, some tribal chiefs began to employ Bengali sharecroppers. Thus by the 1950s plough cultivation became increasingly prevalent. More importantly, after 1947 there was a great influx of Bengalis into CHT. In 1951 the Bengali population of CHT was 9.1 per cent; in 1961 it had increased to 17.7 per cent; and in 1980 it reached 27.5 per cent. More crucially, by the 1980s Bengalis were in control of most of the economy of the CHT.

There were several factors behind the Bengali influx. Apart from the growing problem of land shortage in the plains which encouraged encroachment in the CHT, the thick forest, the extremely heavy rainfall and the Karnafuli river rendered it attractive for the government to develop it for the production of hydro-electric power. The World Bank and other development agencies backed Pakistan's development plans for the CHT. Work on the Kaptai Dam at Karnafuli began in 1956. However, the site chosen for the dam was inhabited by nearly half the population of CHT, mainly the Chakmas. The objections of the local people were overruled and large numbers of Chakmas were displaced. When the dam was completed in 1962 some 1036 sq. km, including 650 sq. km of the best agricultural land, had been submerged under water. It constituted about 40 per cent of the agricultural land of the area. Nearly 100,000 persons were displaced, mostly Chakmas but also 1000 Marma and 8000 Bengali Muslim settlers. Of these, some 55 per cent were engaged in settled plough cultivation. Such change created considerable economic hardship and unemployment in the area. On the other hand, the construction of the Kaptai Dam was a success in terms of greatly increased output of electricity. The Kaptai Dam could generate 80,000 kW, which was over 25 per cent of Bangladesh's total output (Bertocci, 1989: 153–6). However, the electricity was supplied to the suburban areas outside CHT, while the local people were denied access to it.

The development projects associated with the Karnafuli paper mills and other related industries accelerated the activity of non-tribal business interests. Transportation and marketing facilities came increasingly under Bengali control. Also in terms of employment the indigenous people were largely excluded from the opportunities resulting from the new developments. Thus out of a total work force of 6000 only 40 hillmen were employed in the paper mills. President Ziaur Rahman allocated Takas 60 million for settling 30,000 Bengali families in the region. On the other hand, the local people displaced by the Kaptai Dam project were denied any kind of monetary or land compensation (Amin, 1988–89: 113).

The origins of separatism

Separatist ideas were present among the hill people even before the formation of Pakistan. As a Mongoloid people, professing mainly the Buddhist faith, the hill people wanted to be autonomous. The slogan put forward was 'hill tracts for the hillmen' (Bertocci, 1989: 159). Consequently the Pakistani authorities arrested many of the activists and used other high-handed methods to suppress the movement. Sneh Kumar Chakma, who opposed CHT being awarded to Pakistan, fled to India from where he kept drawing attention to the issue of CHT autonomy. The gradual expansion of education in CHT and the opening in 1965 of the Rangamati Government College played an important role in producing an intelligentsia that could articulate the grievances of the tribespeople. The rate of growth of literacy in CHT between 1961 and 1974 was 73 per cent as against 59 per cent for the rest of Bangladesh. How much of it was the result of the influx of educated Bengalis into CHT is difficult to know, but it is important to note that a broad cadre independent of the tribal leaders could gradually emerge in CHT.

During the 1971 civil war Raja Tridev Roy, the Chakma leader, sided with the Pakistani army. Many tribals, however, crossed over to India with the intention of joining the struggle against Pakistan. They were instead treated as collaborators of the Pakistani army. The main liberation force of the Bengali secessionists, the Mukti Bahini, terrorized the tribal people, killing many of them. An anti-Bangladesh and anti-Mukti Bahini feeling therefore developed among them (Banu, 1991: 241). This was exploited by the Pakistani army, which recruited many of them into its voluntary corps of 'Razakars'. After liberation the government of Mujibur Rahman (1972–75) let loose a reign of terror in the CHT area. Many tribespeople crossed over into India. The special status of the CHT granted in 1900, which had been withdrawn in 1964 by the Ayub government, was not restored under the 1972 constitution. Instead all land was placed under a common land law, thus removing all restrictions on free movement of people and goods (Saeed, 1987–88: 75). An impetus was given to greater Bengali settlement in the CHT. Consequently the tribespeople became increasingly worried about Bengali expansionism. In a meeting with Prime Minister Mujibur Rahman on 15 February 1972, Manobendra Narayan Larma, a Chakma member of the Bangladesh Parliament, presented the following four demands (Amin, 1988–89: 114):

1 Autonomy with its own legislature for the Chittagong Hill Tracts.
2 Retention of the 1900 Regulation in the Bangladesh constitution.
3 Tribal chiefs to be allowed to remain in office with full administrative powers.
4 A constitutional guarantee to the effect that the 1900 Regulation shall not be amended and Bengali families will not be allowed to settle in the area.

Mujib rejected these demands outright, branding them as secessionist. The hill people were advised by Mujib to assimilate with mainstream Bengali nationalism (Banu, 1991: 241). The government declared that tribals should have the same Bengali education and identify with the rest of the people. Such a monocultural policy of the government provoked the following response from M.N. Larma: 'I am a Chakma not a Bengali. I am a citizen of Bangladesh, a Bangladeshi. You are also a Bangladeshi but your national identity is Bengali' (Amin, 1988–89: 117). The government ignored the objections.

Consequently a revolt among the tribal people against the Bangladesh government took place. In 1976 the first clash occurred between tribal guerrillas and the Bangladesh army. The successive governments of General Ziaur Rahman (1975–81) and Ershad (1982–90) maintained an uncompromising position on the demands of the CHT people, and as a consequence an armed confrontation has continued between the government and the CHT people. In fact General Ershad greatly exacerbated the already strained relations by establishing, with Saudi Arabian financial support, an Islamic culture centre and a mosque in Rangamati. This was seen by the local people as a move to promote conversions among them. The result was greater resistance from them.

Evolution of organized armed resistance

Notwithstanding their small numbers, the CHT hill people have been successful in developing quite effective resistance to the Bangladesh state. Under the leadership of Manobendra Narayan Larma, Jyotindralal Bodhipriya Larma, Jyotindralal Tripura, Bhavotosh Dewan, Amirya Sen Chakma and Kali Madhav Chakma, efforts were successfully made to unite the various tribes in support of the four-point programme presented earlier to the Bangladesh government. These leaders formed the Rangamati Communist Party (RCS) on 15 May 1972, and a day later the founding was announced of the Parbottya Chattagram Jana Sanghati Samity (PCJSS) as an open platform of the RCP. The ideology adopted derived from both Marxist and nationalist ideas. Although the PCJSS defined feudalism as the main enemy and set itself the task of its liquidation through Maoist guerrilla tactics, it was mainly the conflict with the Bangladesh government and Bengali settlers that dominated its activities. As the confrontation deepened and the level and extent of armed violence increased, the PCJSS began to lay even greater emphasis on the nationalist aspects of its programme. It adopted a modified four-point programme (Amin, 1988–89: 115).

1 Self-determination with a separate legislature.
2 Restoration of the fundamental rights of the tribespeople.
3 Constitutional guarantee assuring the preservation of the national identity of the tribal people.
4 Complete ban on the influx of Bengali outsiders, dismantling of Bengali settlements and transfer of land occupied by the plains people to the tribespeople.

An armed wing, the Gono Mukti Fouj, of the PCJSS, commonly known as the Shanti Bahini, has been carrying out armed struggle since 1972. After the assassination of Mujibur Rahman in 1975, Larma and other leaders of the PCJSS crossed over to India from where they organized guerrilla raids into Bangladesh. The Indian government had been greatly perturbed by the death of Mujib. Relations between the two governments began to cool off thereafter and even became hostile. Indian connivance and support to the PCJSS cadres operating from bases on its territories followed. The Indian press also began to give wide coverage to the struggle of the CHT people (Saeed, 1987–88: 65).

The Ziaur Rahman government embarked upon a policy aiming at, on the one hand, economic uplift and, on the other, greater political and military control of the CHT. In 1976 a large-scale development programme was initiated with a view to increasing local participation in development activities. The Chittagong Hill Tracts Development Board (CHTBD) was established at Rangamati. Although a majority of the Board members were from among the tribal people, the real power resided in the Cabinet Division of the central government. The development schemes did, however, bring economic relief to the people. Simultaneously the presence of government soldiers was increased to the strength of a full division to deal with CHT rebels (Amin, 1988–89: 118).

In 1978 an influential member of the central committee, Priti Kumar Chakma, triggered an ideological conflict on the strategy to emancipate the CHT. He urged that the CHT problem should be solved within a short period on a nationalist basis and the impractical ideas of Marx, Lenin and Mao be abandoned. On the other hand, Manobendra Larma insisted that a protracted struggle based on class struggle should be pursued. The result was a split into a Larma faction and a Priti faction in October 1982. On 10 November 1983 Larma was assassinated by the Priti group. Further splits have followed in both factions.

Escalation of the conflict during the 1980s

The situation in the CHT deteriorated in early 1980 when the Shanti Bahini killed twenty-two army men, including an officer. On 25 March 1980 the Bangladesh army carried out a massacre at Kaokhali Bazar in which, according to Upendralal Chakma, a member of the Bangladesh National Assembly, more than 300 tribal civilians, including women and children, were killed. Upendralal Chakma protested vociferously, demanding neutral inquiry into the incident. The government formed a five-member parliamentary committee to look into the law and order situation in the CHT. The committee, however, did not include a single member from the opposition. The opposition therefore appointed its own three-member fact-finding committee comprising MPs Shahjahan Siraj and Upendralal Chakma of the Jaityo Samajtantrik and Rashed Khan Menon of the Workers Party. The committee observed that the CHT problem should be resolved politically by ensuring the rights of the oppressed tribal people. It recommended the following measures to redress the grievances of the CHT people (Amin, 1988–89: 119):

1 A judicial inquiry into the 25 March 1980 incident and punishment of the guilty.
2 Rehabilitation of the affected people with due security arrangements.
3 Reconstruction of the damaged Buddhist religious institutions, compensation for the losses incurred and apology for hurting religious sentiments.

4   Control on the influx of Bengalis.
5   Immediate withdrawal of the plainspeople settled in the district.
6   Withdrawal of restrictions on the movement of goods in the market and bazaars.

Not only were these recommendations ignored by Ziaur Rahman but he took even harsher measures to quell the disturbances. Some 20,000 soldiers had been deployed in the CHT by the early 1980s. The police force was doubled in size. A new law was proposed in Parliament by the government in December 1980 which conferred unrestricted powers to lower-ranking police and military officers to shoot anyone suspected of anti-state activities. Arrest without warrant was instituted to round up suspects in the disturbed areas. It was not only adopted, but any challenge to it in a court of law was disallowed (Amin, 1988–89: 119). Upendralal Chakma described it as a genocidal solution to the problem of ethnic minorities of the CHT.

The law, however, did not come into effect, because Ziaur Rahman was assassinated in May 1981. On the other hand, by the early 1980s the army had installed modern telecommunication facilities and built better roads in the region. This considerably facilitated its control over the region. By mid-1983 the Ershad government had begun to organize the defence of the Bengali population through the creation of an armed village defence police. In mid-1986 general amnesty was offered to the rebels if they laid down their arms. Some 2500 members of the Priti group took advantage of the offer and surrendered. On the other hand, the Larma group intensified its violent activities with the backing of the Indian government. The Bangladesh government sought to counter the insurrection by soliciting support among less hostile sections of indigenous society. The Tribal Convention with Charu Chauhan Bikash Chakma as its general secretary was one such body which enjoyed government patronage. Its support came from a section of the tiny urban CHT middle class. The Tribal Convention, however, could not succeed in establishing itself as a counter-weight to the Shanti Bahini (Amin, 1988–89: 120).

The Shanti Bahini widened its activities to include kidnapping of foreign personnel working on the various developmental projects. Similar terrorist acts were perpetrated against the Bengali settlers. In 1984, the worst attack on the Bengalis took place. Some 80 persons were killed and 800 injured (Bertocci, 1989: 162). The Bangladesh press reported these cases of rape and brutul killings. On the other hand, acts of state terrorism were almost never reported (*Bangladesh*, 1986: 75–6). The Shanti Bahini was constituted mainly of Chakmas. The Bangladesh government put the number of cadres in arms at 2000. In the *1988 Asia Yearbook of the Far Eastern Economic Review* the estimated number of guerrillas was 8000. Since 1984, the Shanti Bahini itself claims to have 15,000 fighters (Bertocci,

1989: 162). Shanti Bahini established its own administration and judicial system in areas under its control.

Government reconciliatory overtures

The Bangladesh government claims to have spent Bangladeshi Takas 4020 million between 1976 and 1990 on development schemes in the fields of agriculture, education, cottage industry, social welfare, construction of infrastructure and culture in the CHT. The standpoint of the government is that CHT is part of the legally recognized territories of the state. Thus in principle there can be no restrictions on the movement of Bangladeshi citizens from and into the CHT. In sharp contrast to the rest of Bangladesh, the CHT situation presents vast size but scarce population. This has induced landless people from the plains to move into the CHT region. However, as the tribal people are sensitive to the influx of plains people the government has from 1985 stopped non-tribals from settling in the CHT (*Chittagong Hill Tribes and Human Rights*, n.d.). In February 1989 the Bangladesh Parliament passed legislation providing for limited local autonomy through the creation of Hill District Councils. Elections were held, but the Shanti Bahini continued its violent struggle for greater autonomy. In 1989 the Shanti Bahini was responsible for some 133 deaths and in 1990 for another 63 (*Bangladesh*, 1991). There were reports of several deaths and cases of torture and rape at the hands of both the Shanti Bahini and the government troops during 1991–92. The numbers of deaths that the conflict has claimed thus far runs into several thousands. Between 1975 and 1983 some 5000 had occurred. This figure includes the guerrillas as well as government troops (Saeed, 1987–88: 80).

Some positive developments seem to be on the way in the CHT situation. In the past, the CHT people were isolated from mainstream Bangladesh politics. Members elected to the Bangladesh Parliament were nominees of the local parties. In recent years the major Bangladeshi political parties have been trying to establish their support among the tribals. In the 1991 general elections three tribesmen elected to the parliament were members of the Awami League. In August 1992 the Shanti Bahini declared a unilateral ceasefire. High-level talks took place between the government and tribal representatives during November and December 1992, but proved inconclusive (*Bangladesh*, 1993). Negotiations were resumed in 1993 but thus far no definitive result has been reached.

External involvement

From the beginning India has been providing moral, material and logistical support to the CHT militants. The Indian RAW established a clandestine radio station and trained the Chakma guerrillas. On the other hand, Bangladesh has been providing training camps on its territory to Mizo guerrillas fighting against India (Maxwell, 1980: 14). During a visit to India in May 1992 the current prime minister, Mrs Khalida Zia (in office since 1991), discussed with the Indian authorities the problem of the 50,000 tribal refugees from Bangladesh living in camps in the Indian state of Tripura (*Bangladesh*, 1993). Human Rights organizations such as Amnesty International have been monitoring the situation in CHT throughout the 1980s and into the early 1990s. The level of violence has diminished considerably in recent years, but human rights violations occur on the side of both the government troops and the militant tribal population.

References

Ahmed, F. (1973) 'The structural matrix of the struggle in Bangladesh' in K. Gough and H.P. Sharma (eds), *Imperialism and Revolution in South Asia*, New York: Monthly Review Press.

Ahmed, M. (1984) *Bangladesh: Era of Sheikh Mujibur Rahman*, Dhaka: University Press Limited.

Ahmed, R. (1988) 'Conflict and contradictions in Bengali Islam: problems of change and adjustment' in K.P. Ewing (ed.), *Shariat and Ambiguity in South Asian Islam*, Delhi: Oxford University Press.

Ali, T. (1983) *Can Pakistan Survive?*, Harmondsworth: Penguin Books.

Amin, M.N. (1988–89) 'Secessionist movement in the Chittagong Hill Tracts', *Regional Studies*, vol. V11, no. 1.

Asplund, D. (1977) *Bangladesh: Landanalys*, Stockholm: SIDA.

Bangladesh: Country Study and Norwegian Aid Review (1986), Fantoft: The Chr. Michelsen Institute.

Bangladesh: A Summary of Human Rights Violations (April 1993), London: Amnesty International.

Bangladesh: Human Rights in the Chittagong Hill Tracts, 1989–1990 (August 1991), London: Amnesty International.

The Bangladesh Papers (1975?), Lahore: Vanguard.

Banu, R.A. (1991) 'Ethnic conflict, autonomy, democracy and national integration: the case of Chittagong Hill Tracts in Bangladesh' in G.L. Lindgren, K. Nordquist and P. Wallensteen (eds), *Peace Processes in the Third World*, Uppsala: Department of Peace and Conflict Research.

Baxter, C. (1984) *Bangladesh*, Boulder and London: Westview Press.

Bertocci, P.J. (1989) 'Resource development and ethnic conflict in Bangladesh: the case of Chakmas in Chittagong Hill Tracts' in D. Vajpeyi and Y.K. Malik (eds), *Religious and Ethnic Minority Politics in South Asia*, New Delhi: Manohar.

Chittagong Hill Tracts and Human Rights (1992?), Government of Bangladesh.

The Constitution of the People's Republic of Bangladesh (as modified up to 10 October 1991), Dhaka: Government of Bangladesh.

Davies, D. (1989) 'Traveller's tales', *Far Eastern Economic Review*, 23 March.

Gankovsky, Y.V. and Gordon-Polonskaya, L.R. (1972) *A History of Pakistan (1947–1958)*, Lahore: People's Publishing House.

Iftekharuzzaman and Rahman, M. (1986) 'Nation building in Bangladesh: perceptions, problems and an approach' in M.A. Hafiz and A.R. Khan (eds), *Nation Building in Bangladesh: Retrospect and Prospect*, Dhaka: Bangladesh Institute of International and Strategic Studies.

Kabir, M.G. (1986) 'Post-1971 nationalism in Bangladesh: search for a new identity' in M.A. Hafiz and A.R. Khan (eds), *Nation Building in Bangladesh: Retrospect and Prospect*, Dhaka: Bangladesh Institute of International and Strategic Studies.

Khan, M.A. (1983) *Generals in Politics: Pakistan 1958–1982*, New Delhi: Vikas Publishing House PVT Ltd.

Maniruzzaman, T. (1982) *Group Interests and Political Changes: Studies of Pakistan and Bangladesh*, New Delhi: South Asian Publishers.

Maxwell, N. (1980) 'India, the Nagas and the north-east', *Minority Rights Group Report* no.17, London: Minority Rights Group Ltd.

Saeed, A. (1987–88) 'The Chakma unrest in Bangladesh', *Regional Studies*, vol. VI, no. 1.

Interviews May 1990

Professor Salahuddin Ahmed, retired professor of history.
Professor Syed Sajjad Hosain, retired professor of English.
Professor Talukder Maniruzzaman, Department of Political Science, Dhaka University.
Professor Abdur Razzaq, retired national professor.

9

Sri Lanka

On 4 February 1948 the island state of Ceylon (renamed Sri Lanka in 1972) became independent. It is located some 64 km off the southernmost Indian state of Tamil Nadu. The shallow waters of the Palk Strait separate Sri Lanka from the Indian mainland.

The cultural and political heritage of Sri Lanka

The first people to settle on Sri Lanka are believed to have been a Proto-Australoid group known as the Veddas (Bhaduri and Karim, 1990: 12). Not much is known about them except that they were subjugated by immigrants from the Indian mainland. The Sinhalese claim that they arrived on the island from northern India in 500 BC under the leadership of Prince Vijaya. According to Sinhalese mythology, the Buddha visited the island thrice, blessing it as a centre of true Buddhism. The Anuradhapura period (about third century BC to ninth century AD) saw the flowering of a grand Sinhalese-Buddhist civilization in Sri Lanka.

Although canonical Buddhism is not very much concerned with temporal affairs, the Theravada form of Hinayana Buddhism prevalent in Sri Lanka has historically played a very central role in the formation of the cultural identity of the Sinhalese. However, there is evidence to suggest that Hindu religion and gods and Mahayana Buddhism did percolate in some form into the Sri Lankan Buddhist system. Most important in this connection is the fact that the Hindu idea of caste is firmly established in Sinhalese society (Phadnis, 1976: 7–29). On the other hand, the Sri Lankan Tamils claim that they inhabited the island long before the arrival of Vijaya. A Tamil kingdom existed at Anuradhapura until 101 BC when a Sinhala prince, Dutthagamani, captured it and established his own rule (Nissan and Stirrat, 1990: 20). In AD 1215 a Tamil kingdom was again established at Jaffna.

The Sri Lankan Muslims traditionally trace their presence to the settlements established by Muslim Arab traders and émigrés in the very early period of

Islam. They benefited from the religious tolerance of the Sinhalese kings and the local population of those times. Some Muslims prospered as gem traders, but most worked as subsistence farmers. Although small Muslim chiefdoms had existed during the medieval period, the Muslim minority historically has not aspired to create its separate state.

British colonialism and the formation of a unitary state

When the Portuguese came to the island in 1505, they encountered three sovereign kingdoms: two Sinhalese, one based at Kotte near present-day Colombo with control over the south and west of the island, and the other at present-day Kandy ruling the central highlands; and one Tamil, based in Jaffna, ruling over the Tamil-speaking areas of the north and east. The Portuguese were able to subdue the Kotte and Jaffna kingdoms, but ruled them separately. The Kandyan kingdom was able to maintain its independence from both Portuguese and later the Dutch (1658–1796). The British expelled the Dutch in 1796, but could annex Kandy only in 1815. Earlier in 1802 the separate Tamil state had been abolished.

It was in 1815 that the whole island was made a unitary state with a centralized administration under a British Governor. It was named as Ceylon and made a Crown Colony. Thus it was a separate entity and not part of the British Indian Empire. The new administrators were favourably disposed towards encouraging economic activity. The central Kandy region of the island, an essentially Sinhalese area, was found to be particularly suitable for commercial plantation farming. Initially coffee was introduced, and proved quite successful. However, it hit hard at traditional subsistence agriculture, and many Kandyan farmers were dispossessed. However, given the prejudices of the caste system, the Kandyans refused to work as wage labourers on the plantations. The British thus in the 1830s started importing low-caste, debt-ridden impoverished Tamils from southern India. The status of this indentured labour was not much better than that of serfs. Initially this labour force could be used only on a seasonal basis on the coffee plantations. Later when the coffee plant failed owing to disease, tea was introduced. Tea flourished with great ease. Tamil workers were now needed the year round. Consequently a large Indian Tamil population gathered in central Sri Lanka (Fries and Bibin, 1984: 10–13).

The plantations came to include also rubber and coconut production. The chief beneficiaries among Sri Lankans were some upper-caste Sinhalese and Tamil English-speaking families who gained interests in these areas. The scions of these families were welcomed into English-language schools and colleges. There were even conversions to Anglican Christianity from among this élite. A Sri Lankan capitalist élite based on the thriving plantation economy evolved in the process and became the most influential political force in society. Henceforth the indigenous centre of political power in Sri Lanka was located in and around Colombo where this élite was settled. Upper-class Sinhalese also joined the services and professions such as medicine, engineering and the academic field.

On the other hand, the northern and eastern regions constituting Tamil country were arid and infertile and thus provided little scope for agricultural development. The people of these areas therefore looked towards other means of employment. Their opportunity to advance came when American missionaries established several schools and colleges in the Jaffna area. A class of English-educated Tamil professionals and white-collar workers evolved as a result. Conversions to Christianity also took place among Tamils. Élite Tamils usually adopted the Protestant faith, while the poor went over to Catholicism.

British policy tended to favour recruiting Tamils from the American schools in Jaffna into the state services. Thus a modern-educated Tamil élite, largely of the upper caste of *vellala*, came into being. It found access to jobs in the colonial administration and in the various upper-bracket professions. Consequently its ratio in the various services and professions exceeded its ratio of the island's population. Some Jaffna families acquired interests in commerce and trade with India and settled in Colombo. Tamils from more modest backgrounds also moved out and established themselves in petty trading and shopkeeping in Colombo, while the poor sought work as wage-earners in industrial production at the capital. Thus a sizeable Sri Lankan Tamil group had prior to independence moved out of the traditional Tamil areas of north and east and settled among the Sinhalese.

The Muslims supported the British in their bid to oust the Dutch. Consequently they were encouraged by the British to take advantage of the economic opportunities. Some moved into the plantation economy, communication and transport, and packing and fishing as contractors and entrepreneurs. It was however in the gem industry that the Muslims achieved the greatest success, and a Muslim upper class of gem merchants evolved at Colombo.

Evolution of communal identities

From the middle of the nineteenth century Buddhist scholars began addressing the theme that the Sinhalese-Buddhist people (the word used was Sinhalese race) alone had original rights to Sri Lanka. Among them the most influential was Anagarika Dharmapala (1864–1931). In his view there was no place for Tamils, Muslims, Christians or others in Sri Lanka (Ponnombalam, 1983: 88–93). In newspapers, pamphlets and books devotion was lavished on the glory of Buddhism and the Sinhalese language.

Most Sri Lankan Tamils subscribed to a modern south Indian type of Saivaite Hinduism. According to Brahminic Hinduism, Dravidians are placed either in the lowly unclean category of the fourth caste of Sudras or among Untouchables.

Modern Tamil Saivaite Hinduism, set forth in the ideas of Armuka Navalar (1822–79), rejected Brahminic superiority and opposed the growing influence of Christianity. The reforms that he advocated did not aim at the rejection of caste. Rather, instead of the Brahminic caste order an hierarchy of Tamil castes was advanced (Sivathamby, 1990: 176–82). In Sri Lanka, therefore, caste hierarchy and oppression of the low castes was firmly entrenched. Not surprisingly there was little sense of solidarity with the low-caste Plantation Tamils of south Indian extraction. The evolution of a modern Tamil identity, however, was fundamentally associated with the Tamil language and not religion (Hellmann-Rajanayagam, 1991: 41–3).

Exaggerated puritan accounts of Sinhala and Tamil racial differences projected by ideologists of the present-day ethno-nationalist histories of the two sides are quite misleading, however. There is abundant proof of the fact that, while both groups had their distinct cultural specificities, considerable ethno-cultural mixing also took place (interviews, Hellmann-Rajanayagam, 1991; Gabriele Winai-Ström, 1993). The rulers, both Sinhalese and Tamils, largely followed a policy of toleration towards their religious minorities. Consequently some areas have had a continuous Sinhalese and Tamil side-by-side presence, as for example in the eastern parts of Sri Lanka. The popular cultural tradition of Sri Lanka reflects this confluence of both religions.

On the other hand, the Tamil-speaking Muslims emphasized the religious distinction to mark off their distinct identity. A controversy erupted in 1888 between some Tamil and Muslim leaders over the question of the exact ethnic origin of the Muslims. Sir Ponnambalam Ramannathan, a Tamil leader, asserted that the Muslims of Sri Lanka were merely Tamils converted to Islam. The implication of this assertion was that Muslims should assimilate into Tamil society and give up claims to special identity. This position was challenged by I.L.M. Abdul Azeez, who emphasized the Arab ancestry of the Muslims (Mohan, 1986: 119). Beginning in 1889, Muslims were nominated to represent their group in the Legislative Assembly. Later separate electorates were introduced for the minorities, and Muslims were elected on that basis in the expanded Legislative Assembly. On the other hand, the fairly peaceful relations between Muslims and Sinhalese suffered a set-back at the beginning of the twentieth century when rising Sinhalese nationalism began to blame non-Sinhalese and non-Buddhists for the ills of Sinhalese society. In 1915 anti-Muslim riots were instigated by Sinhalese nationalists, especially against the coastal Moors who were recent arrivals from south India (de Silva, 1986: 60–1).

Evolution of a parliamentary political process

From the late nineteenth century, Sinhalese, Tamils, Muslims, Burghers and Europeans were represented in the various councils on a communal basis. English-educated Sinhalese and Tamil élites worked together for constitutional reform at the end of the nineteenth century and the beginning of the twentieth. These activities led to the foundation of the Ceylon National Congress in December 1919. Its first president was a prominent Tamil, Sir Ponnambalam Arunachalam (De Silva, 1981: 386–7). However, differences soon grew over questions of communal representation. While the Sinhalese insisted upon representation according to population strength, the Sri Lankan Tamils wanted representation in excess of their numbers (de Silva, 1986: 99–103). Such differences grew with time as other minorities also disputed communal representation ratios.

The All-Ceylon Malay Association was founded in 1922, the Ceylon Muslim League in 1924, the All-Ceylon Moors' Association in 1935, the Sinhala Maha Sabha (the Great Council of the Sinhalese) in 1937, the Burgher Political Association and the Ceylon Indian Congress (founded by Plantation Tamils) in 1938. The Sri Lankan Tamils founded the All Ceylon Tamil Congress in 1944. Most of these organizations were dominated by the middle classes. Some owed their origin to British sponsorship.

Constitutional developments leading to independence

The Donoughmore Commission (1927–28) arrived from Britain to study the problems of communal representation and to suggest changes. It recommended universal adult franchise, but rejected the principle of communal representation. Universal suffrage was instituted in 1931. However, the minorities were hard hit by such change. The Muslim community, which was dispersed in society, was in particular disadvantaged under the new system. Only one Muslim candidate was elected under the new system to the first assembly, and in the elections to the second assembly none was elected (Mohan, 1986: 120).

Meanwhile the British had been preparing Ceylon for some time for self-rule. In 1944 Lord Soulbury arrived as the head of a new commission that was to draft a constitution for Ceylon. Leaders of the Sri Lankan Tamils pleaded before the Soulbury Commission for a fifty–fifty share in power between the Sinhalese and the rest of the minorities. Muslim leaders did not support such a demand and instead sought to align themselves with the Sinhalese in national politics (de Silva, 1986: 104–5). The Soulbury Commission recommended a constitution which was based essentially on a liberal notion of a multiracial secular democracy. Notwithstanding its democratic tenor, the constitution contained some weaknesses which worked against the interests of the minority groups. Firstly, it prescribed a unitary form of government based on the Westminster model. Secondly, although it expressly forbade discrimination against minorities, a bill of rights clearly defining the rights of individuals and minorities was not included. The constitution was adopted, and enforced in 1947. Sri Lankan independence in 1948 lacked the

Table 12   Religion in Sri Lanka, no. and percentage

Buddhists	10,292,600	70
Hindus	2,295,800	15
Muslims	1,134,600	7.5
Christians	1,111,700	7.5

dramatic showdown between the colonial authorities and the local people, because the British had decided to wind up their empire in South Asia. This way it trod an anomalous path to freedom.

Sri Lankan society and polity

According to the 1981 Census of Sri Lanka the total population of Sri Lanka was 14,850,000. Its total territory comprised only 65,610 sq. km. The annual growth rate of population in 1981 was 1.3 per cent, the lowest in South Asia. The rate of literacy was as high as 87 per cent, which was far ahead of the next highest of 36 per cent for India in South Asia. In 1989 the population was estimated at 16.80 million.

Language and ethnicity

The majority Sinhalese group speaks Sinhala, which is related to north Indian Indo-European languages. The Sinhalese are found in the west, south and central parts of the island. They are usually categorized into low–country Sinhalese (60 per cent) and Kandyan Sinhalese (40 per cent). The second group is the Tamils, who are mostly Saivaite Hindus. The Tamil language belongs to the Dravidian family of languages. The Tamils consist of two groups. The first is the Sri Lankan Tamils, who are concentrated on the northern side of Sri Lanka opposite to Tamil Nadu in India and in lesser numbers in the eastern regions where Muslims and (since independence) Sinhalese settlers are also found in large numbers. The other Tamil group is the so–called Indian Tamils, also called Plantation Tamils, most of whom were brought over as indentured labour from southern India by the British from 1825 onwards to work on the coffee and later tea plantations in the central highlands. Sri Lankan Tamils traditionally consider themselves superior to the Plantation Tamils in terms of caste ranking.

Although the Muslims of Sri Lanka, known as the Moors, are almost entirely Tamil-speaking, they are entered on the basis of religion as a separate ethnic group in Sri Lankan Census records, following British practice. There are Roman Catholic and Protestant Christians among both Sinhalese and Tamils. In fact a noteworthy feature of both Sinhalese and Tamil élite composition has been the

Table 13   Ethnic and linguistic groups in Sri Lanka

Sinhalese	74% (predominantly Buddhists; prominent Christian minority)
Tamils	18% (comprising Sri Lankan Tamils 12.5% and Indian Tamils 5.5%. Predominantly Hindus; sizeable Christian minority)
Sri Lankan Muslims (Moors)	7% (overwhelmingly Tamil-speaking)
Burghers, Malays, Chinese, Veddas and others	1% (English, Malay and Chinese-speaking)

prominent positions occupied by Christians in these strata (Jupp, 1978: 146–51). Some 1 per cent of Sri Lanka's population consists of minor ethnic groups such as the Christian Burghers, who are descendants of mixed European and Sri Lankan parents, Malays, Chinese and the Veddas, who at present comprise some 400 families.

Cultural premisses of the Sri Lankan polity

Sri Lanka is the only country in the world where the followers of Theravada Buddhism constitute a large majority. This fact prompted Sinhalese-Buddhist ideologues in the nineteenth century to propound a theory of cultural nationalism which established a special relationship between Buddhism, the Sinhalese people and the island. By the time of independence, Sinhalese-Buddhist ethno-nationalism had made inroads among the intelligentsia, and a belief in the special relationship had become part of popular thinking. A fear of Indian domination, particularly of being swamped by the Tamils from across the Palk Strait, figured prominently in the Sinhalese-Buddhist political discourse. Paradoxically, a minority complex was deeply ingrained in the Sinhalese majority (Seekins, 1990: 175–6).

The hegemonic–ethnic nation-state project and organizing ideology

Initially, the central Sinhalese political élite and dominant classes can be seen as vacillating between two different models of nation-building. The early governments after independence stood for some sort of composite Sinhalese–Tamil nation. In 1951 S.W.R.D. Bandaranaike, a convert to Buddhism from an upper-class Anglican Christian family, quit the UNP to form the Sri Lanka Freedom Party (SLFP). Sensing the potential for Sinhalese domination in Sri Lankan politics, he evolved a Sinhalese-Buddhist symbolism and discourse. Radical left-of-centre rhetoric and Sinhalese chauvinism were freely mixed in a populist ideology (Ram, 1989: 37–8). In subsequent years this discourse became the inevitable backdrop of political competition between mainstream parties. However, the idea of Buddhist hegemony did not include in a philosophical sense a theological argument about degradation of non-Buddhists to second-rate citizens. The emphasis was on tolerance preached by Buddha. Despite such distinctions made by Buddhist theorists, the mobile Sri Lankan Tamil intelligentsia sensed discrimination in such cultural distinctions.

The Sri Lanka constitution

The Soulbury constitution of 1947 served with minor amendments as the constitution of Ceylon until 1972. The 1972 Constitution effectively declared the country a unitary socialist republic and gave it a Sinhalese name: Sri Lanka. All power was vested in the unicameral National State Assembly. Executive power was to be exercised by an elected prime minister and cabinet. Article 6 recognized the special relationship between Buddhism and the polity, but non-Buddhist Sri Lankans were assured the freedom of worship. Sinhala was declared official language but provisions were made for the limited use of Tamil in the northern and eastern regions. The constitution adopted by the Sri Lanka Parliament was not supported by the Tamil leadership of the Federal Party because it did not establish a federal system which could insure autonomy. A second constitution prescribing a strong president but a cabinet form of executive headed by a relatively weak prime minister, based on the Gaullist model, was adopted in 1978. Sri Lanka was, however, to remain a unitary socialist state. More importantly, the constitution of 1978 went further in cementing a relationship between Sinhala, Buddhism and Sri Lanka:

> Article 9. The Republic of Sri Lanka shall give to Buddhism the foremost place and accordingly it shall be the duty of the state to protect and foster the Buddha *Sasana,* while assuring all religions the rights granted by Articles 10 and 14 (1)(e).
>   10. Every person is entitled to freedom of thought, conscience and religion, including the freedom to have or adopt a religion or belief of his choice.
>   14(1)(e). Every citizen is entitled to . . . the freedom, either by himself or in association with others, and either in public or private, to manifest his religion or belief in worship, observance, practice and teaching. . . .

As regards other fundamental rights, the constitution provided equal civil and political rights to all valid citizens of Sri Lanka. No special qualifications for contesting any public office were laid down.

Sinhala as official language

As regards the question of language, the constitution made a distinction between official language and national languages:

> 18. The Official Language of Sri Lanka shall be Sinhala.
> 19. The National Languages of Sri Lanka shall be Sinhala and Tamil.

The language of administration and of court proceedings was to be Sinhala. Translations of government documents into Tamil were to be made for matters concerning the northern and eastern regions. The Tamil leadership organized in the Federal Party boycotted deliberations on the constitution.

Peter Schalk (1990: 276–95) observes that the 1978 constitution presents a model of an integrative but subordinating hierarchy which, while supporting religious pluralism, sanctions a religious hierarchy with Theravada Buddhism occupying the highest position. Such a constitution reflects the influence of Sinhalese communalist organizations, both clerical as well as lay, which want Sri Lanka to become a *dharmacracy*. The concept of dharmacracy signifies, on the one hand, the rejection of secularism which separates state and religion, and on the other, the elevation of Theravada Buddhism to the position of a supra-ideology permeating all spheres of life: social, economic and political and others.

The political process

Since 1956 the political process in the country has been dominated by two major parties: the United Nation Party (UNP) and the Sri Lanka Freedom Party (SLFP). Both parties are dominated by the Sinhalese. The former is moderate and seeks to enlist Tamils' support. It receives support essentially from those Tamils who are settled in Colombo and have acquired a sizeable stake in business and property. The UNP government has been able to co-opt ministers and other senior incumbents in government from this group of privileged Tamils. The SLFP upholds candidly a Sinhalese populist ideology. There are various Marxist parties of both the parliamentary and revolutionary varieties. Some Marxist parties combine radical social revolution with ethno-nationalism. There are also various communal parties of the Sinhalese, Tamil and Muslim groups. Another important factor in Sri Lankan politics is the prominent and influential role played by the Buddhist clergy. Election issues invariably acquire a religious dimension because of the active role of the Buddhist clericals.

The central élite and politics of ethnicity

The Sri Lankan state has been consistently headed by civilian governments elected on the basis of universal suffrage, although in the Tamil regions opposition to elections became constant after 1977 as the elected governments were seen as representing only Sinhalese nationalist interests. At the time of independence, the Sri Lankan bourgeoisie was constituted by three factions, two Sinhalese, one of plantation owners and the other of businessmen, and, third, the Colombo-based Tamil bourgeoisie with interests in commerce and trade, mainly with India. When the Sinhalese-Buddhist movement rose under the leadership of Bandaranaike, the

Tamil bourgeoisie decided to support the UNP, which represented the more moderate line on the national question. It has continued to follow such a line. However, Sinhalese-Buddhist cultural hegemony began to be reflected in state conduct clearly after the SLFP came to power in 1956.

A significant imbalance in ethnic representation in the Sri Lankan civil bureaucracy devolved upon the state at the time of independence. There was an over-representation of Tamils, although the Sinhalese had an overall preponderance in the administrative services (Olsen, 1989: 35–6). Through changes such as declaration of Sinhalese as official language and in educational policy, the Sinhalese-dominated state tried to rectify this imbalance in favour of the Sinhalese. After 1972 the numbers of Tamils employed by the state and in the various professions began to diminish. In so far as the Sri Lankan armed forces are concerned, they were a tiny force at the time of independence. After 1983 the number of armed personnel increased dramatically from 12,000 to 70,000. It is important to note that Tamils are nearly absent from the armed forces currently (Levy, 1990: 234).

The contradictions of welfare statism

Sri Lanka inherited a functioning democratic system, and a comprehensive welfare system. All education from primary school to university had been free in Sri Lanka since 1945 (Wilson, 1974: 64). In the early years employment was easily available. Nearly half of the labour force was organized in trade unions. The public sector greatly expanded as nationalization of important sectors of the economy was undertaken by the state in the 1960s and 1970s. The state sector was expanded in the transportation and manufacturing sectors (Rogers, 1990: 119). However, it was in the 1970s that the SLFP under Mrs Sirimavo Bandaranaike greatly expanded the state's patronage network: small landowners, school teachers, monks and other lay sections of traditional Sinhalese-Buddhist society were the main recipients of such patronage. For example, the Land Reform Law of 1972 fixed the ceiling at 20 hectares, the lowest in South Asia. The plantations were nationalized, but the Plantation Tamils (who were not considered Sri Lankan citizens) working on these plantations were displaced and the land was distributed among the Sinhalese. However, despite an extensive welfare system Sri Lanka remained essentially a rural society. The patronage of Buddhist-Sinhalese cultural values and hegemony by the élite greatly raised the expectations of Sinhalese youths, but when they could not be provided with employment the result was disenchantment and finally the insurrection of 1971 (Jupp, 1978: 339–55).

Until the end of 1977 the state could expand its welfarist activities. Thereafter, as an economic crisis began to emerge, the new UNP government led by J.R. Jayewardene came under pressure from the World Bank to liberalize the economy. Consequently denationalization of industry and some other sectors began.

However, given the compulsions of maintaining popular support the government continued to expand political patronage. In 1980 about a twelfth of the total population was paid by the state (Moore, 1990: 173).

Ethnic conflict and separatism

Although ethnic tension and conflict in post-independence Sri Lanka has found its main expression along the Sinhalese–Tamil divide, there are other dimensions and cracks in the ethnic mosaic constituting the society. There have been clashes between Sinhalese Buddhists and Sinhalese Christians, Tamil Hindus and Tamil Christians, Christian Sinhalese and Christian Tamils and other similar configurations. Most notably, however, the Muslims have since the mid-1980s been drawn into the ethnic conflict on a large scale.

The evolution of the Sinhalese–Tamil ethnic conflict between 1948 and 1983

In 1946 Don Stephen Senanayake, a Cambridge-University-educated Anglican Sinhalese, formed the United National Party which was dominated by the plantation-owning Sinhalese élite. Support was given to it also by the Sinhalese Maha Sabha, the Ceylon Muslim League and sections of the Sri Lankan and Indian Tamils. It won the elections in 1947 and when the British left in 1948 became the ruling party.

The Ceylon Citizenship Act of 1948

The progeny of the indentured labourers from south India, the Indian Tamils (also known as Plantation Tamils), have historically suffered from all types of social and cultural degradation. Although universal adult franchise was granted in 1931, the status of Indian Tamils had been left unsettled. The Soulbury constitution also left this issue unresolved. Thus, when the Ceylon Citizenship Act of 1948 along with the Indian and Pakistani Residents (Citizenship) Act of 1949 was enacted, most of the progeny of the Indian Tamils were disenfranchised. The government was keen on excluding the plantation workers because of a fear that not doing so would give representation to Indians in the parliament, and thus provide a channel for direct Indian influence in Sri Lankan politics. Some Sinhalese politicians considered the plantation workers, who were a well-organized section of the working class, a fifth column connected to mainland India. Leftist Sinhalese politicians, however, criticized such policy, labelling it as racism (Fries and Bibin, 1984: 17–30; Ram, 1989: 36–7).

On the other hand, the conservative Ceylon Tamil Congress dominated by the upper-caste Jaffna élite, which had won all seats in Tamil constituencies in the 1947 election (i.e. a year before independence), was split on the citizenship question. Two Tamil Ministers voted in favour of the bill, but the leader of the party, G.G. Ponnambalam, voted against it (Vije, 1987: 23). Some Tamils split from the Congress in December 1949 and under the leadership of S.J.V. Chelvanayakam formed the Federal Party. Chelvanayakam put forth the idea of a single Tamil nation comprising both Sri Lankan and Plantation Tamils, and formulated the notion of the 'traditional Tamil homeland' (Wilson, 1994: 21). Although conservative in ideology, the Federal Party became the spokesman of Tamil nationalism. It sought to unite under its banner Tamils of the north and east, the Tamil-speaking Muslims and the Plantation Tamils.

Negotiations between the Sri Lankan and Indian governments on repatriation of Indian Tamils continued for years. Finally in 1964 an agreement was reached. Over a period of 15 years 525,000 Plantation Tamils were to be repatriated to India while 300,000 were to be granted Sri Lankan citizenship. The status of another 150,000 was to be negotiated later (Vije, 1987: 24). Thus while about one-third became Sri Lankan citizens the rest were gradually to be sent to Tamil Nadu. Thus Indian Tamils excluded from Sri Lankan citizenship began to be despatched to the Indian mainland. In the subsequent decades, as the Sinhalese–Tamil conflict worsened, the Plantation Tamils were the worst sufferers. Many migrated to the north-east.

The language issue

An important issue in early Sri Lankan politics was that of national language. English was at that time the state language. The Sinhala-educated intelligentsia and the Buddhist clergy insisted upon Sinhala being declared the only national language of the country. However, the UNP government of Sir John Kotewala (1953–56) took the position that Sinhala and Tamil would be given parity as national languages after English had been phased out. After initially supporting the idea of parity, the main opposition party (the SLFP) changed course and in 1955 began advocating the primacy of Sinhala. On the other hand, the principle of parity put forward by the UNP government was supported by the left parties, the Lanka Sama Samaj Party (LSSP) and the Communist Party.

The 1956 'Sinhala Only' Bill

In the crucial 1956 elections a sharp increase in the activities of Buddhist monks called Bhikkhus took place. Under the leadership of High Priest Buddharakita the Bhikkhus entered the election campaign in support of the SLFP led by S.W.R.D. Bandaranaike, because it had committed itself to Sinhala as the sole national language of Sri Lanka (de Silva, 1986: 174–9). The Mahajan Eksath

Peramuna, a coalition of Bandaranaike's SLFP and the Trotskyist Vilpavakari Lanka Sama Samaj Party (VLSSP), won 51 of the 95 seats in Parliament. It was a major upset for the dominant Sinhalese and Tamil élites who had hitherto arranged power sharing among themselves.

Bandaranaike began his term by moving the 'Sinhala Only' Bill, which stipulated the recognition of Sinhala as the only official language, in Parliament on 5 June 1956. The biggest Tamil party in Parliament, the Federal Party, challenged the constitutionality of the Bill. Furthermore, it demanded greater autonomy for the northern and eastern regions. It also urged Tamils to express their disapproval of the imposition of Sinhala. Federal Party Members of Parliament and other leaders staged sit-down protests near the Parliament building. In 1957 Sinhalese mobs attacked Tamils in Colombo and other parts of the country. Such happenings only made Tamil protests gain pace. In the face of growing Tamil opposition Bandaranaike opened negotiations with the Federal Party leader, Chelvanayakam. In July an accord was reached which placed Sinhala and Tamil on parity. The principle of decentralization of power, with greater authority to the provincial councils in the north and east zones, was also conceded. The UNP, which had been ousted from power in the 1956 election, now denounced the pact as a danger to national unity. Opposition to such concessions also came from some cabinet ministers. Many Buddhist organizations gave a call to scrap the pact. The UNP leader J.R. Jayewardene led a protest march to a holy Buddhist shrine in Kandy to invoke divine blessing for his campaign against the pact. Riots broke out as a result.

At that time, Tamils in southern India were in the forefront of a Dravidian movement against the domination of the Aryan north. The Indian government, fearful of the growth of a greater Tamil movement across borders, pressed the Sri Lankan government to halt further escalation of the conflict. Thus on Indian insistence the Sri Lankan government declared a state of emergency in May 1958. But already thousands of Tamils had been subjected to violent outbursts at the hands of Sinhalese mobs. The government despatched more than 10,000 Tamils from Colombo to safety at Jaffna in the north. Another 12,000 were put in camps. Later that year the pact was repudiated (Ram, 1989: 39–41). Tension between the Sinhalese and Tamils became a regular feature of Sri Lankan politics.

In 1964 Mr Bandaranaike was assassinated by a Buddhist monk. His wife Sirimavo Bandaranaike became the leader of the SLFP. In the March 1965 elections the coalition between SLFP and LSSP was badly defeated, however. The UNP emerged as the biggest party, with 66 seats in Parliament. The Federal Party with 14 seats was the largest Tamil Party. It decided to support the UNP to form the government. A pact between the UNP and the Federal Party was reached which recognized Tamil as the language of the northern and eastern regions, and decentralization of power was to be effected. In addition, restrictions were to be imposed on colonization of the Tamil provinces by the Sinhalese. The government had been settling displaced Sinhalese peasants in traditional Tamil areas, particularly the eastern zone. In 1966, when the government moved a bill which would have sanctioned implementation of the agreement, violent Sinhalese protests broke out. Buddhist monks leading a procession of some 3000 people surrounded the Parliament building. One protester was killed in police firing. Another state of emergency was clamped on the country (Ram, 1989: 43).

The 1971 Sinhalese youths' insurrection

In 1970, Mrs Bandaranaike won the election and formed the government in alliance with the Trotskyist LSSP and the Communist Party. Although the Sri Lankan economy as a whole grew during the 1950s and 1960s at approximately 4.5 per cent per annum, its positive effects were compromised by adverse developments in other sectors of the society. During this period the work force grew at the rate of 2.1 per cent while employment opportunities expanded only at the rate of 1.1 per cent. Considering that the literacy rate was very high in Sri Lanka, unemployment rose dramatically among the young adults aged between 15 and 30. The impact of such changes was particularly felt in agriculture. Pressure on land had been growing with the introduction of the plantation economy in the last century. Over the years the difficulties of smallholders and peasant cultivators had increased, particularly in the Kandyan Sinhalese regions. As a consequence many peasants had been rendered landless. The insurrection was supported by these strata (Marino, 1989: 11).

In May 1965 the Janata Vimukti Peramuna (JVP) was founded by Rohana Wijeweera. Wijeweera had studied at the Patrice Lumumba University in Moscow. Disillusioned with the established left in Ceylon politics, he founded the JVP as a revolutionary party inspired, on the one hand, by Che Guevara, Castro and Mao, and, on the other, by Sinhalese nationalism (Ram, 1989: 98–9). A brilliant orator and skilled organizer, Wijeweera was able quickly to enlist broad support among the growing body of educated but unemployed poor Sinhalese youths of peasant backgrounds. The JVP preached a revolutionary overthrow of the government and identified Indian expansionism as a major external threat to the revolution. It was alleged that the Indian government kept the Plantation Tamils away from joining hands with the indigenous working class. The Plantation Tamils were portrayed as a symbol of Indian expansionism.

The JVP had been gaining quick popularity among the youths and by early 1971 its leaders were preaching revolutionary overthrow of the government of Mrs Bandaranaike. On 14 March Wijeweera and two of his companions were arrested. Two days later a state of emergency was declared. The insurrection led by the JVP began on 5 April. The plan apparently was to attack police stations and capture

Mrs Bandaranaike and her cabinet simultaneously (Gunaratna, 1990: 92–104). The government was taken by surprise and could not control the rebellious situation. An appeal was made for foreign help. International support was forthcoming from many directions irrespective of ideological differences and regional disputes. India, Pakistan, Britain, the USSR, the USA, Egypt, and Yugoslavia helped to provide military equipment. China provided political and economic assistance (Gunaratna, 1990: 1–8–10). Consequently the rebellion was crushed with extreme brutality. An estimated 5000 to 10,000 people were killed (Gunaratna, 1990: 105). The emergency was prolonged and not lifted until 1977. Between 1977 and 1983 the JVP functioned as an electoral party. The Sri Lankan establishment, however, continually harassed the JVP, whose electoral successes improved over the years.

Politics of standardization in education

As elsewhere in South Asia, it was natural for educated youths to turn to the state for employment. The Sinhalese-dominated governments were from the very onset under pressure to provide employment to their youths. A sense of historical wrong had grown among the Sinhalese about the Tamils having been favoured by the British during the colonial period (Olsen, 1989: 35). Now that Sri Lanka was free and sovereign, such wrong had to be corrected. Already the 'Sinhala Only' move of 1956 was a step in this direction. Consequently in 1971 the government introduced the so-called standardization system of selection for admission to higher seats of learning. Quite simply it meant that Tamils had to secure more marks than Sinhalese in order to be admitted to higher seats of learning. Hence a system of affirmative discrimination in favour of Sinhalese was introduced. In 1971, minimum marks for university admission were as in Table 14.

The consequences of such policy were naturally to the detriment of the Tamils. In 1969, that is prior to the introduction of the standardization system, Tamils secured 50 per cent of the admissions to the medical faculty and 48.3 per cent to engineering. After the scheme was implemented their share fell to 28 per cent and 19 per cent respectively. In 1978 this system was scrapped but reintroduced with modifications. By 1980 the Sinhalese (who were 74 per cent of the population) held 85 per cent of all jobs in the state sector, 82 per cent in the professional and technical categories, and 83 per cent in the administrative and managerial spheres (Ram, 1989: 47). In a way, such change brought the representation of the Sri Lankan Tamils down roughly to their 12 per cent ratio of the total population of Sri Lanka. However, as the Sri Lankan Tamils were traditionally dependent on government employment, it hit their intelligentsia devastatingly. Many Tamils emigrated to Australia, Western Europe and North America.

Table 14   Minimum marks for university admission

	Sinhalese students	Tamil students
Medicine and dentistry	229	250
Physical science	183	204
Bio-science	175	184
Engineering	227	250
Veterinary science	181	206
Architecture	180	194

Source: Ponnambalam (1983: 176).

Land colonization

The problem of overpopulation has been a major worry of Sri Lankan govern-ments. A policy of settling Sinhalese in traditional Tamil and Muslim areas was adopted quite early and it continued into the 1980s. Consequently in some districts the Sinhalese became the largest group. On the other hand, in the major land development projects such as the Mahaweli irrigation project which is located in the Sinhalese area, Tamils received a negligible share, only 0.9 per cent (Oberst, 1989: 182–3).

Tamil separatism

In 1972 the Federal Party, the Tamil Congress and the Ceylon Workers Congress, representing the Plantation Tamils, formed an alliance called the Tamil United Front (TUF). It reiterated the typical Tamil demands for parity between Sinhala and Tamil, decentralization of power and creation of a secular state. In 1976 TUF was renamed the Tamil United Liberation Front (TULF). The TULF denounced the 1972 constitution and demanded the 'restoration and reconstruction of the free, sovereign, secular, socialist state of Tamil Eelam based on the right of self-determi-nation inherent to every nation' (Ram, 1989: 48). The TULF did not reject partici-pation in general elections and making representation of its cause in the Sri Lankan Parliament. On the other hand, in the same year Velupillai Prabhakaran, an 18-year old Tamil youth, founded the Tamil New Tigers. It was later renamed Liberation Tigers of Tamil Eelam (LTTE). The Tigers vowed to fight for the interests of the Tamil nation. It is important to note, however, that some sections of Tamil society continued to seek co-operation with Sinhalese-dominated parties, particularly the moderate UNP. This tendency continued into the 1970s and 1980s.

The UNP returns to power

In 1977 new elections were held. During the period 1970–77 an SLFP-led government under Mrs Bandaranaike had been in power. During this period the government had nationalized important sectors of the economy. Economic stagnation and negative growth had set in from the mid-1970s, partly as a reflection of worldwide trends, which imposed severe restraints on state welfarism. Although the 1971 insurrection had been crushed, it left Sri Lanka in a high state of political dissatisfaction and a deteriorating law and order situation. The UNP entered the 1977 election campaign with a promise to revive the economy and restore order. It secured a massive mandate from the electorate: out of a total of 169 National Assembly seats the UNP secured 141. SLFP could secure only eight seats and the Tamil United Liberation Front (TULF) won 18.

Under Mr Junius Jayewardene's leadership some important concessions were offered to the Tamils. Steps were to be taken to use Tamil in the Tamil majority areas of the north. Greater autonomy was to be granted. There were to be elected development committees in every province (Bhaduri and Karim, 1990: 13). Moreover the 1978 constitution accorded Tamil the status of a national language, although Sinhalese was to be the official language. However, these concessions could not be translated into practice because, on the one hand, state functionaries and other Sinhalese nationalists obstructed their implementation and, on the other hand, the Tamil leaders took up extremist separatist positions.

TULF wins Tamil support

The TULF fought the 1977 election with a manifesto which declared the creation of Tamil Eelam as its chief objective. It won 18 out of the 24 contested seats, including all the 14 seats in the northern Tamil areas. It received 71.81 per cent of the vote in Jaffna district, 71.44 per cent in Mannar district, 58.82 per cent in Vavuniya district and 52.16 per cent in Mullaitivu district. In the eastern region, where the population was a mixture of Tamils, Muslims and Sinhalese, the results were less impressive. It won only four out of ten seats, and the UNP won six (Ram, 1989: 49–50). The position of the Tamils living outside the Tamil strongholds was difficult to assess.

The government gets tough

Although the new government was willing to accommodate Tamil demands within some sort of autonomy formula, the separatist stand of the TULF and LTTE was clearly not acceptable to it. Consequently in 1978 the government first enacted the Liberation Tigers of Tamil Eelam Law, which proscribed that organization. In July 1979 the Prevention of Terrorism Act was adopted, giving wide-ranging powers to the police and security forces to suspend civil liberties.

Thus far the armed forces had largely remained neutral and had kept themselves away from direct involvement in ethnic conflicts. In 1981 a Tamil candidate of the

UNP and two policemen were killed by the LTTE in Jaffna. This incident provoked a violent response from the Sinhalese security men stationed in the area. Men in uniform set fire to the famous Jaffna Public Library with its collection of more than 95,000 books, some of rare quality, mainly related to Tamil culture and history (Tambiah, 1986: 19–20). Also reduced to ashes was the office of the *Eelanadu* Tamil daily, and the residence of a TULF Member of Parliament. Anti-Tamil riots spread to other parts of the country. Plantation Tamils, Tamil-speaking Muslims and Christian Tamils — all suffered during this period. A poster put up in 1981 in Colombo warned: 'Aliens, you have danced too much; your destruction is at hand. This is the country of us, the Sinhala' (Ram, 1989: 52).

The 1983 riots

The Sinhalese–Tamil conflict reached extreme proportions with a series of events taking place in 1983. In March the Tigers ambushed a military convoy. In May elections to local bodies were to be held. The Tigers mounted a campaign in favour of boycotting the elections. A Tamil candidate belonging to the UNP was assassinated. Things came to a head when in an ambush on 23 July the Tigers mowed down 13 soldiers of the Sri Lankan army in a hail of machine-gun fire and grenades. Next day began a week-long pogrom of Tamils in Colombo. The contagion spread quickly to other Sinhalese strongholds (Bastian, 1990: 298–304). The JVP, which during this period had been functioning as an electoral party, switched over to violence and converted itself into a Sinhalese-Buddhist ultra-nationalist party. The government reacted quickly and proscribed the JVP on 31 July (Gunaratna, 1990: 187–8).

The evidence collected by several human rights organizations and impartial inquiries established clearly that the operation against Tamils was not spontaneous. Rather it had followed a well-organized plan (*Forty Years*, 1991: 24–9). The police and army remained passive spectators while Sinhalese gangs indulged in a spree of killings and lootings. At least 2000 Tamils lost their lives. Enormous damage was caused to Tamil business and industrial interests located in Colombo and other towns in the Sinhalese areas. At least 100,000 Tamils were driven into refugee camps (Tambiah, 1986: 21–5). On the other hand, Tamil terrorists ruthlessly killed Sinhalese living in the north. Some 24,000 Sinhalese fled southwards and were put up in government refugee camps (Bhaduri and Karim, 1990: 17).

In August 1983 a special session of the Parliament amended the constitution to ban organizations and parties advocating secession. The TULF refused to take the anti-secession oath. This meant that the TULF, which was represented in the Sri Lanka Parliament, was also placed under a ban (Ram, 1989: 53). As a result the TULF leaders and Members of Parliament went into self-exile in Madras in Tamil Nadu.

Proliferation of Tamil guerrilla groups

Several other guerrilla outfits besides the LTTE appeared among Tamils after 1983. Among them was the People's Liberation Organization of Tamil Eelam (PLOTE), founded by Uma Maheswaren who in 1980 had broken away from LTTE. PLOTE concentrated on mass action rather than guerrilla ambush. The Marxist-Leninist Eelam Revolutionary Organization of Students (EROS) claimed links with the Plantation Tamils. The Eelam People's Revolutionary Liberation Front (EPLRM), another Marxist group formed as a result of a split in EROS, was active mostly in the eastern province. Another group, the Tamil Eelam Liberation Organization (TELO), was founded in 1979. However, none could match the LTTE's ability to carry out daring missions in the face of apparently insurmountable odds. It therefore remained the biggest and most influential organization.

The Tamil diaspora

Tamils had been emigrating from Sri Lanka and southern India since the nineteenth century. Along with Tamil functionaries who went to serve the British empire in South-East Asia, particularly Malaysia and Singapore, others emigrated in lesser capacities: contractors, traders, shopkeepers and labourers. Tamil settlements, therefore, also exist in Fiji, South Africa, Guyana in the Caribbean and other places. From the 1970s onwards educated Sri Lankan Tamils started emigrating to North America, Western Europe and also Australia. As the ethnic conflict worsened, the intelligentsia settled abroad became its most vocal and active support base internationally (de Silva, 1986: 329). As the civil war intensified, a stream of Tamils seeking asylum in the West developed and several thousands left the island in the 1980s. In 1989 alone 20,000 Tamils sought asylum in Europe. The numbers allowed into the West decreased in the 1990s as these countries tightened their asylum policies.

Thus several hundred thousand diaspora Tamils are now settled outside Sri Lanka. They have played an important role in the provision of material and moral support to the separatist movement in Sri Lanka. Tamil activists have been arrested many times in South-East Asia and elsewhere trying to purchase weapons for the LTTE (*Sri Lanka Monitor*, November 1991: 2; Pfaffenberger, 1993: 19). The large diaspora Tamil community has thus played an important role in supplying money and arms to Tamils in Sri Lanka.

International dimension

Given the concerns and strategic interests of the superpowers during the 1980s in South Asia there was also a high level of international involvement in the Sri

Lankan civil war. Friendly countries such as China, Britain, Pakistan and South Korea helped to modernize the Sri Lankan army. Israel's Mossad and Shin Beth provided training in intelligence gathering. Other Western powers, including South Africa and mercenaries of the Rhodesian war, were also reported in the Indian press to be involved in the campaign against the Tamils (Ram, 1989: 89). Some Tamil guerrilla groups were believed to have received training with the PLO.

The Indian connection

Tamils living in Sri Lanka and on the Indian mainland have maintained regular contacts all through history, although interaction in pre-modern times between the two groups was not so frequent. After the British began to recruit Tamils from the mainland to work on the plantations in Sri Lanka, contacts became more regular. The expulsion of Plantation Tamils and the recurrent Tamil riots in Sri Lanka created a support base for the victims in Tamil Nadu. Thus the TULF, LTTE and other Tamil groups were provided with sanctuary and bases in Tamil Nadu. Moreover, the Indian state has had to demonstrate a concern for Tamils in Sri Lanka in order to placate its own 60 million Tamils, among whom separatism had been a strong attraction in the 1950s. Thus the central government had connived at the establishment of militant Tamil resistance. Some of the guerrilla groups were directly patronized and protected by the Indians (Jayaweera, 1991: 19–20). The LTTE also received material and moral support but, because it would not submit to their control, it was treated with suspicion and even hostility by the Indian establishment.

Eschewing direct confrontation with the Sri Lanka government but maintaining pressure on it had been the strategy which the Indian government normally pursued in relation to Sri Lanka. While Mrs Gandhi was tilted more towards the Tamil separatists, her successor, Rajiv Gandhi, was less inclined to encourage them (Vanniasingham, 1988: 137–40). Instead Rajiv Gandhi offered his good offices for exploring the possibility of a political settlement. The TULF played a prominent role in the negotiations. The main guerrilla groups, including LTTE, authorized the TULF to negotiate on their behalf. Several schemes and formulae were put forward between 1983 and 1986, but an agreement could not be reached. President Jayewardene even tried secret negotiations with the LTTE. However, after three years of tiresome but fruitless negotiations, a settlement had not been agreed. In exasperation the Delhi government in December 1986 started disarming the Tiger cadres based in Tamil Nadu and ordered them out of India.

The Tigers moved back to Jaffna and announced they were taking over the administration of the Jaffna region from New Year's Day, 1987. This move was interpreted by the Sri Lanka government as virtually a declaration of a separate state. It imposed a tight economic blockade on the Jaffna peninsula. In April a major military assault was launched on Jaffna. Fearing that this might mean a defeat for the guerrillas — a prospect which could reduce the Indian role in Sri Lanka as well as agitate India's own Tamil people — the Indian government dispatched five transport planes and two fighter aircraft over the Jaffna peninsula, ostensibly to supply relief but in reality to intimidate the Sri Lankan government (Ram, 1989: 94). Jayewardene, who had publicly been criticizing Indian inter-ference in the internal matters of Sri Lanka, now changed course and sought Indian help in establishing the peace in his country.

Indian intervention

An agreement was reached between India and Sri Lanka on 29 July 1987 to work together to establish durable peace in the region (Ram, 1989: 140–6). The pact recognized the unity and sovereign status of Sri Lanka. On the other hand, the Sri Lankan government recognized the multi-ethnic and multi-religious nature of Sri Lankan society. The idea of a Tamil homeland was also recognized, albeit within Sri Lanka. Devolution of power was to be implemented. A referendum was to be held in the Eastern Province to ascertain if the people living there wanted to link their province with the Northern Province or not. On the other hand, India was to play an active role in establishing the peace. The militants were to be denied help and sanctuary in India. Further, India was to disarm the Tamil militants in the north and east. For doing this India was to send a peace-keeping force to Sri Lanka.

The accord between the Sri Lankan and Indian governments was assailed from both Tamil and Sinhalese directions. Some members of the government, including Prime Minister Premadasa, displayed their displeasure by staying away from the formal signing ceremony between President Julius Jayewardene and the Indian Prime Minister Rajiv Gandhi. The SLFP launched a political offensive against the alleged capitulation of Sri Lankan sovereignty by Jayewardene to India.

Ultra-nationalist opposition to the Agreement

But the most intense opposition to the Agreement came from the JVP. A written statement signed by the leaders of the JVP was circulated throughout the country in which the people were urged to oppose Indian intervention. Scathing criticism was made of the 'illegal, treacherous, murderous, fascist, Jayewardene–Thonda-man Government' (Gunaratna, 1990: 252). The JVP launched what was described as a 'Patriotic War'. Once again it was poor unemployed Sinhalese youths from peasant backgrounds who constituted its main support base. Land scarcity and employment opportunities had worsened over the years and thousands of unemployed youths were available for mobilization. The JVP movement was joined by several other ultra-nationalist Sinhalese parties and factions of both clerical and lay persuasions. The ultra-nationalists launched a terror campaign against government functionaries as well as the activists of the ruling UNP. Killings, bombings and abductions were undertaken on a large scale. Cadres of the SLFP also indulged in these killings.

The state, having reposed the responsibility of disarming the Tamil militants of the north and east in the Indian government, turned its full fury on the Sinhalese ultra-nationalists (Marino, 1989: 2–3). Between 1987 and 1991 some 40,000 to 60,000 people disappeared or died in the south (*Sri Lanka Monitor*, October 1990 and December 1991; *Sri Lanka Human Rights Situation*, January 1992). By 1991 the ultra-nationalists had been successfully crushed, although low-level action on the part of the JVP continued into 1993.

The IPFK operation and LTTE resistance

On 30 July 1987 India dispatched 6000 of its best equipped soldiers to the northern province. Later this number was to rise constantly until by 1990 70,000 troops were placed in the north and east of the island. Initially the LTTE leader, Velupillai Prabhakaran, assumed a somewhat confusing position: he rejected the accord but expressed an intention not to fight India. Thus when the Indian Peace-Keeping Force (IPKF) started collecting arms from all Tamil groups, the Tigers on 5 August 1987 also made a token gesture of publicly surrendering their weapons. However, things got out of hand when a Sri Lankan patrol intercepted a Tamil boat and captured twelve LTTE members. They were initially put in Indian custody but later were allowed to be taken to Colombo by Sri Lankan forces. This was in contravention of the accord as amnesty had been promised to LTTE's cadres. On their way to Colombo the twelve Tigers committed suicide by swallowing cyanide capsules (Ram, 1989: 66). On several other issues disagreement developed between the LTTE and the Indian government. In the meantime the Tigers wiped out all the other guerrilla groups from the Jaffna area. Relations between the IPKF and the LTTE turned hostile rapidly as both competed with each other to establish their writ in the region.

Despite laying a siege to Jaffna and causing considerable damage to Tamil life and property, the Sri Lankan army had failed to dislodge the Tigers from there. Now the IPKF decided to wrest Jaffna from them. In early October the IPKF launched an invasion on Jaffna. Two thousand LTTE cadres faced a superior Indian force which was additionally backed by the Indian Air Force. After heavy fighting, which included considerable civilian casualties, the Indian forces took Jaffna city on 25 October. An estimated 700 cadres of the Tigers were killed out of a total strength of a fighting force of 2500. The Tigers now withdrew into the thick jungle and retreated to the eastern province, from where they continued to attack Indian positions. During 1988 the IPKF scored several successes against the LTTE. At the same time negotiations continued between Indian secret agencies and political functionaries and the LTTE, both in Sri Lanka and in Madras. The IPFK earned the considerable ill will of the Tamil civilians when cases of rape, torture and killing at the hands of the Indian soldiers began to be reported (*Massacre at Valvettiturai*, 1989).

Although the Tigers surrendered Jaffna, they did not give up harassing and attacking the IPKF. They continuously launched surprise attacks with deadly accuracy, causing havoc among the Indians. The local Tamil population tended to side with the Tigers. Moreover they could easily find cover in thick jungle in the region. The war dragged on. India not only failed to defeat the Tigers but was made to pay a heavy penalty in terms of casualties, including at least 2500 troops killed in action.

President Premadasa and the concept of multi-ethnic democracy

In the 1988 presidential election the nominee of Junius Jayewardene for the president post, the sitting prime minister, Ranasinghe Premadasa, won by a narrow margin over Mrs Bandaranaike. A devout Buddhist, President Premadasa was also known for his opposition to the presence of the IPKF. In an interview given in 1989 to a research team commissioned by the Peace Research Institute Oslo (PRIO) to investigate into the possibilities of establishing peace on the island, Premadasa spoke in favour of reconciliation and concord with the Tamils and for establishing a multi-ethnic democracy (Jayaweera, 1991: 121–6). As regards the central role accorded to Buddhism in the constitution, he pointed out that such a commitment did not violate the rights of minorities to religious freedom, because Buddhism believed in tolerance and peaceful co-existence. His willingness to negotiate with the LTTE was defended by him on grounds that it might lead to the establishment of durable peace. Whereas devolution of power to the northeast was acceptable, it had to be within the framework of a united Sri Lanka. On the language question, he emphasized the restoration of English as a means of gaining modern knowledge but also as a 'middle ground for the Sinhala and Tamil people'. But ultimately 'the best ground for the Sinhala and Tamil people is the knowledge of each other's language. Only then will we become one nation, as a Sri Lanka nation' (Jayaweera, 1991: 123).

Withdrawal of the IPKF — but the conflict drags on

In the 1989 Indian national elections Rajiv Gandhi was defeated and V.P. Singh became prime minister. Thus the key political actors involved in bringing the

Indian soldiers to Sri Lanka had been removed from centre stage and the climate improved for an Indian withdrawal. Premadasa invited the LTTE and JVP for talks. While the JVP declined the offer, LTTE accepted it. For the LTTE this meant a recognition of their status as the main party representing the Tamils. In March 1990 the IPKF withdrew, but peace eluded all later initiatives of President Premadasa. Within his government and administration there was strong opposition to any concessions to the Tamils. The large politicized Buddhist clergy also opposed such reconciliatory overtures. The Tigers too refused to lay down their arms and order cessation of violent activities. The conflict dragged on.

Sri Lankan help to the Tamil Tigers

A most peculiar and bizarre aspect of the IPKF–LTTE armed confrontation that came out later in public was that, during the critical period when the Tigers were faring badly against the Indians, the Sri Lankan state had secretly been helping the Tigers with arms and other facilities from certain quarters close to Prime Minister Premadasa (Gunaratna, 1993: 386–7). Apparently this was done so that the Tigers would not be defeated by a foreign power, something which could have reflected adversely on the ability of the Sri Lankan state to demonstrate its sovereign authority over its territory. It was suspected that a defeat would only strengthen Indian hegemony and facilitate its expansionist designs.

The Muslim question

Although Muslims are to be found all over the country, they are concentrated mainly in the eastern districts of Amaparai (41.53 per cent), Trincomalee (28.97 per cent), and Batticalo (23.97 per cent) and in the northern district of Mannar (26.62 per cent). The Muslim élite and merchant class is concentrated in the capital, Colombo. Most Muslims in the east are agriculturists, often poor peasants. There is, however, a large body of small traders and shopkeepers who are spread all over the villages and towns in both Sinhalese and Tamil areas. Although the mother tongue of the Moors is almost invariably Tamil, many of them who are settled in Sinhalese areas are bilingual. The Moors are almost entirely Sunnis (Mohan, 1986: 123). There are also some Muslims among the Plantation Tamils, and a small number of Indian and Malay Muslims are also settled in Sri Lanka.

Muslims in post-independence Sri Lanka

The Colombo-based Muslim leadership continued in the post-independence period to align itself with the Sinhalese. The Sinhalese responded by including some Muslim ministers in the government. Amid the intensified ethno-nationalist hostilities between the Sinhalese and Tamils, the Muslims also revitalized their Islamic identity (Mohan, 1986: 135–41). Partly such identity was a reflection of the exposure of many Sri Lankan Muslims to Arab culture. From the 1970 onwards Sri Lankan Muslims had been in large numbers seeking employment in the Persian Gulf region. Those who stayed there a few years returned home groomed in Islamic culture and practices. Muslim youths, alienated from the growing Sinhalese–Tamil polarization, and frequently exposed to brutal attacks from both sides, were easily attracted to the Islamic discourse of the returnees from the Arab countries.

The escalation of ethnic conflict between Sinhalese and Tamils inevitably dragged the Muslim community into its orbit. Moreover, the policy of Sinhalese colonization in the east and north also hurt the Muslim population living there. Consequently, as Muslims became politicized, both Sinhalese and Tamil extremists intensified their terror tactics against them. Consequently the Muslims established their own militias and began to organize defence committees. However, as most of them were settled among Tamils, the main confrontation took place between them and the Tamils.

The policy of ethnic cleansing which the Tamil separatists had been pursuing since 1988 in the north and east led to considerable loss of life and property of the Muslim minority. In October the LTTE issued an ultimatum to Muslims in Mannar, Mullaitivu, Kilinochchi and Jaffna districts to leave or be killed (*Summary Human Rights*, February 1991). Since 1990 more than 50,000 Muslims have been driven out of their villages in the north alone. Several pogroms of Muslims have taken place at the hands of the Tamil Tigers. For example, 170 Muslims were slaughtered in the Polonnaruwa district by the Tamil Tigers on 15 October 1992 (*Sri Lanka Monitor*, October 1992). There have also been some Muslim reprisals against the Tamils, but their ability to retaliate is hopelessly limited. Thus Muslims have been demanding the creation of a separate Muslim province or council in the east and north.

The protraction of the conflict

Although the Sri Lankan government is in principle committed to devolution, it has made it conditional on the Tigers first surrendering their weapons, something which LTTE has refused to do thus far (Jayaweera, 1991: 22). On the one hand, a strong ultra-nationalist Sinhalese lobby exists within the government. With the support of the politicized Buddhist clergy it can be a real obstacle to the peace process. On the other hand, in spite of the fact that the LTTE has effectively been controlling the north and parts of the eastern regions, the Sri Lankan state has continued to perform some of its functions unmolested. For example, the management of hospitals and schools continues to reside with the government. It also maintains some other offices and pays the pensions and other allowances to the people. The Tigers are simply in no position in economic terms to sustain the whole range of state activities. The departure of the Indian troops was followed by renewed military action of the Sri Lankan armed forces against the Tigers. Skirmishes and battles between the Tigers and the army and security forces have continued and it seems impossible that Tamil separatism can be contained through military action. Some 40,000 people were killed between 1987 and 1993 in the north-east alone.

On the other hand, surviving JVP cadres have continued to indulge in militant activities though on a very low scale. Arrests of suspected ultra-nationalists continued into 1993. The ultra-nationalist forces have persisted with acts of banditry and arson, and bomb explosions have continued to be reported in the press and in the government-controlled mass media. Similarly, violent confrontations between Muslims and Tamil militants have continued.

The LTTE remains in the lead

The LTTE was able to maintain its leading position despite all odds. The supreme leader of the LTTE, Prabhakaran, emerged almost as a messianic figure among his followers. In a way, many Tamils came to associate their survival with the LTTE. Many young men and women, some of them only children, joined its training camps to receive guerrilla training. Tamils settled abroad returned to join the movement. The LTTE developed an extraordinarily effective and integrated leadership. Upon completion of the training each guerrilla was given a cyanide capsule which was to be swallowed in order to avoid arrest by government forces. Martyrdom was to be preferred to the humiliation of being arrested and tortured. In this regard the heroic tales from the *Mahabharata* have been employed to instil a love for martyrdom (Schalk, 1991). A core group called Black Tigers was assigned key missions which involved a high probability of death. The most terrifying of all Tiger operations have been the suicide bombers: cadres who tie explosives to their bodies and blow up themselves and their victims. With such tactics the LTTE organizers built up a small but extremely effective fighting force. Tamils who oppose the Tigers are intimidated and terrorized. Liquidation of dissidents and opponents is part of the LTTE's standard practices. Thus the Tigers have gained notoriety as a vengeful and cruel terrorist organization (*Inside Story*, 1991).

Assassinations by suspected LTTE squads

On 2 March 1991 the Sri Lankan defence minister, Ranjan Wijeratne, died in a suspected LTTE bomb blast. Tamil vengeance for what they perceived as a betrayal by the Delhi regime of their cause claimed the life of Prime Minister Rajiv Gandhi on 21 May 1991. A woman suicide bomber killed herself, Rajiv Gandhi and several other people during an election meeting in Tamil Nadu. The police inquiry report, which was based on substantial circumstantial evidence, incriminated the Tigers for the assassination (Mitra, 1991: 82–9). Consequently LTTE bases in Tamil Nadu were abolished, and it was banned from India. The LTTE, however, denied any involvement in the murder. In February 1993 Prabhakaran announced that the LTTE was ready to forgo its goal of complete separation and independence in favour of a federal arrangement with substantial autonomy within a united Sri Lankan state (*Sri Lanka Monitor*, February 1993). However the assassination of President Premadasa by a suicide bomber on 1 May 1993, in typical Tiger style, marred the possibility of an early solution of the Sri Lankan ethnic war. President Premadasa was blown up by a suicide bomber while taking part in the May Day rally in Colombo. The LTTE denied any involvement in that murder, too. At present, lasting peace does not seem to be in the offing.

Ideology and programme of the LTTE

A Marxist-oriented socio-economic programme but with strong emphasis on political democracy is set forth in the programme of the proposed Eelam state. The *Socialist Tamil Eelam* declares its main objective as the creation of 'an independent sovereign socialist State of Tamil Eelam'. It is further asserted:

> We have a homeland, a historically constituted habitation with a well defined territory embracing the Northern and Eastern provinces, distinct language, a rich culture and tradition, a unique economic life and a lengthy history extending to over three thousand years. As a nation, we have the inalienable right of self-determination. . . . The independent State of Eelam as envisioned by the LTTE shall be a people's State, a secular democratic, socialist State created by the will of the people, administered by the people; a State that will guarantee all democratic liberties and freedoms of its citizens.

All forms of exploitation and social oppression are to be abolished. As regards the Sinhalese people, only the chauvinistic ruling class is described as the enemy of all the working and toiling people of Sri Lanka. On the other hand, state-organized Sinhalese colonization of Tamil areas is to be opposed. As regards the Muslim people, their distinct ethnic identity is recognized. Tamil Eelam is also to be the homeland of the Muslim people. Citizenship rights are to be conferred on all Plantation Tamils in Tamil Eelam. They are to be encouraged to migrate to Tamil Eelam once independence has been achieved.

All forms of female exploitation prevalent among Tamils are to be eradicated. The socialist economy of Tamil Eelam is not to be based on a rigid centralized plan. People's participation at all levels in the socio-economic transformation of the nation will be necessary. 'While ensuring equal distribution of national wealth, the LTTE will provide incentives for expatriate Tamil patriots to contribute to the development of the national economy.'

Bryan Pfaffenberger (1993: 13) has worked out that the territorial claims of LTTE for Tamil Eelam require a secession of 28.7 per cent of the area, which includes 60 per cent of the coastline, of Sri Lanka.

Interview with Krishnakumar alias Kittu

I interviewed Mr Krishnakumar alias Kittu, International Spokesperson of the LTTE, in May 1991 in London. A summary is presented below.

The Buddhist scriptures from the pre-colonial period are full of hatred against Tamils and South Indians. Sinhalese kings have in the past fought attempts by Tamil kings of south India to extend their influence on Sri Lanka. During the nineteenth century Buddhist ideologues continued to emphasize the anti-Tamil sentiment in their nationalist writings. But among the common Sinhalese and Tamil people there was no animosity or ill will. It all started with the coming into power of the SLFP-led government in 1956. Mr Bandaranaike exploited the ethnic issue to get votes. The 1958 anti-Tamil riots impelled Tamils to seek safeguards for their security. At that time UNP was not against Tamils and the Sinhalese people had no animosity against Tamils. When Tamil youths started agitating peacefully against the standardization policy of 1972 they were beaten by the essentially Sinhalese police. Thereafter the Tamils took to arms to defend their democratic rights.

There is a difference between the economic and social structure of the northern and eastern Tamil societies. The north is unfit for profitable agriculture. The east is rich because water is available in abundance from the rivers flowing through it. Tricommeelee has the best natural harbour in the region. Several hundred ships can dock in it. Sinhalese colonization in the east began after independence. In 1948 only 10 per cent of the population of Tricommeelee was Sinhalese, now one-third are Tamils, one-third Tamil Muslims and one-third Sinhalese colonizers. In Amaparai district the Sinhalese are now in a majority. Even in the north, Sinhalese have been settled by the government. The Sinhalese settlers carry guns and attack Tamils. As a result many Tamils have fled from these areas. More than 400,000 Tamils are refugees in Tamil Nadu.

The LTTE is a secular nationalist organization open to all Tamil-speaking peoples of Sri Lanka. Tamil Muslims also joined our organization. Many of them died fighting the Indian and Sri Lankan armies. During 1987–90 everybody joined ranks to resist the Indians. Thereupon the Sri Lankan government embarked upon a policy of driving a wedge among Tamils and Muslims. Now it is only Hindu and Christian Tamils who are active in the liberation struggle.

The Tigers first started receiving arms from the Indian government in 1983. At that time the Sri Lankan government was providing several military and intelligence gathering facilities to the USA. The Indians wanted to pressure Sri Lanka by bracing the Tigers militarily. However, the Tigers did not agree to becoming a tool of Indian foreign policy and maintained their independent initiative. As far as the question of the main objective of the movement is concerned, it is simply the security of the Tamil people. During the whole post-independence period the pacts and agreements negotiated by Tamils with the Sri Lankan government have come to naught. How can the Tamils rely on any other people for their security? Tamil Eelam is the expression of the need for security of Tamils.

On 15 January 1993 Krishnakumar Kittu was killed when the boat he was travelling on to Jaffna was intercepted by the Indian navy. Apparently the guerrillas themselves blew up their boat (*Sri Lanka Monitor*, January 1993: 1).

References

Bastian, S. (1990) 'Political economy of ethnic violence in Sri Lanka: the July 1983 riots' in V. Das (ed.), *Mirrors of Violence: Communities, Riots, and Survivors in South Asia*, Delhi: Oxford University Press.

Bhaduri, S. and Karim, A. (1990) *The Sri Lankan Crisis*, New Delhi: Lancer International.

The Constitution of the Democratic Socialist Republic of Sri Lanka, certified on 31 August 1978, Colombo: Government Publications Bureau.

De Silva, K.M. (1981) *A History of Sri Lanka*, London: C. Hurst.

de Silva, K.M. (1986) *Managing Ethnic Tensions in Multi-Ethnic Societies: Sri Lanka 1880–1985*, London: University Press of America.

Forty Years of Human Rights Violations by Sri Lanka — What Is to be Done (1991), Surrey: International Federation of Tamils.

Fries, Y. and Bibin, T. (1984) *The Undesirables: The Expatriation of the Tamil People 'of Recent Indian Origin' from the Plantations in Sri Lanka to India*, Calcutta: K.P. Bagchi & Company.

Gunaratna, R. (1990) *Sri Lanka, a Lost Revolution: The Inside Story of the JVP*, Colombo: Institute of Fundamental Studies.

Gunaratna, R. (1993) *Indian Intervention in Sri Lanka: The Role of India's Intelligence Agencies*, Colombo: South Asian Network on Conflict Research.

Hellmann-Rajanayagam, D. (1991) 'Ethnicity and nationalism — the Sri Lanka Tamils in the late nineteenth century: some theoretical questions' in D. Weidemann, *Nationalism, Ethnicity and Political Development: South Asian Perspectives*, New Delhi: Manohar.

Inside Story: Suicide Killers (a BBC production, 1991), telecast on Swedish TV 2 on 27 April 1993.

Jayaweera, N. (1991) *Sri Lanka: Towards a Multi-ethnic Democracy?*, Oslo: PRIO.

Jupp, J. (1978) *Sri Lanka — Third World Democracy*, London: Frank Cass.

Levy, R.J. (1990) 'National security' in *Sri Lanka: A Country Study*, Washington, DC: United States Government.

Marino, E. (1989) *Political Killings in Southern Sri Lanka*, London: International Alert Publication.

Massacre at Valvettiturai: India's Mylai (1989), Bombay: Hind Mazdoor Kissan Panchayat.

Mitra, A. (1991) 'Rajiv assassination: the inside story', *India Today*, 15 July.

Mohan, D.V. (1986) 'Islam in Sri Lanka' in A. Engineer (ed.), *Islam in Asia*, Lahore: Vanguard.

Moore, M. (1985) *The State and Peasant Politics in Sri Lanka*, Cambridge: Cambridge University Press.

Moore, M. (1990) 'Sri Lanka: the contradictions of the social democratic state' in S.K. Mitra (ed.), *The Post-Colonial State in Asia*, New York: Harvester Wheatsheaf.

Nissan, E. and Stirrat, R.L. (1990) 'The generation of communal identities' in J. Spencer (ed.), *Sri Lanka: History and the Roots of the Conflict*, London and New York: Routledge.

Oberst, R.C. (1989) 'Tamil militancy and youth insurgency in Sri Lanka' in D. Vajpeyi and Y.K. Malik (eds), *Religious and Ethnic Minority Politics in South Asia*, New Delhi: Manohar.

Olsen, B. (1989) *The Sri Lanka Conflict: A Study of Elite Perceptions*, Fantoft: Chr. Michelsen Institute.

Pfaffenberger, B. (1993) 'The structure of protracted conflict: the case of Sri Lanka', paper presented at the conference, State Formation and Institution Building in South Asia, Sunnersta, Sweden, 9 October 1993.

Phadnis, U. (1976) *Religion and Politics in Sri Lanka*, New Delhi: Manohar.

Ponnambalam, S. (1983) *Sri Lanka: The National Question and the Tamil Liberation Struggle*, London: Zed Books.

Ram, M. (1989) *Sri Lanka: The Fractured Island*, New Delhi: Penguin Books.

Rogers, J.D. (1990) 'The economy' in *Sri Lanka: A Country Study*, Washington, DC: United States Government.

Schalk, P. (1990) 'Articles 9 and 18 of the Constitution of Lanka as obstacles to peace' in P. Schalk (ed.), *Lanka*, December, Uppsala.

Schalk, P. (1991) 'The concept of martyrdom and resistance of the Liberation Tigers of Tamil Eelam (LTTE)', paper presented at the conference on Ethnicity, Identity and Development in South Asia, held at Postgaarden, Denmark in October 1991.

Seekins, D.M. (1990) 'Government and politics' in *Sri Lanka: A Country Study*, Washington, DC: United States Government.

Sivathamby, K. (1990) 'The ideology of Saiva–Tamil integrality: its socio-historical significance in the study of Yalppanam Tamil society' in P. Schalk (ed.), *Lanka*, December, Uppsala.

Sri Lanka Human Rights Situation (January 1992), prepared on behalf of the European NGO Forum on Sri Lanka by the Country Working Group on Sri Lanka, Geneva.

Sri Lanka Monitor, London, October 1990, November and December 1991, October 1992, January 1993, February 1993.

Sri Lanka: Summary of Human Rights Concerns During 1990 (February 1991), London: Amnesty International.

Tambiah, S.J. (1986) *Sri Lanka: Ethnic Fratricide and the Dismantling of Democracy*, Delhi: Oxford University Press.

Tamil Eelam: Political Programme of the LTTE (1990?).

Vanniasingham, S. (1988) *Sri Lanka: The Conflict Within*, New Delhi: Lancer.

Vije, M. (1987) *Where Serfdom Thrives*, Madras: TIRU.

Wilson, A.J. (1974) *Politics in Sri Lanka: 1947–1973*, London: Macmillan.

Wilson, A.J. (1994) *S.J.V. Chelvanayakam and the Crisis of Sri Lankan Tamil Nationalism, 1947–77*, London: Hurst & Company.

Interviews

Dr Dagmar Hellmann-Rajanayagam, London (1991)
Krishnakumar alias Kittu, International Secretary, LTTE (1991)
Professor Peter Schalk, Uppsala University (1993)
Dr Gabriele Winai-Ström, Uppsala University (1993)

10

A Comparative Analysis

This chapter presents a comparative analysis of the state–society contradictions manifesting in the form of ethnic conflicts and separatist movements in contemporary South Asia. A conclusion is drawn and some measures are suggested which might help reduce regional and inter-state tension and contribute to the peaceful resolution of ethnic conflicts and confrontations between the state and separatist movements. The aim is to stimulate the efforts of all those who might have an interest in peace and humane development in South Asia and elsewhere in the world.

Historical roots of state–society incongruence

The ruling élites of India, Pakistan and Sri Lanka set about to rectify the incongruence between state and society which occurred during the colonial period. The British policy of communal representation had thoroughly politicized ethnic identity and built it into the politics of the successor South Asian states. Because the British were an alien, ethnically discrete ruling group they could pretend to be neutral arbiters of societal disputes. The indigenous power élites of the successor states could not fit into the role of neutral arbiters. They had to propound their own strategies of controlling and leading society. This was by no means an easy task. The departure of the British not only jolted the power balance among social forces within states but also shattered the overall power structure in South Asia. The destabilizing repercussions of the colonial withdrawal were considerable both within them and between them.

Predicaments of modernization and development under peripheral capitalism

The new states were obliged to construct nation-state models and use their monopoly over state power to secure compliance from the people. Irrespective of the specific problems and circumstances of each state, their common aim of ensuring their survival necessitated the accomplishment of two main objectives: firstly, to bring about economic growth through modernization and industrialization, and, secondly, to consolidate the disparate cultural entities — all-inclusively or selectively — that constituted their population into an integrated political nation. With an all-inclusive territorial democratic nation-state project, equal rights of citizens and in the case of a selective nation-state project differential or discriminatory distribution of rights followed logically. However, irrespective of the ideological concerns, the modernization and development processes generated a complex clash of interest and identity. The state began to intervene increasingly in people's lifestyles and established means of earning a livelihood, and in the process affected their lives in a more substantial manner. Above all it meant greater centralization of power — with all the possibilities of such power being used arbitrarily.

On the other hand, state-led modernization and development released new social forces which acquired group interests and developed collective identity not readily compatible with the nation-state project. In multicultural societies the processes of modernization and uneven development were bound to have ramifications on cultural identity. As greater centralization of power occurred or the state simply behaved arbitrarily or rashly, regional élites and intelligentsia of unranked cultural groups concentrated in large numbers in specific geographical areas began to assert their separate cultural identity in relation to the state. Their communal and regional identities had already been recognized as valid basis for political claims during the colonial period (communal in terms of ethnic or religious groups and regional in terms of the creation of separate provinces on the basis of language, for example separation of Sindh from Bombay in 1936), and therefore could potentially serve as the basis of continuing communal and regional interests *vis-à-vis* the state. The more ardent cultural nationalists among them began to assert their claim to nationness and alluded to the right of self-determination. By re-reading colonial and pre-colonial history, invoking ethnic markers and selectively quoting Western political theory on nationalism and group rights, Sikh, Kashmiri, Sindhi, Mohajir, Tamil and even the tribal peoples of the Chittagong Hill Tracts could assert a separate nationalism. The claim to being a nation with the right to secede from the state was a matter of further ideological construction. Such an opportunity arrived with the growing crisis of modernization.

Initially, however, the state was successful in leading society. In the 1950s and until the mid-1960s the respective states seemed assured that they were on the way to the consolidation of their support base in the larger society. Although ethnic tension and separatist movements did exist during this period, these tendencies were rather easily brought under control. Thus India was able to contain the Naga insurgency, merge the princely states and resolve subnationalist aspirations through the creation of linguistic states. In Punjab this could be done first in

1966 — only after mass agitations had been staged by the Sikhs. In Kashmir, Article 370 had been agreed to define the special relation between India and the Jammu and Kashmir State. The arrest of Sheikh Abdullah in 1953 was indicative of the peculiar difficulties present in that situation. Pakistan rode roughshod over the objections of the regional nationalists and could with impunity merge the various provinces and princely States of its western wing into the single province of West Pakistan during the mid-1950s. Sri Lanka could pass the 'Sinhala Only' Bill in 1956 with utter disregard for Tamil sensibilities. Until the middle of the 1960s, therefore, the state was strong in relation to society in general, but especially *vis-à-vis* the cultural minorities and nationalities; the strength of the state being its ability to impose its will on society and the various units without any, or more than limited, resistance from them.

From the mid-1960s the inherent contradictions of peripheral capitalism began to emerge with force in India, Pakistan and Sri Lanka. The wars between India and Pakistan in 1965 and 1971 were expressions of the disputes bequeathed by the colonial legacy. The mass democratic movements and revolutionary struggles in India, similar trends in Pakistan, and the youth insurrection in Sri Lanka in 1971 were indicative of how the politics of these societies were influencing each other. In the face of the growing crisis the states began to employ force and violence on a massive scale in order to regain control over society. It did not matter whether the respective states subscribed to a democratic or an authoritarian model of nation building. The upshot of structural incapacity deriving from peripheral capitalism was that the South Asian states began increasingly to fail to act as effective solvers of the multiplying societal problems.

The intensification of the Cold War, the rise of fundamentalist Islam from the late 1970s in and around South Asia and the revolution in communication technology tended to aid the emerging separatist movements. Cheaper air travel made physical movement of people swift and unproblematic. Commercial production of cassette radios and later in the 1980s of video systems meant that news and propaganda could be transmitted easily. The groups which made the most of the new facilities were the Tamils, Sikhs, and Kashmiris — in the chronological order of the origins of their separatist movements — which had large diaspora support groups present in the West. On the other hand, groups such as the Sindhis and the CHT tribals, who lacked the support of diaspora communities and had lagged behind in modernization with the result that their intelligentsia was small, were disadvantaged in exploiting effectively the communications facilities. The Mohajirs in Pakistan were of course the most advanced group in Pakistan, and the MQM made full use of the communications facilities to build up a solid support among the Mohajir community. However, since the MQM lacked diaspora support and additionally was the creature of the ISI, its actual ability to defy the state was precarious.

As ethnic conflict intensified and separatist movements gained momentum, the nation-state projects of the four South Asian states were adjusted, revised or abandoned, if not in theory then definitely in practice. The paramount intention of the state in such behaviour was to prevent the loss of territory in a region where mutual hostility had only deepened, and where actors from outside the region were gaining access easily. By the early 1980s state–society incongruence had taken the form mainly of centre–periphery contradictions in the politics of India, Pakistan, Bangladesh and Sri Lanka.

International and regional linkages and separatist conflicts

State–society contradictions were aggravated partly by Cold War confrontational politics. Thus, since India was aligned to the Soviet Union, the Sikh and Kashmiri separatist movements looked towards the West for material and other assistance. How much was provided, if any at all, remains unknown. In its 1984 report on the Punjab problem the Indian government mentioned that diaspora Sikhs were trying to lobby members of the US Congress. In the Sikh Charter published by the Khalistan Council an offer was made to provide Sikh soldiers to NATO. As regards Kashmir, the Americans once supported the plebiscite demand of Pakistan and the Kashmiris, but no longer. Additionally, in both the cases large diaspora communities were settled in the West which played an important role in supporting the separatist movements. In the case of Kashmir support for the militants was forthcoming also from the Pakistani state, Azad Kashmir and the Pakistani Punjab, where ethnic Kashmiris are settled in large numbers.

On the other hand, since Pakistan had a pro-Western stance and during the Afghanistan conflict received US military aid, the Sindhi secessionists tried to attract Indian help. In this they were rather unsuccessful. On the other hand both Sindhis and Mohajirs lacked the support of diaspora communities. Consequently the availability of arms remained limited and the level of conflict did not assume such proportions as happened in the case of the Sikh, Kashmiri or Tamil confrontations with the state. In the case of Sri Lanka, while the state received help from Western countries and Israel, some Tamil factions were backed by Palestinian guerrilla groups. Additionally the help from Tamil Nadu, the Indian government (at times) and the large well-educated Tamil diaspora has meant that the Tamils have been able to fight the Sri Lankan state with considerable effectiveness. The CHT guerrilla movement was also able to sustain its low-level conflict with the Bangladesh state because it received training and arms from India. Thus the external linkages have been crucial in determining the level of conflict.

Now when the Cold War is over and the world is dominated by the USA the support for internal civil wars in South Asia may have little attraction for the big powers. In its unique role as sole superpower, the USA is in a position to defuse tension or to exacerbate it. How it will relate to South Asia remains to be seen. In the longer run, as new power blocs emerge, the need again to control South Asian societies may again render exploitation of their intra-state and inter-state conflicts an effective means to such an end. On the other hand, the surge of fundamentalism in South Asia is likely to prevail for some time as no signs of it subsiding are in sight.

The nation-state project and the survival of the state

An important point to note is that the overriding need for survival has meant that all the four states have opposed secession of territory. On the other hand, if some ambiguity existed about the legality of claims, these states did not hesitate in exploiting the situation. Such ambiguity inhered in the vagaries of the British withdrawal from South Asia. Consequently India, the biggest and most powerful among them, used various opportunities to annex such territory. Pakistan behaved in a similar manner, and the hope of incorporating the Indian Kashmir into its jurisdiction has led it to initiate several military adventures. Bangladesh and Sri Lanka have not been less protective of their territorial interests. They do not apparently entertain expansionist designs, but are willing to employ maximum force to hold on to territories under their jurisdiction.

A bizarre aspect of such fear is that it haunts states the same way as it haunts individuals — exaggerated in case of bad experience and overly reactive or overly protective to future repetitions. Thus India is haunted by the Partition scenario, and its involvement in Sri Lanka, Bangladesh and earlier on in East Pakistan stems from a mixture of fear and vengeance and an overconfidence about its own power. No doubt Pakistan views India as a major threat to its security. The loss of East Pakistan is rationalized in terms of Indian aggression. Consequently, both countries are looking for opportunities of weakening each other, and therefore making the adversary suffer loss of territory fascinates their defence planners. Needless to mention, Bangladesh and Sri Lanka are always concerned about Indian designs in the region.

The role of violence and the leadership role model

The hallmark of the élites which received power in 1947–48 was their adherence to peaceful agitation and parliamentary methods during the freedom struggle. However, on the Indian subcontinent Partition had already left a legacy of violence. After 16 August 1946, when Suhrawardy ordered his goons to bleed Calcutta in communal hatred, things got out of hand and the civilized politics of the freedom struggle simply collapsed in the face of collective madness. The post-independence societal upheavals in all the four countries developed gradually, came to a head in the 1970s and were crushed by the state through draconian laws and violence. This propensity continued and the ethnic conflicts and separatist struggles of the 1980s became thoroughly steeped in violence and brutality. The recourse to violence has come to be a sinister but typical feature of the contemporary separatist struggles. In some cases the state was provoked to react violently. For example it was only after the JKLF carried out bomb blasts in Srinagar in 1988 that the Indian state dispatched its various police and military forces in large numbers into Kashmir. Thereafter violence and terror became endemic in the Kashmir situation and the various Kashmiri outfits and the Indian forces were drawn into a bloody and brutal armed conflict.

The leadership role model of such violent separatist movements required a person who could appear to run the government personally. If established élite leaders were not willing to undertake daring and risky missions, a new leadership could emerge from among more modest sections of society. Something of the sort happened among most separatist movements of the 1980s. A new type of ruthless leader emerged to whom disciples rendered fanatical obedience and upon whose instructions they were willing to let loose vengeance and terror. The classic examples are Velupillai Prabhakaran of the Tamil Tigers, Sant Jarnail Singh Bhindranwale of the Sikh militants and Altaf Hussain of the Mohajir Quomi Movement (MQM). In one sense, the psychological profile of the separatist leader was a mirror image of the most nefarious component of the modern state: the various key intelligence services representing the state within the state; in other words of the ultimate instruments of brute power.

The power and weakness of state and society

Returning to the fundamental question of the power of the state and of society, it can be asserted that it is a question more about the relative strengths and weaknesses of the two. All the four states were able to advance gradually along the road to modernization and development within a framework circumscribed by peripheral capitalism, some doing better than the others.

On the other hand, the non-Westernized traditional élite and intelligentsia, which had been sidelined during the freedom struggle, sprung back into action as the nation-state projects ran into difficulties. The influence or power which these traditional strata gained over the state can in one sense be considered a movement towards greater interpenetration between state and society, which in turn can be interpreted as an improvement in state–society congruence: the state becoming like the society. Such an inference is only partially valid because it tends to ignore the fact that the state is also the arena where ideas and ideals concerning the shape of society receive authoritative backing or are rejected. In an ideal Hegelian sense the state is the site where universal altruism receives fulfilment. In other words the state forms and constructs society. It can do it effectively if it is autonomous of the society. The post-colonial states of South Asia, however, compromised their autonomy rather than enhancing it. In the case of India, the universal nation-state project was not revised or abandoned, but extensive digressions from it occurred in practice. On the other hand, Pakistan, Bangladesh and Sri Lanka seemed to have capitulated their autonomy to the larger society. The most glaring failure or weakness of the state became apparent in its inability to impose law and order on the society. A general decline in the 'rule of law' occurred in all the four states, and corruption seemed to pervade their routine conduct.

Rather than a concerted will of the state and chain of command, there seem to be several wills of the state: its various organs and political cliques sometimes work in co-ordination and at other times in an anarchical manner. Thus in the case of India, the widespread violation of human rights in Punjab and Kashmir is indicative of a wide latitude of lawless behaviour of security forces and the corrupt police establishments. Pakistan, Bangladesh and Sri Lanka have also flouted constitutional and legal restraints in their treatment of ethnic conflict and separatist struggles.

However, the area in which all the four states acquired overwhelming power over society was in their ability to maintain territorial integrity — the exception being Pakistan, which lost East Pakistan. This was able to happen because India intervened militarily in support of the Bangladeshi resistance. External assistance to revolutionary movements and separatist struggles can be difficult for the state to control. However, as the general disposition of the international system is to maintain the territorial integrity of established states, the significance of such international norms in bolstering the strength of contemporary states *vis-à-vis* their constituent societal units should not be discounted.

Ethnicity, state, society and nation

The fact of ethnicity as a basis of political and social interaction in all societies, and of the majoritarian ethnic dimension having significance in the shaping of state power, need not be elaborated again. However, it does not follow that in normal states, in which the ethnic majority is well entrenched in terms of control over state power, the minorities are excluded *ipso facto* from the nation. The nation as such is a political construction. It is a political declaration about rights and duties and is not therefore simply reducible to so-called objective ethnic groups. A democratic territorial concept of nation which confers equal rights on all citizens irrespective of their caste, colour or creed needs to be distinguished from one which explicitly draws a line among its population — placing some within the nation, others without. Thus, although the democratic territorial concept of nation is likely to function better if the majority group is well represented in government and the state, ways and means of including ethnic minorities into the nation of equal citizens can be devised. The rights of minorities are a matter of ideology, élite preference and the moral persuasion of the majority mainstream society.

The state can promote a special type of group identity based on equal rights: a group identifiable by its common civic culture. The citizens may continue to belong to other ethnic groups such as the Hindu majority or Muslim minority in India, but as citizens their common identity would be defined in terms of their rights. Such a project would not be ethnic, notwithstanding the inevitable cultural hegemony of the majority ethnic group. States may of course prefer selective nation-building, in which case it would be an ethnic nation-state project. The current structure of power in India, Pakistan, Bangladesh and Sri Lanka conforms to the normal type of positive relationship between ethnicity and state power. Currently, therefore, ethnic majorities are firmly in power in each South Asian state. A brief critical review is undertaken below of the ideological and political aspects of the nation-state projects adopted by each state. They are then compared to the separatist projects which challenged the state.

India

The rational and scientific principles of the Enlightenment, progressive and universal views on citizenship and rights derivative of the philosophies of the American and French Revolutions, the patriotic ideology of the anti-colonial struggle influenced largely by Leninist ideas of imperialism, and the Gandhian ideology of peaceful resistance — all contributed to the pristine nation-state project. Thus the Indian nation-state project was a unique fusion of several philosophical and historical influences. The adoption by the Indian Parliament of laws criminalizing the practice of untouchability and various measures on positive discrimination in behalf of the scheduled castes and tribes were extraordinary achievements which boldly rejected the worst forms of the Hindu ethos. The ability to institutionalize democratic procedures such as free, periodic elections on a multi-party basis were further remarkable achievements of the state.

The weakness of the state was its inability to democratize society in general. Constitutional provisions and the main instrument of political socialization which the élite sanctioned — periodic elections based on universal adult franchise — could not suffice to dislodge the influence of ethnic and parochial ties on voting behaviour. Rather the electoral system itself adjusted to such reality, and Indian democracy and the state have been affected by society's particularism. An ethnic dimension was discernible in the behaviour of the state as it increasingly resorted to force and terror to stifle large-scale discontent in both

Punjab and Kashmir. However, thus far a consensus apparently exists among mainstream élite Hindus in favour of secularism and democracy. Even beyond élite consensus, secularism and democracy are now internalized by the Indian political system. Even the Hindu nationalists do not categorically reject secularism or democracy: only the alleged perverted type of secularism based on appeasement of minorities practised by Congress is to be rejected and instead respect for Hinduism established.

In any case, India's future progress towards a fuller democracy would depend on its ability to eliminate the crushing poverty sprawling among the bulk of its population, and the ability of mainstream society to internalize democratic values. Egalitarian processes set in motion by the state at the time of independence would not suffice. Social equality has yet to establish itself as a norm in Hindu society. The scheduled castes and tribes and non-Hindus, particularly Muslims, would have to be integrated into society as equal members. Scholars of Hinduism usually either emphasize the rigidity of the caste system, suggesting that Hinduism as a belief system cannot survive without its caste system, that Hinduism is an ethnic religion based on notions of racial purity and pollution, and, therefore, social equality cannot be established among Hindus; or lean in the other direction and assert that Hinduism lacks a central orthodoxy and, therefore, is amenable to very diverse and radical interpretations, that the caste system is a negation of higher Hinduism and can be eliminated from its belief system. The highly complex and apparently contradictory nature of Hinduism is admitted by all its serious students. It remains to be seen which feature of Hinduism will be adhered to by the future generations of Hindus.

In a more immediate political sense there seems to be the need of a strategy aiming at integrating Indian Muslims into national politics. Isolating the conservative Muslim leadership and instead promoting secular-minded Muslims would be the task for the various secular political parties, including, of course, the Congress Party, to give priority to. Thus far the Muslims have been treated in Indian politics either as an unfortunate cultural group deserving the sympathy and protection of the secular state (the Nehruvian legacy) or as a despised and disloyal one fit to be relegated to an even more excluded and marginal position (the Hindu fundamentalist legacy). Both legacies are logical offshoots of the Partition tragedy. It remains to be seen whether the democratic and secular forces can regain the initiative and push back the Hindu fundamentalist onslaught. At any rate, the policy thus far of tolerating various different civil codes seems dysfunctional to the nation-state project. A common civil code based on a strict distinction between spheres of citizenship and religious community is *ipso facto* imperative to such a strategy. Muslim conservative opposition can be overruled because India is after all a sovereign state and sovereignty entitles it to act in a determined manner in the pursuit of its national self-interest and democratic goals.

The Khalistan project

The Khalistan project has its roots in the communal politics of Punjab going back to the 1920s. The claim to being a nation is justified in terms of religion and special relationship with the Punjabi language written in the Gurmukhi script. In terms of historical proof of the Sikhs' claim to a separate state is mentioned the existence of the kingdom of Ranjit Singh. On the other hand, the ideal political ruler is Guru Gobind Singh. As regards the territorial extent of Khalistan, it is not clear what are envisaged as its precise boundaries. The Sikh kingdom at its height included the whole of Punjab, much of NWFP and parts of Sindh in Pakistan, and some parts of present-day Afghanistan. Punjab was partitioned in 1947. In 1966 East Punjab was reorganized. Which Punjab the Khalistanis have in mind is difficult to establish. In any case, Khalistan is bound to include a substantial Hindu minority unless wholesale forced expulsions or extermination are undertaken. Because the Khalistan movement originated in a religious revival, there is the additional problem of the protection of the civil and political rights of free-thinking Sikhs and of sects such as the Nirankaris. These sections of Sikh society are likely to be subjected to censure and very probably persecution in a purist Sikh theocracy.

Sikhs as a whole cannot reasonably complain of discrimination and deprivation. If any part of India has benefited from development and any minority has gained the most economically, it is the Sikhs. The role of the landowning Sikh élite organized in the various Akali factions in fomenting communal tension has been considerable. It has been the main gainer from the Green Revolution and today constitutes a robust class of prosperous capitalist farmers. However, in cultural and ideological terms the Akalis cling on to religion as a means of enhancing political support. In the 1980s the political initiative on Sikh nationalism was pre-empted by the fundamentalists and diaspora Sikhs who wanted separatism to lead to some sort of a Sikh state. The Punjab Congress Party also exploited communalism to its advantage. In addition, Hindu communal parties, previously the Jana Sangh and now the BJP, have been a source of constant communal tension in Punjab. The communal rivalries of old pre-Partition Punjab have continued to persist into the present times and a real break with the past has yet to come.

The Khalistan project faces many internal difficulties. The Sikh community never as a whole supported the Akalis. Substantial numbers voted for Congress and two Communist parties. This can partly be explained by the divisive role which caste and class play in Sikh society. Sikh society is marked by social distinctions between landowning castes, the business community (many of which migrated from West Punjab), the artisan castes and the Mazhabi Sikhs. These strata have seldom worked together politically. Moreover, more than 3 million Sikhs are settled outside Punjab in different parts of India. Sikh business and transport interests are spread all over India and, as mentioned earlier, large numbers of Sikhs are employed in the army. The transport sector is dominated by Sikhs. In industry, business and commerce Sikhs are to be found all over India. Thus very different receptions of the Khalistan idea can be found among the Sikhs. By ordering military action on the Golden Temple and later acquiescing in the Sikh massacres in November 1984, the Indian state antagonized the vast majority of Sikhs. Were it not for these atrocities the Khalistan project would have in all likelihood remained an extremist idea with much of its support resting outside India. At any rate, without external military help the possibility of realization of the Khalistan project is rather remote. Diaspora Sikhs by themselves cannot sustain large-scale assistance to the Sikh separatists in India. Now, when the Cold War is over and India is no more aligned to a hostile power bloc, a continuing Western interest in Khalistan is most unlikely.

The initiative to a peaceful resolution needs to come from the Indian state. Politically the secular tradition still exists as a major force among Sikhs. Substantial numbers had been voting for Congress and the Communist parties and, given an opportunity, may continue to do so in the future. The restoration of the democratic process, in a proper sense, should be able to play some role in reconciliation between Sikhs and the Indian state. Also, implementation of the Longowal accord of 1985 could alleviate many grievances of the Sikhs.

The Kashmir project

The Kashmir separatist project derives its legitimacy from the Two-Nation Theory, which continues to constitute its basic logical thrust, as well as the fact that it is a dispute which is recognized by international law by virtue of it being placed before the United Nations by India. The Kashmiri Muslim opinion is definitely turned against India currently. The ethnic revival going on around and in South Asia has impacted on the new generation of Kashmiri Muslims, who tend to see their identity in Islamic terms. Kashmiri perceptions are also partly a product of the rise of Hindu nationalism in mainstream Indian society. On the other hand the Hindus of Jammu and the Buddhists of Ladakh cannot reasonably be expected to support the creation of a separate Jammu and Kashmir state, which will be dominated by Muslims; much less would they be enthusiastic about the state joining Pakistan. The idea of a 'Kashmiri nation' including Muslims, Hindus, Buddhists, Sikhs and others, which the JKLF upholds officially, does not have any basis in history. The Jammu and Kashmir State of the colonial period was a patchwork of regional entities which had been put together through conquest and expansion mainly during the Sikh and Dogra periods. The disparate subjects of the Dogras never shared a sense of common identity in the past, and the events after the colonial withdrawal do not suggest that such an identity was consolidated later.

In ideological terms, however, the idea of a Kashmiri nation has been employed widely in State politics. Sheikh Abdullah employed it but vacillated between autonomy and independence as the goal of the Kashmiri nation. Moreover he failed to develop a support base beyond the Muslim constituency of Jammu and Kashmir. His radical policies were seen by the Hindus of Jammu and the Buddhists of Ladakh as biased in favour of the Muslims. It seems that the changing balance of power in South Asia played a major role in fashioning the positions of the Indian central government and Sheikh Abdullah on the question of Kashmir. In a queer manner the arrangement between India and Kashmir in the form of Article 370 appears to its opponents as implicit affirmation of the controversial relationship between the two entities. Hindu nationalists consider it the greatest hindrance to Kashmir's integration into India while the separatists see it as proof of the disputed nature of India's claims on it. At any rate, since only Kashmir has been given special status, it stands out conspicuously as an anomaly. Popular wisdom would rather that either all states within the Indian Union be granted the same latitude of autonomy under a general Article 370 or none should.

It is ironic that in their changing historical identity from Hindus to Buddhists back to Hindus and then to Muslims the people of the Kashmir Valley have never been afforded a better standard of living or provided greater religious freedom than during the current period. This assertion is supported by the fact that the Kashmiri militants have not made any allegations of religious persecution by the Indian state. Also, the level of autonomy provided to Kashmir has no parallels elsewhere in South Asia. Pakistan has functioned more or less like a unitary state for most of its post-independence history. The creation of the West Pakistan province under One-Unit in 1955 was a negation of federalism in the extreme. Thus provinces which had voted in favour of joining Pakistan in the hope of preserving their autonomy ceased to exist altogether under One-Unit. Furthermore the majority province of East Pakistan was treated virtually like a colony by the ruling West Pakistani oligarchy. Furthermore, Azad Kashmir has been fully integrated into the Pakistani economy. As far as Sri Lanka is concerned, it not only openly declared itself a unitary state but has been fighting a bloody civil war with the Tamils on such a basis. Bangladesh is also a unitary state which thus far has not been able to work out an autonomy formula which can accommodate the legitimate economic, cultural and political interests of the CHT tribal peoples. Thus by South Asian standards India's respect for Kashmiri autonomy and self-rule has been singularly generous.

It is not, therefore, from discrimination, exploitation and oppression in the ordinary sense of the words that Kashmiri separatism derives its political legitimacy. Rather it is the Partition syndrome of religious identity being recognized as basis of nationness that fuels its ideological dynamics. Additionally it is India's inconsistent record on Kashmir which furnishes the separatists the moral high ground. India first refused to recognize the accession of Junagarh and Manavadar to Pakistan on the grounds that such decisions were not consistent with the principle of Hindu majority areas going to India and Muslim majority areas to Pakistan. It committed itself to a plebiscite in the Security Council but subsequently reneged on such a commitment. Constant central government interference in the form of, among other things, election rigging, promotion of stooges and so on, are presented as further arguments about illegitimate Indian occupation. However, it was not until 1990, when the Indian security forces went on a rampage of indiscriminate killing, raping and destruction of property, that the Kashmir Muslims turned demonstrably against India. It is another matter whether the provocation came in the form of bomb blasts arranged in 1988 in Srinagar by JKLF and other activists.

Although support of diaspora Kashmiris has been important, the help and facilities furnished by Pakistan have been decisive for them to sustain the armed struggle against India. On the other hand, it is not clear what is the current US policy on the Kashmir dispute.

Pakistan

In a philosophical and ideological sense the Pakistani nation-state project descends from the German Romantic type of nationalism exalting ethnic particularity, in the case of Pakistan that of religion. Its historical roots stem from the Two-Nation theory, the *raison d'être* of the state. In the post-independence period the inability of the various élite factions to agree on Islamic democracy paved the way for a more authoritarian and theocratic type of state ideology. How broad-based is the support for Islamization is most difficult to say. Nevertheless the faith in the superiority of the Islamic state model — modernist or fundamentalist — obtains among all sections of society. Consequently even though the strength or power of the state over society is based on its punitive capabilities rather than persuasive ones, and separatist movements have arisen seeking to break away from the state, the Islamic factor has helped it build up its support in society by directly appealing to religious affiliations.

In a country which has a 96.7 per cent Muslim population and there is no problem of a large atypical cultural group being located in a sensitive border area, the adoption of Islam as the ideological framework for the nation-state project would seem to suggest rather easy integration. However, the situation in Pakistan is not so simple. Since Pakistani Muslims subscribe to different sectarian branches of Islam, the efforts to create a purer Islamic nation have usually led to widening the cleavages between the various sects. On the other hand, the emergence of various separatist movements throughout Pakistan's history is proof that the

Islamic bond has failed to dissolve subnational identity deriving from common language and the culture associated with it.

The main casualty of the Pakistani nation-state project has been democracy. Since traditional Islamic law discriminates fundamentally between the rights of men and women, half the population is disadvantaged on a gender basis and disqualified from the enjoyment of equal rights. Now if the religious minorities, minority sects and Muslim women are counted together, the nation-state project technically disqualifies more than half the population of Pakistan from enjoying equal civil, political and economic rights. However, as Pakistan has never categorically rejected the ambition to develop a model of Islamic democracy, women and non-Muslims have not been disenfranchised in accordance with the extremist demands of some *ulama*. Ironically, the right to vote has enabled the people of Pakistan to elect Benazir Bhutto twice as their prime minister even when in a court of law her evidence is half in worth of that given by a man.

The main challenge to the Pakistani Muslim modernists is to evolve a model of Islamic democracy which fulfils the minimum requirements of a modern civilized polity: that the *bona fide* residents of Pakistan are not denied the dignity to be members of the Pakistani nation simply because they have been born into a religion the state considers improper, or on a gender basis women are discriminated against in a court of law and socially segregated. Disentangling the state from such a relationship with society is not, of course, easy since Pakistan in a logical sense is the fulfilment of a religious notion of nation. However, while the Muslim élite consisting of Jinnah and others successfully exploited the Islamic factor to create a separate state, it is now for their disciples to prove that the whole exercise was not just a cynical manipulation of emotive ties whose main aim was not to ameliorate Muslim poverty and backwardness but to satisfy the urge for power of the Muslim élite which felt alienated from Congress.

The Sindhi project

The authoritarian and strongly centrist policies of the state have been largely responsible for the alienation of the subordinate provinces of Pakistan. Nowhere is the contrast so starkly manifest than in Sindh. The rapid transformation of Karachi into the industrial capital of Pakistan brought little benefit to the indigenous Sindhis. The land development schemes have also been biased in the favour of the settlers, whether Punjabis or others. The various settler ethnic groups are entrenched in the modern industrial sector while the indigenous Sindhis are confined largely to the rural interior. The continued absence of Sindhis in state employment, and their not getting a reasonable share of the wealth produced by its cities, is sufficient ground for frustration and grievances.

The intriguing aspect of the Sindh situation is that notwithstanding genuine grievances the Sindhi nationalists have been unable to develop a mass support base. A plausible explanation could be that factionalism and hierarchy pervade the upper crust of Sindhi society and sectional interests tend to prevail over Sindhi nationalist ones. The central government has, therefore, always found sizeable numbers of landowners willing to join ranks with it against rival landlords. Apart from the factionalism of the landlords, the emergence of the PPP as a radical party which could skilfully combine nationalist grievances with the social question, and upon that basis sought power within a united Pakistan, has meant that popular Sindhi political energies have been deflected away from separatism. Additionally, the moderate Sindhi nationalist leaders such as Mumtaz Ali Bhutto and Abdul Hafeez Pirzada have been talking in terms of a loose federation or confederation. Rasul Baksh Palejo even denies allegations of Sindhi separatism. All these various leaders have some popular support behind them. Consequently the outright secessionists are just one of the various political tendencies among Sindhis. Unlike the Tamil Tigers who have been able to crush dissent within the Tamil community, the Sindhi secessionists are one group among many competing for popular support. More significant in this connection is that in the realm of political power important changes have been occurring since the early 1970s. A share in political power at the centre as well as at the provincial level is usually available to some of the various Sindhi landlord factions.

At the level of ideology also the Sindhi secessionists have not been able to construct a formula that can excite the fantasies of the people. The ancient historical, cultural and ideological bases of Sindhu Desh traced by G.M. Sayed are perhaps more elegant than the intellectual merits of the Two-Nation Theory, but learning to think of Raja Dahir (a Hindu whom the Arabs vanquished 1200 years ago) as a Sindhi hero must in all probability be incomprehensible to ordinary Sindhi Muslims. Sindhi leaders such as G.M. Sayed themselves drove away the Hindus from Sindh less than 50 years ago and thus lent respectability and legitimacy to communalism. The subsequent invocation of Stalinist criteria on nation has not helped the secessionists broaden their support base. The radical socio-economic programme has also not been able to attract the support of the Sindhi masses, because the PPP continues to be perceived as the radical party in the province. Consequently the Jiye Sindh candidates have repeatedly been rejected at the polls. The support base for mounting a major challenge to the Pakistani state therefore does not exist and the state has been able to bring Sindh under control rather easily. Thus, even when oppression against Sindhis was at its worst during the Zia period and thousands were put in jail, the number of people killed or injured has been counted in the hundreds and not thousands. This stands in sharp contrast to more serious confrontations such as that between the Indian state and the Sikh or Kashmiri militants or the Sri Lankan state and the Tamil Tigers.

In this regard the historically evolved social structure of Sindh has been a major hindrance to the evolution of Sindhi nationalism. The life of ease and pleasure discouraged the Waderas from investing their capital in risky enterprises. Consequently a Sindhi bourgeoisie was not at hand to exploit the development opportunities that were created by the state in the 1950s and 1960s. Of course the authoritarian state patronized the ethnic minorities of Memons, Ismailis and Bohras and the Punjabi Chinioti sheikhs but there was no law or regulation prohibiting Sindhis from investing in industry. The Wadera system also obstructed the evolution both of a proletariat, because the Hari was kept bonded on the land, and of a large intelligentsia, because no interest was taken in the spread of education. In the absence of a large intelligentsia and proletariat the support base for mass action was limited. The external environment has also not been conducive to the secessionists. In the absence of a large and prosperous diaspora community, superpower backing or effective help from India with arms and bases, the secessionist bid stands no reasonable chance against the organized might of the Pakistani state. The Indian RAW has been reported to be active in Sindh. Apparently it has been successful in infiltrating both the Sindhi nationalist organizations and the MQM. In helping to arouse a major secessionist bid it does not seem to have been very effective.

It is in the realm of economic transformation that the future of the Sindhi nationalist movement will be determined. It can be defused if Sindhis are enabled to increase their stake in the all-Pakistan economy, as happened for the Pukhtuns in the 1960s, or it can be accentuated if the irreversible process of modernization penetrating interior Sindh generates only a potential intelligentsia and a proletariat which cannot find employment.

The MQM project

The Mohajir élite and intelligentsia opted for a Pakistan where the phantom of Mughul glory could be resurrected under their leadership. In many ways their cultural ascendancy was acknowledged by the state, which declared their mother-tongue as the national language of Pakistan. The subsequent crisis of identity which occurred among them can be made sense of from the very peculiar nature of the Pakistani state formation and nation-state project. The Mohajirs can correctly claim that they migrated to Pakistan out of voluntary choice. As Azim Ahmed Tariq mentions, and as is widely known, Nehru and many other leaders of Congress such as Abul Kalam Azad urged the Muslims to stay on in India, but they preferred to migrate to Pakistan. Not only is Jinnah on record for inviting Muslim bureaucrats from UP to migrate to Pakistan, but even G.M. Sayed in 1943 looked forward to the more educated Muslims of northern India coming and settling in Sindh and helping its development. This trust, however, was abused by the Mohajir élite, which took full advantage of its control over the bureaucracy and established its hold over the most advanced areas of Sindh: Karachi, Hyderabad and other urban centres.

Subsequent developments, however, were to dislodge the Mohajirs from such a vantage position. Uneven modernization and development enabled the much larger nationalities of Punjabis and Pukhtuns to move up and expand while the Mohajir hold began to shrink. The new generations of Mohajirs led by the MQM now started reverting, in a political sense, to their northern Indian identity in the hope of negotiating a deal on power sharing which was advantageous to them; threatening with bloodshed and secession if such were not conceded.

The MQM represents, therefore, the most infamous type of ethno–nationalism which has surfaced in the modern world: settler groups who employ all means to take control of a territory to which they are recent arrivals. This is patently manifest from the way the MQM intends to bring about demographic change in its favour. Thus, while it shares with the Sindhi nationalists and secessionists an interest in opposing further influx into Sindh from Punjab and other Pakistani provinces, it favours the repatriation of the 250,000 Biharis stranded in Bangladesh since 1971 to Pakistan with the right to settle in Sindh. The Biharis, being northern Indian Urdu speakers, are likely to prefer settling in Karachi or Hyderabad, thereby improving the Urdu-speaking component of the Sindh population.

The idea of separating Karachi and Hyderabad from the rest of Sindh and creating a new province which the MQM keeps projecting can only be achieved through force, because no Sindhi politician or party is likely to go along with it. No major world power or India seem interested in such a project at present. The Mohajirs also lack the support of a prosperous diaspora community. On the other hand strategic co-operation between all shades of Sindhi opinion and the army is likely to prevent a violent disruption of the present administrative structure. Any rational strategy of keeping Pakistan united would require not antagonizing the Sindhis too deeply, because they share a long, porous border with India and the Pakistani state cannot possibly afford a total Sindhi revolt. This assertion is corroborated by the way the military acted in 1992 against the MQM. Inciting Mohajirs to various acts of defiance via telephone calls from Britain might be testimony of Altaf Husain's ability to fend novelty, but such antics make no serious political strategy. Rather they are symptomatic of impending disaster.

Bangladesh

The unusually high degree of ethnic, linguistic and religious homogeneity in Bangladesh stands out as an exception in South Asia. Bangladesh began its experiment in nation-building with a leaning towards the libertarian ideals of the French

Revolution. In subsequent years it increasingly acquired Islamic features. Thus far, in principle, Hindus and other minorities have not been disqualified constitutionally from contesting public office. On the other hand, the continued flight of Hindus to India is indicative of the fears and apprehensions of a sizeable minority who feel alienated from the state. The spill effect of Hindu–Muslim confrontation in Ayodhya has been communal violence against the Hindus. Extreme poverty, an inchoate industrial base, a relatively small and weak defence structure and, above all, a long border with a regional giant such as India has meant that Bangladesh has been much more susceptible to external pressures and threats. On the one hand, Bangladesh faces pressure from the international Islamic movement backed by the oil wealth of Saudi Arabia and Iran to move in the theocratic direction. On the other hand, continuing tension with India also tends to push it towards an Islamic identity.

The future shape of the majoritarian–syncretic nation-state project will depend on whether the ruling élite can agree among themselves regarding the choice between democracy and an Islamic polity. The secular forces are by no means so weak as in Pakistan. The liberation struggle was spearheaded by secular nationalists, and they still have a stronghold in the Awami League, the main opposition party currently.

The CHT project

The separatist movement of the Chittagong Hill Tracts is a case of ethnic and class oppression coinciding. The state represents the overwhelmingly large superordinate cultural group, and the tribals the tiny subordinate cultural group. For its developmental needs the state has been intervening in the traditional natural economy of a small marginalized group of people which lacks a diversified production base. Consequently such drastic changes occurred that the only option left for the affected tribal population has been either to fight to prevent a total collapse of its traditional system or to perish as a cultural entity.

In their dispute with the state the tribals have been able to invoke the historical precedent of a treaty with the British which recognized their autonomy over that area. On the other hand, the fact that less than 1 per cent of the population claims autonomy over some one-tenth of the land as its own exclusively, of course, makes it particularly difficult to handle by a country which is not only one of the poorest in the developing world but also has one of the highest population densities. At any rate, the hill people stand no chance of gaining an independent state with Indian help, which is motivated by the latter's own interests. Some autonomy formula is what they can at most negotiate with the state.

Sri Lanka

In the absence of a freedom struggle, Sri Lankans did not have nationalist symbols and references readily available upon which to found their national identity. Although Sinhalese-Buddhist nationalism had been growing against over-representation of Tamils in the various services and professions, it was ignored by the British, who handed over full control to the conservative Sinhalese—Tamil élite who were agreed among themselves upon a composite territorial nation-state model fashioned by the principles of the French Revolution. Such optimism was, however, misplaced because the Bandaranaike regime of 1956 could successfully place the Sinhalese-Buddhist nation-state project in the centre of Sri Lankan electoral politics. The hegemonic nation-state project was a drastic shift to the particularist, ethnic type of nationalism related to the German Romantic tradition. It appropriately glorified a mythical Sinhalese past. Thus in the case of Sri Lanka the shift from a universal to a particularist type of state nationalism was most dramatic.

Putting it simply, the majority was not going to allow the minority to continue enjoying over-representation in the public sector and the higher-bracket professions. The notion of 'tyranny of the majority' became truly institutionalized through elections and other means. Thus, even when Sri Lanka was the most advanced welfare state in the region, the Sinhalese élite developed a patronage system which effectively discriminated between Sinhalese and non-Sinhalese. On the other hand, the state was no less merciless to the ultra-nationalism of the JVP. Thus the central élite, while committed to a hegemonic role for Buddhism, was not willing to go along with the most extreme form of Sinhalese-Buddhist chauvinism.

What is characteristic of modern Sri Lanka is the ubiquity of violence. The state and the JVP zealots have been practising the creed of violence on an island claiming to inherit the mantle of the Buddha, one of the greatest paragons of non-violence and peace. It is quite clear that such wide discrepancy between professed ideals and concrete practice cannot serve as the basis of a stable political order. The state will have to seek peaceful solutions to the question of devolution and power-sharing with the Tamils. Moderate Tamil forces and the TULF still exist and it should be possible to enlist their participation in any negotiations on autonomy. As India does not lay claim to any part of the island, and in practice has shown no interest in the creation of a separate Tamil Eelam, the external environment also seems conducive to reconciliation.

The Tamil Eelam project

The Tamils' separatist project evolved in reaction to the biased and high-handed policies of the Sri Lankan state. Until the late 1970s, moderate Tamils were willing to work out a federal arrangement, but the state failed to accommodate their legitimate demands. Accumulated grievances finally erupted in the form of LTTE and other guerrilla outfits. The Tamils invoke the existence of a Tamil state at Jaffna before the colonial period as historical evidence of their separate nationhood. The restoration of that Tamil state in some modern form is asserted as a legitimate claim. The LTTE would additionally like Tamil Eelam to be based on radical socialist ideas aiming at a programme for reconstruction of the social order along egalitarian lines. On the other hand, the Tamil Eelam project aiming for independence in the Tamil majority north-eastern zones of the island seems a highly unreasonable demand in terms of its territorial claims: two-thirds of the coastline for 12.5 per cent of the population. The Plantation Tamils living in the central areas of the island cannot directly benefit from such a reorganization of the Sri Lankan state, unless there is a complete transfer of populations. Moreover the substantial Muslim minority would not be willing to live in such a state, considering that they have been victimized by the Tigers in recent years.

As regards the means towards such a goal, the Tigers have been particularly prone to the employment of violence and terror. A martyr discourse was developed from the *Mahabharata*, and cadres were indoctrinated with fanatical devotion, preparing some for suicidal missions. All opposition within their strongholds, whether emanating amongst Sinhalese, Tamils or Muslims, has been met with exceptionally cruel reprisals. The Muslims have in particular suffered greatly at the hands of the Tigers.

As regards external help, India should have little reason to back a separatist movement which could boomerang, reviving separatism among the Tamils in India and perhaps other groups. On the other hand, the diaspora Tamils and those of Tamil Nadu will not stand by and see their fellow Tamils capitulate to Sri Lanka. Any Western interest in Tamil Eelam in the post-Cold-War era seems very unlikely. Ultimately the Tamils will have to agree a peace with the state which safeguards their autonomy and cultural freedoms.

The pliability of ethnic identity and ethno-nationalist mixes

Since ethnic identity is multidimensional and is usually constituted by more than one element, the invocation of language or religion as basis for separatist national identity in contemporary South Asia has not been consistent. Rather, competition for resources and power has made groups of people sharing a common but multiple cultural identity shift from one composite element to the other. Where people share the same religion a shift in emphasis can occur on the division of language, as happened in the case of the East Pakistan secession or is currently happening between Sindhis and Mohajirs. Both Sindhis and Mohajirs are predominantly Sunni Muslims but they speak different languages. Their competition for power and resources has led them to tone down religious commonality and instead emphasize, even exaggerate, the division of language. The same is possible when it is a common language but several religious groups use it. The conflict between Sikh and Hindu communalists in Punjab underscores this point. Where religion and language combine, as in the case of the conflict between Kashmiri Muslims and the Indian state and between the Tamils and the Sri Lankan state, and external linkages with diaspora groups and neighbouring states are also available, the separatist challenge to the state is the most intense.

On the other hand, the implications of identities deriving from common language or religion have been important for the state to consider in its formulation and implementation of the nation-state project, particularly because the separatist movements which have emerged were also centred on language and/or religion. These are examined below.

Language

India largely solved the problem of linguistic nationalism by, on the one hand, creating linguistic states and, on the other hand, by agreeing not to impose Hindi on the non-Hindi speaking nationalities of southern India. Pakistan made similar arrangements with the Bengalis, and both Urdu and Bengali were declared national languages in 1954. In West Pakistan Urdu is practically the only link language among the various provinces and regions and therefore its status as the national language is no longer disputed in present-day Pakistan. As far as Bangladesh is concerned, the status of Bengali or 'Bangla' as national language is obvious. The only state where language has been employed as a means of a major cultural offensive of the majority against a minority is Sri Lanka. The result was the rise of the Tamil separatist movement. In the 1978 Sri Lanka Constitution a clause was included which purported to re-establish some sort of parity between Sinhala and Tamil. Thus, while Sinhala was declared as the official state language, both Sinhala and Tamil were recognized as national languages. In practice, however, Tamil was neglected. The late President Premadasa was favourably inclined to the employment of English as the chief means of communication between the Sinhalese and Tamils, at least during an interim period during which both groups were to be encouraged to learn each other's language.

The interesting fact is that, irrespective of the formal recognition of some language as official state or national language (or languages as in the case of Sri Lanka which formally recognizes both Sinhala and Tamil), English is still used routinely in official communication. Surprisingly, even in Bangladesh, where more than 98 per cent of the population speaks Bengali (or Bangla, the official designation), English is the main language of official communication at the higher level. Thus, whatever the emotional attachment to national language, its relevance to the states is more political and cultural — in the sense of a common national identity — rather than functional.

Among the contemporary separatist movements, neither the Sikh nor the Kashmiri movement in India is fired by linguistic passion. In the case of the Sikhs, Punjabi written in Gurmukhi has been accepted as the official language of Punjab. The India state went out of its way to Kashmir to accommodate Muslim sensibilities: thus when the Kashmir State Assembly adopted Urdu as the official language, although it was not the mother-tongue of any local people, it was accepted. As regards Sindh in Pakistan, since the early 1970s both Sindhi and Urdu have been recognized as the official languages of the province. The PPP and moderate Sindhi nationalists and others accept such an arrangement. Only ultranationalist Sindhis such as G.M. Sayed insist on Sindhi being the sole language of the proposed Sindhu Desh. As regards the Mohajirs, their mother-tongue, Urdu, is the official national language of Pakistan, notwithstanding the fact that the Mohajirs are a tiny portion of the Pakistani population. The two-language formula adopted in 1972 seems to be a reasonable and fair arrangement for both Mohajirs and Sindhis. However, whereas educated Sindhis are fluent in Urdu, the Mohajirs settled in Karachi and Hyderabad have generally been hostile to learning Sindhi. On the other hand, Mohajirs settled in Sindh interior are usually bilingual. In Bangladesh the CHT tribals are resistant to forced assimilation, and the question of preserving their languages is only a part of the overall question of economic and cultural right. The Tamil separatist movement has always insisted on parity between Sinhala and Tamil and on the use of the latter in official communications in the Tamil strongholds.

Religion

Religion is undoubtedly an important factor in the cultural identity of a people and it does constitute an important source from which people derive their moral values and political attitudes. If society is secularized and democratic values pervade popular culture, it does not matter if the state by historical tradition retains a religious character, because the state does not any longer impose the doctrines of the church. Sweden and the UK are cases in point. There is also the special case of the USA as a society with strong religious sensibilities as well as established democratic norms, values and procedures in the political system. The US Constitution not only strictly separates religion and state but lays great emphasis on freedom of conscience and individual autonomy, ideals which are widely shared in society. Nevertheless Protestant priests and fundamentalist groups play quite an important role in politics. Even the US presidents employ religious vocabulary in their official pronouncements.

However, if the state is secular but the society is deeply religious, the consolidation of secularism and the dissemination of democratic values in society is likely to be quite difficult. In these circumstances the élite can either through force ban the exploitation of religion for political purposes, as happened when Atatürk founded the Turkish secular national state in 1924, or it can try to develop a popular support base for secularism which does not offend religion. India has done this by adopting the formula of equal respect for all religions. Thus not only Hindu religious festivals and holy days are declared public holidays but the main Islamic festivals of Eid-ul-Fitr and Eid-ul-Zuha and the Shia holy day of 10th Muharram are also public holidays. So are the birthday of Guru Nanak on 18 November and the Christian festivals of Good Friday, Easter and Christmas. Thus, despite a culture which is deeply steeped in religion and where Hinduism (in its various forms) is the faith of an overwhelming majority of the population, the state policy of equal respect for all religions is observed. This contrasts with the discrimination and persecution built into the Pakistani constitution. Bangladesh has thus far resisted pressure from the fundamentalists to declare it an Islamic state. Sri Lanka has adopted a Buddhist national identity which has played an important part in the estrangement between Sinhalese and Tamils.

Religion, collective identity and cultural fascism

As regards the role of religion in the contemporary ethnic conflicts and separatist movements, except for Sindh (where it has adversely affected the rights of the Hindu minority), it has assumed a very central role. Thus the emergence of Hindu militancy in India cannot be separated from the fact that Pakistan was created as a separate Muslim state out of the partition of British India. Any further break-up of India on a religious basis is considered too devastating a blow by Hindus; hence the militancy of Hindu nationalists. The Islamic wave rising in West Asia and the Arab world in the 1980s also impacted profoundly on South Asia. While Pakistan and Bangladesh have been pushed towards greater compliance with fundamentalism, Hindu nationalists have been able to capitalize on the fear of a perceived Muslim thrust into India and promoted the idea of Hindutva (Hindu nation). On the other hand, the emergence of Islamic militancy in Kashmir cannot be understood in isolation from the overall Muslim revival in West and South Asia or the Hindu revival in India. Sinhalese apprehensions about being swarmed by Tamils from southern India are partly a religious fear of Buddhism losing its pre-eminence on the island. Thus one reason why religion has assumed a central role in contemporary ethnic conflicts and separatist struggles is that the political environment is charged with religious frenzy. Under the circumstances collective identity deriving from religion is easily prone to politicization.

Although the Indian state is secular the Hindu connection has increasingly been exploited to win elections and to gain cheap popularity. That the attack on the Golden Temple was partly motivated by the intention of appeasing Hindu sensibilities, as Talveen Singh suggests, if it is true, shows only how cynical the exploitation of religion in South Asian politics can be. Pakistan has openly been trying to become an Islamic state and has in the process trampled underfoot democratic values. Bangladesh has also acquired greater Islamic characteristics and moved away from its original commitment to secularism. Sri Lanka's experiment in dharmacracy (Schalk, 1990: 276–95) has been accompanied by growth of aggressive and intolerant Buddhist nationalism.

As regards the separatists, the Sikh and Kashmiri separatist movements are inspired by religious ideology. Not by any means because they are persecuted on such a basis, however. On the contrary, in the name of religion both the Sikh and Kashmiri militants have carried out various dastardly acts of sheer terror against their opponents. The Tamil nationalist movement is not ideologically inspired by religious zeal but is essentially a reaction to Sinhalese-Buddhist hegemony. Thus narration of heroic tales from the *Mahabharata* is meant to promote total devotion among the cadres and among some a willingness to carry out suicide missions. Separatism among the tribal people of the CHT is also not about a religious crusade but, in the face of increasing Islamization at the centre, contains a reactive religious dimension.

In all those cases where religion is employed as the main denominator of national identity, it is not religion as higher morality or as a search for metaphysical truths which is invoked. On the contrary it is in the form of a militarist, authoritarian or totalitarian political ideology that it has gained prominence. Hindu fundamentalists and Tamil separatists have been busy in developing a martial discourse out of the *Mahabharata* epic. Muslim fundamentalist ideologues recognize God as the only source of truth and from such a position arrive at the modern doctrine of the sovereignty of God, a concept which is easily exploited to derive totalitarian state ideology. The Akal Takht symbolizes for the Sikhs a union of state and church, and from that Sikh ideologues derive their fundamentalist ideology of the state. The politicized clergy of Sri Lanka has developed its own discourse of ethnic nationalism. The political project underlying all such reform, whether initiated by the ruling élites or by other forces trying to capture the state, is to use the concentrated power of the state in favour of a particular religion or sect — in short, to undo whatever democratic practices and institutions exist and instead create a polity based on cultural fascism.

Recommendations

The recommendations which follow from the above analysis suggest that peaceful resolutions of ethnic conflicts and separatist demands can be achieved only through initiatives across societies and states within the South Asian region and their linkage with worldwide movements engaged in human rights causes. Before more is said on this, the creation of new ethnic states as one possible solution is examined.

Establishment of new ethnic states

Can a radical restructuring of the present political map of South Asia on ethnic lines improve regional stability and promote communal harmony? Simply put, the answer is no. This may seem to contradict one major argument of the book, that ethnicity is intrinsic to politics and to state composition. However, another argument of the book, and the more crucial one, is that ethnicity is multi-dimensional and because of its highly emotional nature easy to manipulate during periods of stress and crisis. It is not, therefore, a stable basis for rational politics. At any rate, reorganization of the South Asian political map in terms of discrete ethnic states would be even more complicated given the peculiar cultural and historical legacy of the region. In both diachronic and synchronic senses cultural overlap is universal in South Asia. The Hindu, Muslim (Sunni or Shia), Sikh, Buddhist, Sindhi, Sinhalese, Tamil and other forms of historical states and societies were based on some form of cultural pluralism. In a segmented, religiously diverse, social order the traditional political sovereign acted as the protector of all the subjects.

In contrast to South Asia, where several religions have co-existed historically, Christianity was the only major religion of Western Europe, and the nation-states could emerge in that part of the world on the basis of language and sect as capitalism undermined the cultural unity of Europe deriving from adherence to Roman Catholicism. The terrible fate of minority Christian sects, Jews and other smaller ethnic groups during this long period of transformation is all too well known and need not be taken up here. Similarly, European interventions in the Americas and Australia wiped out cultural diversity through, among other means, direct genocide. The 'homogeneity' thus achieved was the social background against which secularism and liberal democracy evolved from the eighteenth century onwards. It was only after the Second World War that the pluralist model based on secularism and liberal democracy was further elaborated and incorporated in the Western democracies. The incoming labourers from the poorer parts of Europe and the Third World could now be accommodated within a multi-ethnic civic nation conferring more or less equal rights on all citizens.

However, distinctions such as that between natural-born citizens and naturalized citizens are observed in some parts of the world. For example, a naturalized citizen cannot contest the US presidency. Such distinctions are likely to prevail in the future too as the historical circumstances of each society are so very different. In any case, the co-extension of the whole population with the nation is now the presumed basis of the advanced industrialized democratic states. By law such rights have been conferred on all citizens in Western democracies. The real enjoyment of rights is of course another matter, and how society in general treats minorities is also another matter. It is perhaps more realistic to assert that a situation in which ethnic differences would cease to influence the way states distribute rewards and penalties is a utopia. The nearest human societies can come towards this ideal is to adopt laws and other enlightened policies supportive of such change.

In contrast to Western development, the pre-colonial South Asian tradition was based on cultural pluralism, although it required ideologically the non-mixture of the various cultures. During the British period mobility of people from one part of South Asia to another increased. Many different cultural groups can therefore be found living side by side in all parts of the area. A neat separation of people on the basis of cultural differences is therefore wellnigh impossible. The partition of India in 1947 clearly illustrates this fact. Ironically Pakistan was created for the Muslim nation of India whose leaders felt that they could not trust the Hindu majority. In other words 'minority fears' were at the bottom of the demand for Pakistan. Yet the Pakistan which finally came into being was situated in the Muslim-majority regions, where the Muslims least needed protection from the Hindus. The worst sufferers in the creation of Pakistan have been the millions of the poorest Muslims living in the Hindu majority provinces who had neither the means nor the connections nor the patronage of the Muslim élite to migrate to Pakistan, and were abandoned by Jinnah and other leaders of the Muslim League without too much concern.

One can speculate what might have happened if British India had remained undivided. It would have meant a population ratio of seven to three between Hindus and Muslims. In addition there were the Christians, Sikhs and others. For such a state to survive and stabilize, a pluralist democracy, respecting regional interests and accommodating the various groups into the state services, would have been necessary or else disintegration would have been a serious possibility. How such a state and society would have behaved in the face of modernization, uneven development and external pressures is, of course, a highly conjectural question, but unity through pluralist democracy could have avoided the antagonisms which the division of India brought.

Now let us consider the Kashmir problem. It captures the intractability of conflicts emerging from diverse interpretations of ethnic identity and nationalism. Its resolution apparently should help reduce drastically tension between India and Pakistan. However, prestige, self-righteousness, suspicion and fear prevent the two states from agreeing conclusively to a mutually acceptable solution. It can even be suspected that the military establishments of both the states may have an interest in keeping such tension high. At least in the case of Pakistan the high profile of the army in politics leaves no doubt that the Kashmir policy is determined on its discretion.

Of all the separatist movements obtaining in contemporary South Asia the Kashmiri separatist movement is the only one which has emerged in a territory which at the termination of British colonialism was disputed territory. It was, strictly speaking, not within the international boundaries of India, and, additionally, Indian annexation was not consistent with the underlying principles of Partition. On the other hand the Sikh, Sindhi, Mohajir, CHT tribal and Tamil separatist movements emanated from within territories which are within the fully legal jurisdiction of the countries concerned. This of course does not give licence to the respective states to treat the Sikh, Sindhi, Mohajir, CHT tribals or Tamil peoples harshly or cruelly. Despite the fact that these conflicts have emerged within the recognized borders of the sovereign states, the international system can be expected to favour the claims of states. In the case of Kashmir, Indian annexation poses extremely intricate problems of interpretation of legal documents, political history and conflicting interests.

Notwithstanding popular belief about the ethnic affiliation of Jawaharlal Nehru to Kashmir and the emotional attachment which he and the Gandhi family are alleged to have felt for it, the main Indian concerns in Kashmir are security, power balance and economic interests. The whole state going to Pakistan would mean several military and economic disadvantages to India, as several rivers which pass through India and Pakistan originate in Kashmir. An independent Muslim-dominated Jammu and Kashmir would mean the creation of another hostile state adjacent to India. Indian officials point out (see T.N. Kaul's article) that in the case of Kashmir breaking away a Hindu backlash against the hundred million Muslims scattered throughout the towns and villages of India would be impossible for the state to control. How many Muslims would be killed by paranoid Hindus — already grieved because of the 1947 division of India — is a matter of speculation. At any rate, it would make the moral case for secularism and tolerance hollow because it would have demonstrated that Muslims are not loyal to India. This suspicion merits serious thought. The rise of the BJP and other Hindu nationalist social and cultural movements are symptomatic of a growing fear deeply ingrained in Indian thinking. If secularism and democracy are subverted and India becomes a Hindu nationalist state the consequences for the Muslim minority could be catastrophic.

As argued earlier, the subjectivity of ethnic perceptions makes rational communication difficult. For example, Kashmiri Muslims want to separate from India because they have developed a strong sense of national identity. They obviously do not identify themselves with other Indian Muslims. The JKLF even tries to argue in terms of a secular territorial Kashmiri identity, but without demonstrating that the Hindus of Jammu and the Buddhists of Ladakh share such an identity with it. However, Indian Muslims can be held responsible for the acts of the Kashmiri Muslims by the Hindu nationalists because they may not see the Kashmiri Muslims as a separate group. They may argue that Muslims as a whole are disloyal to India and point out Kashmiri separatism as corroboration of such a suspicion. Given the peculiar colonial history of India, all such arguments and inferences contain a mixture of truth and untruth.

The worst scenario may be Pakistan having to receive refugees on a massive scale from India. It does not seem that Pakistan is prepared for such an eventuality. The 250,000 Biharis who supported the unity of Pakistan and, therefore, sided with the Pakistan army during the East Pakistan civil war have not been permitted to immigrate to Pakistan even when they have expressed such a wish. In fact Pakistan (like Israel for Jews) is under moral obligation to accept all Muslims of India to come and settle in the land which was created specifically for the Muslim nation of the subcontinent. To that extent the MQM's position is entirely logical and historically accurate, although its invocation of Muslim nationalism on the whole is by no means an honest and sincere one. Thus, on the one hand, it supports repatriation of Biharis to Pakistan, but has used all means to keep Sindhis out of Karachi and Hyderabad cities, and opposes Punjabi and Pukhtun influx into Sindh. Thus it applies the segregational and discriminatory nature of Muslim ethno-nationalism in its own selective and arbitrary manner. Even Zia-ul-Haq, who became passionately involved in the Afghan war, apparently out of commitment to Islamic solidarity, ignored the Biharis. At any rate, since 1954 free inflow of Indian Muslims is not permitted, and public opinion in Pakistan (except for the Mohajirs) is by no means favourably inclined to such influx of Muslims from across the border.

A war between India and Pakistan over Kashmir is likely to cause enormous damage because both states are armed with sophisticated weapons (nuclear weapons perhaps) and have huge armies at their disposal. Attempts at secession, therefore, are a daunting undertaking with far-reaching consequences for the economic, political and security interests of existing states, and have ramifications for the regional balance of power and indeed for global stability. There may even be a new wave of refugees fleeing in thousands from such a situation. Any reasonable peaceful solution of the Kashmir problem, other than the present one of both states preserving the existing line of control, would have to look into the security fears and economic interests of the two states as well as the communal interests of the Azad Kashmiris, Muslims of the Kashmir Valley, the Kashmiri pundits, Hindus, Muslims and Sikhs of Jammu and the Buddhists and Muslims of Ladakh.

Without wholesale destruction, therefore, of the historically evolved South Asian society the criterion of ethnic exclusivity as basis of state-building cannot be applied successfully. On the other hand, less than extreme measures would leave many people, particularly the vast assortment of minor tribes, ethnic groups, religious sects and popular cults, living within larger socio-cultural wholes. The distinction between nations and minorities, with the former entitled to sovereignty in a state and the others simply to some group rights is patently biased in favour of the ethnic majority. Moreover, there are good practical reasons for opposing ethnic identity as sufficient basis for nationhood. Quite simply there are far too many more fairly sizeable ethnic groups in the world than can be allotted separate states. According to one estimate there are some 10,000 ethnic groups in the world (Eriksen, 1993: 45). Gellner mentions 8000 language groups. It would be surprising if several hundred such groups are not found in South Asia.

The balkanization of South Asia would mean ever greater expenditure on maintaining the state, especially its military apparatuses and other punitive organs. The main beneficiaries of the creation of new states would be the élites and intelligentsia which can operate its various control levers. On the other hand, as Ernest Gellner points out (1964), the vast majority of peasants and workers are not likely to see their grievances reduced or resolved. It can be argued, of course, that overall economic development will be hastened as each new ethnic state will have a smaller area and perhaps a more compact population to take care of. This aspect has to be weighed against the possibilities that nationalist rivalries, arms purchase and concomitant fears are likely to multiply if there are more rather than fewer states in South Asia. The case against the creation of new ethnic states is, therefore, a strong one.

In the postwar period the old type of nationalism based on the nation-state model has been gradually giving way in Europe to the notion of a decentralized but united Europe in the form of the European Union. If this process continues it will mean a significant decline if not complete disappearance of the nation-state model in the region where it was born, and from where it later travelled to all corners of the world as an intellectual and political movement, with both good and bad consequences. Why the old type of nationalism is subsiding in Europe can be understood in terms of the evolution of advanced capitalism. It is currently evolving in the direction of regional economic blocs, and the whole world is bound to be impacted by the latest structure of capitalism.

There are no reasons for not looking at ways and means of bringing the South Asia states and peoples closer to one another even though at the present time in South Asian history such musings seem an exercise in futility, since not only is capitalism poorly and unevenly developed but, as Zoya Hasan rightly suggests, pre-modern social and cultural forms weigh heavily on these societies and states. The result is a great difficulty in rational communication. At any rate, the Gellnerian model of the political and the national unit coinciding in the nation-state under impact of modernization applies only partially to the present reality of South Asia. It can be argued that the present spate of separatist movements in South Asia derive their strength from a combination of an overcharged political sphere and pre-modern cultural and social values rather than only the contradictions deriving from uneven economic development. The pressures exerted by international actors on South Asia have played a major role in exacerbating state–society contradictions. More importantly, for a long time to come incomplete industrialization is likely to persist. The politics of South Asia will therefore have to take cognition of the ethnic plurality. Apart from downright genocide, therefore, some formulae of accommodation will have to be evolved.

Power sharing and autonomy

The role of politics in the realm of authoritative decisions of states, governments, élites and so on needs to be put into perspective. Of course structural constraints and historical contexts circumscribe the freedom of action and restrict the options available in a given situation. The important thing is, however, that a number of options are usually available and the decisions of powerholders play a significant role in influencing and shaping social reality. Proceeding from a realistic position on South Asia regarding the power of the states to maintain territorial integrity, it seems that most cultural groups will in any event have to seek solutions within the existing territorial framework. This applies particularly to the vast number of smaller ethnic groups, religious sects and so on, which, although they may be the most deprived in an objective sense, have no chance of winning an armed battle against the state. A greater share in development coupled with cultural and regional autonomy appears to be the only formula that can create stability and peace within the states and in the South Asian region.

Arend Lijphart (1977: 1–52) presents the model of a consociational democracy as a possible solution to the instability and breakdown of democracy in societies marked by social, ethnic and political differences. The four main features of consociational democracy are: (a) a high degree of co-operation among leaders of different segments of pluralist society to counteract the separatist tendencies inherent in pluralist societies (this would require a government of a grand coalition of the political leaders of all significant sections of society); (b) mutual veto, which additionally protects vital minority interests; (c) proportional representation as the principle according to which political office, civil service appointments and public funds are allocated; and (d) a high degree of autonomy for each segment to manage its own internal affairs.

Such a model certainly deserves serious consideration as it prescribes concrete steps to offset majoritarian monopoly over state power. The problem with it is that the most crucial precondition — requiring a high degree of co-operation among leaders of different segments of society — is not easy to achieve in South Asia, given its very complex historical legacies of religious conflicts, sectarian affiliations and regional loyalties. During a period of stress and internal and external pressure élite consensus is particularly difficult to maintain. The break-down of the political fabric in the Lebanon is a case in point of such élite discord. If anything, élite competition has been at the bottom of the separatist struggles in South Asia. Without a consensus on how state and society are to change and trans-form, sustained co-operation among the culturally variegated élites of South Asia is most difficult.

The choice seems to be between a secular-democratic pluralist model of devel-opment and a particularistic ethnic model of development. As long as the élites are not agreed on whether secularism or religious nationalism is the goal, co-operation among leaders of the various groups would be most precarious.

Proceeding from an overall critique of the Indian polity T.K. Oommen (1990: 111) argues for a radical transformation of the socio-economic and political orders:

> for authentic social transformation to take place what we need in India is not state capitalism but a cooperative economy in which the primary producers directly own the means of production more or less equitably; a decentralized rather than a delegated polity, which gives maximum opportunity to the men at the grass-roots to shape their destiny, and a secular pluralist society which permits optimum elasticity to maintain diversities of culture.

Oommen's prescription, or at least elements of it, can be fruitfully applied not just to India but also to the whole South Asian region. A peaceful solution to these problems can be expedited if a concerted effort is made by all the states to work together to improve their societies in the light of enlightened humanist ideals. The South Asian heritage is not deficient in this respect, but universal values of democracy and equality need to be given much greater emphasis than is done cur-rently. In the meantime the question of cultural and regional autonomy has to be tackled in a more concrete manner.

Autonomy

As far as the concept of autonomy is concerned, it contains an in-built tension. By its very definition autonomy denotes limitation on interference of one entity into another's domain. In the context of the territorial state, it refers to a relationship which recognizes, on the one hand, the existence of several parts possessing special properties of their own and, on the other hand, that together these parts constitute a whole which is not simply the sum total of the parts but a distinct being in its own right with authority over the parts. Underlying such a conception is the awareness that members have conflicting interests and preferences but at the same time share an interest in seeking collectivist solutions to their common problems and aspirations.

Cultural autonomy

Cultural autonomy refers essentially to matters such as the freedom to practise a religion or speak a language or use a script and other such demands referring to the aesthetic and spiritual identity of a group. In ordinary circumstances group assertion may not entail more than an innocuous measure at enhancing self-esteem. A case in point is the demand of the Sikhs living in Europe to be allowed to wear turbans at their work place. This demand has not been met with easy approval from the authorities and has resulted in some agitation on the part of Sikhs. The political importance of such particularist assertion, however, is marginal in the context of Europe. However, in the wake of the Shah Bano case the assertion of the Muslim minority in India about cultural autonomy in the sphere of marriage and divorce clearly collided with Indian law, which placed such matters within the purview of secular law. The question of cultural freedom therefore is not always easy to settle. However, each state has to handle such demands within the framework of its nation-state project. Even a confessional state such as Pakistan does not deny the right to cultural autonomy; therefore clearer legislation on such autonomy needs to be adopted.

Regional autonomy

Demands for cultural autonomy with a view to avoiding assimilation into mainstream society require some agreement between the state and concerned cultural groups over an exclusive cultural space to which that group can withdraw. Demands for regional autonomy require the state to concede economic and political space to cultural groups over specific territorial space. In particular the problem of land colonization has to be handled carefully. Thus in the case of Pakistan, Bangladesh and Sri Lanka there are genuine grievances of the dominated Sindhi, tribal people and Tamils and Muslims respectively of the state using its power to relocate people from the majority group in their traditional areas.

Generally if autonomy is granted at an early stage and respected by the state there are good chances of defusing the separatist tendency. In a purely systemic sense, however, autonomy can be granted more substantially by a developed socio-political system. Systems which are still in the process of acquiring such capability usually pre-empt autonomy by greater centralization of power and control over scarce resources. This has been happening in all the four South Asian states analysed in this investigation. However, political sagacity and proper policy can enable developing states to work out some regional or local autonomy formula. India did evolve one in the form of linguistic states, but, as is obvious from Punjab and Kashmir, it subsequently violated such autonomy. Somehow in the Indian situation the interests of the Congress Party and the Indian state have been confused. Pakistan remains committed to a federal structure since 1969 and currently elected provincial governments are in power. However, federalism, like democracy in Pakistan, is precarious because of the *de facto* veto powers held by the military–bureaucratic oligarchy. Even the unitary states such as Bangladesh and Sri Lanka have to consider regional autonomy because the minorities of the tribal people and the Sri Lankan Tamils demand such an arrangement. In the case of Sri Lanka, a federal framework appears to be the only workable formula. That groups are concentrated in specific regions is a fact in all the four states. External pressure and interference, however, make states overly protective and they can violate the autonomy agreement purely out of security and defence considerations. The establishment of regional stability and order can have a benign influence on the centre–regional relationships in South Asia.

Regional peace and stability

In 1985 the South Asian Association of Regional Co-operation (SAARC) was established by the South Asian states as a platform for promoting regional co-operation and understanding. So far it is a weak and ineffective organization, but if properly promoted could serve a useful purpose in reducing tension and conflict. Greater economic co-operation and exchange in the fields of culture and education can promote understanding. It is amazing that so little interaction takes place in these spheres between India, Pakistan, Bangladesh and Sri Lanka. In any case the South Asian states will need to pool their resources if they are to improve their terms of trade *vis-à-vis* the rest of the world, which is fast organizing itself into regional systems of economic co-operation.

Towards civil society

In recent years, the idea of a civil society has been advanced in opposition to the interventionist state. The argument is that the authoritarian tendencies of the state can be kept in check if a strong civil society is consolidated. Georg Wilhelm Friedrich Hegel (1770–1831), who laid a major emphasis on the distinction between state and civil society, associated universal altruism with the state, which was to work for the common good, and universal egoism with the civil society, in which people were to be free to seek personal gain and self-interest, but according to universal rules ultimately upheld by the state. Thus the ultimate guarantee for the working of the civil society was the higher realm of intellectual universalism represented by the state (Avineri, 1991: 196–8). Marx employed the term civil society in a pejorative sense — as one in which the sense of community is supplanted by individualism. Typically the civil society emerges during the period of capitalism and is the 'site of crass materialism' of the private individual (Sassoon,

1985: 73). In sharp contrast to Marx, Gramsci employs the concept of civil society in a positive sense. It refers to the existence of autonomous organizations and to the rational self-regulation of society and individuals. For him, the civil society is a realm of freedom preserved under the law. However, Gramsci is well aware of the fact that the distinction between state and society is only methodological, since whatever freedom society enjoys is established and sustained by the state itself, and is therefore a political arrangement (1976: 160). Thus the Gramscian civil society is dependent upon the democratic state exercising self-restraint. The distinction between state and civil society is nevertheless important because it refers to the overall gains made by society in relation to the inherently coercive nature of the state.

The recent revival of the civil society concept took place in Eastern Europe. It was conceived as part of a political strategy to create democratic space *vis-à-vis* the totalitarian state. In the World Bank and IMF discussions it has been used generally as an argument to promote the evolution of autonomous organizations, but the main emphasis is on the economic realm being freed from state intervention. In South Asian, particularly Indian, discussion the civil society stands for an intermediary space occupied by voluntary organizations, especially those dealing with human rights issues, between the total state and the larger society. The argument in all cases is that the scope of state activities has to be reduced in favour of civil society.

As argued earlier, South Asia has never been under totalitarian rule although authoritarian features have always been present. A basic commitment to a free press and elections has been maintained by all the four states. India leads in the area of voluntary organizations. A fairly well educated middle class and a large group of academics and professionals — social scientists, historians, lawyers, retired judges and people belonging to the world of art and cinema — constitute an intermediary stratum which upholds Gandhian non-violence and Nehruvian rationalism. From among this stratum have evolved citizen committees, human rights organizations and a variety of other civil liberties social movements. Additionally, responsible newspapers, magazines and scholarly journals provide analyses and critiques of the political scene. Finally the Union and State parliaments provide forum for open debate. A fairly sophisticated democratic institutional network is evolving in the process.

As regards Pakistan, notwithstanding declarations of Islamizing it, no regime has gone so far as to emulate Iran and Saudi Arabia in a comprehensive manner. The free press exists and academic freedom has not been usurped altogether by ideological falsification or spurious scholarly production. It is all the more admirable that human rights organizations have also sprung up in Pakistan and taken up bold, critical positions on human rights violations by the state. In Bangladesh too, similar organizations are emerging. The fact that the writer Taslima Nasrin received support from some women's organizations and intellectuals while the fundamentalists were out to kill her in 1994 is indicative of a potential organizational basis for working towards the civil society. Civil liberties, human rights organizations and similar bodies are active in Sri Lanka and have played an important role in drawing world attention to the tragic civil war in that country.

The consolidation of the civil society, however, does not preclude a strong state. During this long period of transformation from an agrarian to an industrial economy the strong state will be needed to lead and consolidate such gigantic change. A strong state in the sense of one headed by a dedicated élite would also be necessary to keep in check the more rash and fanatical tendencies in the larger society. The civil society cannot take over the fundamental responsibility of controlling the society at large. An interventionist state which promotes the civil society cannot be a contradiction in terms. Rather the evolution of both is a matter of overall democratization with initiatives coming from either side. Moreover, the state still remains the main guarantee of welfare activities in modern societies. There is no reason why it should not have similar responsibilities in developing societies.

An agenda for humane development

In the case of South Asia and many parts of the Third World, where human rights violations are extensive, and indigenous people and the poor in general are made to pay a heavy price for the development schemes of the state, the outstanding problems of poverty, illiteracy, brutality, police and paramilitary terror and so on call for alternative strategies of development. What needs to be done is to delegitimize violence, especially that practised by the state which in its role as the legitimate monopolizer of power bears greater responsibility for its abuse. The routine involvement of the military, paramilitary forces and security services such as the RAW and ISI in ethnic conflicts clearly show how violent the state has become. Although violence and terror have been employed extensively in the Indian Punjab, Kashmir and Tamil situations, there are cases of criminal activity from both sides. In the Tamil situation, however, clearly the Sri Lankan state bears the greater responsibility for the escalation in violence. The Sindh and CHT situations have been less violent, not because the concerned states in question are more restrained but because the challengers were weak and isolated.

The huge amounts of money spent on buying arms and other instruments of destruction and torture has to be opposed by concerned intellectuals and opinion-builders. Such initiatives will not come from the power élites, because of their vested interests and the prestige involved. The initiatives have to come from the civil society. A new development strategy based on the notion of humane development needs to be adopted. Humane development can be considered as a new programme of reconstruction agreed between the state, autonomous organizations and international development and human rights organizations. Such a strategy would have to address egregious iniquities such as the oppression of women, manifest in their being forced to give birth to many babies, and in other cultural forms, exploitation of ethnic minorities and subordinate classes, indigenous people being robbed of their habitats and natural resources by the state and transnational companies and such similar gross violations of human rights. Nationalist struggles and ethnic hatred tend to eclipse the more fundamental social and class inequalities prevailing in society. Unless these are tackled successfully the inherent tensions in society are very likely to erupt into violent confrontations of one sort or the other fired by irrational ideologies and atavistic passions. In the same way that the earlier notion of individual rights associated with the bourgeois civil society has been abandoned in favour of a more comprehensive notion of both freedom and protection and named as 'human rights' in the UN declarations of Universal Human Rights (1948) and later conventions, the idea of humane development (rather than just economic development) leading to a humane society deserves a thought.

International inputs to the reduction of tension

The involvement of international human rights organizations becomes inevitable as human rights violations take place and refugees flee the troubled areas to neighbouring states and to Europe and North America. If this argument be granted, that conflicts between the state and separatist movements can be settled peacefully only within some autonomy formula, the role of international actors can be more positive if:

1   The violations of human rights by the state and the militant groups are monitored impartially and these organizations are not perceived to be taking biased positions on the question of self-determination. In this connection it is equally important that the invocation of sovereignty by the state to justify human rights violations of innocent people is not accepted by the world community.

2   Activities are co-ordinated and organized so that the political and social forces within the Western societies which are contributing to the aggravation of conflicts are exposed and held answerable for such misdoings. The weapons with which the post-colonial state and its opponents fight their war games are often purchased from countries where the main human rights organizations such as Amnesty International, International Alert, Minority Rights Group, Asia Watch, Africa Watch and others are based.

3   More concretely, the supply of funds and weapons via the diaspora communities and hostile states has to be watched and appropriate action by the international community on such matters co-ordinated.

A queer angle to attitudes of Western governments has been the reluctance to see things in their totality or wholeness. Many conflicts which we have studied in this inquiry would perhaps not have taken such an ugly turn had the weapons produced in the West or the former Soviet bloc not been available. However, arguments such as national self-interest, economic compulsions, the need to maintain technological competitiveness and so on are always readily available for these states and their spokespeople to justify weapon exports. At bottom what determines Western priorities is greed and profit. The appalling poverty of Third World societies is a reflection of the way the developed industrialized world continues to draw maximum advantage from the world economy. The spiralling debt burden, the population explosion and other egregious problems drive individuals, groups and states in many parts of the Third World to desperate acts. Without these problems being addressed on a global level no stability and peace can be established.

Right of self-determination and state sovereignty

The only situation where no state should be left unpunished is when it has ordered a genocide or has forcibly expelled a people from its traditional homeland. In the aftermath of the Second World War and during the Nuremberg trials a principle was recognized that states and their functionaries can under no circumstance justify massive aggression and human rights violations against unarmed people. This principle has not been given proper legal recognition, and states can get away with many acts of terror and brutality against people living within their territories.

On the other hand, the demand for national self-determination has to be carefully assessed and evaluated in the light of historical circumstances. The right to secede from an existing state becomes worthy of international sympathy and support when a cultural group has been living in a specific territory for a long historical period and the following conditions obtain:

1 If it can demonstrate that the state has adopted laws and constitutional provisions to discriminate against it in matters of employment and/or in practice it has been denied the ways and means of earning a reasonable livelihood.
2 If the exploitation of that group, either through the production process or its natural resources, has led to the appropriation of the economic surplus by the state, and it has been reduced to a permanent under-class.
3 If the state has adopted explicit laws and constitutional provisions to legitimize the persecution of that group on the basis of its religious beliefs, race or ethnic origin.

When discrimination, exploitation and oppression coincide, the case for secession is the strongest. There is no reason to consider the existing states and their territories sacred. The right to self-determination can be raised by any group of people and the merits of their claim can be judged only in the light of the concrete conditions obtaining in a society and the actual practice of the state. This book, however, clearly demonstrates how difficult it is to create ethnically or culturally pure states, no matter whether ethnicity is employed in a narrow sense to cover 'purely' ethnic groups or whether it is used in a wider sense to cover large religious communities and linguistic nationalities. Whether such a project is worthy of international solidarity and support is also to be questioned, because ethnonationalism can rather easily succumb to fascistic obsession for cultural chastity of one sort or another. The effort should be, therefore, to find peaceful resolution of ethnic conflicts and separatist demands within the framework of existing South Asian states. More importantly, the democratization of state and society should always be encouraged and supported. As Björn Beckman aptly remarks (1989: 96): 'The democratic space has to be protected in order to be expanded.' Only then would objective conditions for the peaceful resolution of conflicts really exist.

References

Avineri, S. (1991) 'Hegel, Georg Wilhelm Friedrich' in D. Miller, J. Coleman, W. Connolly and A. Ryan (eds), *The Blackwell Encyclopaedia of Political Thought*, Oxford: Basil Blackwell.

Beckman, B. (1989) 'Whose democracy? Bourgeois vs popular democracy', *Review of African Political Economy*, no. 45/46, Sheffield: The Review of African Political Economy.

Eriksen, T.H. (1993) 'Ethnicity and nationalism: definition and critical reflections' in H. Lindholm (ed.), *Ethnicity and Nationalism: Formation of Identity and Dynamics of Conflict in the 1990s*, Göteborg: Nordnes.

Gramsci, A. (1976) *Selections from the Prison Notebooks*, London: Lawrence and Wishart.

Lijphart, A. (1977) *Democracy in Plural Societies: A Comparative Exploration*, New Haven and London: Yale University Press.

Oommen, T.K. (1990) *State and Society in India: Studies in Nation-building*, New Delhi/ Newbury Park/London: Sage Publications.

Sassoon, A.S. (1985) 'Civil society' in T. Bottomore (ed.), *A Dictionary of Marxist Thought*, Oxford: Basil Blackwell.

Schalk, P. (1990) 'Articles 9 and 18 of the Constitution of Lanka as obstacles to peace' in P. Schalk (ed.), *Lanka*, December, Uppsala.

Bibliography of cited sources

Interviews

India

Sikhs: UK, July 1986

Dr Jagjit Singh Chauhan
Gurmej Singh Gill
Manmoham Singh Khalsa
Davinder Singh Parmar
Harbans Singh Ruprah
Gurdeep Singh
Indarjit Singh

Stockholm, June 1987

Lachman Singh Anjala
Dr Chanan Singh Chan

Kashmiris: London, June 1991

Raja Zafar Khan, JKLF

Dalits and indigenous peoples: Stockholm, October 1994

E. Ezhil Caroline, Dalit Women's Organization of South India
Saral K. Chatterji, Director, the Christian Institute for the
    Study of Religion and Society (CISRS), New Delhi
Samar Bosu Mullick, Consultant on Tribal Studies for
    CISRS, Ranchi University, Bihar
Ram Dayal Munda, President, the Indian Confederation of
    Indigenous and Tribal Peoples, Ranchi, Bihar

Pakistan

Karachi and Lahore, March—April 1990

Azim Ahmed Tariq, Chairman MQM (Mohajir)
Professor Azizuddin Ahmed, political activist on the left (Punjabi)
Mumtaz Ali Bhutto, chief minister of Sindh in 1972 (Sindhi)
Rafiq Khan, PPP activist and political refugee in Sweden (Punjabi)
Dr Hamida Khuhro, academic, Sindhi historian (Sindhi)
Professor Hamid Hasan Kizilbash, political scientist (Punjabi)
Faqir Muhammad Lashari, journalist (Sindhi)
Rao Tariq Latif, labour leader and political activist (Urdu-speaking refugee, settled in Lahore, Punjab and assimilated into Punjabi culture)
Professor Khalid Mahmud, political scientist (Punjabi-speaking Azad Kashmiri)
Hussain Naqi, journalist (Urdu-speaking refugee, settled in Lahore, Shia)
Abdul Hafeez Pirzada, ex-law minister in PPP government (Sindhi)
Hanif Ramay, ex-chief minister of Punjab and PPP leader (Punjabi)
Junaid Bakhsh Soomro, ex-member Sindh Legislative Assembly (Sindhi)
Mir Thebo, Sindhi political activist
S. Akbar Zaidi, Senior Research Officer, Department of Applied Economics, Karachi University (Urdu-speaking refugee settled in Karachi)
Fakhar Zaman, poet, writer and politician, President of Punjab PPP in 1990 (Punjabi)

Bangladesh (late April—early May 1990, Dhaka)

Professor Salahuddin Ahmed, retired professor of history
Professor Syed Sajjad Hosain, retired professor of English
Professor Talukder Maniruzzaman, Department of Political Science, Dhaka University
Professor Abdur Razzaq, retired national professor

Sri Lanka

Dr Dagmar Hellmann-Rajanayagam, London (June 1991)
Krishnakumar alias Kittu, International Secretary, LTTE (June 1991)
Professor Peter Schalk, Uppsala University (1993)
Dr Gabriele Winai-Ström, Uppsala University (1993)

Audio and video cassette tapes

Kushwant Singh, journalist, writer and historian (videotape: *Bleeding Punjab in Search of Peace*)
Tavleen Singh, journalist (videotape: *Bleeding Punjab in Search of Peace*)
Sant Jarnail Singh Bhindranwale radio (1–13) and video (1–3) cassette tapes

TV programme

Inside Story: Suicide Killers (BBC-produced programme on the Tamil Tigers from 1991) relayed at 21.50 hrs on 27 April 1993 by Swedish Television TV 2.

Documents and reports issued by governments and organizations

Bangladesh

1989 Statistical Yearbook of Bangladesh, Dhaka: Bangladesh Bureau of Statistics, 1989.
The Constitution of the People's Republic of Bangladesh (as modified up to 10 October 1991), Dhaka.
Chittagong Hill Tracts and Human Rights (n.d., 1992?; supplied by the Bangladesh embassy in Stockholm).

India

Arms Supply from Pakistan and Narco-Terrorist Links (n.d.; supplied by the Indian embassy in Stockholm).
The Constitution of India, New Delhi: Universal Book Traders, 1992.
Pakistan Abetting Terrorism in Jammu and Kashmir (n.d.; supplied by the Indian embassy in Stockholm).
Punjab Settlement, 24 July 1985, Delhi.
Simla Agreement, 2 July 1972, Delhi.
Statistical Outline of India 1989–90, Bombay, 1989.
Strategic Analysis, vol. XIII, no. II, Delhi, 1990.
Terrorist Revelations — the Pakistani Connection (n.d.; supplied by the Indian embassy in Stockholm).
White Paper on the Punjab Agitation, 10 July 1984, New Delhi: Government of India.

Khalistan Council

Khalistan News (December 1987–January 1988), Kent: Khalistan Council, 1987–88.

Jammu Kashmir Liberation Front (JKLF)

Khan, A., *Underlying Causes of Kashmir Dispute (and Reasons for Its Remaining Unresolved)*, Brussels: JKLF, 1993.
Khan, R.Z., *The Kashmir Question and Struggle for Identity*, JKLF, 1992.

Pakistan

The Constitution of the Islamic Republic of Pakistan, 1956, 1962 and 1973.
Pakistan Statistical Yearbook 1989.
Regional Studies (several issues), Islamabad.
Report of the Court of Inquiry constituted under Punjab Act II of 1954 to Enquire into the Punjab Disturbances of 1953, Lahore, 1954.
Rizvi, A.H., *India: A Terrorist State* (n.d.; supplied by the Pakistan Embassy in Stockholm).

Christian organizations

Saavan (bilingual Urdu–English monthly Christian publication), Lahore.

Mohajir Quomi Movement (MQM)

Hussain, A., *Safr-e-Zindagi*, Lahore: Jang Publishers, 1988.

Sindhi organizations

Bhutto, M.A., *Manifesto of the Sindh National Front*, Karachi, 1989.
Sayed, G.M. (Jiye Sindh), *A Case for Sindhu Desh*, Bombay: Sorath Publication, 1985.

Sri Lanka

The Constitution of the Democratic Socialist Republic of Sri Lanka, Certified on 31 August, 1978, Colombo, 1978.
Census of Population and Housing 1981, Colombo, 1981.

Tamil organizations

Forty Years of Human Rights Violations by Sri Lanka — What Is to be Done, Surrey: International Federation of Tamils, 1991.
Tamil Eelam: Political Programme of the LTTE (n.d.; supplied by LTTE London office).

Documents and reports of human rights organizations: international and South Asian

Bangladesh: A Summary of Human Rights Violations, London: Amnesty International, April 1993.
Bangladesh: Human Rights in the Chittagong Hill Tracts 1989–1990, London: Amnesty International, August 1991.
The 'Blasphemy' Episode, Lahore: Human Rights Commission of Pakistan, 1992.
Gopsill, T., *'Heaven on Fire'*, London (report prepared for British Parliamentary Committee), 1993.
Hiro, D., *The Untouchables of India*, London: Minority Rights Group, 1982.
Human Rights in India: Kashmir Under Siege, Asia Watch Report, 1991.
India: Uri Hydroelectric Power Project, Report no. 9, Stockholm, 1994.
India's Kashmir War, Delhi Committee for Initiative on Kashmir, 1990.
Kashmir Bleeds, Srinagar: Human Rights Commission, 1990.
Kashmir: A Land Ruled by the Gun, Delhi: Committee for Initiative on Kashmir, 1991.
Kashmir 1991, report by Physicians for Human Rights, UK, 1991.
Kashmir Under Siege, Punjab Human Rights Organisation, 1990.
Marino, A., *Political Killings in Southern Sri Lanka*, London: International Alert Publication, 1989.
Massacre at Valvettiturai: India's Mylai, Bombay: Hind Mazdoor Kissan Panchayat, 1989.
Maxwell, N., 'India, the Nagas and the north-east', *Minority Rights Group Report* no. 17, London, 1980.
Oppression in Punjab, Birmingham: Hind Mazdoor Kisan Panchayat, 1985.
Report of the Citizens' Commission (on Delhi riots, 31 October–4 November), Delhi, 1985.
Sindh Inquiry: Summer 1990, Lahore: Human Rights Commission of Pakistan, 1990.

Sri Lanka Human Rights Situation, Geneva, 1992.
Sri Lanka Monitor (several issues), British Refugee Council, London.
Sri Lanka: Summary of Human Rights Concerns During 1990, February 1991, London: Amnesty International, 1991.
Truth About Delhi Riots, Delhi: Citizens for Democracy, 1985.
The United Nations Charter, 1945.
The United Nations International Covenant on Civil and Political Rights, 1966.
The United Nations International Covenant on Economic, Social, and Cultural Rights, 1966.
The United Nations Universal Declaration of Human Rights, 1948.

Independent journals, magazines and newspapers: international and South Asian

AI & Society, London: Springer-Verlag London Ltd, 1993.
British Journal of Sociology, 7, 1957.
The Daily Jang (Urdu-language), London.
Economic and Political Weekly (several issues), Bombay.
Far Eastern Economic Review, 23 March, 1989.
Hindustan Times, 23 September, 1992.
India Today, New Delhi, 1991.
Indian Express (several issues).
Journal of Contemporary Asia, vol. 19, no. 3, 1989.
Journal of Education Planning and Administration, vol. V, no. 3 (July 1991), Delhi.
Journal of Refugee Studies, vol. 3, no. 1 (1990), Oxford.
New Community, vol. XI (1983), London.
Review of African Political Economy, no. 45/46 (1989), Sheffield.
Sydasien, nr 3 (1994), Lund.
Times of India, 27, 28 October 1992, 2 January 1993, 19 October 1993.
Tribune (Indian), 4 February 1993.
Viewpoint (several issues), Lahore.

Books

Agarwala, B.R. (ed.), *Shah Bano Case*, New Delhi: Arnold-Heinemann, 1986.
Ahmad, I., *Pakistan General Elections 1970*, Lahore: South Asia Institute, 1976.
Ahmed, A.S., *Pakistan Society: Islam, Ethnicity and Leadership in South Asia*, Delhi: Oxford University Press, 1988.
Ahmed, F. (ed.), *Focus on Baluchistan and Pushtoon Question*, Lahore: People's Publishing House, 1975.
Ahmed, I., *The Concept of an Islamic State: An Analysis of the Ideological Controversy in Pakistan*, London: Frances Pinter, 1987.
Ahmed, M., *Bangladesh: Era of Sheikh Mujibur Rahman*, Dhaka: University Press Limited, 1984.
Ahmed, P.A., *Kaya Hum Ikhatay Reh Saktay Hein?*, Lahore: Maktab-e-Fikr-o-Danish, 1988.
Ahmed, V. and Amjad, R., *The Management of Pakistan's Economy 1947–82*, Karachi: Oxford University Press, 1984.

Akbar, M.J., *India: The Siege Within*, Harmondsworth: Penguin Books, 1985.

Akbar, M.J., *Kashmir: Behind the Vale*, New Delhi: Viking, 1991.

Alavi, H. and Halliday, F. (eds), *State and Ideology in the Middle East and Pakistan*, London: Macmillan, 1988.

Alavi, H. and Harriss, J., *Sociology of 'Developing Societies': South Asia*, London: Macmillan, 1989.

Ali, T., *Can Pakistan Survive?*, Harmondsworth: Penguin Books, 1983.

Allana, G. (ed.), *Pakistan Movement: Historic Documents*, Lahore: Islamic Book Service, 1977.

Altekar, A.S., *State and Government in Ancient India*, Delhi: Motilal Banarsidass, 1962.

Andersen, P.B., 'Theoretical reflections on Santal and Hindu elements in the Santal Karam ritual', unpublished paper presented at the Seventh Annual Conference of the Nordic Association of South East Asian Studies, held at Klintholm Haven, 1990.

Anderson, B., *Imagined Communities*, London: Verso, 1983.

Antonova, K., Bongard-Levin, G. and Kotovsky, G., *A History of India*, Book 4, Moscow: Progress Publishers, 1979.

Apter, D.E., *Some Conceptual Approaches to the Study of Modernization*, Englewood Cliffs, New Jersey: Prentice-Hall, Inc., 1968.

Arendt, H., *On Violence*, New York and London: Harvest/HBJ, 1970.

Asplund, D., *Bangladesh: Landanalys*, Stockholm: SIDA, 1977.

Bahadur, K. and Singh, U. (eds), *Pakistan: Transition to Democracy*, New Delhi: Patriot Publishers, 1989.

Ball, T., *Transforming Political Discourse*, Oxford: Basil Blackwell, 1980.

Banerjee, S., *India's Simmering Revolution: The Naxalite Uprising*, London: Zed Books, 1984.

Bangladesh: Country Study and Norwegian Aid Review, Fantoft: Chr. Michelsen Institute, 1986.

The Bangladesh Papers, Lahore: Vanguard, 1975?

Barnett, M.R., *The Politics of Cultural Nationalism in South India*, Princeton: Princeton University Press, 1976.

Barrier, N.G. and Dusenbery, V.A. (eds), *The Sikh Diaspora: Migration and the Experience Beyond Punjab*, Delhi: Chanakya Publications, 1989.

Baxter, C., *Bangladesh*, Boulder and London: Westview Press, 1984.

Baxter, C. (ed.), *Zia's Pakistan: Politics in a Frontline State*, Lahore: Vanguard, 1985.

Bhaduri, S. and Karim, A., *The Sri Lankan Crisis*, New Delhi: Lancer International, 1990.

Bhatia, S., *Social Change and Politics in Punjab: 1898–1910*, New Delhi: Enkay Publishers PVT Ltd, 1987.

Bhutto, B., *Daughter of Destiny*, New York: Simon and Schuster, 1989.

Binder, L., *Religion and Politics in Pakistan*, Berkeley: University of California Press, 1961.

Blomquist, H., *The Soft State: Housing Reform and State Capacity in Urban India*, Uppsala: Uppsala University, 1988.

Bottomore, T. (ed.), *A Dictionary of Marxist Thought*, Oxford: Basil Blackwell, 1985.

Brass, P.R., *Language, Religion and Politics in North India*, Cambridge: Cambridge University Press, 1974.

Brass, P.R., *Ethnicity and Nationalism: Theory and Practice*, New Delhi: Sage Publications, 1991.

Breuilly, J., *Nationalism and the State*, Manchester: Manchester University Press, 1982.

Brown, J.M., *Modern India: The Origins of an Asian Democracy*, Delhi: Oxford University Press, 1985.

Brzoska, M. and Ohlson, T. (eds), *Arms Trade in the Third World*, Stockholm: SIPRI, 1986.

Burke, S.M., *Pakistan's Foreign Policy*, London: Oxford University Press, 1973.

Buzan, B., *People, States and Fear*, London: Harvester Wheatsheaf, 1991.

Buzan, B. and Rizvi, G., *South Asian Insecurity and the Great Powers*, London: Macmillan, 1986.

Cashmore, E., *Dictionary of Race and Ethnic Relations*, London: Routledge, 1988.

Chandra, B., *Communalism in Modern India*, New Delhi: Vikas Publishing House Pvt Ltd, 1989.

Char, S.V.D. (ed.), *Readings in the Constitutional History of India 1757–1947*, Delhi: Oxford University Press, 1983.

Chaudhry, N.A., *Development of Urdu as Official Language in the Punjab (1849–1974)*, Lahore: Government of the Punjab, 1977.

Chennakesavan, S., *A Critical Study of Hinduism*, Motilal Banarsidass: Delhi, 1980.

Chopra, V.D., Mishra, R.K. and Singh, N. (eds), *Agony of Punjab*, New Delhi: Patriot Publishers, 1984.

Choudhary, G.W., *Constitutional Development in Pakistan*, Lahore: Longman, 1969.

Choudhary, S., *What Is the Kashmir Problem?*, Luton: Jammu Kashmir Liberation Front, 1991.

Clapham, C., *Third World Politics*, London and Sydney: Croom Helm, 1985.

Cunningham, J.D., *A History of the Sikhs*, London: Humphrey Milford/Oxford University Press, 1918.

Das, V. (ed.), *Mirrors of Violence: Communities, Riots, and Survivors in South Asia*, Delhi: Oxford University Press, 1990.

Davidson, S., *Human Rights: Law and Political Change*, Buckingham: Open University Press, 1993.

Demokrati och Makt i Sverige (report prepared by Yvonne Hirdman, Johan P. Olsen, Inga Persson, Olof Petersson and Anders Westholm), Stockholm: SOU, 1990.

De Silva, K.M., *A History of Sri Lanka*, London: C. Hurst, 1981.

de Silva, K.M., *Managing Ethnic Tensions in Multi-ethnic Societies: Sri Lanka 1880–1985*, London: University Press of America, 1986.

Deutsch, K.W., *Nationalism and Social Communication*, Cambridge, Mass.: MIT Press, 1966.

Dobbin, C.E., *Basic Documents in the Development of Modern India and Pakistan, 1835–1947*, London: Van Nostrand Reinhold Company, 1970.

Easton, D., *A System Analysis of Political Life*, New York: John Wiley and Sons, 1965.

Eaton, R.H., 'Indo Muslim state formation, temple destruction, and the historiography of holy warrior', unpublished paper presented at the Conference: State Formation and Institution Building in South Asia, held at Sunnersta Herrgård, Uppsala, 1993.

Engineer, A.A. (ed.), *Secular Crown on Fire: The Kashmir Problem*, Delhi: Ajanta Publications, 1991.

Enloe, C.H., *Ethnic Soldiers*, London: Penguin, 1980.

Ewing, K.P. (ed.), *Shariat and Ambiguity in South Asian Islam*, Delhi: Oxford University Press, 1988.

Farquhar, J.N., *Modern Religious Movements in India*, Delhi: Munshiram Manoharlal, 1967.

Finsk-Ungriska Småskrifter, Lund: Finsk-ugriska Institutionen, 1991.

Frankel, F.R., *India's Political Economy, 1947–1977: The Gradual Revolution*, Princeton: Princeton University Press, 1978.

Franklin, B. (ed.), *The Essential Stalin*, New York: Anchor Books, 1972.

Fries, Y. and Bibin, T., *The Undesirables: The Expatriation of the Tamil People 'of Recent Indian Origin' from the Plantations in Sri Lanka to India*, Calcutta: K.P. Bagchi & Company, 1984.

Gankovsky, Y.V. and Gordon-Polonskaya, L.R., *A History of Pakistan (1947–1958)*, Lahore: People's Publishing House, 1972.

Gankovsky, Y.V. and Moskalenko, V.N., *The Three Constitutions of Pakistan*, Lahore: People's Publishing House, 1978.

Gardezi, H. and Rashid, J. (eds), *Pakistan, the Roots of Dictatorship: The Political Economy of a Praetorian State*, London: Zed Books, 1983.

Geertz, C. (ed.), *Old Societies and New State*, New York: Free Press, 1963.

Gellner, E., *Thought and Change*, London: Weidenfeld and Nicolson, 1964.

Gellner, E., *Nations and Nationalism*, Oxford: Basil Blackwell Ltd, 1983.

Ghosh, P.S., *Cooperation and Conflict in South Asia*, New Delhi: Manohar Publications, 1989.

Giddens, A., *The Nation-State and Violence*, Cambridge: Polity Press, 1985.

Gill, S.S., 'Development experience of a fast growing region in a slow growing backward economy: recent socio-economic changes in the Punjab', conference paper presented at the Indian Institute of Advanced Studies, Shimla, 1992.

Gilmartin, D., *Empire and Islam: Punjab and the Making of Pakistan*, Delhi: Oxford University Press, 1989.

Glazer, N. and Moynihan, D.P. (eds), *Ethnicity: Theory and Experience*, Cambridge, Mass.: Harvard University Press, 1975.

Gopal, R., *Indian Muslims: A Political History (1858–1947)*, Lahore: Book Traders, 1976.

Gopal, S. (ed.), *Anatomy of a Confrontation: The Babri Masjid–Ramjanmabhumi Issue*, New Delhi: Viking, 1991.

Gough, K. and Sharma, H.P. (eds), *Imperialism and Revolution in South Asia*, New York: Monthly Review Press, 1973.

Graham, B.D., *Hindu Nationalism and Indian Politics: The Origins and Developments of the Bharatiya Jana Sangh*, Cambridge: Cambridge University Press, 1990.

Gramsci, A., *Selections from the Prison Notebooks*, London: Lawrence and Wishart, 1976.

Gunaratna, R., *Sri Lanka a Lost Revolution: The Inside Story of the JVP*, Colombo: Institute of Fundamental Studies, 1990.

Gunaratna, R., *Indian Intervention in Sri Lanka: The Role of India's Intelligence Agencies*, Colombo: South Asian Network on Conflict Research, 1993.

Gupta, S., *Kashmir: A Study in India–Pakistan Relations*, Bombay: Asia Publishing House, 1966.

Gurr, T.D., *Why Men Rebel*, Princeton: Princeton University Press, 1971.

Haellquist, K.R. (ed.), *NIAS Report 1990*, Copenhagen: Nordic Institute of Asian Studies, 1990.

Hafiz, M.A. and Khan, A.R. (eds), *Nation Building in Bangladesh: Retrospect and Prospect*, Dhaka: Bangladesh Institute of International and Strategic Studies, 1986.

Harrison, S.S., *In Afghanistan's Shadow: Baluch Nationalism and Soviet Temptations*, New York and Washington, DC: Carnegie Endowment for International Peace, 1981.

Hasan, Z., Jha, S.N. and Khan, R. (eds), *The State, Political Processes, and Identity: Reflections on Modern India*, New Delhi: Sage Publications, 1989.

Held, D. *et al.* (eds), *States and Societies*, Oxford: Martin Robertson and Company, 1983.

Hellman, E., *Political Hinduism: The Challenge of the Viśva Hindu Parisad*, Uppsala: Uppsala University, 1993.

Hiro, D., *Inside India Today*, London: Routledge & Kegan Paul, 1976.

Hobsbawm, E.J., *Nations and Nationalism Since 1780*, Cambridge: Cambridge University Press, 1992.

Horowitz, D.L., *Ethnic Groups in Conflict*, Berkeley and Los Angeles: University of California Press, 1985.

Huntington, S.P., *Political Order in Changing Societies*, New Haven: Yale University Press, 1968.

Hussain, A., *Safr-e-Zindagi*, Lahore: Jang Publishers, 1988.

Jafery, Z., *Saraiki, Sind, Baluchistan: S.S.B. and National Question*, Multan: Melluha Publications, 1986.

Jalal, A., *The Sole Spokesman*, Cambridge: Cambridge University Press, 1985.

Jalal, A., *The State of Martial Law: The Origins of Pakistan's Political Economy of Defence*, Cambridge: Cambridge University Press, 1990.

Jansson, E., *India, Pakistan or Pakhtunistan?*, Uppsala: Acta Universitatis Upsaliensis, 1981.

Jayaweera, N., *Sri Lanka: Towards a Multi-ethnic Democracy?*, Oslo: PRIO, 1991.

Jeffrey, R., *What's Happening to India?*, London: Macmillan, 1986.

Jinnah, M.A., *Speeches and Writings of Mr Jinnah*, vol. 2, Lahore: Sh. Muhammad Ashraf, 1976.

Johal, S., *Conflict and Integration in Indo-Pakistan Relations*, Berkeley: University of California, 1989.

Jones, A.K., *Muslim Politics and the Growth of the Muslim League in Sind, 1935–1941*, PhD thesis, Duke University, 1977.

Josh, S.S., *Hindustan Gadar Party: A Short History*, New Delhi: People's Publishing House, 1977.

Juergensmeyer, M., *Religious Rebels in the Punjab: The Social Vision of Untouchables*, Delhi: Ajanta Publications, 1988.

Jupp, J., *Sri Lanka — Third World Democracy*, London: Frank Cass, 1978.

Kapur, R., *Sikh Separatism: The Politics of Faith*, London: Allen and Unwin, 1986.

Kaur, A. *et al.* (eds), *The Punjab Story*, New Delhi: Roli Books International, 1990.

Kennedy, C.H., *Pakistan: 1992*, Boulder: Westview Press, 1992.

Khan, M.A., *Generals in Politics: Pakistan 1958–1982*, New Delhi: Vikas Publishing House Pvt Ltd, 1983.

Khan, M.A. (ed.), *Islam, Politics and the State: The Pakistan Experience*, London: Zed Books, 1985.

Khan, W., *Facts Are Facts: The Untold Story of India's Partition*, New Delhi: Vikas Publishing House Pvt Ltd, 1987.

Khawar, M. and Shaheed, F., *Women of Pakistan: Two Steps Forward, One Step Back?*, Lahore: Vanguard, 1987.

Khosla, G.D., *Stern Reckoning: A Survey of the Events Leading up to and Following the Partition of India*, Delhi: Oxford University Press, 1989.

Khuhro, H. (ed.), *Sindh: Through the Centuries*, Karachi: Oxford University Press, 1981.

Kohli, A., *The State and Poverty in India: The Politics of Reform*, Cambridge: Cambridge University Press, 1989.

Kohli, A., *Democracy and Discontent: India's Growing Crisis of Governability*, Cambridge: Cambridge University Press, 1990.

Kosambi, D.D., *An Introduction to the Study of Indian History*, Bombay: Popular Prakash, 1975.

Kothari, R., *Politics in India*, New Delhi: Orient Longman, 1970.

Kumar, R.N. and Sieberer, G., *The Sikh Struggle: Origin, Evolution and Present Phase*, Delhi: Chanakya Publications, 1991.

Leigh, M.S., *The Punjab and the War*, Lahore: Government Printing Press, 1922.

Lenin, V.I., *The National Liberation Movement in the East*, Moscow: Progress Publishers, 1969.

Lijphart, A., *Democracy in Plural Societies: A Comparative Exploration*, New Haven and London: Yale University Press, 1977.

Lindgren, G.L., Nordquist, K. and Wallensteen, P. (eds), *Peace Processes in the Third World*, Uppsala: Department of Peace and Conflict Research, 1991.

Lindholm, H. (ed.), *Ethnicity and Nationalism: Formation of Identity and Dynamics of Conflict in the 1990s*, Göteborg: Nordnes, 1993.

Macauliffe, M.A., *The Sikh Religion*, vol. 1, Oxford: Clarendon Press, 1909.

Mahmud, K., *Indian Political Scene, 1989: Main Contenders for Power*, Islamabad: Institute for Regional Studies, 1989.

Malik, R., *The Politics of One Unit, 1955–58*, Lahore: University of the Punjab, 1988.

Maniruzzaman, T., *Group Interests and Political Changes: Studies of Pakistan and Bangladesh*, New Delhi: South Asian Publishers, 1982.

Mann, M. (ed.), *Macmillan Student Encyclopedia of Sociology*, London: Macmillan, 1983.

Martinussen, J., *Staten i perifere og post-koloniale samfund: Indien og Pakistan*, Århus: Forlaget Politica, 1980.

Marty, M.E. and Appleby, R.C. (eds), *Fundamentalisms and the State: Remaking Polities, Economics, and Militance*, Chicago and London: University of Chicago Press, 1993.

Marx, K. and Engels, F., *Collected Works*, vol. 5, Moscow: Progress Publishers, 1976.

Marx, K. and Engels, F., *Selected Works*, Moscow: Progress Publishers, 1970.

Mehdi, S., *Politics Without Parties: A Report on the 1985 Partyless Election in Pakistan*, Lahore: SAHE, 1988.

Mehkri, G.M., *Sorrows of Sindh*, Hyderabad Sind: Sind Friends Circle, 1987.

Midgal, J.S., *Strong Societies and Weak States*, Princeton: Princeton University Press, 1988.

Miller, D., Coleman, J., Connally, W. and Ryan, A. (eds), *The Blackwell Encyclopaedia of Political Thought*, Oxford: Blackwell Reference, 1991.

Mirza, M., *Aaj Ka Sindh*, Lahore: Progressive Publishers, 1987.

Mitra, S.K. (ed.), *The Post-colonial State in Asia: Dialectics of Politics and Culture*, New York: Harvester Wheatsheaf, 1990.

Moore Jr, B., *Social Origins of Dictatorship and Democracy: Lord and Peasant in the Making of the Modern World*, Harmondsworth: Penguin University Books, 1966.

Moore, M., *The State and Peasant Politics in Sri Lanka*, Cambridge: Cambridge University Press, 1985.

Morgan, K.W. (ed.), *The Religion of Hindus*, New York: The Ronald Press, 1953.

Mukherjee, R., *The Rise and Fall of the East India Company*, New York and London: Monthly Review Press, 1974.

Myrdal, G., *Asian Drama*, vol. I, New York: Pantheon, 1968.

Nayar, B.R., *Minority Politics in the Punjab*, Princeton: Princeton University Press, 1966.

Noman, O., *The Political Economy of Pakistan 1947–85*, London: KPI, 1988.

O'Connell, J.T., Israel, M., Oxtoby, W.G., McLeod, W.H. and Grewal, J.S. (eds), *Sikh History and Religion in the Twentieth Century*, New Delhi: Manohar, 1990.

Oddie, G.A. (ed.), *Religion in South Asia*, New Delhi: Manohar, 1991.

Olsen, B., *The Sri Lanka Conflict: A Study of Elite Perceptions*, Fantoft: Chr. Michelsen Institute, 1989.

Oommen, T.K., *State and Society in India: Studies in Nation-Building*, New Delhi/ Newbury Park/London: Sage Publications, 1990.

Pettigrew, J., *Robber Noblemen*, London: Routledge and Kegan Paul, 1975.

Pfaffenberger, B., 'The structure of protracted conflict: the case of Sri Lanka', paper presented at the conference, State Formation and Institution Building in South Asia, Sunnersta, Sweden, 9 October 1993.

Phadnis, U., *Religion and Politics in Sri Lanka*, New Delhi: Manohar, 1976.

Phadnis, U., *Ethnicity and Nation-building in South Asia*, New Delhi: Sage Publications, 1989.

Ponnambalam, S., *Sri Lanka: National Conflict and the Tamil Liberation Struggle*, London: Zed Books, 1983.

Qureshi, I.A., *The Struggle for Pakistan*, Karachi: University of Karachi, 1979.

Ram, M., *Sri Lanka: The Fractured Island*, New Delhi: Penguin Books, 1989.

Rousseau, J.-J., *The Social Contract and Discourses*, London: Everyman, 1990.

Rudebeck, L. (ed.), *When Democracy Makes Sense*, Uppsala: AKUT, 1992.

Rudolph, L.I. and Rudolph, S.H., *In Pursuit of Lakshmi: The Political Economy of India*, Chicago and London: University of Chicago, 1987.

Runciman, W.G. (ed.), *Weber Selections in Translation*, Cambridge: Cambridge University Press, 1978.

Sabine, G.H. and Thorson, T.L., *A History of Political Theory*, Hinsdale: Dryden Press, 1973.

Sayed, G.M., *A Case for Sindhu Desh*, Bombay: Sorath Publication, 1985.

Sayeed, K.B., *Pakistan: The Formative Phase 1857–1948*, Karachi: Oxford University Press, 1978.

Sayeed, K.B., *Politics in Pakistan: The Nature and Direction of Change*, New York: Praeger Publishers, 1980.

Schalk, P. (ed.), *Lanka*, Uppsala, 1990.

Schalk, P., 'The concept of martyrdom and resistance of the Liberation Tigers of Tamil Eelam (LTTE)', paper presented at the conference on Ethnicity, Identity and Development in South Asia, held at Postgaarden, Denmark in October 1991.

Seervai, H.M., *Partition of India: Legend and Reality*, Bombay: Emmanem Publications, 1989.

Shackle, C., *The Siraiki Language of Central Pakistan: A Reference Grammar*, London: School of Oriental and African Studies, 1976.

Shakdher, S.L. (ed.), *The Constitution and the Parliament in India*, New Delhi: National Publishing House, 1976.

Shakir, M. (ed.), *Religion, State and Politics in India*, Delhi: Ajanta Books, 1989.

Singh, A. (ed.), *Punjab in Indian Politics: Issues and Trends*, Delhi: Ajanta Publications, 1985.

Singh, B., *State Politics in India: Explorations in Political Processes in Jammu and Kashmir*, New Delhi: Macmillan India Ltd, 1982.

Singh, G., *Religion and Politics in the Punjab*, New Delhi: Deep & Deep Publications, 1986.

Singh, G., *History of Sikh Struggles*, vol. 1, *1946–1966*, New Delhi: Atlantic Publishers & Distributors, 1989.

Singh, K., *A History of the Sikhs*, vol. 1, *1469–1839*, Princeton: Princeton University Press, 1963.

Singh, K., *A History of the Sikhs*, vol. 2, *1839–1964*, Princeton: Princeton University Press, 1966.

Singh, K., *Ranjit Singh: Maharajah of the Punjab 1780–1839*, New Delhi: Orient Longman, 1985.

Singh, S.K., *Sachi Sakhi* (in Punjabi), Vancouver: Modern Printing House, 1982.

Skinner, Q., *The Foundations of Modern Political Thought*, vols 1 and 2, Cambridge: Cambridge University Press, 1978.

Skocpol, T., *States and Social Revolutions*, Cambridge: Cambridge University Press, 1979.

Smith, A.D., *State and Nation in the Third World*, London: Wheatsheaf Books, 1983.

Smith, A.D., *Theories of Nationalism*, London: Duckworth, 1983.

Smith, A.D., *The Ethnic Origins of Nations*, Oxford: Basil Blackwell Ltd, 1986.

Smith, D.E., *India as a Secular State*, Princeton: Princeton University Press, 1963.

Snyder, L.L., *Varieties of Nationalism: A Comparative Study*, New York: Holt, Rinehart and Winston, 1976.

Spencer, J. (ed.), *Sri Lanka: History and the Roots of the Conflict*, London and New York: Routledge, 1990.

Sri Lanka: A Country Study, Washington, DC: United States Government, 1990.

Tambiah, S.J., *Sri Lanka: Ethnic Fratricide and the Dismantling of Democracy*, Delhi: Oxford University Press, 1986.

Taylor, D. and Jupp, M. (eds), *Political Identity in South Asia*, London: Curzon Press, 1979.

Teng, M.K., *Kashmir Article 370*, New Delhi: Anmol Publications, 1990.

Thapar, R., *Ancient Indian Social History: Some Interpretations*, New Delhi: Orient Longman Ltd, 1979.

The Truth: an International Magazine on Sikhism, vol. 2, December 1985 and April 1986, nos 3 and 4, Quebec.

Tully, M. and Jacob, S., *Amritsar: Mrs Gandhi's Last Battle*, London: Jonathan Cape, 1985.

Vajpeyi, D. and Malik, Y.K. (eds), *Religious and Ethnic Minority Politics in South Asia*, New Delhi: Manohar, 1989.

Vanniasingham, S., *Sri Lanka: The Conflict Within*, New Delhi: Lancer, 1988.

Vije, M., *Where Serfdom Thrives*, Madras: TIRU, 1987.

Wali, K., *Facts Are Facts: The Untold Story of India's Partition*, New Delhi: Vikas Publishing House Pvt Ltd, 1987.

Wallace, P. and Chopra, S., *Political Dynamics of Punjab*, Amritsar: Guru Nanak Dev University, 1981.

Waseem, M., *Politics and the State in Pakistan*, Lahore: Progressive, 1989.

Weidemann, D. (ed.), *Nationalism, Ethnicity and Political Development: South Asian Perspectives*, New Delhi: Manohar, 1991.

Wilson, A.J., *Politics in Sri Lanka 1947–1973*, London: Macmillan, 1974.

Wilson, A.J., *S.J.V. Chelvanayakam and the Crisis of Sri Lankan Tamil Nationalism, 1947–77*, London: Hurst & Company, 1994.

Winai-Ström, G. (ed.), *Konfliktlösning i det flerkulturella samhället*, Uppsala: Uppsala Universitet, 1988.

Wolpert, S., *A New History of India*, New York: Oxford University Press, 1982.

Young, C., *The Politics of Cultural Pluralism*, Madison: University of Wisconsin Press, 1976.

Zaidi, S.A. (ed.), *Regional Imbalances and the National Question in Pakistan*, Lahore: Vanguard, 1992.

Index